Pro Android

Sayed Y. Hashimi and Satya Komatineni

Apress®

Pro Android

Copyright © 2009 by Sayed Y. Hashimi and Satya Komatineni

ISBN-13 (pbk): 978-1-4302-1596-7

ISBN-13 (electronic): 978-1-4302-1597-4

Printed and bound in the United States of America 9 8 7 6 5 4 3 2 1

Trademarked names may appear in this book. Rather than use a trademark symbol with every occurrence of a trademarked name, we use the names only in an editorial fashion and to the benefit of the trademark owner, with no intention of infringement of the trademark.

Java™ and all Java™-based marks are trademarks or registered trademarks of Sun Microsystems, Inc., in the United States and other countries.

Apress, Inc., is not affiliated with Sun Microsystems, Inc., and this book was written without endorsement from Sun Microsystems, Inc.

Lead Editor: Steve Anglin
Development Editor: Douglas Pundick
Technical Reviewer: Vikram Goyal
Editorial Board: Clay Andres, Steve Anglin, Mark Beckner, Ewan Buckingham, Tony Campbell,
    Gary Cornell, Jonathan Gennick, Michelle Lowman, Matthew Moodie, Jeffrey Pepper,
    Frank Pohlmann, Ben Renow-Clarke, Dominic Shakeshaft, Matt Wade, Tom Welsh
Project Manager: Richard Dal Porto
Copy Editor: Nina Goldschlager Perry
Associate Production Director: Kari Brooks-Copony
Production Editor: Candace English
Compositor: Patrick Cunningham
Proofreader: Lisa Hamilton
Indexer: Ron Strauss
Artist: April Milne
Cover Designer: Kurt Krames
Manufacturing Director: Tom Debolski

Distributed to the book trade worldwide by Springer-Verlag New York, Inc., 233 Spring Street, 6th Floor, New York, NY 10013. Phone 1-800-SPRINGER, fax 201-348-4505, e-mail orders-ny@springer-sbm.com, or visit http://www.springeronline.com.

For information on translations, please contact Apress directly at 2855 Telegraph Avenue, Suite 600, Berkeley, CA 94705. Phone 510-549-5930, fax 510-549-5939, e-mail info@apress.com, or visit http://www.apress.com.

Apress and friends of ED books may be purchased in bulk for academic, corporate, or promotional use. eBook versions and licenses are also available for most titles. For more information, reference our Special Bulk Sales–eBook Licensing web page at http://www.apress.com/info/bulksales.

The information in this book is distributed on an "as is" basis, without warranty. Although every precaution has been taken in the preparation of this work, neither the author(s) nor Apress shall have any liability to any person or entity with respect to any loss or damage caused or alleged to be caused directly or indirectly by the information contained in this work.

The source code for this book is available to readers at http://www.apress.com.

To my son: Sayed-Adieb

—Sayed Y. Hashimi

To my family: Narayan Komatineni, Kavitha Komatineni, Nikolas Perez,
Ashley Perez, and AnnMarie Komatineni

—Satya Komatineni

Contents at a Glance

Contents

About the Authors

SAYED Y. HASHIMI was born in Afghanistan and now resides in Jacksonville, Florida. His expertise spans the fields of health care, financials, logistics, service-oriented architecture, and mobile application development. In his professional career, Sayed has developed large-scale distributed applications with a variety of programming languages and platforms, including C/C++, MFC, J2EE, and .NET. He has published articles in major software journals and has written several other popular Apress titles. Sayed holds a master's degree in engineering from the University of Florida. You can reach Sayed by visiting http://www.sayedhashimi.com.

SATYA KOMATINENI (http://www.satyakomatineni.com) has more than 20 years of programming experience working with small and large corporations. Satya has published more than 30 articles about web development using Java and .NET technologies. He is a frequent speaker at industry conferences on innovative technologies and a regular contributor to the weblogs on java.net. He is the author of AspireWeb (http://www.activeintellect.com/aspire), an open sourced, simplified tool for Java web development. In addition, Satya is the creator of Aspire Knowledge Central (http://www.knowledgefolders.com), an open sourced "personal web OS" with a focus on individual productivity. He is also a contributing member to a number of Phase I proposals and one Phase II proposal for the U.S. Small Business Innovation Research Program (http://www.sbir.gov/).

About the Technical Reviewer

■**VIKRAM GOYAL** is the author of the Apress book *Pro Java™ ME MMAPI: Mobile Media API for Java™ Micro Edition*, as well as a technical writer and blogger. Vikram lives in Brisbane, Australia, with his wife and baby daughter.

Acknowledgments

Writing this book took effort not only from the authors, but also from some of the very talented staff at Apress and the technical reviewer. Therefore, we would like to thank Steve Anglin, Douglas Pundick, Richard Dal Porto, Nina Goldschlager Perry, and Candace English from Apress. We would also like to extend our appreciation to the technical reviewer, Vikram Goyal, for the work he did on the book. His commentary and corrections were invaluable.

Introduction

At a high level, this book is about writing mobile applications for devices that support the Android Platform. Specifically, the book teaches you how to write applications using the Android SDK.

Who This Book Is For

This book is for software developers interested in writing mobile applications with the Android SDK. Because Android is a fairly new technology, anyone interested in building mobile applications using the Java™ platform will also benefit from this book. In addition, software architects and business-development professionals can use this book to get an understanding of the Android Platform's capabilities.

What This Book Covers

This book covers the Android SDK. It's broken up into 13 chapters, as follows:

- Chapter 1, "Introducing the Android Computing Platform"

  This chapter introduces you to the Android Platform and its basic building blocks. It also gives you an overview of the Android subsystems by showing you the high-level packages within the Android SDK. Plus, we provide information on Android's specialized virtual machine that addresses the limitations of handheld devices.

- Chapter 2, "Getting Your Feet Wet"

  In this chapter, we show you how to set up a development environment for Android programming. We then walk you through a basic application and introduce you to some of the Android components. We also cover the application lifecycle and familiarize you with some debugging tools.

- Chapter 3, "Using Resources, Content Providers, and Intents"

  Here we cover several of the fundamental pillars of the Android Platform—resources, content providers, and intents. We explain what resources are and how they function in an Android application. We demonstrate how to use content providers as a mechanism for abstracting data into services. We define intents and show you how to use them as a generic way to request action.

- Chapter 4, "Building User Interfaces and Using Controls"

  This chapter is all about building user interfaces with the Android widget toolkit. We first cover building UIs programmatically, then cover Android's preferred way of defining UIs—in XML layout files. We also discuss Android's layout managers and view adapters. Plus, this chapter provides an introduction to the Hierarchy Viewer tool, which you use to optimize UIs.

- Chapter 5, "Working with Menus and Dialogs"

  Here we extend our discussion on UI programming in Android by talking about menus and dialogs. We show you Android's philosophy on building menus, and then discuss the various types of menus available in the Android SDK. We also talk about dialog components.

- Chapter 6, "Unveiling 2D Animation"

  In this chapter, we discuss Android's 2D animation capabilities. We show you how to animate views to make your applications more appealing. Specifically, we cover three categories of animation: frame-by-frame animation, layout animation, and view animation.

- Chapter 7, "Exploring Security and Location-Based Services"

  This chapter covers Android's security model and location-based services. In the first part, we show you Android's security requirements and then show you how to secure your applications. In the second part, we talk about location-based services, which is a fundamental aspect of a mobile device. We show you Android's support for mapping and then show you how to customize a map with data specific to your application. We also cover geocoding in this chapter.

- Chapter 8, "Building and Consuming Services"

  This chapter is about building background services in Android. Here, we talk about building services that are local to your application, as well as remote services— services that can be consumed by other applications running on the device. Remote services are based on Android Interface Definition Language (AIDL), so we show you how to define AIDL types and files. We also describe how to pass types across process boundaries.

- Chapter 9, "Using the Media Framework and Telephony APIs"

  This chapter shows you how to build media-capable applications with the Android SDK. We talk about playing audio and video and then show you how to record audio. We cover text messaging in the telephony part of the chapter.

- Chapter 10, "Programming 3D Graphics with OpenGL"

  Here, you learn how to implement 3D graphics using OpenGL. We show you how to set up OpenGL with your applications and then cover the basics of OpenGL and OpenGL ES. We cover some of the essential OpenGL ES APIs and build a test harness that you can use to exercise those APIs.

- Chapter 11, "Managing and Organizing Preferences"

  In this chapter, we talk about Android's preferences framework. We show you that Android has built-in support for displaying and persisting preferences. We discuss three types of UI elements: CheckBoxPreference, EditTextPreference, and RingtonePreference. We also talk about organizing preferences within your applications.

- Chapter 12, "Coming to Grips with 1.5"

  Chapter 12 discusses some of the changes in the Android 1.5 SDK. Specifically, we talk about some of the SDK's new tools and a few of the most exciting APIs. For example, you'll learn about the new UI wizard that creates Android resources, the new speech-recognition intent, intents to record audio and video, video capture using the MediaRecorder, and more. You'll also get a short introduction to Android's input-method framework (IMF) implementation.

- Chapter 13, "Simplifying OpenGL and Exploring Live Folders"

  This chapter begins by covering the OpenGL-related changes in Android 1.5 and then discusses the new live-folder framework. As you'll see, the Android 1.5 SDK offers some additional abstractions to the OpenGL APIs that make it easier for you to build applications that utilize 3D graphics. We also talk at length about a new concept called *live folders*, which allow you to expose content providers such as contacts, notes, and media on the device's default opening screen.

After reading this book, you'll have a good understanding of the fundamentals of Android. You will be able to utilize the various types of components available in the Android SDK to build your mobile applications. You will also know how to deploy and version your applications.

How to Contact the Authors

You can reach Sayed Y. Hashimi through his web site at http://www.sayedhashimi.com or by e-mail at hashimisayed@gmail.com. You can reach Satya Komatineni through his web site at http://www.satyakomatineni.com or by e-mail at satya.komatineni@gmail.com.

■ ■ ■

CHAPTER 1

Introducing the Android Computing Platform

Personal computing continues to become more "personal" in that computers are becoming increasingly accessible anytime, anywhere. At the forefront of this advancement are handheld devices that are transforming into computing platforms. Mobile phones are no longer just for talking—they have been capable of carrying data and video for some time. More significantly, the mobile device is now becoming so capable of general-purpose computing that it's destined to become the next PC. It is also anticipated that a number of manufacturers such as ASUS, HP, and Dell will be producing netbooks based on the Android OS. So the battle lines of operating systems, computing platforms, programming languages, and development frameworks are being shifted and reapplied to mobile devices.

We are also expecting a surge in mobile programming in the IT industry as more and more IT applications start to offer mobile counterparts. To help you profit from this trend, we'll show you how to use Java to write programs for devices that run on Google's Android Platform (http://code.google.com/android/), an open source platform for mobile development. We are excited about Android because it is an advanced platform that introduces a number of new paradigms in framework design. In this chapter, we'll provide an overview of Android and its SDK, show you how to take advantage of Android source code, and highlight the benefits of programming for the Android Platform.

The fact that hitherto dedicated devices such as mobile phones can now count themselves among other venerable general-computing platforms is great news for programmers (see Figure 1-1). This new trend makes mobile devices accessible through general-purpose computing languages and therefore increases the range and market share for mobile applications.

The Android Platform fully embraces this idea of general-purpose computing for handheld devices. It is indeed a comprehensive platform that features a Linux-based operating system stack for managing devices, memory, and processes. Android's libraries cover telephony, video, graphics, UI programming, and every other aspect of the physical device.

The Android Platform, although built for mobile devices, exhibits the characteristics of a full-featured desktop framework. Google makes this framework available to Java programmers through a software development kit called the Android SDK. When you are working with the Android SDK, you rarely feel that you are writing to a mobile device because you have access to most of the class libraries that you use on a desktop or a server—including a relational database.

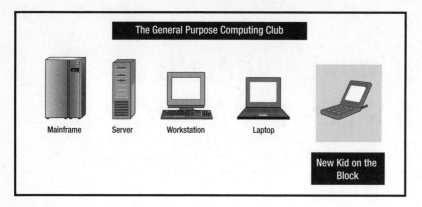

Figure 1-1. *Handheld is the new PC.*

The Android SDK supports most of Java Platform, Standard Edition (Java SE) except for the Abstract Window Toolkit (AWT) and Swing. In place of the AWT and Swing, the Android SDK has its own extensive modern UI framework. Because you're programming your applications in Java, you might expect to need a Java Virtual Machine (JVM) that is responsible for interpreting the runtime Java bytecode. A JVM typically provides necessary optimization to help Java reach performance levels comparable to compiled languages such as C and C++. Android offers its own optimized JVM to run the compiled Java class files in order to counter the handheld device limitations such as memory, processor speed, and power. This virtual machine is called the Dalvik VM, which we'll explore in the section "Delving Into the Dalvik VM."

The familiarity and simplicity of the Java programming language coupled with Android's extensive class library makes Android a compelling platform to write programs for. Figure 1-2 provides an overview of the Android software stack. (We'll provide further details in the section "Understanding the Android Software Stack.")

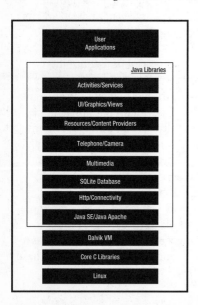

Figure 1-2. *High-level view of the Android software stack*

History of Android

Now that we've provided a brief introduction to the Android Platform, we'll describe how it appeared on the mobile-development scene. Mobile phones use a variety of operating systems such as Symbian OS, Microsoft's Windows Mobile, Mobile Linux, iPhone OS (based on Mac OS X), and many other proprietary OSs. Supporting standards and publishing APIs would greatly encourage widespread, low-cost development of mobile applications, but none of these OSs has taken a clear lead in doing so. Then Google entered the space with its Android Platform, promising openness, affordability, open source code, and a high-end development framework.

Google acquired the startup company Android Inc. in 2005 to start the development of the Android Platform (see Figure 1-3). The key players at Android Inc. included Andy Rubin, Rich Miner, Nick Sears, and Chris White.

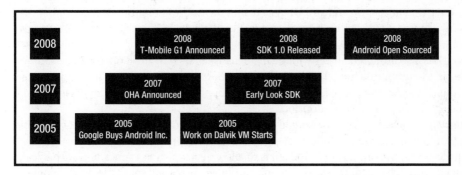

Figure 1-3. *Android timeline*

In late 2007, a group of industry leaders came together around the Android Platform to form the Open Handset Alliance (http://www.openhandsetalliance.com). Some of the alliance's prominent members include

- Sprint Nextel
- T-Mobile
- Motorola
- Samsung
- Sony Ericsson
- Toshiba
- Vodafone
- Google
- Intel
- Texas Instruments

Part of the alliance's goal is to innovate rapidly and respond better to consumer needs, and its first key outcome was the Android Platform. Android was designed to serve the needs of mobile operators, handset manufacturers, and application developers. The members have committed to release significant intellectual property through the open source Apache License, Version 2.0.

■**Note** Handset manufacturers do not need to pay any licensing fees to load Android on their handsets or devices.

The Android SDK was first issued as an "early look" release in November 2007. In September 2008, T-Mobile announced the availability of the T-Mobile G1, the first smartphone based on the Android Platform. A few days after that, Google announced the availability of Android SDK Release Candidate 1.0. In October 2008, Google made the source code of the Android Platform available under Apache's open source license.

When Android was released, one of its key architectural goals was to allow applications to interact with one another and reuse components from one another. This reuse not only applies to services, but also to data and UI. As a result, the Android Platform has a number of architectural features that keep this openness a reality. We'll delve into some of these features in Chapter 3.

Android has also attracted an early following because of its fully developed features to exploit the cloud-computing model offered by web resources and to enhance that experience with local data stores on the handset itself. Android's support for a relational database on the handset also played a part in early adoption.

In late 2008 Google released a handheld device called Android Dev Phone 1 that is capable of running Android applications without being tied to any cell phone provider network. The goal of this device (approximate cost $400.00) is to allow developers to experiment with a real device that can run the Android OS with out any contracts. At around the same time, Google also released a bug fix version 1.1 of the OS that is solely based on 1.0. In releases 1.0 and 1.1 Android did not support soft keyboards, requiring the devices to carry physical keys. Android fixed this issue by releasing the 1.5 SDK in April of 2009, along with a number of other features, such as advanced media-recording capabilities, widgets, and live folders. The last two chapters of this book are dedicated to exploring the features from this 1.5 SDK.

Delving into the Dalvik VM

Google has spent a lot of time thinking about optimizing designs for low-powered handheld devices. Handheld devices lag behind their desktop counterparts in memory and speed by eight to ten years. They also have limited power for computation; a handheld device's total RAM might be as little as 64MB, and its available space for applications might be as little as 20MB.

■**Note** For example, the T-Mobile G1 phone, released in late 2008, comes with 192MB of RAM, a 1GB SD card, and a 528 MHz Qualcomm MSM7201A processor. Compare that to the lowest-priced Dell laptop, which comes with a 2.1 GHz dual-core processor and 2GB of RAM.

The performance requirements on handsets are severe as a result, requiring handset designers to optimize everything. If you look at the list of packages in Android, you'll see that they are full-featured and extensive in number. According to Google, these system libraries might use as much as 10MB, even with their optimized JVM.

These issues led Google to revisit the standard JVM implementation in many respects. (The key figure in Google's implementation of this JVM is Dan Bornstein, who wrote the Dalvik VM and named it after a town in Iceland.) First, the Dalvik VM takes the generated Java class files and combines them into one or more Dalvik Executable (.dex) files. It reuses duplicate information from multiple class files, effectively reducing the space requirement (uncompressed) by half from a traditional .jar file. For example, the .dex file of the web-browser app in Android is about 200K, whereas the equivalent uncompressed .jar version is about 500K. The .dex file of the alarm-clock app is about 50K, and roughly twice that size in its .jar version.

Second, Google has fine-tuned the garbage collection in the Dalvik VM, but it has chosen to omit a just-in-time (JIT) compiler, in this release at least. The company can justify this choice because many of Android's core libraries, including the graphics libraries, are implemented in C and C++. For example, the Java graphics APIs are actually thin wrapper classes around the native code using the Java Native Interface (JNI). Similarly, Android provides an optimized C-based native library to access the SQLite database, but this library is encapsulated in a higher-level Java API. Because most of the core code is in C and C++, Google reasoned that the impact of JIT compilation would not be significant.

Finally, the Dalvik VM uses a different kind of assembly-code generation, in which it uses registers as the primary units of data storage instead of the stack. Google is hoping to accomplish 30 percent fewer instructions as a result.

We should point out that the final executable code in Android, as a result of the Dalvik VM, is based not on Java bytecode but on .dex files instead. This means you cannot directly execute Java bytecode; you have to start with Java class files and then convert them to linkable .dex files.

This extreme performance paranoia extends into the rest of the Android SDK. For example, the Android SDK uses XML extensively to define UI layouts. However, all of this XML is compiled to binary files before these binary files become resident on the devices. Android provides special mechanisms to use this XML data.

While we are on the subject of Android's design considerations, we should answer this question: How would one compare and contrast Android to Java Platform, Micro Edition (Java ME)?

Comparing Android and Java ME

As you have seen so far in this chapter, Android has taken a dedicated and focused approach to its mobile-platform efforts that goes beyond a simple JVM-based solution. The Android Platform comes with everything you need in a single package: the OS, device drivers, core libraries, the JNI, the optimized Dalvik VM, and the Java development environment. Developers can be assured that when they develop new applications, all key libraries will be available on the device.

Let us offer a brief overview of Java ME before comparing the two approaches. Figure 1-4 shows the availability of Java for various computing configurations. Java Platform, Standard Edition (Java SE) is suitable for desktop and workstation configurations. Java Platform, Enterprise Edition (Java EE) is designed for server configurations.

Java Platform, Micro Edition (Java ME) is an edition of Java that is pared down for smaller devices. Furthermore, two configuration sets are available for Java ME. The first configuration is called the Connected Device Configuration (CDC). Java ME for CDC involves a pared down version of Java SE with fewer packages, fewer classes within those packages, and even fewer fields and methods within those classes. For appliances and devices that are further constrained, Java defines a configuration called Connected Limited Device Configuration (CLDC). The available APIs for various Java configurations are contrasted in Figure 1-5.

Any optional packages that are installed on top of the base CDC and CLDC APIs are treated as "profiles" that are standardized using the JSR process. Each defined profile makes an additional set of APIs available to the developer.

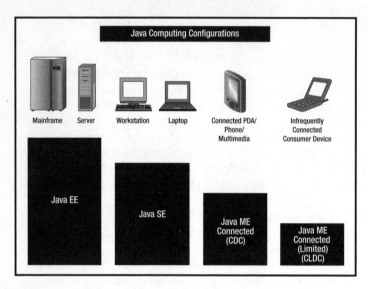

Figure 1-4. *Java computing configurations*

▨**Caution** Both CLDC and CDC might support some Java APIs outside Java SE, and their classes might not start with the `java.*` namespace. As a consequence, if you have a Java program that runs on your desktop, there are no guarantees that it will run on devices supporting only micro editions.

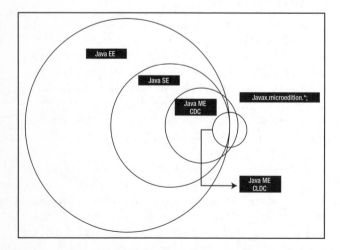

Figure 1-5. *Java API availability*

The CLDC Java platform is hosted on a specialized and much reduced JVM called the K Virtual Machine (KVM), which is capable of running on devices whose memory is as low as 128K. (The "K" in "KVM" stands for "kilobytes.") CLDC can run additional APIs under MIDP (Mobile Information Device Profile) 2.0. This API includes a number of packages under `javax.microedition.*`. The key packages are MIDlets (simple applications), a UI package called LCDUI, gaming, and media.

The CDC configuration APIs include the `java.awt` API, the `java.net` API, and more security APIs in addition to the CLDC configuration APIs. The additional profiles available on top of CDC make the `javax.microedition.xlet` API available to application programmers (Xlets represent applications in the CDC configuration). On top of a CDC configuration you'll find about ten more optional packages that you can run, including Bluetooth, Media API, OpenGL for Embedded Systems (OpenGL ES), Java API for XML Processing (JAXP), JAXP-RPC, Java 2D, Swing, Java Remote Method Invocation (Java RMI), and Java Database Connectivity {JDBC). Overall the Java ME specification includes more than 20 JSRs. It is also expected that JavaFX (`http://javafx.com`) will play an increasing role in the mobile space for Java.

■**Note** JavaFX is a new UI effort from Sun to dramatically improve applet-like functionality in browsers. It offers a declarative UI programming model that is also friendlier to designers. A mobile version of JavaFX is expected to be released sometime in 2009.

Now that you have a background on Java ME, look at how it compares to Android:

- *Multiple device configurations*: Java ME addresses two classes of micro devices and offers standardized and distinct solutions for each. Android, on the other hand, applies to just one model. It won't run on low-end devices unless or until the configurations of those devices improve.

- *Ease of understanding*: Because Android is geared toward only one device model, it's easier to understand than Java ME. Java ME has multiple UI models for each configuration, depending on the features supported by the device: MIDlets, Xlets, the AWT, and Swing. The JSRs for each Java ME specification are harder to follow; they take longer to mature; and finding implementations for them can be difficult.

- *Responsiveness*: The Dalvik VM is more optimized and more responsive compared to the standard JVM supported on a similarly configured device. You can compare the Dalvik VM to the KVM, but the KVM addresses a lower-level device with much less memory.

- *Java compatibility*: Because of the Dalvik VM, Android runs .dex bytecode instead of Java bytecode. This should not be a major concern as long as Java is compiled to standard Java class files. Only runtime interpretation of Java bytecode is not possible.

- *Adoption*: There is widespread support for Java ME on mobile devices because most mobile phones support it. But the uniformity, cost, and ease of development in Android are compelling reasons for Java developers to program for it.

- *Java SE support*: Compared to the support for Java SE in CDC, the Android support for Java SE is a bit more complete, except for the AWT and Swing. As we mentioned earlier, Android has its own UI approach instead. In fact, Android's declarative UI resembles the JavaFX approach.

Understanding the Android Software Stack

So far we've covered Android's history and its optimization features including the Dalvik VM, and we've hinted at the Java programming stack available. In this section, we would like to cover the development aspect of Android. Figure 1-6 is a good place to start this discussion.

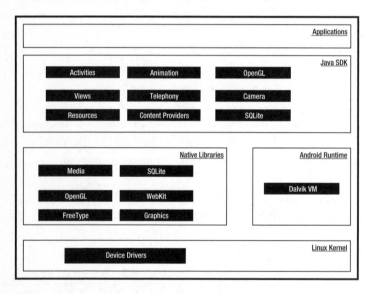

Figure 1-6. *Detailed Android SDK software stack*

At the core of the Android Platform is Linux kernel version 2.6, responsible for device drivers, resource access, power management, and other OS duties. The supplied device drivers include Display, Camera, Keypad, WiFi, Flash Memory, Audio, and IPC (interprocess communication). Although the core is Linux, the majority—if not all—of the applications on an Android device such as the T-Mobile G1 are developed in Java and run through the Dalvik VM.

Sitting at the next level, on top of the kernel, are a number of C/C++ libraries such as OpenGL, WebKit, FreeType, Secure Sockets Layer (SSL), the C runtime library (libc), SQLite, and Media. The system C library based on Berkeley Software Distribution (BSD) is tuned (to roughly half its original size) for embedded Linux-based devices. The media libraries are based on PacketVideo's (http://www.packetvideo.com/) OpenCORE. These libraries are responsible for recording and playback of audio and video formats. A library called Surface Manager controls access to the display system and supports 2D and 3D.

The WebKit library is responsible for browser support; it is the same library that supports Google Chrome and Apple Inc.'s Safari. The FreeType library is responsible for font support. SQLite (http://www.sqlite.org/) is a relational database that is available on the device itself. SQLite is also an independent open source effort for relational databases and not directly tied to Android. You can acquire and use tools meant for SQLite for Android databases as well.

Most of the application framework accesses these core libraries through the Dalvik VM, the gateway to the Android Platform. As we indicated in the previous sections, Dalvik is optimized to run multiple instances of VMs. As Java applications access these core libraries, each application gets its own VM instance. The Dalvik VM is backward-compatible with Java SE Development Kit (JDK) 5.0 but optimized for the Android Platform. However, some features of the Java experience might differ because the version of Java SE on Android is a subset of the full platform.

The Android Java API's main libraries include telephony, resources, locations, UI, content providers (data), and package managers (installation, security, and so on). Programmers develop end-user applications on top of this Java API. Some examples of end-user applications on the device include Home, Contacts, Phone, Browser, and so on.

Android also supports a custom Google 2D graphics library called Skia, which is written in C and C++. Skia also forms the core of the Google Chrome browser. The 3D APIs in Android, however, are based on an implementation of OpenGL ES from the Khronos group (http://www.khronos.org). OpenGL ES contains subsets of OpenGL that are targeted toward embedded systems.

From a media perspective, the Android Platform supports the most common formats for audio, video, and images. From a wireless perspective, Android has APIs to support Bluetooth, EDGE, 3G, WiFi, and Global System for Mobile Communication (GSM) telephony, depending on the hardware.

Developing an End-User Application with the Android SDK

In this section, we'll introduce you to the high-level Android Java APIs that you'll use to develop end-user applications for an Android handheld. We will briefly talk about the Android phone emulator and foundational components, UI programming, services, media, telephony, animation, and OpenGL. We will also show you some code snippets when they are helpful.

The Android Emulator

The Android SDK ships with an Eclipse plug-in called Android Development Tools (ADT). You will use this Integrated Development Environment (IDE) tool for developing, debugging, and testing your Java applications. (We'll cover ADT in depth in Chapter 2.)

You can also use the Android SDK without using ADT; you'd use command-line tools instead. Both approaches support an emulator that you can use to run, debug, and test your applications. You will not even need the real device for 90 percent of your application development.

The full-featured Android emulator mimics most of the device features, but you'll encounter some limitations regarding USB connections, camera and video capture, headphones, battery simulation, and Bluetooth.

The Android emulator accomplishes its work through an open source "processor emulator" technology called QEMU (http://bellard.org/qemu/) developed by Fabrice Bellard. This is the same technology that allows emulation of one operating system on top of another, irrespective of the processor. QEMU allows emulation at the CPU level.

In the case of the Android emulator, the processor is based on ARM (Advanced RISC Machine). ARM is a 32-bit microprocessor architecture based on RISC (Reduced Instruction Set Computer), in which design simplicity and speed is achieved through a reduced number of instructions in an instruction set. The emulator actually runs the Android version of Linux on this simulated processor. PowerPCs supporting Apple Macs and SPARC chips supporting Sun workstations are examples of RISC architectures.

ARM is widely used in handhelds and other embedded electronics where lower power consumption is important. Much of the mobile market uses processors based on this architecture. For example, Apple Newton is based on the ARM6 processor. Devices such as the iPod, Nintendo DS, and Game Boy Advance run on ARM architecture version 4 with approximately 30,000 transistors. Compared to that, the Pentium classic contains 3,200,000 (3.2 million) transistors.

You can find more details about the emulator in the Android SDK documentation at http://code.google.com/android/reference/emulator.html.

The Android UI

Android uses a UI framework that resembles other desktop-based, full-featured UI frameworks, but it's more modern and more asynchronous in nature. Android is almost a fourth-generation UI framework if you were to call the traditional C-based Microsoft Windows API the first generation and the C++-based MFC (Microsoft Foundation Classes) the second generation. The Java-based Swing UI framework would be the third generation, introducing design flexibility far beyond that offered by MFC. The Android UI, JavaFX, Microsoft Silverlight, and Mozilla XML User Interface Language (XUL) fall under this new type of fourth-generation UI framework in which the UI is declarative and independently themed.

■**Note** The noteworthy aspect of UI programming in Android is that you are programming in a modern UI paradigm even though the device happens to be a handheld.

Programming in the Android UI involves declaring the interface in XML files. You will then load these XML view definitions as windows in your UI application. Even menus in your application are loaded from XML files. Screens or windows in Android are often referred to as *activities*, which comprise multiple views that a user needs in order to accomplish a logical unit of action. *Views* are Android's basic UI building blocks, and you can further combine them to form composite views called *view groups*. Views internally use the familiar concepts of canvases, painting, and user interaction. An activity hosting these composite views, which include views and view groups, is the logical replaceable UI component in Android.

One of the Android framework's key concepts is the lifecycle management of activity windows. Protocols are put in place so that Android can manage state as users hide, restore, stop, and close activity windows. You will get a feel for these basic ideas in Chapter 2, along with an introduction to setting up the Android development environment.

The Android Foundational Components

The Android UI framework, along with other parts of Android, relies on a new concept called an *intent*. An intent is an amalgamation of ideas such as windowing messages, actions, publish-and-subscribe models, interprocess communications, and application registries. Here is an example of using the Intent class to invoke or start a web browser:

```
public static void invokeWebBrowser(Activity activity)
{
    Intent intent = new Intent(Intent.ACTION_VIEW);
    intent.setData(Uri.parse("http://www.google.com"));
    activity.startActivity(intent);
}
```

Through an intent, we are asking Android to start a suitable window to display the content of a web site. Depending on the list of browsers that are installed on the device, Android will choose a suitable one to display the site. You will learn more about intents in Chapter 3.

Android also has extensive support for *resources*, which include familiar elements and files such as strings and bitmaps, as well as some not-so-familiar items such as XML-based view definitions. The framework makes use of resources in a novel way to make their usage easy, intuitive, and convenient. Here is an example where IDs are automatically generated for resources defined in XML files:

```
public final class R {
    public static final class attr { }
    public static final class drawable {
        public static final int myanimation=0x7f020001;
        public static final int numbers19=0x7f02000e;
    }

    public static final class id {
        public static final int textViewId1=0x7f080003;
    }
    public static final class layout {
        public static final int frame_animations_layout=0x7f030001;
        public static final int main=0x7f030002;
    }
    public static final class string {
        public static final int hello=0x7f070000;
    }
}
```

Each auto-generated ID in this class corresponds to either an element in an XML file or a whole file itself. Wherever you would like to use those XML definitions, you can use these generated IDs instead. This indirection helps a great deal when it comes to localization. (Chapter 3 covers the R.java file and resources in more detail.)

Another new concept in Android is the *content provider*. A content provider is an abstraction on a data source that makes it look like an emitter and consumer of RESTful services. The underlying SQLite database makes this facility of content providers a powerful tool for application developers. (In Chapter 3, we'll discuss how intents, resources, and content providers promote openness in the Android Platform.)

Advanced UI Concepts

We have pointed out that XML plays a role in describing the Android UI. Look at an example of how XML does this for a simple layout containing a text view:

```
<?xml version="1.0" encoding="utf-8"?>
<LinearLayout xmlns:android=http://schemas.android.com/apk/res/android>
<TextView android:id="@+id/textViewId"
    android:layout_width="fill_parent"    android:layout_height="wrap_content"
    android:text="@string/hello"
    />
</LinearLayout>
```

You will then use an ID generated for this XML file to load this layout into an activity window. (We'll cover these ideas further in Chapter 4.)

Android also provides extensive support for menus, from standard menus to context menus. You'll find it convenient to work with menus in Android because they are also loaded as XML files and because resource IDs for those menus are auto-generated. Here's how you would declare menus in an XML file:

```
<menu xmlns:android="http://schemas.android.com/apk/res/android">
    <!-- This group uses the default category. -->
    <group android:id="@+id/menuGroup_Main">
        <item android:id="@+id/menu_clear"
            android:orderInCategory="10"
            android:title="clear" />
        <item android:id="@+id/menu_show_browser"
            android:orderInCategory="5"
            android:title="show browser" />
    </group>
</menu>
```

Although Android supports dialogs, all dialogs in Android are asynchronous. These asynchronous dialogs present a special challenge to developers accustomed to the synchronous modal dialogs in some windowing frameworks. We'll address menus and dialogs more extensively in Chapter 5, where we'll also provide a number of mechanisms to deal with asynchronous-dialog protocols.

Android also offers support for animation as part of its UI stack based on views and drawable objects. Android supports two kinds of animation: *tweening* animation and frame-by-frame animation.

"Tweening" is a term in animation that refers to the drawings that are "in between" the key drawings. You accomplish this with computers by changing the intermediate values at regular intervals and redrawing the surface. Frame-by-frame animation occurs when a series of frames is drawn one after the other at regular intervals. Android enables both animation approaches through animation callbacks, interpolators, and transformation matrices. Moreover, Android allows you to define these animations in an XML resource file. Check out this example, in which a series of numbered images is played in frame-by-frame animation:

```
<animation-list xmlns:android="http://schemas.android.com/apk/res/android"
        android:oneshot="false">
    <item android:drawable="@drawable/numbers11" android:duration="50" />
    ......
    <item android:drawable="@drawable/numbers19" android:duration="50" />
</animation-list>
```

The underlying graphics libraries support the standard transformation matrices, allowing scaling, movement, and rotation. A Camera object in the graphics library provides support for depth and projection, which allows 3D-like simulation on a 2D surface. (We'll explore animation further in Chapter 6.)

Android also supports 3D graphics through its implementation of the OpenGL ES 1.0 standard. OpenGL ES, like OpenGL, is a C-based flat API. The Android SDK, because it's a Java-based programming API, needs to use Java binding to access the OpenGL ES. Java ME has already defined this binding through Java Specification Request (JSR) 239 for OpenGL ES, and Android uses the same Java binding for OpenGL ES in its implementation. If you are not familiar with OpenGL programming, the learning curve is steep. But we've reviewed the basics here, so you'll be ready to start programming in OpenGL for Android in Chapter 10.

Starting with release 1.5 Android has simplified OpenGL so that it is approachable to beginning OpenGL programmers. We will cover these improvements in Chapter 13. Additionally, that SDK introduced a new concept called live folders, which we will also cover in Chapter 13.

Android Service Components

Security is a fundamental part of the Android Platform. In Android, security spans all phases of the application lifecycle—from design-time policy considerations to runtime boundary checks. Location-based service is another one of the more exciting pieces of the Android SDK. This portion of the SDK provides application developers APIs to display and manipulate maps, as well as obtain real-time device-location information. We'll cover these ideas in detail in Chapter 7.

In Chapter 8, we'll show you how to build and consume services in Android, specifically HTTP services. The chapter will also cover interprocess communication (communication between applications on the same device). Here is an example of doing an HttpPost in Android:

```
InputStream is = this.getAssets().open("data.xml");
HttpClient httpClient = new DefaultHttpClient();
HttpPost postRequest = new HttpPost("http://192.178.10.131/WS2/Upload.aspx");

byte[] data = IOUtils.toByteArray(is);

InputStreamBody isb = new InputStreamBody(
        new ByteArrayInputStream(data),"uploadedFile");
StringBody sb1 = new StringBody("someTextGoesHere");
StringBody sb2 = new StringBody("someTextGoesHere too");

MultipartEntity multipartContent = new MultipartEntity();
multipartContent.addPart("uploadedFile", isb);
multipartContent.addPart("one", sb1);
multipartContent.addPart("two", sb2);
```

```
postRequest.setEntity(multipartContent);
HttpResponse res =httpClient.execute(postRequest);
res.getEntity().getContent().close();
```

Android Media and Telephony Components

Android has APIs that cover audio, video, and telephony components. Here is a quick example of how to play an audio file from an Internet URL:

```
private void playAudio(String url)throws Exception
{
    mediaPlayer = new MediaPlayer();
    mediaPlayer.setDataSource(internetUrl);
    mediaPlayer.prepare();
    mediaPlayer.start();
}
```

And here's an example of playing an audio file from the local device:

```
private void playLocalAudio()throws Exception
{
    //The file is located in the /res/raw directory and called "music_file.mp3"
     mediaPlayer = MediaPlayer.create(this, R.raw.music_file);
     mediaPlayer.start();
}
```

We'll cover these audio and video APIs extensively in Chapter 9. The chapter will also address the following aspects of the telephony API:

- Sending and receiving Short Message Service (SMS) messages

- Monitoring SMS messages

- Managing SMS folders

- Placing and receiving phone calls

Here is an example taken from that chapter on sending an SMS message:

```
private void sendSmsMessage(String address,String message)throws Exception
{
    SmsManager smsMgr = SmsManager.getDefault();
    smsMgr.sendTextMessage(address, null, message, null, null);
}
```

Prior to the 1.5 release you could record audio but not video. Both audio and video recording are accommodated in 1.5 through MediaRecorder. This is covered with examples in Chapter 12. Chapter 12 also covers voice recognition, along with the input-method framework (IMF), which allows a variety of inputs to be interpreted as text while typing into text controls. The input methods include keyboard, voice, pen device, mouse, etc. This framework was originally designed as part of Java API 1.4; you can read more about it at the following Java site:

```
http://java.sun.com/j2se/1.4.2/docs/guide/imf/overview.html
```

Last but not least, Android ties all these concepts into an application by creating a single XML file that defines what an application package is. This file is called the application's manifest file (AndroidManifest.xml). Here is an example:

```xml
<?xml version="1.0" encoding="utf-8"?>
<manifest xmlns:android="http://schemas.android.com/apk/res/android"
    package="com.ai.android.HelloWorld"
    android:versionCode="1"
    android:versionName="1.0.0">
  <application android:icon="@drawable/icon" android:label="@string/app_name">
      <activity android:name=".HelloWorld"
              android:label="@string/app_name">
        <intent-filter>
            <action android:name="android.intent.action.MAIN" />
            <category android:name="android.intent.category.LAUNCHER" />
        </intent-filter>
      </activity>
  </application>
</manifest>
```

The Android manifest file is where activities are defined, where services and content providers are registered, and where permissions are declared. Details about the manifest file will emerge throughout the book as we develop each idea.

Android Java Packages

One way to get a quick snapshot of the Android Platform is to look at the structure of Java packages. Because Android deviates from the standard JDK distribution, it is important to know at a high level what is supported and what is not. Here's a brief description of the important Java packages that are included in the Android SDK:

- *android.app*: Implements the Application model for Android. Primary classes include Application, representing the start and stop semantics, as well as a number of activity-related classes, controls, dialogs, alerts, and notifications.

- *android.appwidget*: Implements the mechanism for allowing applications to publish their views in other applications, such as the home page. The primary classes include AppWidgetHost, AppWidgetHostView, AppWidgetManager, AppWidgetProvider, and AppWidgetProviderInfo. This package is available only in SDK 1.5.

- *android.content*: Implements the concepts of content providers. Content providers abstract out data access from data stores. This package also implements the central ideas around intents and Android Uniform Resource Identifiers (URIs).

- *android.content.pm*: Implements Package Manager–related classes. A package manager knows about permissions, installed packages, installed providers, installed services, installed components such as activities, and installed applications.

- *android.content.res*: Provides access to resource files both structured and unstructured. The primary classes are AssetManager (for unstructured resources) and Resources.

- *android.database*: Implements the idea of an abstract database. The primary interface is the `Cursor` interface.

- *android.database.sqlite*: Implements the concepts from the `android.database` package using SQLite as the physical database. Primary classes are `SQLiteCursor`, `SQLiteDatabase`, `SQLiteQuery`, `SQLiteQueryBuilder`, and `SQLiteStatement`. However, most of your interaction is going to be with classes from the abstract `android.database` package.

- *android.graphics*: Contains the classes `Bitmap`, `Canvas`, `Camera`, `Color`, `Matrix`, `Movie`, `Paint`, `Path`, `Rasterizer`, `Shader`, `SweepGradient`, and `TypeFace`.

- *android.graphics.drawable*: Implements drawing protocols and background images, and allows animation of drawable objects.

- *android.graphics.drawable.shapes*: Implements shapes including `ArcShape`, `OvalShape`, `PathShape`, `RectShape`, and `RoundRectShape`.

- *android.hardware*: Implements the physical `Camera`-related classes. This `Camera` represents the hardware camera, whereas `android.graphics.Camera` represents a graphical concept that's not related to a physical camera at all.

- *android.inputmethodservice*: Implements the interfaces and base abstract classes necessary for writing input methods.

- *android.location*: Contains the classes `Address`, `GeoCoder`, `Location`, `LocationManager`, and `LocationProvider`. The `Address` class represents the simplified XAL (Extensible Address Language). `GeoCoder` allows you to get a latitude/longitude coordinate given an address, and vice versa. `Location` represents the latitude/longitude.

- *android.media*: Contains the classes `MediaPlayer`, `MediaRecorder`, `Ringtone`, `AudioManager`, and `FaceDetector`. `MediaPlayer`, which supports streaming, is used to play audio and video. `MediaRecorder` is used to record audio and video. The `Ringtone` class is used to play short sound snippets that could serve as ringtones and notifications. `AudioManager` is responsible for volume controls. You can use `FaceDetector` to detect people's faces in a bitmap.

- *android.net*: Implements the basic socket-level network APIs. Primary classes include `Uri`, `ConnectivityManager`, `LocalSocket`, and `LocalServerSocket`.

- *android.net.wifi*: Manages WiFi connectivity. Primary classes include `WifiManager` and `WifiConfiguration`. `WifiManager` is responsible for listing the configured networks and the currently active WiFi network.

- *android.opengl*: Contains utility classes surrounding OpenGL ES operations. The primary classes of OpenGL ES are implemented in a different set of packages borrowed from JSR 239. These packages are `javax.microedition.khronos.opengles`, `javax.microedition.khronos.egl`, and `javax.microedition.khronos.nio`. These packages are thin wrappers around the Khronos implementation of OpenGL ES in C and C++.

- *android.os*: Represents the OS services accessible through the Java programming language. Some important classes include `BatteryManager`, `Binder`, `FileObserver`, `Handler`, `Looper`, and `PowerManager`. `Binder` is a class that allows interprocess communication. `FileObserver` keeps tabs on changes to files. You use `Handler` classes to run tasks on the message thread, and `Looper` to run a message thread.

- *android.preference*: Allows applications the ability to have users manage their preferences for that application in a uniform way. The primary classes are `PreferenceActivity`, `PreferenceScreen`, and various `Preference`-derived classes such as `CheckBoxPreference` and `SharedPreferences`.

- *android.provider*: Comprises a set of prebuilt content providers adhering to the `android.content.ContentProvider` interface. The content providers include `Contacts`, `MediaStore`, `Browser`, and `Settings`. This set of interfaces and classes stores the metadata for the underlying data structures.

- *android.sax*: Contains an efficient set of Simple API for XML (SAX) parsing utility classes. Primary classes include `Element`, `RootElement`, and a number of `ElementListener` interfaces.

- *android.speech*: Contains constants for use with speech recognition. This package is available only in releases 1.5 and later.

- *android.telephony*: Contains the classes `CellLocation`, `PhoneNumberUtils`, and `TelephonyManager`. A `TelephonyManager` lets you determine cell location, phone number, network-operator name, network type, phone type, and Subscriber Identity Module (SIM) serial number.

- *android.telephony.gsm*: Allows you to gather cell location based on cell towers and also hosts classes responsible for SMS messaging. This package is called GSM because Global System for Mobile Communication is the technology that originally defined the SMS data-messaging standard.

- *android.text*: Contains text-processing classes.

- *android.text.method*: Provides classes for entering text input for a variety of controls.

- *android.text.style*: Provides a number of styling mechanisms for a span of text.

- *android.utils*: Contains the classes `Log`, `DebugUtils`, `TimeUtils`, and `Xml`.

- *android.view*: Contains the classes `Menu`, `View`, `ViewGroup`, and a series of listeners and callbacks.

- *android.view.animation*: Provides support for tweening animation. The main classes include `Animation`, a series of interpolators for animation, and a set of specific animator classes that include `AlphaAnimation`, `ScaleAnimation`, `TranslationAnimation`, and `RotationAnimation`.

- *android.view.inputmethod*: Implements the input-method framework architecture. This package is available only in releases 1.5 and later.

- *android.webkit*: Contains classes representing the web browser. The primary classes include `WebView`, `CacheManager`, and `CookieManager`.

- *android.widget*: Contains all of the UI controls usually derived from the `View` class. Primary widgets include `Button`, `Checkbox`, `Chronometer`, `AnalogClock`, `DatePicker`, `DigitalClock`, `EditText`, `ListView`, `FrameLayout`, `GridView`, `ImageButton`, `MediaController`, `ProgressBar`, `RadioButton`, `RadioGroup`, `RatingButton`, `Scroller`, `ScrollView`, `Spinner`, `TabWidget`, `TextView`, `TimePicker`, `VideoView`, and `ZoomButton`.

- *com.google.android.maps*: Contains the classes `MapView`, `MapController`, and `MapActivity`, essentially classes required to work with Google maps.

These are some of the critical Android-specific packages. From this list you can see the depth of the Android core platform.

▨**Note** In all, the Android Java API contains more than 36 packages and more than 700 classes.

In addition, Android provides a number of packages in the `java.*` namespace. These include `awt.font`, `io`, `lang`, `lang.annotation`, `lang.ref`, `lang.reflect`, `math`, `net`, `nio`, `nio.channels`, `nio.channels.spi`, `nio.charset`, `security`, `security.acl`, `security.cert`, `security.interfaces`, `security.spec`, `sql`, `text`, `util`, `util.concurrent`, `util.concurrent.atomic`, `util.concurrent.locks`, `util.jar`, `util.logging`, `util.prefs`, `util.regex`, and `util.zip`.

Android comes with these packages from the `javax` namespace: `crypto`, `crypto.spec`, `microedition.khronos.egl`, `microedition.khronos.opengles`, `net`, `net.ssl`, `security.auth`, `security.auth.callback`, `security.auth.login`, `security.auth.x500`, `security.cert`, `sql`, `xml`, and `xmlparsers`.

In addition, it contains a lot of packages from `org.apache.http.*`. It also carries `org.json`, `org.w3c.dom`, `org.xml.sax`, `org.xml.sax.ext`, `org.xml.sax.helpers`, `org.xmlpull.v1`, and `org.xmlpull.v1.sax2`.

Together, these numerous packages provide a rich computing platform to write applications for handheld devices.

Taking Advantage of Android Source Code

During these early releases of Android, documentation is a bit "wanting" in places. When you run into that situation, it is worthwhile exploring Android source code to fill the gaps.

The details of the Android source distribution are published at `http://source.android.com`. The code was open sourced around October 2008 (read the announcement at `http://source.android.com/posts/opensource`). One of the Open Handset Alliance's goals was to make Android a free and fully customizable mobile platform. The announcement strongly suggests that the Android Platform is a fully capable mobile computing platform with no gaps. The open source model allows contributions from noncore team members within the public communities.

As indicated, Android is a platform and not just one project. You can see the scope and the number of projects at `http://source.android.com/projects`.

The source code of Android and all its projects is managed by the Git source-code control system. Git (`http://git.or.cz/`) is an open source source-control system designed to handle large and small projects with speed and convenience. The Linux kernel and Ruby on Rails projects also rely on Git for version control. The complete list of Android projects in the Git repository appears at `http://android.git.kernel.org/`.

You can download any of these projects using the tools provided by Git and described at the product's web site. Some of the primary projects include Dalvik, `frameworks/base` (the `android.jar` file), Linux kernel, and a number of external libraries such as Apache HTTP libraries (apache-http). The core Android applications are also hosted here. Some of these core applications include: AlarmClock, Browser, Calculator, Calendar, Camera, Contacts, Email, GoogleSearch, HTML Viewer, IM, Launcher, Mms, Music, PackageInstaller, Phone, Settings, SoundRecorder, Stk, Sync, Updater, and VoiceDialer.

The Android projects also include the "Provider" projects. "Provider" projects are like databases in Android that wrap their data into RESTful services. These projects are CalendarProvider, ContactsProvider, DownloadProvider, DrmProvider, GoogleContactsProvider, GoogleSubscribedFeedsProvider, ImProvider, MediaProvider, SettingsProvider, SubscribedFeedsProvider, and TelephonyProvider.

As a programmer, you will be most interested in the source code that makes up the `android.jar` file. (If you'd rather download the entire platform and build it yourself, refer to the documentation available at `http://source.android.com/download`.) You can download the source for this .jar file by typing in the following URL:

```
http://git.source.android.com/➥
?p=platform/frameworks/base.git;a=snapshot;h=HEAD;sf=tgz
```

This is one of the general-purpose URLs you can use to download Git projects. On Windows, you can unzip this file using `pkzip`. Although you can download and unzip the source, it might be more convenient to just look at these files online if you don't need to debug the source code through your IDE. Git also allows you to do this. For example, you can browse through `android.jar` source files by visiting this URL:

```
http://android.git.kernel.org/?p=platform/frameworks/base.git;a=summary
```

However, you have to do some work after you visit this page. Pick `grep` from the dropdown list and enter some text in the search box. Click one of the resulting file names to open that source file in your browser. This facility is convenient for a quick lookup of source code.

At times the file you are looking for might not be in the `frameworks/base` directory or project. In that case, you need to find the list of projects and search each one step by step. The URL for this list is `http://android.git.kernel.org/`.

You cannot `grep` across all projects, so you will need to know which project belongs to which facility in Android. For example, the graphics-related libraries in the Skia project are available here:

```
http://android.git.kernel.org/?p=platform/external/skia.git;a=summary
```

Summary

In this chapter, we wanted to pique your curiosity about Android. You learned that Android programming is done in Java and how the Open Handset Alliance is propelling the Android effort. You saw how handhelds are becoming general-purpose computing devices, and you got an overview of the Dalvik VM, which makes it possible to run a complex framework on a constrained handset.

You also saw how Android's approach compares to that of Java ME. You explored Android's software stack and got a taste of its programming concepts, which we'll cover in subsequent chapters. You saw some sample code and learned where to find and download Android source code.

We hope this chapter has convinced you that you can program productively for the Android Platform without facing too many hurdles. With confidence, we welcome you to step into the rest of the book for an in-depth understanding of the Android SDK.

CHAPTER 2

Getting Your Feet Wet

In the last chapter, we provided an overview of Android's history and we hinted at concepts we'll cover in the rest of the book. So by this point, you're probably eager to get your hands on some code. We'll start by showing you what you need to start building applications with the Android Software Development Kit (SDK) and help you set up your development environment. Next, we'll baby-step you through a "Hello World!" application and dissect a slightly larger application after that. Then we'll explain the Android application lifecycle and end with a brief discussion about debugging your applications.

To build applications for Android, you'll need the Java SE Development Kit (JDK), the Android SDK, and a development environment. Strictly speaking, you can develop your applications using a primitive text editor, but for the purposes of this book, we'll use the commonly available Eclipse IDE. The examples in this book target Android SDKs 1.1 and 1.5. (Chapters 12 and 13 focus on material specific to Android 1.5.) The Android SDK requires JDK 5 or higher, and we use JDK 6 with the examples. Moreover, the Android SDK requires Eclipse 3.3 or higher; we use Eclipse 3.4 (Ganymede).

Finally, to make your life easier, you'll want to use Android Development Tools (ADT). ADT is an Eclipse plug-in that supports building Android applications with the Eclipse IDE. In fact, we built all the examples in this book using the Eclipse IDE (version 3.4) with the ADT tool.

Setting Up Your Environment

To build Android applications, you need to establish a development environment. In this section, we are going to walk you through downloading JDK 6, the Eclipse IDE, the Android SDK, and ADT. We'll also help you configure Eclipse to build Android applications.

Downloading JDK 6 and Eclipse 3.4

The first thing you'll need is the JDK. As we said earlier, the Android SDK 1.0 requires JDK 5 or higher, and we developed the examples using JDK 6. To get started, download JDK 6 from the Sun web site: `http://java.sun.com/javase/downloads/index.jsp`.

After you download the JDK, you'll want to install it and set the JAVA_HOME environment variable to point to the JDK install folder. On a Windows machine, you can do this from a command line by typing this code:

```
set JAVA_HOME=[YOUR JDK_PATH_GOES_HERE]
```

Now, you can download the Eclipse IDE for Java Developers (not the edition for Java EE). Again, the examples in this book use Eclipse 3.4 (on a Windows environment), which you can download from http://www.eclipse.org/downloads/.

Downloading the Android SDK

To build applications for Android, you need the Android SDK. The SDK includes an emulator so you don't need a mobile device with the Android OS to develop Android applications. In fact, we developed the examples in this book on a Windows XP machine.

You can download the Android SDK from http://code.google.com/android/download.html. The Android SDK ships as a .zip file for Windows, so you need to unzip it. Unzip the file to c:\AndroidSDK\, after which you should see the files shown in Figure 2-1.

Figure 2-1. *Contents of the Android SDK*

Installing Android Development Tools (ADT)

Now you need to install ADT, an Eclipse plug-in that helps you build Android applications. Specifically, ADT integrates with Eclipse to provide facilities for you to create, test, and debug Android applications. You'll need to use the Software Updates facility within Eclipse to perform the installation. If you are using Android 1.1, follow the instructions below. If you are using Android 1.5, refer to Chapter 12 for ADT installation. To get started, launch the Eclipse IDE and follow these instructions:

1. Select the Help menu item and choose the "Software Updates..." option.

2. In the "Software Updates and Add-ons" dialog, select the "Available Software" tab.

3. Click the "Add Site..." button and set the "Location" field to the ADT download site: https://dl-ssl.google.com/android/eclipse/. Click the "OK" button to add the site. You should now see the corresponding entry in the "Available Software" list as shown in Figure 2-2.

4. Expand the added entry by selecting the node in the list. You should see an entry named "Developer Tools" with two child nodes: "Android Development Tools" and "Android Editors." Select the parent node "Developer Tools" and click the "Install" button to install ADT.

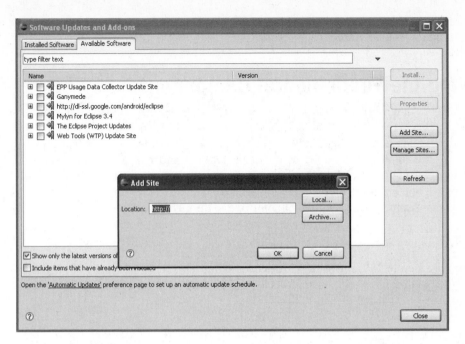

Figure 2-2. *Installing ADT using the Software Updates feature in Eclipse*

Eclipse will then download ADT and install it. You'll need to restart Eclipse for the new plug-in to show up in the IDE. The final step to get ADT functional is to point it to the Android SDK. Select the Window menu and choose Preferences. In the "Preferences" dialog box, select the "Android" node and set the "SDK Location" field to the path of the Android SDK (see Figure 2-3). Then click the "OK" button. Note that you might see a dialog box asking if you want to send usage statistics to Google concerning the Android SDK.

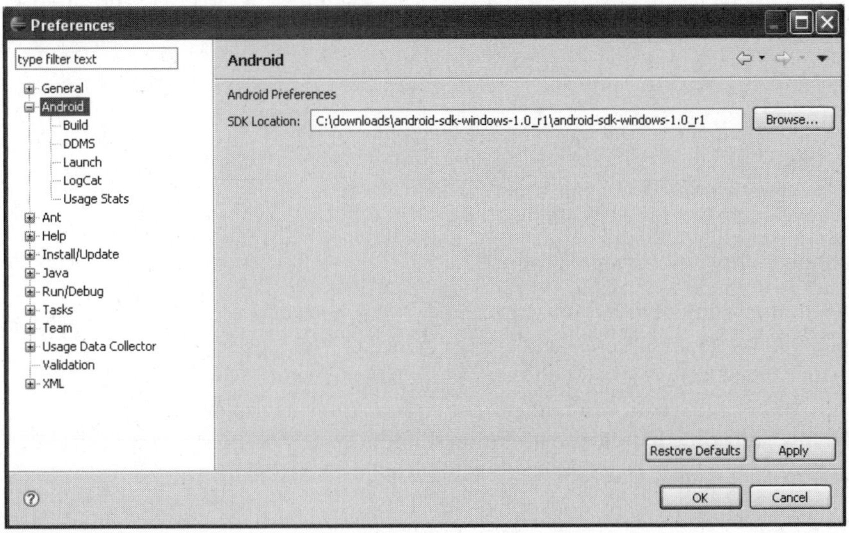

Figure 2-3. *Pointing ADT to the Android SDK*

You are almost ready for your first Android application—we have to briefly discuss the fundamental concepts of an Android application first.

Learning the Fundamental Components

Every application framework has some key components that developers need to understand before they can begin to write applications based on the framework. For example, you would need to understand JavaServer Pages (JSP) and servlets in order to write Java 2 Platform, Enterprise Edition (J2EE) applications. Similarly, you need to understand activities, views, intents, content providers, services, and the `AndroidManifest.xml` file when you build applications for Android. We will briefly discuss these fundamental concepts here so that you can follow the rest of this chapter, and we'll discuss them in more detail throughout the book.

View

The concept of a view in J2EE and Swing carries over to Android. Views are UI elements that form the basic building blocks of a user interface. Views are hierarchical and they know how to draw themselves.

Activity

An activity is a user interface concept. An activity usually represents a single screen in your application. It generally contains one or more views, but it doesn't have to. Moreover, other concepts in Android could better represent a viewless activity (as you'll see in the "Service" section shortly).

Intent

An intent generically defines an "intention" to do some work. Intents encapsulate several concepts, so the best approach to understanding them is to see examples of their use. You can use intents to perform the following tasks, for instance:

- Broadcast a message

- Start a service

- Launch an activity

- Display a web page or a list of contacts

- Dial a phone number or answer a phone call

Intents are not always initiated by your application—they're also used by the system to notify your application of specific events (such as the arrival of a text message).

Intents can be explicit or implicit. If you simply say that you want to display a URL, the system will decide what component will fulfill the intention. You can also provide specific information about what should handle the intention. Intents loosely couple the action and action handler.

Content Provider

Data sharing among mobile applications on a device is common. Therefore, Android defines a standard mechanism for applications to share data (such as a list of contacts) without exposing the underlying storage, structure, and implementation. Through content providers, you can expose your data and have your applications use data from other applications.

Service

Services in Android resemble services you see in Windows or other platforms—they're background processes that can potentially run for a long time. Android defines two types of services: local services and remote services. Local services are components that are only accessible by the application that is hosting the service. Conversely, remote services are services that are meant to be accessed remotely by other applications running on the device.

An example of a service is a component that is used by an e-mail application to poll for new messages. This kind of service might be a local service if the service is not used by other applications running on the device. If several applications use the service, then the service would be implemented as a remote service. The difference, as you'll see in Chapter 8, is in `startService()` vs. `bindService()`.

You can use existing services and also write your own services by extending the `Service` class.

AndroidManifest.xml

`AndroidManifest.xml`, which is similar to the `web.xml` file in the J2EE world, defines the contents and behavior of your application. For example, it lists your app's activities and services, along with the permissions the application needs to run.

Hello World!

Now you're ready to build your first Android application. You'll start by building a simple "Hello World!" program. Create the skeleton of the application by following these steps:

1. Launch Eclipse and select File ➤ New ➤ Project. In the "New Project" dialog box, select "Android" and then click "Next." You will then see the "New Android Project" dialog box, as shown in Figure 2-4.

2. As shown in Figure 2-4, enter **HelloAndroid** as the project name, **pro.android** as the package name, **HelloActivity** as the activity name, and **HelloAndroidApp** as the application name. Note that for a real application, you'll want to use a meaningful application name because it will appear in the application's title bar. Also note that the default location for the project will be derived from the Eclipse workspace location. In this case, your Eclipse workspace is `c:\Android`, and the New Project Wizard appends the name of the new application to the workspace location to come up with `c:\Android\HelloAndroid\`.

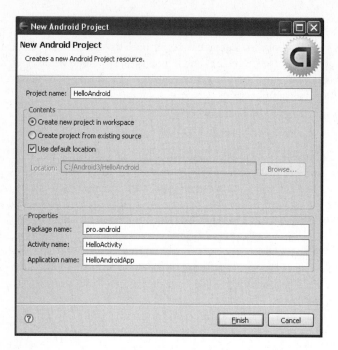

Figure 2-4. *Using the New Project Wizard to create an Android application*

3. Click the "Finish" button, which tells ADT to generate the project skeleton for you. For now, open the HelloActivity.java file under the src folder and modify the onCreate() method as follows:

```
/** Called when the activity is first created. */
@Override
public void onCreate(Bundle savedInstanceState) {
    super.onCreate(savedInstanceState);
    /** create a TextView and write Hello World! */
    TextView tv = new TextView(this);
    tv.setText("Hello World!");
    /** set the content view to the TextView */
    setContentView(tv);
}
```

Add an import statement for android.widget.TextView. To run the application, you'll need to create an Eclipse launch configuration (see Figure 2-5).

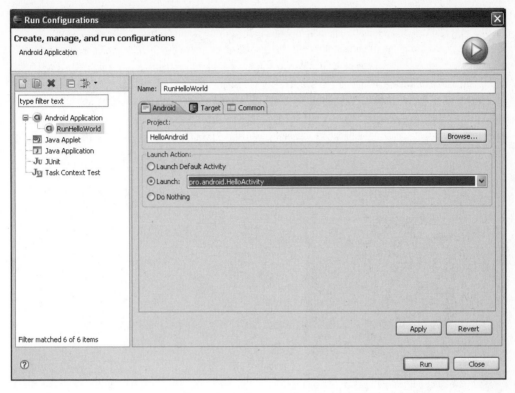

Figure 2-5. *Configuring an Eclipse launch configuration to run the "Hello World!" app*

Create the Eclipse launch configuration by following these steps:

1. Select Run ➤ Run Configurations.

2. In the "Run Configurations" dialog box, double-click "Android Application" in the left pane. The wizard will insert a new configuration named "New Configuration."

3. Rename the configuration **RunHelloWorld**.

4. Click the "Browse…" button and select the HelloAndroid project.

5. Under "Launch Action," select "Launch" and select "pro.android.HelloActivity" from the drop-down list.

6. Click "Apply" and then "Run." You should see the emulator launched with the HelloAndroid project (see Figure 2-6).

▓**Note** It might take the emulator a minute to emulate the device-bootup process. After starting up, you should see HelloAndroidApp running in the emulator, as shown in Figure 2-6. In addition, be aware that the emulator starts other applications in the background during the startup process, so you might see a warning or error message from time to time. If you see an error message, you can generally dismiss it to allow the emulator to go to the next step in the startup process. For example, if you run the emulator and see a message like "application abc is not responding," you can either wait for the application to start or simply ask the emulator to forcefully close the application. Generally, you should wait and let the emulator start up cleanly if you have the patience.

Figure 2-6. *HelloAndroidApp running in the emulator*

Now you know how to create a new Android application and run it in the emulator. Next, we'll discuss the pieces that make the simple program display in the emulator. We'll begin by talking about an Android application's artifacts and structure.

Exploring the Structure of an Android Application

Although the size and complexity of Android applications can vary greatly, their structures will be similar. Figure 2-7 shows the structure of the "Hello World!" app you just built.

Figure 2-7. *The structure of the "Hello World!" app*

Android applications have some artifacts that are required and some that are optional. Table 2-1 summarizes the elements of an Android application. (Note that Android 1.5 adds a few elements; see Chapter 12 for details.)

Table 2-1. *The Artifacts of an Android Application*

Artifact	Description	Required?
AndroidManifest.xml	The Android application descriptor file. This file defines the activities, content providers, services, and intent receivers of the application. You can also use this file to declaratively define permissions required by the application, as well as grant specific permissions to other applications using the services of the application. Moreover, the file can contain instrumentation detail that you can use to test the application or another application.	Yes
src	A folder containing all of the source code of the application.	Yes
assets	An arbitrary collection of folders and files.	No
res	A folder containing the resources of the application. It's the parent folder of drawable, anim, layout, values, xml, and raw.	Yes
drawable	A folder containing the images or image-descriptor files used by the application.	No
anim	A folder containing the XML-descriptor files that describe the animations used by the application.	No
layout	A folder containing views of the application. You should create your application's views by using XML descriptors rather than coding them.	No
values	A folder containing other resources used by the application. All the resources in the folder are also defined with XML descriptors. Examples of resources included in this folder include strings, styles, and colors.	No
xml	A folder containing additional XML files used by the application.	No
raw	A folder containing additional data—possibly non-XML data—that is required by the application.	No

As you can see from Table 2-1, an Android application is primarily made up of three pieces: the application descriptor, a collection of various resources, and the application's source code. If you put aside the `AndroidManifest.xml` file for a moment, you can view an Android app in this simple way: you have some business logic implemented in code, and everything else is a resource. This basic structure resembles the basic structure of a J2EE app, where the resources correlate to JSPs, the business logic correlates to servlets, and the `AndroidManifest.xml` file correlates to the `web.xml` file.

You can also compare J2EE's development model to Android's development model. In J2EE, the philosophy of building views is to build them using markup language. Android has also adopted this approach, although the markup in Android is XML. You benefit from this approach because you don't have to hard-code your application's views; you can modify the look and feel of the application by editing the markup.

It is also worth noting a few constraints regarding resources. First, Android supports only a linear list of files within the predefined folders under `res`. For example, it does not support nested folders under the `layout` folder (or the other folders under `res`). Second, there are some similarities between the `assets` folder and the `raw` folder under `res`. Both folders can contain raw files, but the files within `raw` are considered resources and the files within `assets` are not. So the files within `raw` will be localized, accessible through resource IDs, and so on. But the contents of the `assets` folder are considered general-purpose contents, to be used without resource constraints and support. Note that because the contents of the `assets` folder are not considered resources, you can put an arbitrary hierarchy of folders and files within it. (We'll talk a lot more about resources in Chapter 3.)

■**Note** You might have noticed that XML is used quite heavily with Android. We all know that XML is a bloated data format, so this begs the question, "Does it make sense to rely on XML when you know your target is going to be a device with limited resources?" It turns out that the XML we create during development is actually compiled down to binary using the Android Asset Packaging Tool (AAPT). Therefore, when your application is installed on a device, the files on the device are stored as binary. When the file is needed at runtime, the file is read in its binary form and is not transformed back into XML. This gives us the benefits of both worlds—we get to work with XML and not have to worry about taking up valuable resources on the device.

Analyzing the Notepad Application

Not only do you know how to create a new Android application and run it in the emulator, but you also have a feel for the artifacts of an Android application. Next, we are going to look at the Notepad application that ships with the Android SDK. Notepad's complexity falls between that of the "Hello World!" app and a full-blown Android application, so analyzing its components will give you some realistic insight into Android development.

Loading and Running the Notepad Application

In this section, we'll show you how to load the Notepad application into the Eclipse IDE and run it in the emulator. Before we start, you should know that the Notepad application implements several use cases. For example, the user can create a new note, edit an existing note, delete a note, view the list of created notes, and so on. When the user launches the application, there aren't any saved notes yet, so the user sees an empty note list. If the user presses the Menu key, the application presents him with a list of actions, one of which allows him to add a new note. After he adds the note, he can edit or delete the note by selecting the corresponding menu option.

Follow these steps to load the Notepad sample into the Eclipse IDE:

1. Start Eclipse.

2. Go to File ➤ New ➤ Project.

3. In the "New Project" dialog, select Android ➤ Android Project.

4. In the "New Android Project" dialog, select "Create project from existing source" and set the "Location" field to the path of the Notepad application. Note that the Notepad application is located in `c:\AndroidSDK\samples\`, which you downloaded earlier. After you set the path, the dialog reads the `AndroidManifest.xml` file and prepopulates the remaining fields in the "New Android Project" dialog box.

5. Click the "Finish" button.

You should now see the NotesList application in your Eclipse IDE. To run the application, you could create a launch configuration (as you did for the "Hello World!" application), or you can simply right-click the project, choose Run As, and select Android Application. This will launch the emulator and install the application on it. After the emulator has completed loading (you'll see the date and time displayed in the center of the emulator's screen), press the Menu button to view the Notepad application. Play around with the application for a few minutes to become familiar with it.

Dissecting the Application

Now let's study the contents of the application (see Figure 2-8).

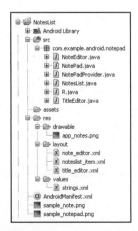

Figure 2-8. *Contents of the Notepad application*

As you can see, the application contains several .java files, a few .png images, three views (under the layout folder), and the AndroidManifest.xml file. If this were a command-line application, you would start looking for the class with the Main method. So what's the equivalent of a Main method in Android?

Android defines an entry-point activity, also called the top-level activity. If you look in the AndroidManifest.xml file, you'll find one provider and three activities. The NotesList activity defines an intent-filter for the action android.intent.action.MAIN and for the category android.intent.category.LAUNCHER. When an Android application is asked to run, the host loads the application and reads the AndroidManifest.xml file. It then looks for, and starts, an activity or activities with an intent-filter that has the MAIN action with a category of LAUNCHER, as shown here:

```
<intent-filter>
    <action android:name="android.intent.action.MAIN" />
    <category android:name="android.intent.category.LAUNCHER" />
</intent-filter>
```

After the host finds the activity it wants to run, it must resolve the defined activity to an actual class. It does this by combining the root package name and the activity name, which in this case is com.example.android.notepad.NotesList (see Listing 2-1).

Listing 2-1. *The AndroidManfiest.xml File*

```
<manifest xmlns:android="http://schemas.android.com/apk/res/android"
    package="com.example.android.notepad"
>
    <application android:icon="@drawable/app_notes"
        android:label="@string/app_name"
    >
        <provider android:name="NotePadProvider"
            android:authorities="com.google.provider.NotePad"
        />
        <activity android:name="NotesList"
                    android:label="@string/title_notes_list">
            <intent-filter>
                <action android:name="android.intent.action.MAIN" />
                <category
                    android:name="android.intent.category.LAUNCHER" />
            </intent-filter>
            <intent-filter>
                <action android:name="android.intent.action.VIEW" />
                <action android:name="android.intent.action.EDIT" />
                <action android:name ="android.intent.category.DEFAULT" />
                <data android:mimeTyp="android.intent.action.PICK" />
                <category android:name
                    e="vnd.android.cursor.dir/vnd.google.note" />
            </intent-filter>
```

```
            <intent-filter>
                <action android:name="android.intent.action.GET_CONTENT" />
                <category android:name="android.intent.category.DEFAULT" />
                <data
               android:mimeType="vnd.android.cursor.item/vnd.google.note" />
            </intent-filter>
        </activity>
    ...
</manfiest>
```

The application's root package name is defined as an attribute of the `<manifest>` element in the `AndroidManifest.xml` file, and each activity has a name attribute.

Once the entry-point activity is determined, the host starts the activity and the `onCreate()` method is called. Let's have a look at `NotesList.onCreate()`, shown in Listing 2-2.

Listing 2-2. *The onCreate Method*

```
public class NotesList extends ListActivity {
@Override
protected void onCreate(Bundle savedInstanceState) {
        super.onCreate(savedInstanceState);

        setDefaultKeyMode(DEFAULT_KEYS_SHORTCUT);
        Intent intent = getIntent();
        if (intent.getData() == null) {
            intent.setData(Notes.CONTENT_URI);
        }

        getListView().setOnCreateContextMenuListener(this);

        Cursor cursor = managedQuery(getIntent().getData(),
PROJECTION, null, null,
                Notes.DEFAULT_SORT_ORDER);

        SimpleCursorAdapter adapter = new SimpleCursorAdapter(this,
R.layout.noteslist_item, cursor, new String[] { Notes.TITLE },
new int[] { android.R.id.text1 });
        setListAdapter(adapter);
}
}
```

Activities in Android are usually started with an intent, and one activity can start another activity. The `onCreate()` method checks whether the current activity's intent has data (notes). If not, it sets the URI to retrieve the data on the intent. We'll learn in Chapter 3 that Android accesses data through content providers that operate on URIs. In this case, the URI provides enough information to retrieve data from a database. The constant `Notes.CONTENT_URI` is defined as a `static final` in `Notepad.java`:

```
public static final Uri CONTENT_URI =
        Uri.parse("content://" + AUTHORITY + "/notes");
```

The Notes class is an inner class of the Notepad class. For now, know that the preceding URI tells the content provider to get all of the notes. If the URI looked something like this

```
public static final Uri CONTENT_URI =
    Uri.parse("content://" + AUTHORITY + "/notes/11");
```

then the consuming content provider would return (update or delete) the note with an ID equal to 11. We will discuss content providers and URIs in depth in Chapter 3.

The NotesList class extends the ListActivity class, which knows how to display list-oriented data. The items in the list are managed by an internal ListView (a UI component), which displays the notes in the list vertically (by default). After setting the URI on the activity's intent, the activity registers to build the context menu for notes. If you've played with the application, you probably noticed that context-sensitive menu items are displayed depending on your selection. For example, if you select an existing note, the application displays "Edit note" and "Edit title." Similarly, if you don't select a note, the application shows you the "Add note" option.

Next, we see the activity execute a managed query and get a cursor for the result. A managed query means that Android will manage the returned cursor. In other words, if the application has to be unloaded or reloaded, neither the application nor the activity has to worry about positioning the cursor, loading it, or unloading it. The parameters to managedQuery(), shown in Table 2-2, are interesting.

Table 2-2. *Parameters to Activity.managedQuery()*

Parameter	Data Type	Description
URI	Uri	URI of the content provider
projection	String[]	The column to return (column names)
selection	String	Optional where clause
selectionArgs	String[]	The arguments to the selection, if the query contains ?s
sortOrder	String	Sort order to be used on the result set

We will discuss managedQuery() and its sibling query() later in this section and also in Chapter 3. For now, realize that a query in Android returns tabular data. The projection parameter allows you to define the columns you are interested in. You can also reduce the overall result set and sort the result set using a SQL order-by clause (such as asc or desc). Also note that an Android query must return a column named _ID to support retrieving an individual record. Moreover, you must know the type of data returned by the content provider—whether a column contains a string, int, binary, or the like.

After the query is executed, the returned cursor is passed to the constructor of SimpleCursorAdapter, which adapts records in the dataset to items in the user interface (ListView). Look closely at the parameters passed to the constructor of SimpleCursorAdapter:

```
SimpleCursorAdapter adapter =
 new SimpleCursorAdapter(this, R.layout.noteslist_item,
cursor, new String[] { Notes.TITLE }, new int[] { android.R.id.text1 });
```

Specifically, look at the second parameter: an identifier to the view that represents the items in the ListView. As you'll see in Chapter 3, Android provides an auto-generated utility class that provides references to the resources in your project. This utility class is called the R class because its name is R.java. When you compile your project, the AAPT generates the R class for you from the resources defined within your res folder. For example, you could put all your string resources into the values folder and the AAPT will generate a public static identifier for each string. Android supports this generically for all of your resources. For example, in the constructor of SimpleCursorAdapter, the NotesList activity passes in the identifier of the view that displays an item from the notes list. The benefit of this utility class is that you don't have to hard-code your resources and you get compile-time reference checking. In other words, if a resource is deleted, the R class will lose the reference and any code referring to the resource will not compile.

Let's look at another important concept in Android that we alluded to earlier: the onListItemClick method of NotesList (see Listing 2-3).

Listing 2-3. *The onListItemClick Method*

```
@Override
    protected void onListItemClick(ListView l, View v, int position, long id) {
        Uri uri = ContentUris.withAppendedId(getIntent().getData(), id);

        String action = getIntent().getAction();
        if (Intent.ACTION_PICK.equals(action) ||
Intent.ACTION_GET_CONTENT.equals(action)) {
            setResult(RESULT_OK, new Intent().setData(uri));
        } else {
            startActivity(new Intent(Intent.ACTION_EDIT, uri));
        }
    }
```

The onListItemClick method is called when a user selects a note in the UI. The method demonstrates that one activity can start another activity. When a note is selected, the method creates a URI by taking the base URI and appending the selected note's ID to it. The URI is then passed to startActivity() with a new intent. startActivity() is one way to start an activity: it starts an activity but doesn't report on the results of the activity after it completes. Another way to start an activity is to use startActivityForResult(). With this method, you can start another activity and register a callback to be used when the activity completes. For example, you'll want to use startActivityForResult() to start an activity to select a contact because you want that contact after the activity completes.

At this point, you might be wondering about user interaction with respect to activities. For example, if the running activity starts another activity, and *that* activity starts an activity, and so on, then what activity can the user work with? Can she manipulate all the activities simultaneously, or is she restricted to a single activity? Actually, activities have a defined lifecycle. They're maintained on an activity stack, with the running activity at the top. If the running activity starts another activity, the first running activity moves down the stack and the new activity moves to the top. Activities lower in the stack can be in a so-called "paused" or "stopped" state. A paused activity is partially or fully visible to the user; a stopped activity is not visible to the user. The system can kill paused or stopped activities if it deems that resources are needed elsewhere.

Let's move on to data persistence now. The notes that a user creates are saved to an actual database on the device. Specifically, the Notepad application's backing store is a SQLite database. The managedQuery() method that we discussed earlier eventually resolves to data in a database, via a content provider. Let's examine how the URI, passed to managedQuery(), results in the execution of a query against a SQLite database. Recall that the URI passed to managedQuery() looks like this:

```
public static final Uri CONTENT_URI =
Uri.parse("content://" + AUTHORITY + "/notes");
```

Content URIs always have this form: content://, followed by the authority, followed by a general segment (context-specific). Because the URI doesn't contain the actual data, it somehow results in the execution of code that produces data. What is this connection? How is the URI reference resolved to code that produces data? Is the URI an HTTP service or a web service? Actually, the URI, or the authority portion of the URI, is configured in the AndroidManifest.xml file as a content provider:

```
<provider android:name="NotePadProvider"
    android:authorities="com.google.provider.NotePad"/>
```

When Android sees a URI that needs to be resolved, it pulls out the authority portion of it and looks up the ContentProvider class configured for the authority. In the Notepad application, the AndroidManifest.xml file contains a class called NotePadProvider configured for the com.google.provider.NotePad authority. Listing 2-4 shows a small portion of the class.

Listing 2-4. *The NotePadProvider Class*

```
public class NotePadProvider extends ContentProvider
{

    @Override
    public Cursor query(Uri uri, String[] projection, String selection,
  String[] selectionArgs,String sortOrder) {}

    @Override
    public Uri insert(Uri uri, ContentValues initialValues) {}

    @Override
    public int update(Uri uri, ContentValues values, String where,
String[] whereArgs) {}

    @Override
    public int delete(Uri uri, String where, String[] whereArgs) {}

    @Override
    public String getType(Uri uri) {}

    @Override
    public boolean onCreate() {}
```

```
    private static class DatabaseHelper extends SQLiteOpenHelper {}

    @Override
        public void onCreate(SQLiteDatabase db) {}

        @Override
        public void onUpgrade(SQLiteDatabase db,
int oldVersion, int newVersion) {
            //...
        }
    }
}
```

Clearly, you can see that the NotePadProvider class extends the ContentProvider class. The ContentProvider class defines six abstract methods, four of which are CRUD (Create, Read, Update, Delete) operations. The other two abstract methods are onCreate() and getType(). onCreate() is called when the content provider is created for the first time. getType() provides the MIME type for the result set (you'll see how MIME types work when you read Chapter 3).

The other interesting thing about the NotePadProvider class is the internal DatabaseHelper class, which extends the SQLiteOpenHelper class. Together, the two classes take care of initializing the Notepad database, opening and closing it, and performing other database tasks. Interestingly, the DatabaseHelper class is just a few lines of custom code (see Listing 2-5), while the Android implementation of SQLiteOpenHelper does most of the heavy lifting.

Listing 2-5. *The DatabaseHelper Class*

```
 private static class DatabaseHelper extends SQLiteOpenHelper {

        DatabaseHelper(Context context) {
            super(context, DATABASE_NAME, null, DATABASE_VERSION);
        }

        @Override
        public void onCreate(SQLiteDatabase db) {
            db.execSQL("CREATE TABLE " + NOTES_TABLE_NAME + " ("
                    + Notes._ID + " INTEGER PRIMARY KEY,"
                    + Notes.TITLE + " TEXT,"
                    + Notes.NOTE + " TEXT,"
                    + Notes.CREATED_DATE + " INTEGER,"
                    + Notes.MODIFIED_DATE + " INTEGER"
                    + ");");
        }

        //…
}
```

As shown in Listing 2-5, the onCreate() method creates the Notepad table. Notice that the class's constructor calls the superclass's constructor with the name of the table. The superclass will call the onCreate() method only if the table does not exist in the database. Also notice that one of the columns in the Notepad table is the _ID column we discussed in the section "Dissecting the Application."

Now let's look at one of the CRUD operations: the insert() method (see Listing 2-6).

Listing 2-6. *The insert() Method*

```
//…
SQLiteDatabase db = mOpenHelper.getWritableDatabase();
      long rowId = db.insert(NOTES_TABLE_NAME, Notes.NOTE, values);
      if (rowId > 0) {
          Uri noteUri = ContentUris.withAppendedId(
NotePad.Notes.CONTENT_URI, rowId);
              getContext().getContentResolver().notifyChange(noteUri, null);
              return noteUri;
      }
```

The insert() method uses its internal DatabaseHelper instance to access the database and then inserts a notes record. The returned row ID is then appended to the URI and a new URI is returned to the caller.

At this point, you should be familiar with how an Android application is laid out. You should be able to navigate your way around Notepad, as well as some of the other samples in the Android SDK. You should be able to run the samples and play with them. Now let's look at the overall lifecycle of an Android application.

Examining the Application Lifecycle

The lifecycle of Android applications differs greatly from the lifecycle of web-based J2EE applications. J2EE apps are loosely managed by the container they run in. For example, a J2EE container can remove an application from memory if it sits idle for a predetermined time period. But the container generally won't move applications in and out of memory based on load and/or available resources. In other words, it's up to the application owners to ensure that resources are available.

The lifecycle of an Android application, on the other hand, is strictly managed by the system, based on the user's needs, available resources, and so on. A user might want to launch a web browser, for example, but the system ultimately decides whether to start the application. Although the system is the ultimate manager, it adheres to some defined and logical guidelines to determine whether an application can be loaded, paused, or stopped. If the user is currently working with an activity, the system will give high priority to that application. Conversely, if an activity is not visible and the system determines that an application must be shut down to free up resources, it will shut down the lower-priority application.

■**Note** Android runs each application in a separate process, each of which hosts its own virtual machine. This provides a protected-memory environment. Moreover, by isolating applications to an individual process, the system can control which application deserves higher priority. For example, a background process that's doing a CPU-intensive task cannot block an incoming phone call.

The concept of application lifecycle is logical, but a fundamental aspect of Android applications complicates matters. Specifically, the Android application architecture is component- and integration-oriented. This allows a rich user experience, seamless reuse, and easy application integration, but creates a complex task for the application-lifecycle manager.

Let's consider a typical scenario. A user is talking to someone on the phone and needs to open an e-mail message to answer a question. She goes to the home screen, opens the mail application, opens the e-mail message, clicks a link in the e-mail, and answers her friend's question by reading a stock quote from a web page. This scenario would require four applications: the home application, a talk application, an e-mail application, and a browser application. As the user navigates from one application to the next, her experience is seamless. In the background, however, the system is saving and restoring application state. For instance, when the user clicks the link in the e-mail message, the system saves metadata on the running e-mail–message activity before starting the browser-application activity to launch a URL. In fact, the system saves metadata on any activity before starting another, so that it can come back to the activity (when the user backtracks, for example). If memory becomes an issue, the system will have to shut down a process running an activity and resume it as necessary.

Android is sensitive to the lifecycle of an application and its components. Therefore, you'll need to understand and handle lifecycle events in order to build a stable application. The processes running your Android application and its components go through various lifecycle events, and Android provides callbacks that you can implement to handle state changes. For starters, you'll want to become familiar with the various lifecycle callbacks for an activity (see Listing 2-7).

Listing 2-7. *Lifecycle Methods of an Activity*

```
protected void onCreate(Bundle savedInstanceState);
protected void onStart();

protected void onRestart();
protected void onResume();
protected void onPause();
protected void onStop();
protected void onDestroy();
```

Listing 2-7 shows the list of lifecycle methods that Android calls during the life of an activity. It's important to understand when each of the methods is called by the system to ensure that you implement a stable application. Note that you do not need to react to all of these methods. If you do, however, be sure to call the superclass versions as well. Figure 2-9 shows the transitions between states.

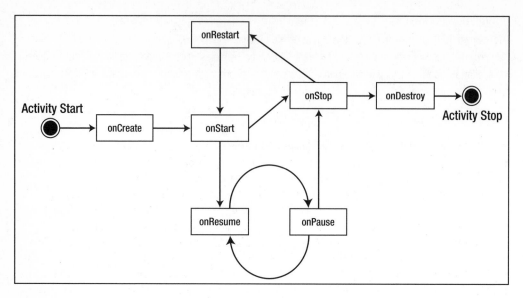

Figure 2-9. *State transitions of an activity*

The system can start and stop your activities based on what else is happening. Android calls the onCreate() method when the activity is freshly created. onCreate() is always followed by a call to onStart(), but onStart() is not always preceded by a call to onCreate() because onStart() can be called if your application was stopped (from onStop()). When onStart() is called, your activity is not visible to the user, but it's about to be. onResume() is called after onStart(), just when the activity is in the foreground and accessible to the user. At this point, the user is interacting with your activity.

When the user decides to move to another activity, the system will call your activity's onPause() method. From onPause(), you can expect either onResume() or onStop() to be called. onResume() is called, for example, if the user brings your activity back to the foreground. onStop() is called if your activity becomes invisible to the user. If your activity is brought back to the foreground, after a call to onStop(), then onRestart() will be called. If your activity sits on the activity stack but is not visible to the user, and the system decides to kill your activity, onDestroy() will be called.

The state model described for an activity appears complex, but you are not required to deal with every possible scenario. In fact, you will mostly handle onCreate() and onPause(). You will handle onCreate() to create the user interface for your activity. In this method, you will bind data to your widgets and wire up any event handlers for your UI components. In onPause(), you will want to persist critical data to your application's data store. It's the last safe method that will get called before the system kills your application. onStop() and onDestroy() are not guaranteed to be called, so don't rely on these methods for critical logic.

The takeaway from this discussion? The system manages your application, and it can start, stop, or resume an application component at any time. Although the system controls your components, they don't run in complete isolation with respect to your application. In other words, if the system starts an activity in your application, you can count on an application context in your activity. For example, it's not uncommon to have global variables shared among the activities in your application. You can share a global variable by writing an extension of the android.app.Application class and then initializing the global variable in the onCreate() method (see Listing 2-8). Activities and other components in your application can then access these references with confidence when they are executing.

Listing 2-8. *An Extension of the Application Class*

```
public class MyApplication extends Application
{
    // global variable
    private static final String myGlobalVariable;

    @Override
    public void onCreate()
    {
        super.onCreate();
        //... initialize global variables here
        myGlobalVariable = loadCacheData();
    }

    public static String getMyGlobalVariable() {
        return myGlobalVariable;
    }

}
```

In the next section, we'll give you some armor to help you develop Android applications—we will discuss debugging.

Debugging Your App

After you write a few lines of code for your first application, you'll start wondering if it's possible to have a debug session while you interact with your application in the emulator. Shortly after that, you'll instinctively run to System.out.println(), which will fail because the code is running on the emulator and the sys-out statement is not fed back to the IDE. But don't worry; the Android SDK includes a host of applications that you can use for debugging purposes.

To log messages from your application, you'll want to use the android.util.Log class. This class defines the familiar informational, warning, and error methods. You can also get detailed tracing information by using the android.os.Debug class, which provides a start-tracing method (Debug.startMethodTracing()) and a stop-tracing method (Debug.stopMethodTracing()). You can then view the tracer output using the trace-viewer tool included in the Android SDK. The SDK also includes a file-explorer tool that you can use to view files on the device. These tools are integrated with the Eclipse IDE (see Figure 2-10).

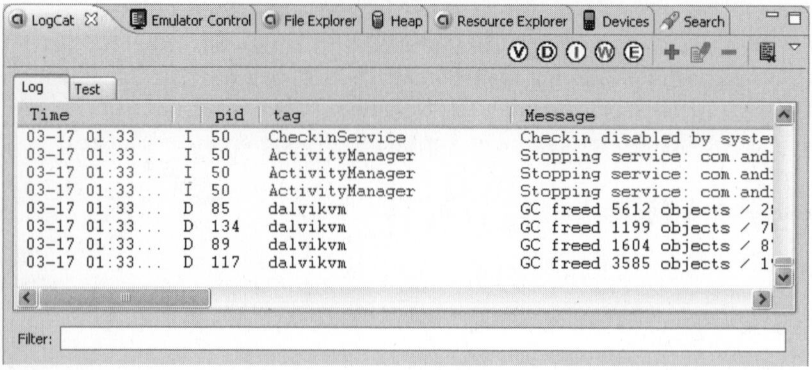

Figure 2-10. *Debugging tools that you can use while building Android applications*

You can view the tools by selecting the Debug perspective in Eclipse. You can also launch each tool by going to Window ➤ Show View ➤ Other ➤ Android.

One of the tools that you'll use throughout your Android development is LogCat. This tool displays the log messages that you emit using `android.util.Log`, exceptions, and so on. We will introduce the other tools throughout the book.

Summary

In this chapter, we showed you how to set up your development environment for building Android applications. We discussed some of the basic building blocks of the Android APIs, and introduced views, activities, intents, content providers, and services. We then analyzed the Notepad application in terms of the aforementioned building blocks and application components. Next, we talked about the importance of the Android application lifecycle. Finally, we briefly mentioned some of the Android SDK's debugging tools that integrate with the Eclipse IDE.

And so begins the foundation of your Android development. The next chapter will discuss content providers, resources, and intents in great detail.

CHAPTER 3

■■■

Using Resources, Content Providers, and Intents

In Chapter 2, you got an overview of an Android application and a quick look at some of its underlying concepts. Among these, resources, content providers, and intents form the three primary pillars of Android UI programming. Android depends on resources for look-and-feel flexibility, content providers for abstracting data into services, and intents for interoperability and UI reuse. You must fully understand these three concepts in order to build successful Android applications, so we'll discuss them in depth here.

Understanding Resources

Resources are critical to the Android architecture. In this section, you'll learn what resources are and how to create them using resource files. You'll find out that resources are declarative, and that Android creates resource IDs for convenient use in your Java programs. You'll also see how the R.java source file mediates the generation and usage of these resource IDs. Then you'll learn how to define resources in XML files, reuse resources in other resource XML definitions, and reuse resources in Java programs. In addition to these XML-based resources, this chapter also covers two other types of resources: *raw* resources and *assets*.

String Resources

A resource in Android is a file (like a music file) or a value (like the title of a dialog box) that is bound to an executable application. These files and values are bound to the executable in such a way that you can change them without recompiling and redeploying the application.

Resources play a part in many, if not all, familiar UI frameworks. Familiar examples of resources include strings, colors, and bitmaps. Instead of hard-coding strings in an application, for example, you can use their IDs instead. This indirection lets you change the text of the string resource without changing the source code.

Let's start with strings and see how they are used as resources. Android allows you to define multiple strings in one or more XML resource files. These XML files containing string-resource definitions reside in the /res/values subdirectory. The names of the XML files are arbitrary, although you will commonly see the file name as strings.xml. Listing 3-1 shows an example of a string-resource file.

Listing 3-1. *Example strings.xml File*

```
<?xml version="1.0" encoding="utf-8"?>
<resources>
    <string name="hello">hello</string>
    <string name="app_name">hello appname</string>
</resources>
```

When this file is created or updated, the Eclipse ADT plug-in will automatically update a Java class in your application's root package called R.java with unique IDs for the two string resources specified.

■**Note** Regardless of the number of resource files, there is only one R.java file. In releases 1.5 and up the file R.java is generated in a separate subdirectory at the same level as the Java source-code root for your application. This generated separate subdirectory is called "gen." Under this subdirectory the package name in R.java continues to be the same as in previous releases, which is the root package name for your application.

For the string-resource file in Listing 3-1, the updated R.java file would have these entries:

```
public final class R {
    ...other entries depending on your project and application

    public static final class string
    {
        ...other entries depending on your project and application

        public static final int hello=0x7f040000;
        public static final int app_name=0x7f040001;

        ...other entries depending on your project and application
    }
    ...other entries depending on your project and application
}
```

Let's focus on the static definition for static final class string. R.java creates this inner static class as a namespace to hold string-resource IDs. The two static final ints defined with variable names hello and app_name are the resource IDs that represent the corresponding string resources. You could use these resource IDs anywhere in the source code through the following code structure:

```
R.string.hello
```

Note that these generated IDs point to ints rather than strings. Most methods that take strings also take these resource identifiers as inputs. Android will resolve those ints to strings where needed.

It is merely a convention that most sample applications define all strings in one strings.xml file. Android takes any number of arbitrary files as long as the structure of the XML file looks like Listing 3-1 and the file resides in the /res/values subdirectory.

The structure of this file is easy to follow. You have the root node of `<resources>` followed by one or more of its child elements of `<string>`. Each `<string>` element or node has a property called name that will end up as the id attribute in R.java and the actual text for that string ID.

To see that multiple string-resource files are allowed in this subdirectory, you can place another file with the following content in the same subdirectory and call it strings1.xml:

```
<?xml version="1.0" encoding="utf-8"?>
<resources>
    <string name="hello1">hello 1</string>
    <string name="app_name1">hello appname 1</string>
</resources>
```

The Eclipse ADT plug-in will validate the uniqueness of these IDs at compile time and place them in R.java as two additional constants: R.string.hello1 and R.string.app_name1.

Layout Resources

A layout resource is another key resource commonly used in Android programming. In Android, the view for a screen is often loaded from an XML file as a resource. These XML files are called *layout resources*. Consider this code segment for a sample Android activity:

```
public class HelloWorldActivity extends Activity
{
    @Override
    public void onCreate(Bundle savedInstanceState)
    {
        super.onCreate(savedInstanceState);
        setContentView(R.layout.main);
        TextView tv = (TextView)this.findViewById(R.id.text1);
        tv.setText("Try this text instead");
    }
    ........
}
```

The line setContentView(R.layout.main) points out that there is a static class called R.layout, and within that class there is a constant called main (an integer) pointing to a View defined by an XML layout-resource file. The name of the XML file would be main.xml, which needs to be placed in the resources' layout subdirectory. In other words, this statement would expect the programmer to create the file /res/layout/main.xml and place the necessary layout definition in that file. The contents of the main.xml layout file could look like Listing 3-2.

Listing 3-2. *Example main.xml Layout File*

```
<?xml version="1.0" encoding="utf-8"?>
<LinearLayout xmlns:android="http://schemas.android.com/apk/res/android"
    android:orientation="vertical"
    android:layout_width="fill_parent"
    android:layout_height="fill_parent"
    >
```

```
<TextView    android:id="@+id/text1"
    android:layout_width="fill_parent"
    android:layout_height="wrap_content"
    android:text="@string/hello"
    />
 <Button    android:id="@+id/b1"
    android:layout_width="fill_parent"
    android:layout_height="wrap_content"
    android:text="@+string/hello"
    />
</LinearLayout>
```

The layout file in Listing 3-2 defines a root node called LinearLayout, which contains a TextView followed by a Button. A LinearLayout lays out its children vertically or horizontally—vertically, in this example.

You will need to define a separate layout file for each screen. More accurately, each layout needs a dedicated file. If you are painting two screens, you will likely need two layout files such as /res/layout/screen1_layout.xml and /res/layout/screen2_layout.xml.

■**Note** Each file in the /res/layout/ subdirectory generates a unique constant based on the name of the file (extension excluded). With layouts, what matters is the number of files; with string resources, what matters is the number of individual string resources *inside* the files.

For example, if you have two files under /res/layout/ called file1.xml and file2.xml, you'll have the following entries in R.java:

```
public static final class layout {
    .... any other files
      public static final int file1=0x7f030000;
      public static final int file2=0x7f030001;
}
```

The views defined in these layout files are accessible in code if you reference their IDs from R.java:

```
TextView tv = (TextView)this.findViewById(R.id.text1);
tv.setText("Try this text instead");
```

In this example, you locate the TextView by using the findViewById method of the Activity class. The constant R.id.text1 corresponds to the ID defined for the TextView. The id for the TextView in the layout file is as follows:

```
<TextView android:id="@+id/text1"
..
</TextView>
```

The attribute value for the id attribute indicates that a constant called text1 will be used to uniquely identify this view among other views hosted by that activity. The plus sign (+) in @+id/text1 means that text1 will be created if it doesn't exist already. There is more to this syntax, in which ids are assigned to resources. We'll talk about that next.

Resource-Reference Syntax

Irrespective of the type of resource, all Android resources are identified (or referenced) by their id in Java source code. The syntax you use to allocate an id to a resource in the XML file is called *resource-reference syntax*. The id attribute syntax in the previous example @+id/text1 has the following formal structure:

```
@[package:]type/name
```

The type corresponds to one of the resource-type namespaces available in R.java, such as the following:

- R.drawable
- R.id
- R.layout
- R.string
- R.attr

The corresponding types in XML resource-reference syntax are as follows:

- drawable
- id
- layout
- string
- attr

The name part in the resource reference @[package:]type/name is the name given to the resource; it also gets represented as an int constant in R.java. Now we have come to the important part of this syntax: the package. If you don't specify any package, then the pair type/name will be resolved based on local resources and the application's local R.java package.

If you specify android:type/name, on the other hand, the reference will look in the package identified by android: the android.R.java file, to be precise. So you can use any Java package name in place of the package placeholder to locate the right R.java file to resolve the reference. Based on this information, let's analyze a few examples:

```
<TextView id="text">
// Compile error, as id will not take raw text strings

<TextView id="@text">
// wrong syntax. It is missing a type name
// you will get an error "No Resource type specified
```

```
<TextView id="@id/text">
//Error: No Resource found that matches id "text"
//Unless you have taken care to define "text" before

<TextView id="@android:id/text">
// Error: Resource is not public
// indicating that there is no such id in android.R.id
// Of course this would be valid if Android R.java were to define
// an id with this name

<TextView id="@+id/text">
//Success: Creates an id called "text" in the local package
```

Defining Your Own Resource IDs for Later Use

The general pattern for allocating an id is either to create a new one or to use the one created by the Android package. However, it is possible to create ids beforehand and use them later in your own packages.

The line <TextView id="@+id/text"> in the preceding code segment indicates that an id named text is going to be used if one already exists. If the id doesn't exist, then a new one is going to be created. So when might an id such as text already exist in R.java for it to be reused?

You might be inclined to put a constant like R.id.text in R.java, but R.java is not editable. Even if it were, it gets regenerated every time something gets changed, added, or deleted in the /res/* subdirectory. However, you can use a resource tag called item to define an id without attaching to any particular resource. Here is an example:

```
<resources>
<item type="id" name="text"/>
</resources>
```

The type refers to the type of resource—an id in this case. Once this id is in place, the following View definition would work:

```
<TextView android:id="@id/text">
..
</TextView>
```

Compiled and Noncompiled Android Resources

Android supports a number of other resources in addition to string resources and layout resources. The general process of creating and using these various resources is similar.

However, it is worthwhile to consider some differences. Android supports all these resources through XML files, bitmap files for images, and raw files (examples of which could include audio and video). Within the set of XML files, you'll find two types: one gets compiled into binary format, and the other gets copied as is. The examples you have seen so far—the string-resource XML files and the layout-resource XML files—get compiled into binary format before becoming part of the installable package. You can also place `raw` XML files in the `/res/xml/` subdirectory to have them compiled into binary format. But if you place files, including XML files, in the `/res/raw/` directory instead, they don't get compiled into binary format. You must use explicit stream-based APIs to read these files.

As we mentioned in Table 2-1 in the previous chapter, resource files are housed in various subdirectories based on their type. Here are some important subdirectories in the `/res` folder and the types of resources they host:

- `anim`: Compiled animation files
- `drawable`: Bitmaps
- `layout`: UI/view definitions
- `values`: Arrays, colors, dimensions, strings, and styles
- `xml`: Compiled arbitrary raw XML files
- `raw`: Noncompiled raw files

The resource compiler in the Android Asset Packaging Tool (AAPT) compiles all the resources except the `raw` resources and places them into the final .apk file. This file, which contains the Android application's code and resources, correlates to Java's .jar file ("apk" stands for "Android Package"). The .apk file is what gets installed onto the device. In addition to gathering raw assets into a final compressed file, the AAPT also parses resource definitions into binary asset data.

Note Although the XML resource parser allows resource names such as `hello-string`, you will see a compile-time error in `R.java`. You can fix this by renaming your resource to `hello_string` (replacing the dash with an underscore).

Enumerating Key Android Resources

Now that we've been through the basics of resources, we'll enumerate some of the other key resources that Android supports, their XML representations, and the way they're used in Java code. (You can use this section as a quick reference as you write resource files for each resource.) To start with, take a quick glance at the types of resources and what they are used for (see Table 3-1).

Table 3-1. *Types of Resources*

Resource Type	Location	Description
Color	/res/values/any-file	Represents color identifiers pointing to color codes. These resource IDs are exposed in R.java as R.color.*.
String	/res/values/any-file	Represents string resources. String resources allow Java-formatted strings and raw HTML in addition to simple strings. These resource IDs are exposed in R.java as R.string.*.
Dimension	/res/values/any-file	Represents dimensions or sizes of various elements or views in Android. Supports pixels, inches, millimeters, density-independent pixels, and scale-independent pixels. These resource IDs are exposed in R.java as R.dimen.*.
Image	/res/drawable/multiple-files	Represents image resources. Supported images include .jpg, .gif, and .png. Each image is in a separate file and gets its own ID based on the file name. These resource IDs are exposed in R.java as R.drawable.*. The image support also includes an image type called a *stretchable* image that allows portions of an image to stretch while other portions of that image stay static.
Color Drawable	/res/values/any-file also /res/drawable/multiple-files	Represents rectangle of colors to be used as view backgrounds or general drawables like bitmaps. You can use this instead of specifying a single colored bitmap as a background. In Java, this is equivalent to creating a colored rectangle and setting it as a background for a view. The <drawable> value tag in the values subdirectory supports this. These resource IDs are exposed in R.java as R.drawable.*. Android also supports rounded rectangles and gradient rectangles through XML files placed in /res/drawable with the root XML tag <shape>. These resource IDs are also exposed in R.java as R.drawable.*. Each file name in this case translates to a unique drawable ID.
Arbitrary XML Files	/res/xml/*.xml	Android allows arbitrary XML files as resources. These files will be compiled by the AAPT compiler. These resource IDs are exposed in R.java as R.xml.*.
Arbitrary Raw Resources	/res/raw/*.*	Android allows arbitrary *noncompiled* binary or text files under this directory. Each file gets a unique resource ID. These resource IDs are exposed in R.java as R.raw.*.
Arbitrary Raw Assets	/assets/*.*/*.*	Android allows arbitrary files in arbitrary subdirectories, starting at the /assets subdirectory. These are not really resources, but raw files. This directory, unlike the /res subdirectory, allows an arbitrary depth of subdirectories. These files do not generate any resource IDs. You have to use a relative path name starting at and excluding /assets.

Each of the resources specified in this table are further elaborated in the following sections with XML and Java code snippets.

Color Resources

As you can do with string resources, you can use reference identifiers to indirectly reference colors. Doing this enables Android to localize colors and apply themes. Once you've defined and identified colors in resource files, you can access them in Java code through their IDs. Whereas string-resource IDs are available under the *<your-package>*.R.string namespace, the color IDs are available under the *<your-package>*.R.color namespace.

See Listing 3-3 for some examples of specifying color in an XML resource file.

Listing 3-3. *XML Syntax for Defining Color Resources*

```
<resources>
    <color name="red">#f00</color>
    <color name="blue">#0000ff</color>
    <color name="green">#f0f0</color>
    <color name="main_back_ground_color">#ffffff00</color>
</resources>
```

The entries in Listing 3-3 need to be in a file residing in the /res/values subdirectory. The name of the file is arbitrary, meaning the file name can be anything you choose.

Listing 3-4 shows an example of using a color resource in Java code.

Listing 3-4. *Color Resources in Java code*

```
int mainBackGroundColor
    = activity.getResources.getColor(R.color.main_back_ground_color);
```

Listing 3-5 shows how you would use a color resource in a view definition.

Listing 3-5. *Using Colors in View Definitions*

```
<TextView android:layout_width="fill_parent"
        android:layout_height="wrap_content"
        android:textColor="@color/ red"
        android:text="Sample Text to Show Red Color"/>
```

More on String Resources

We covered string resources briefly when we introduced resources at the beginning of this chapter. Let us revisit them in order to provide some more detail. We will show you how to define and use HTML strings, as well as how to substitute variables in string resources.

Note Unlike other UI frameworks, Android offers the ability to quickly associate IDs with string resources through R.java. So using strings as resources is that much easier in Android.

Let us start by showing how you can define normal strings, quoted strings, HTML strings, and substitutable strings in an XML resource file (see Listing 3-6).

Listing 3-6. *XML Syntax for Defining String Resources*

```xml
<resources>
    <string name="simple_string">simple string</string>
    <string name="quoted_string">"quoted'string"</string>
    <string name="double_quoted_string">\"double quotes\"</string>
    <string name="java_format_string">
        hello %2$s java format string. %1$s again
    </string>
    <string name="tagged_string">
        Hello <b><i>Slanted Android</i></b>, You are bold.
    </string>
</resources>
```

This XML string-resource file needs to be in the /res/values subdirectory. The name of the file is arbitrary.

Notice how quoted strings need to be either escaped or placed in alternate quotes. The string definitions also allow standard Java string-formatting sequences.

Android also allows child XML elements such as <b>, <i>, and other simple text-formatting HTML within the <string> node. You can use this compound HTML string to style the text before painting in a text view.

The Java examples in Listing 3-7 illustrate each usage.

Listing 3-7. *Using String Resources in Java Code*

```java
//Read a simple string and set it in a text view
String simpleString = activity.getString(R.string.simple_string);
textView.setText(simpleString);

//Read a quoted string and set it in a text view
String quotedString = activity.getString(R.string.quoted_string);
textView.setText(quotedString);

//Read a double quoted string and set it in a text view
String doubleQuotedString = activity.getString(R.string.double_quoted_string);
textView.setText(doubleQuotedString);

//Read a Java format string
String javaFormatString = activity.getString(R.string.java_format_string);
//Convert the formatted string by passing in arguments
String substitutedString = String.format(javaFormatString, "Hello" , "Android");
//set the output in a text view
textView.setText(substitutedString);
```

```
//Read an html string from the resource and set it in a text view
String htmlTaggedString = activity.getString(R.string.tagged_string);
//Convert it to a text span so that it can be set in a text view
//android.text.Html class allows painting of "html" strings
//This is strictly an Android class and does not support all html tags
Spanned textSpan = android.text.Html.fromHtml(htmlTaggedString);
//Set it in a text view
textView.setText(textSpan);
```

Once you've defined the strings as resources, you can set them directly on a view such as TextView in the XML layout definition for that TextView. Listing 3-8 shows an example where an HTML string is set as the text content of a TextView.

Listing 3-8. *Using String Resources in XML*

```
<TextView android:layout_width="fill_parent"
          android:layout_height="wrap_content"
          android:textAlign="center"
          android:text="@string/tagged_string"/>
```

TextView automatically realizes that this string is an HTML string, and honors its formatting accordingly. This is nice because you can quickly set attractive text in your views as part of the layout.

Dimension Resources

Pixels, inches, and points are all examples of dimensions that can play a part in XML layouts or Java code. You can use these dimension resources to style and localize Android UIs without changing the source code.

Listing 3-9 shows how you can use dimension resources in XML.

Listing 3-9. *XML Syntax for Defining Dimension Resources*

```
<resources>
    <dimen name="mysize_in_pixels">1px</dimen>
    <dimen name="mysize_in_dp">5dp</dimen>
    <dimen name="medium_size">100sp</dimen>
</resources>
```

You could specify the dimensions in any of the following units:

- *px*: Pixels

- *in*: Inches

- *mm*: Millimeters

- *pt*: Points

- *dp*: Density-independent pixels based on a 160-dpi (pixel density per inch) screen (dimensions adjust to screen density)

- *sp*: Scale-independent pixels (dimensions that allow for user sizing; helpful for use in fonts)

In Java, you need to access your Resources object instance to retrieve a dimension. You can do this by calling getResources on an activity object (see Listing 3-10).

Listing 3-10. *Using Dimension Resources in Java Code*

```
float dimen = activity.getResources().getDimension(R.dimen.mysize_in_pixels);
```

■**Note** The method call uses Dimension whereas the R.java namespace uses the shortened version dimen to represent "dimension."

As in Java, the resource reference for a dimension in XML uses dimen as opposed to the full word "dimension" (see Listing 3-11).

Listing 3-11. *Using Dimension Resources in XML*

```
<TextView android:layout_width="fill_parent"
        android:layout_height="wrap_content"
        android:textSize="@dimen/medium_size"/>
```

Image Resources

Android generates resource IDs for image files placed in the /res/drawable subdirectory. The supported image types include .gif, .jpg, and .png. Each image file in this directory generates a unique ID from its base file name. If the image file name is sample_image.jpg, for example, then the resource ID generated will be R.drawable.sample_image.

■**Caution** You'll get an error if you have two file names with the same base file name. Also, files in subdirectories underneath /res/drawable will be ignored.

You can then reference these images in other XML layout definitions, as shown in Listing 3-12.

Listing 3-12. *Using Image Resources in XML*

```
<Button
      android:id="@+id/button1"
      android:layout_width="fill_parent"
      android:layout_height="wrap_content"
      android:text="Dial"
      android:background="@drawable/sample_image"
/>
```

You can also retrieve the image programmatically and set it yourself in Java (see Listing 3-13).

Listing 3-13. *Using Image Resources in Java*

```
//Call getDrawable to get the image
BitmapDrawable d = activity.getResources().getDrawable(R.drawable.sample_image);

//You can use the drawable then to set the background
button.setBackgroundDrawable(d);

//or you can set the background directly from the Resource Id
button.setBackgroundResource(R.drawable.icon);
```

■**Note** These background methods go all the way back to the View class. As a result, most of the UI controls have this background support.

Android also supports a special type of image called a *stretchable* image. This is simply a kind of .png where parts of the image can be specified as static and stretchable. Android provides a tool called the Draw 9-patch tool to specify these regions. (You can read more about it at http://developer.android.com/guide/developing/tools/draw9patch.html.)

Once the .png image is made available, you can use it as any other image. It comes in handy when used as background for buttons where the button has to stretch itself to accommodate the text.

Color-Drawable Resources

In Android, an image is one type of a drawable resource. Android supports another drawable resource called a color-drawable resource; it's essentially a colored rectangle.

■**Caution** The Android documentation seems to suggest that rounded corners are possible. At least in releases 1.0, 1.1, and 1.5, that is not the case. The documentation also suggests that the instantiated Java class is PaintDrawable, but the code returns a ColorDrawable.

To define one of these color rectangles, you define an XML element by the node name of drawable in any XML file in the /res/values subdirectory. Listing 3-14 shows a couple of color-drawable resource examples.

Listing 3-14. *XML Syntax for Defining Color-Drawable Resources*

```
<resources>
    <drawable name="red_rectangle">#f00</drawable>
    <drawable name="blue_rectangle">#0000ff</drawable>
    <drawable name="green_rectangle">#f0f0</drawable>
</resources>
```

Listings 3-15 and 3-16 show how you can use a color-drawable resource in Java and XML, respectively.

Listing 3-15. *Using Color-Drawable Resources in Java Code*

```
// Get a drawable
ColorDrawble redDrawable =
(ColorDrawable)
activity.getResources().getDrawable(R.drawable.red_rectnagle);

//Set it as a background to a text view
textView.setBackground(redDrawable);
```

Listing 3-16. *Using Color-Drawable Resources in XML Code*

```
<TextView android:layout_width="fill_parent"
        android:layout_height="wrap_content"
        android:textAlign="center"
        android:background="@drawable/red_rectangle"/>
```

To achieve the rounded corners in your drawable, you can use the currently undocumented <shape> tag. However, this tag needs to reside in a file by itself in the /res/drawable directory. Listing 3-17 shows how you can use the <shape> tag to define a rounded rectangle in a file called /res/drawable/my_rounded_rectangle.xml.

Listing 3-17. *Defining a Rounded Rectangle*

```
<shape xmlns:android="http://schemas.android.com/apk/res/android">
    <solid android:color="#f0600000"/>
    <stroke android:width="3dp" color="#ffff8080"/>
    <corners android:radius="13dp" />
    <padding android:left="10dp" android:top="10dp"
        android:right="10dp" android:bottom="10dp" />
</shape>
```

You can then use this drawable resource as a background of the previous text-view example:

```
// Get a drawable
GradientDrawable roundedRectangle =
(GradientDrawable)
activity.getResources().getDrawable(R.drawable.red_rectnagle);

//Set it as a background to a text view
textView.setBackground(roundedRectangle);
```

■**Note** It is not necessary to cast the returned base Drawable to a GradientDrawable, but it was done to show you that this `<shape>` tag becomes a GradientDrawable. This information is important because you can look up the Java API documentation for this class to know the XML tags it defines.

Working with Arbitrary XML Resource Files

Android also allows arbitrary XML files as resources. This approach offers three distinct advantages. First, it provides a quick way to reference these files based on their generated resource IDs. Second, the approach allows you to localize these resource XML files. Third, you can compile and store these XML files on the device efficiently.

XML files that need to be read in this fashion are stored under the /res/xml subdirectory. Here is an example XML file called /res/xml/test.xml:

```
<rootelem1>
    <subelem1>
        Hello World from an xml sub element
    </subelem1>
</rootelem1>
```

As it does with other Android XML resource files, the AAPT will compile this XML file before placing it in the application package. You will need to use an instance of XmlPullParser if you want to parse these files. You can get an instance of the XmlPullParser implementation using this code from any context (including activity):

```
Resources res = activity.getResources();
XmlResourceParser xpp = res.getXml(R.xml.test);
```

The returned XmlResourceParser is an instance of XmlPullParser, and it also implements java.util.AttributeSet. Listing 3-18 shows a more complete code snippet that reads the test.xml file.

Listing 3-18. *Using XmlPullParser*

```
private String getEventsFromAnXMLFile(Activity activity)
throws XmlPullParserException, IOException
{
    StringBuffer sb = new StringBuffer();
    Resources res = activity.getResources();
    XmlResourceParser xpp = res.getXml(R.xml.test);

    xpp.next();
    int eventType = xpp.getEventType();
    while (eventType != XmlPullParser.END_DOCUMENT)
    {
        if(eventType == XmlPullParser.START_DOCUMENT)
        {
            sb.append("******Start document");
        }
        else if(eventType == XmlPullParser.START_TAG)
        {
            sb.append("\nStart tag "+xpp.getName());
        }
        else if(eventType == XmlPullParser.END_TAG)
        {
            sb.append("\nEnd tag "+xpp.getName());
        }
        else if(eventType == XmlPullParser.TEXT)
        {
            sb.append("\nText "+xpp.getText());
        }
        eventType = xpp.next();
    }//eof-while
    sb.append("\n******End document");
    return sb.toString();
}//eof-function
```

In Listing 3-18, you can see how to get XmlPullParser, how to use XmlPullParser to navigate the XML elements in the XML document, and how to use additional methods of XmlPullParser to access the details of the XML elements. If you want to run this code, you must create an XML file as shown earlier and call the getEventsFromAnXMLFile function from any menu item or button click. It will return a string, which you can print out to the log stream using the Log.d debug method.

Working with Raw Resources

Android also allows raw files in addition to raw XML files. These raw resources, placed in /res/raw, are arbitrary file resources such as audio, video, or text files that require localization or references through resource IDs. Unlike the raw XML files placed in /res/xml, these files are not compiled but moved to the application package as is. However, each file will have an identifier generated in R.java. If you were to place a text file at /res/raw/test.txt, you would be able to read that file using the code in Listing 3-19.

Listing 3-19. *Reading a Raw Resource*

```
String getStringFromRawFile(Activity activity)
{
    Resources r = activity.getResources();
    InputStream is = r.openRawResource(R.raw.test);
    String myText = convertStreamToString(is);
    is.close();
    return myText;
}

String convertStreamToString(InputStream is)
{
    ByteArrayOutputStream baos = new ByteArrayOutputStream();
    int i = is.read();
    while (i != -1)
    {
        baos.write(i);
        i = baos.read();
    }
    return baos.toString();
}
```

■**Caution**   File names with duplicate base names generate a build error in the Eclipse ADT plug-in. This is the case for all resource IDs generated for resources that are based on files.

Working with Assets

Android offers one more directory where you can keep files to be included in the package: /assets. It's at the same level as /res, meaning it's not part of the /res subdirectories. The files in /assets do not generate IDs in R.java; you must specify the file path to read them. The file path is a relative path starting at /assets. You will use the AssetManager class to access these files:

```
//Note: Exceptions are not shown in the code
String getStringFromAssetFile(Activity activity)
{
    AssetManager am = activity.getAssets();
    InputStream is = am.open("test.txt");
    String s = convertStreamToString(is);
    is.close();
    return s;
}
```

Reviewing the Resources Directory Structure

In summary, here is a quick look at the overall resources directory structure:

```
/res/values/strings.xml
         /colors.xml
         /dimens.xml
         /attrs.xml
         /styles.xml
    /drawable/*.png
            /*.jpg
            /*.gif
            /*.9.png
    /anim/*.xml
    /layout/*.xml
    /raw/*.*
    /xml/*.xml
/assets/*.*/*.*
```

■Note Only the `/assets` directory, because it's not under the `/res` directory, can contain an arbitrary list of subdirectories. Every other directory can have files only at the level of that directory and no deeper. This is how `R.java` generates identifiers for those files.

Let us conclude this section on resources by quickly enumerating what you have learned about resources so far. You know the types of resources supported in Android and you know how to create these resources in XML files. You know how resource IDs are generated and how to use them in Java code. You also learned that resource ID generation is a convenient scheme that simplifies resource usage in Android. Finally, you learned how to work with raw resources and assets. With that, we will now turn our attention to the section on content providers, where you will learn to work with data on Android.

Understanding Content Providers

Android allows you to expose your data sources (or data providers) through a representational state transfer–like (REST-like) abstraction called a *content provider*. A SQLite database on an Android device is an example of a data source that you can encapsulate into a content provider. To retrieve data from a content provider or save data into a content provider, you will need to use a set of REST-like URIs. For example, if you were to retrieve a set of books from a content provider that is an encapsulation of a book database, you will need to use a URI like this:

```
content://com.android.book.BookProvider/books
```

To retrieve a specific book from the book database (book 23), you will need to use a URI like this:

```
content://com.android.book.BookProvider/books/23
```

You will see in this section how these URIs translate to underlying database-access mechanisms. Any application on the device can make use of these URIs to access and manipulate data. As a consequence, content providers play a significant role in sharing data between applications.

Strictly speaking, though, the content providers' responsibilities comprise more of an encapsulation mechanism than a data-access mechanism. You'll need an actual data-access mechanism such as SQLite or network access to get to the underlying data sources. So, content-provider abstraction is required only if you want to share data externally or between applications. For internal data access, an application can use any data storage/access mechanism that it deems suitable, such as the following:

- *Preferences*: A set of key/value pairs that you can persist to store application preferences

- *Files*: Files internal to applications, which you can store on a removable storage medium

- *SQLite*: SQLite databases, each of which is private to the package that creates that database

- *Network*: A mechanism that lets you retrieve or store data externally through the Internet

Note Despite the number of data-access mechanisms allowed in Android, this chapter focuses on SQLite and the content-provider abstraction because content providers form the basis of data sharing, which is much more common in the Android framework compared to other UI frameworks. We'll cover the network approach in Chapter 8 and the preferences mechanism in Chapter 11.

As we go through this section, we will show you the content providers that come with Android and how to explore them. We will discuss in detail the structure of content URIs and how these URIs are linked with MIME types. After covering these content-provider concepts in detail, we will show you how to build a content provider from scratch that encapsulates a simple book database.

Exploring Android's Built-in Providers

Android comes with a number of built-in content providers, which are documented in the SDK's android.provider Java package. You can view the list of these providers here:

```
http://developer.android.com/reference/android/provider/package-summary.html
```

Here are a few of the providers listed on that documentation page:

```
Browser
CallLog
Contacts
    People
    Phones
    Photos
    Groups
MediaStore
    Audio
        Albums
        Artists
        Genres
        Playlists
    Images
        Thumbnails
    Video
Settings
```

■**Note** Android has added a new provider called "Dictionary" in SDK 1.5.

The top-level items are databases and the lower-level items are tables. So Browser, CallLog, Contacts, MediaStore, and Settings are individual SQLite databases encapsulated as providers. These SQLite databases typically have an extension of .db and are accessible only from the implementation package. Any access outside that package must go through the content-provider interface.

Exploring Databases on the Emulator and Available Devices

Because many content providers in Android use SQLite databases (http://www.sqlite.org/), you can use tools provided both by Android and by SQLite to examine the databases. Many of these tools reside in the \android-sdk-install-directory\tools subdirectory.

One of the tools is a remote shell on the device that allows you to execute a command-line SQLite tool against a specified database. You'll see in this section how to use this command-line utility to examine the built-in Android databases.

Android uses another command-line tool called Android Debug Bridge (adb), which is available as

```
tools\adb.exe
```

adb is a special tool in the Android toolkit that most other tools go through to get to the device. However, you must have an emulator running or an Android device connected for adb to work. You can find out whether you have running devices or emulators by typing this at the command line:

```
adb devices
```

If the emulator is not running, you can start the emulator by typing this at the command line:

```
\tools\emulator.exe
```

Note You should specify the Android Virtual Device (AVD) name to the emulator in SDK 1.5. See Chapter 12 for information on creating and naming virtual devices. Once you have the name of a virtual device, you can invoke the emulator as follows in SDK 1.5:

```
\tools\emulator.exe your-avd-name
```

You can also start the emulator through the Eclipse ADT plug-in. This automatically happens when you choose a program to run or debug in the emulator. Once the emulator is up and running, you can test again for a list of running devices by typing this:

```
\tools\adb.exe devices
```

Now you should see a printout that looks like this:

```
List of devices attached
emulator-5554 device
```

You can see the many options and commands that you can run with adb by typing this at the command line:

```
adb help
```

You can also visit the following URL for many of the runtime options for adb:

```
http://developer.android.com/guide/developing/tools/adb.html
```

You can use adb to open a shell on the connected device by typing this:

```
\tools\adb.exe shell
```

Note This shell is essentially a Unix ash, albeit with a limited command set. You can do ls, for example, but find, grep, and awk are not available in the shell.

You can see the available command set in the shell by typing this at the shell prompt:

```
#ls    /system/bin
```

The # sign is the prompt for the shell. For brevity, we will omit this prompt in some of the following examples. In release 1.0 and 1.1, the preceding line brings up the commands:

dumpcrash	toolbox
am	hcid
dumpstate	route
input	setprop
itr	sleep
monkey	setconsole
pm	smd
svc	stop
ssltest	top
debuggerd	start
dhcpcd	umount
hostapd_cli	vmstat
fillup	wipe
linker	watchprops
logwrapper	sync
telnetd	netcfg
iftop	chmod
mkdosfs	date
mount	dd
mv	cmp
notify	cat
netstat	dmesg
printenv	df
reboot	getevent
ps	getprop
renice	hd
rm	id
rmdir	ifconfig
rmmod	insmod
sendevent	ioctl
schedtop	kill
ping	ln
sh	log
hciattach	lsmod
sdptool	ls
logcat	mkdir
servicemanager	dumpsys
dbus-daemon	service
debug_tool	playmp3
flash_image	sdutil
installd	rild
dvz	dalvikvm
hostapd	dexopt
htclogkernel	surfaceflinger
mountd	app_process
qemud	mediaserver
radiooptions	system_server

■**Note** The commands here are from the 1.1 release. For the 1.5 release this list may vary slightly.

To see a list of root-level directories and files, you can type the following in the shell:

```
ls    -l
```

You'll need to access this directory to see the list of databases:

```
ls    /data/data
```

This directory contains the list of packages on the device. Let's look at an example by exploring the com.android.providers.contacts package:

```
ls   /data/data/com.android.providers.contacts/databases
```

This will list a database file called contacts.db, which is a SQLite database. If there were a find command in the included ash, you could look at all the *.db files. But there is no good way to do this with ls alone. The nearest thing you can do is this:

```
ls -R /data/data/*/databases
```

In releases 1.0 and 1.1 of the emulator, you will notice that the Android distribution has the following databases:

```
alarms.db
contacts.db
downloads.db
internal.db
settings.db
mmssms.db
telephony.db
```

■**Note** You will see two additional databases in release 1.5: user_dict.db and launcher.db.

Unlike traditional databases on servers and desktops, SQLite databases on the device are created as needed. You might not see some database files unless you have accessed the database at least once, thereby instigating its creation. You can invoke sqlite3 on one of these databases inside the adb shell by typing this:

```
#sqlite3   /data/data/com.android.providers.contacts/databases/contacts.db
```

You can exit sqlite3 by typing this:

```
sqlite>.exit
```

Notice that the prompt for adb is # and the prompt for sqlite3 is sqlite>. You can read about the various sqlite3 commands by visiting http://www.sqlite.org/sqlite.html. However, we will list a few important commands here so that you don't have to make a trip to the web. You can see a list of tables by typing

```
sqlite> .tables
```

This command is a shortcut for

```
SELECT name FROM sqlite_master
WHERE type IN ('table','view') AND name NOT LIKE 'sqlite_%'
UNION ALL
SELECT name FROM sqlite_temp_master
WHERE type IN ('table','view')
ORDER BY 1
```

As you probably guessed, the table sqlite_master is a master table that keeps track of tables and views in the database. The following command line prints out a create statement for a table called people in contacts.db:

```
.schema people
```

This is one way to get at the column names of a table in SQLite. This will also print out the column data types. While working with content providers, you should note these column types because access methods depend on them.

However, it is pretty tedious to humanly parse through this long create statement just to learn the column names and their types. Luckily, there is a workaround: you can pull contacts.db down to your local box and then examine the database using any number of GUI tools for SQLite version 3. You can issue the following command from your OS command prompt to pull down the contacts.db file:

```
adb pull  /data/data/com.android.providers.contacts/databases/contacts.db ➥
c:/somelocaldir/contacts.db
```

We used a free download of Sqliteman (http://sqliteman.com/), a GUI tool for SQLite databases, which seemed to work fine. We experienced a few crashes but otherwise found the tool completely usable for exploring Android SQLite databases.

Quick SQLite Primer

The following sample SQL statements could help you navigate through the SQLite databases quickly:

```
//Set the column headers to show in the tool
sqlite>.headers on

//select all rows from a table
select * from table1;

//count the number of rows in a table
select count(*) from table1;
```

```
//select a specific set of columns
select col1, col2 from table1;

//Select distinct values in a column
select distinct col1 from table1;

//counting the distinct values
select count(col1) from (select distinct col1  from table1);

//group by
select count(*), col1 from table1 group by col1;

//regular inner join
select * from table1 t1, table2 t2
where t1.col1 = t2.col1;

//left outer join
//Give me everything in t1 even though there are no rows in t2
select * from table t1 left outer join table2 t2
on t1.col1 = t2.col1
where ....
```

Architecture of Content Providers

You now know what content providers are and how to explore existing content providers through Android and SQLite tools. Next, we'll examine some of the architectural elements of content providers and how these content providers relate to other data-access facilities in the industry.

Content providers expose their data to their clients through a URI, similar to the way a web site exposes its content through URLs. Overall, the content-provider approach has parallels to the following:

- Web sites

- REST

- Web services

- Stored procedures

Each content provider on a device registers itself like a web site with a string (akin to a domain name) and a set of URIs. Here are two examples of providers registered in AndroidManifest.xml:

```
<provider android:name="SomeProvider"
        android:authorities="com.your-company.SomeProvider" />

<provider android:name="NotePadProvider"
    android:authorities="com.google.provider.NotePad"
/>
```

An *authority* is like a domain name for that content provider. Given the preceding authority registration, these providers will honor URLs starting with that authority prefix:

```
content://com.your-company.SomeProvider/
content://com.google.provider.NotePad/
```

Content providers also provide REST-like URLs to retrieve or manipulate data. For the preceding registration, the URI to identify a directory or a collection of notes in the NotePadProvider database is

```
content://com.google.provider.NotePad/Notes
```

The URL to identify a specific note is

```
content://com.google.provider.NotePad/Notes/#
```

where # is the id of a particular note. Here are some additional examples of URIs that some data providers accept:

```
content://media/internal/images
content://media/external/images
content://contacts/people/
content://contacts/people/23
```

Content providers exhibit characteristics of web services as well. A content provider, through its URIs, exposes internal data as a service. But the output from the URL of a content provider is not typed data, as is the case for a SOAP-based web-service call. Nor do the content provider's URIs define the structure of the data that they return. But as you will see in this chapter's "Structure of Android MIME Types" section, a content provider has a built-in mechanism to determine the Multipurpose Internet Mail Extensions (MIME) type of the data represented by this URI. In short, the content provider has an ability to receive inputs via the URI and return outputs as a set of columns and rows, but it does not have a Web Service Definition Language (WSDL). The caller is expected to know the structure of the rows and columns that are returned.

In addition to resembling web sites, REST, and web services, a content provider's URIs also resemble the names of stored procedures in a database. Stored procedures present service-based access to the underlying relational data. URIs are similar to stored procedures because URI calls against a content provider return a cursor. However, content providers differ from stored procedures in that the input to a service call in a content provider is typically embedded in the URI itself.

We've provided these comparisons to give you an idea of the broader scope of content providers and their limitations.

Structure of Android Content URIs

We compared a content provider to a web site because it responds to incoming URIs. So, to retrieve data from a content provider, all you have to do is invoke a URI. The retrieved data in the case of a content provider, however, is in the form of a set of rows and columns represented by an Android cursor object. In this context, we'll examine the structure of the URIs that you could use to retrieve data.

Content URIs in Android look similar to HTTP URIs, except that they start with content and have this general form:

```
content://*/*/*
```

Here's an example URI that identifies a note numbered 23 in a database of notes:

```
content://com.google.provider.NotePad/notes/23
```

After content:, the URI contains a unique identifier for the authority, which is used to locate the provider in the provider registry. In the preceding example, com.google.provider. NotePad is the authority portion of the URI.

/notes/23 is the path section of the URI that is specific to each provider. The notes and 23 portions of the path section are called path segments. It is the responsibility of the provider to document and interpret the path section and path segments of the URIs. The developer of the content provider usually does this by declaring constants in a Java class or a Java interface in that provider's implementation Java package. Furthermore, the first portion of the path might point to a collection of objects. For example, /notes indicates a collection or a directory of notes, whereas /23 points to a specific note item.

Given this URI, a provider is expected to retrieve rows that the URI identifies. The provider is also expected to alter content at this URI using any of the state-change methods: insert, update, or delete.

Structure of Android MIME Types

Just as a web site returns a MIME type for a given URL, a content provider has an added responsibility to return the MIME type for a given URI. MIME types work in Android similar to how they work in HTTP. You ask a provider for the MIME type of a given URI that it supports, and the provider returns a two-part string identifying its MIME type according to the standard web MIME conventions. You can find the MIME-type standard here:

```
http://tools.ietf.org/html/rfc2046
```

According to the MIME-type specification, a MIME type has two parts: a type and a sub-type. Here are some examples of well-known MIME-type pairs:

```
text/html
text/css
text/xml
text/vnd.curl
application/pdf
application/rtf
application/vnd.ms-excel
```

You can see a complete list of registered types and subtypes at the Internet Assigned Numbers Authority (IANA) web site:

```
http://www.iana.org/assignments/media-types/
```

The primary registered content types are

```
application
audio
example
image
message
model
multipart
text
video
```

Each of these primary types has subtypes. But if a vendor has proprietary data formats, the subtype name begins with vnd. For example, Microsoft Excel spreadsheets are identified by the subtype vnd.ms-excel, whereas pdf is considered a nonvendor standard and is represented as such without any vendor-specific prefix.

Some subtypes start with x-; these are nonstandard subtypes that don't have to be registered. They're considered private values that are bilaterally defined between two collaborating agents. Here are a few examples:

```
application/x-tar
audio/x-aiff
video/x-msvideo
```

Android follows a similar convention to define MIME types. The vnd in Android MIME types indicates that these types and subtypes are nonstandard, vendor-specific forms. To provide uniqueness, Android further demarcates the types and subtypes with multiple parts similar to a domain spec. Furthermore, the Android MIME type for each content type has two forms: one for a specific record, and one for multiple records.

For a single record, the MIME type looks like this:

```
vnd.android.cursor.item/vnd.yourcompanyname.contenttype
```

For a collection of records or rows, the MIME type looks like this:

```
vnd.android.cursor.dir/vnd.yourcompanyname.contenttype
```

Here are a couple examples:

```
//One single note
vnd.android.cursor.item/vnd.google.note
```

```
//A collection or a directory of notes
vnd.android.cursor.dir/vnd.google.note
```

MIME types are extensively used in Android, especially in intents, where the system figures out what activity to invoke based on the MIME type of data. MIME types are invariably derived from their URIs through content providers. You need to keep three things in mind when you work with MIME types:

- The type and subtype need to be unique for what they represent.

- As mentioned earlier, they need to be preceded with vnd if they are not standard (which is usually the case when you talk about specific records).

- They are typically namespaced for your specific need.

You should also note that the primary MIME type for a collection of items returned through an Android cursor should always be vnd.android.cursor.dir, and the primary MIME type of a single item retrieved through an Android cursor should be vnd.android.cursor.item. You have more wiggle room when it comes to the subtype, as in vnd.google.note; after the vnd. part, you are free to subtype it with anything you'd like.

Reading Data Using URIs

Now you know how to retrieve data from a content provider using URIs. Just as a web site can allow a number of different URLs based at a certain root URL, a content provider can also allow a number of URIs. Because the URIs defined by a content provider are unique to that provider, it is important that these URIs are documented and available for clients to see and then call. The providers that come with Android make this easier by defining constants representing these URI strings.

Consider these three URIs defined by helper classes in the Android SDK:

```
MediaStore.Images.Media.INTERNAL_CONTENT_URI
MediaStore.Images.Media.EXTERNAL_CONTENT_URI
Contacts.People.CONTENT_URI
```

The equivalent textual URI strings would be as follows:

```
content://media/internal/images
content://media/external/images
content://contacts/people/
```

The MediaStore provider defines two URIs and the Contacts provider defines one URI. Given these URIs, the code to retrieve a single row of contacts looks like this:

```
Uri peopleBaseUri = Contacts.People.CONTENT_URI;
Uri myPersonUri = peopleBaseUri.withAppendedId(Contacts.People.CONTENT_URI, 23);

//Query for this record.
//managedQuery is a method on Activity class
Cursor cur = managedQuery(myPersonUri, null, null, null);
```

Notice how the Contacts.People.CONTENT_URI is predefined as a constant in the People class. In this example, the code takes the root URI, adds a specific person ID to it, and makes a call to the managedQuery method.

As part of the managed query against this URI, it is possible to specify a sort order, the columns to select, and a where clause. These additional parameters are set to null in this example.

A content provider should list which columns it supports by implementing a set of interfaces or by listing the column names as constants. However, the class or interface that defines constants for columns should also make the column types clear.

Listing 3-20 shows how to retrieve a cursor with a specific list of columns from the People provider, based on the previous example.

Listing 3-20. *Retrieving a Cursor from a Content Provider*

```
// An array specifying which columns to return.
string[] projection = new string[] {
    People._ID,
    People.NAME,
    People.NUMBER,
};

// Get the base URI for People table in Contacts Content Provider.
// ie. content://contacts/people/
Uri mContactsUri = People.CONTENT_URI;

// Best way to retrieve a query; returns a managed query.
Cursor managedCursor = managedQuery( mContactsUri,
                        projection, //Which columns to return.
                        null,      // WHERE clause
                        People.NAME + " ASC"); // Order-by clause.
```

Notice how a projection is merely an array of strings representing column names. So unless you know what these columns are, you'll find it difficult to create a projection. You should look for these column names in the same class that provides the URI, in this case the People class. Let's look at the other column names defined in this class:

```
CUSTOM_RINGTONE
DISPLAY_NAME
LAST_TIME_CONTACTED
NAME
NOTES
PHOTO_VERSION
SEND_TO_VOICE_MAIL
STARRED
TIMES_CONTACTED
```

You can discover more about each of these columns by looking at the SDK documentation for the android.provider.Contacts.PeopleColumns class, available at this URL:

```
http://code.google.com/android/reference/android/provider/➥
Contacts.PeopleColumns.html
```

It is also important to note that a database like contacts contains several tables, each of which is represented by a class or an interface to describe its columns and their types. Let's take a look at the package android.providers.Contacts, documented at the following URL:

```
http://code.google.com/android/reference/android/provider/Contacts.html
```

You will see that this package has the following nested classes or interfaces:

```
ContactMethods
Extensions
Groups
Organizations
People
Phones
Photos
Settings
```

Each of these classes represents a table name in the `contacts.db` database, and each table is responsible for describing its own URI structure. Plus, a corresponding `Columns` interface is defined for each class to identify the column names, such as `PeopleColumns`.

Let's revisit the `cursor` that is returned: it contains zero or more records. Column names, order, and type are provider-specific. However, every row returned has a default column called `_id` representing a unique ID for that row.

Using the Cursor

Before you access a cursor, you should know a few things about an Android cursor:

- A cursor is a collection of rows.
- You need to use `moveToFirst()` because the cursor is positioned before the first row.
- You need to know the column names.
- You need to know the column types.
- All field-access methods are based on column number, so you must convert the column name to a column number first.
- The cursor is a random cursor (you can move forward and backward, and you can jump).
- Because the cursor is a random cursor, you can ask it for a row count.

An Android cursor has a number of methods that allow you to navigate through it. Listing 3-21 shows you how to check if a cursor is empty, and how to walk through the cursor row by row when it is not empty.

Listing 3-21. *Navigating Through a Cursor Using a while Loop*

```
if (cur.moveToFirst() == false)
{
   //no rows empty cursor
   return;
}

//The cursor is already pointing to the first row
//let's access a few columns
int nameColumnIndex = cur.getColumnIndex(People.NAME);
String name = cur.getString(nameColumnIndex);
```

```
//let's now see how we can loop through a cursor

while(cur.moveToNext())
{
   //cursor moved successfully
   //access fields
}
```

The assumption at the beginning of Listing 3-21 is that the cursor has been positioned before the first row. To position the cursor on the first row, we use the moveToFirst() method on the cursor object. This method returns false if the cursor is empty. We then use the moveToNext() method repetitively to walk through the cursor.

To help you learn where the cursor is, Android provides the following methods:

```
isBeforeFirst()
isAfterLast()
isClosed()
```

Using these methods, you can also use a for loop as in Listing 3-22 to navigate through the cursor instead of the while loop used in Listing 3-21.

Listing 3-22. *Navigating Through a Cursor Using a for Loop*

```
for(cur.moveToFirst();!cur.isAfterLast();cur.moveToNext())
{
   int nameColumn = cur.getColumnIndex(People.NAME);
   int phoneColumn = cur.getColumnIndex(People.NUMBER);

   String name = cur.getString(nameColumn);
   String phoneNumber = cur.getString(phoneColumn);
}
```

To find the number of rows in a cursor, Android provides a method on the cursor object called getCount().

Working with the where Clause

Content providers offer two ways of passing a where clause:

- Through the URI

- Through the combination of a string clause and a set of replaceable string-array arguments

We will cover both of these approaches through some sample code.

Passing a where Clause Through a URI

Imagine you want to retrieve a note whose ID is 23 from the Google notes database. You'd use the code in Listing 3-23 to retrieve a cursor containing one row corresponding to row 23 in the notes table.

Listing 3-23. *Passing SQL WHERE Clauses Through the URI*

```
Activity someActivity;
//..initialize someActivity
String noteUri = "content://com.google.provider.NotePad/notes/23";
Cursor managedCursor = someActivity.managedQuery( noteUri,
                        projection, //Which columns to return.
                        null,       // WHERE clause
                        null); // Order-by clause.
```

We left the where clause argument of the managedQuery method null because in this case, we assumed that the note provider is smart enough to figure out the id of the book we wanted. This id is embedded in the URI itself. In a sense, we used the URI as a vehicle to pass the where clause. This becomes apparent when you notice how the notes provider implements the corresponding query method. Here is a code snippet from that query method:

```
//Retrieve a note id from the incoming uri that looks like
//content://.../notes/23
int noteId = uri.getPathSegments().get(1);

//ask a query builder to build a query
//specify a table name
queryBuilder.setTables(NOTES_TABLE_NAME);

//use the noteid to put a where clause
queryBuilder.appendWhere(Notes._ID + "=" + );
```

Notice how the id of a note is extracted from the URI. The Uri class representing the incoming argument uri has a method to extract the portions of a URI after the root content://com.google.provider.NotePad. These portions are called path segments; they're strings between / separators such as /seg1/seg3/seg4/ and they're indexed by their positions. For the URI here, the first path segment would be 23. We then used this ID of 23 to append to the where clause specified to the QueryBuilder class. In the end, the equivalent select statement would be

```
select * from notes where _id == 23
```

■**Note** The classes Uri and UriMatcher are used to identify URIs and extract parameters from them. (We'll cover UriMatcher further in the section "Using UriMatcher to Figure Out the URIs.") SQLiteQueryBuilder is a helper class in android.database.sqlite that allows you to construct SQL queries to be executed by SQLiteDatabase on a SQLite database instance.

Using Explicit WHERE Clauses

Now that you have seen how to use a URI to send in a where clause, consider the other method by which Android lets us send a list of explicit columns and their corresponding values as a where clause. To explore this, let's take another look at the managedQuery method of the Activity class that we used in Listing 3-23. Here's its signature:

```
public final Cursor managedQuery(Uri uri,
    String[] projection,
    String selection,
    String[] selectionArgs,
    String sortOrder)
```

Notice the argument named selection, which is of type String. This selection string represents a filter (where clause, essentially) declaring which rows to return, formatted as a SQL WHERE clause (excluding the WHERE itself). Passing null will return all rows for the given URI. In the selection string you can include ?s, which will be replaced by the values from selectionArgs in the order that they appear in the selection. The values will be bound as Strings.

Because you have two ways of specifying a where clause, you might find it difficult to determine how a provider has used these where clauses and which where clause takes precedence if both where clauses are utilized.

For example, you can query for a note whose ID is 23 using either of these two methods:

```
//URI method
managedQuery("content://com.google.provider.NotePad/notes/23"
,null
,null
,null
,null);
```

or

```
//explicit where clause
managedQuery("content://com.google.provider.NotePad/notes"
,null
,"_id=?"
,new String[] {23}
,null);
```

The convention is to use where clauses through URIs where applicable and use the explicit option as a special case.

Inserting Records

So far we have talked about how to retrieve data from content providers using URIs. Let us turn our attention to inserts, updates, and deletes. Let us start with insert first.

Android uses a class called android.content.ContentValues to hold the values for a single record, which is to be inserted. ContentValues is a dictionary of key/value pairs, much like column names and their values. You insert records by first populating a record into ContentValues and then asking android.content.ContentResolver to insert that record using a URI.

■**Note** You need to locate ContentResolver because at this level of abstraction, you are not asking a database to insert a record; instead, you are asking to insert a record into a provider identified by a URI. ContentResolver is responsible for resolving the URI reference to the right provider and then passing on the ContentValues object to that specific provider.

Here is an example of populating a single row of notes in ContentValues in preparation for an insert:

```
ContentValues values = new ContentValues();
values.put("title", "New note");
values.put("note","This is a new note");

//values object is now ready to be inserted
```

Although we have hard-coded the column names, you can use constants defined in your Notepad application instead. You can get a reference to ContentResolver by asking the Activity class:

```
ContentResolver contentResolver = activity.getContentResolver();
```

Now all you need is a URI to tell ContentResolver to insert the row. These URIs are defined in a class corresponding to the Notes table. In the Notepad example, this URI is

```
Notepad.Notes.CONTENT_URI
```

We can take this URI and the ContentValues we have, and make a call to insert the row:

```
Uri uri = contentResolver.insert(Notepad.Notes.CONTENT_URI, values);
```

This call returns a URI pointing to the newly inserted record. This returned URI would match the following structure:

```
Notepad.Notes.CONTENT_URI/new_id
```

Adding a File to a Content Provider

Occasionally you might need to store a file in a database. The usual approach is to save the file to disk and then update the record in the database that points to the corresponding file name.

Android takes this protocol and automates it by defining a specific procedure for saving and retrieving these files. Android uses a convention where a reference to the file name is saved in a record with a reserved column name of _data.

When a record is inserted into that table, Android returns the URI to the caller. Once you save the record using this mechanism, you also need to follow it up by saving the file in that location. To do this, Android allows ContentResolver to take the Uri of the database record and return a writable output stream. Behind the scenes, Android allocates an internal file and stores the reference to that file name in the _data field.

If you were to extend the Notepad example to store an image for a given note, you could create an additional column called _data and run an insert first to get a URI back. The following code demonstrates this part of the protocol:

```
ContentValues values = new ContentValues();
values.put("title", "New note");
values.put("note","This is a new note");

//Use a content resolver to insert the record
ContentResolver contentResolver = activity.getContentResolver();
Uri newUri = contentResolver.insert(Notepad.Notes.CONTENT_URI, values);
```

Once you have the URI of the record, the following code asks the ContentResolver to get a reference to the file output stream:

```
….
//Use the content resolver to get an output stream directly
//ContentResolver hides the access to the _data field where
//it stores the real file reference.
OutputStream outStream = activity.getContentResolver().openOutputStream(newUri);
someSourceBitmap.compress(Bitmap.CompressFormat.JPEG, 50, outStream);
outStream.close();
```

The code then uses that output stream to write to.

Updates and Deletes

So far we have talked about queries and inserts; updates and deletes are fairly straightforward. Performing an update is similar to performing an insert, in which changed column values are passed through a ContentValues object. Here is the signature of an update method on the ContentResolver object:

```
int numberOfRowsUpdated =
activity.getContentResolver().update(
    Uri uri,
    ContentValues values,
    String whereClause,
    String[] selectionArgs )
```

The whereClause argument will constrain the update to the pertinent rows. Similarly, the signature for the delete method is

```
int numberOfRowsDeleted =
activity.getContentResolver().update(
    Uri uri,
    String whereClause,
    String[] selectionArgs )
```

Clearly a delete method will not require the ContentValues argument because you will not need to specify the columns you want when you are deleting a record.

Almost all the calls from managedQuery and ContentResolver are directed eventually to the provider class. Knowing how a provider implements each of these methods gives us enough clues as to how those methods are used by a client. In the next section, we'll cover the implementation from scratch of an example content provider called BookProvider.

Implementing Content Providers

So we've discussed how to interact with a content provider for our data needs, but haven't yet discussed how to write a content provider. To write a content provider, you have to extend android.content.ContentProvider and implement the following key methods:

```
query
insert
update
delete
getType
```

However, to make these methods work, you'll have to set up a number of things before implementing them. We will illustrate all the details of a content-provider implementation by describing the steps you'll need to take:

1. Plan your database, URIs, column names, and so on, and create a metadata class that defines constants for all of these metadata elements.

2. Extend the abstract class ContentProvider.

3. Implement these methods: query, insert, update, delete, and getType.

4. Register the provider in the manifest file.

Planning a Database

To explore this topic, we'll create a database that contains a collection of books. The book database contains only one table called books, and its columns are name, isbn, and author. You'll define this sort of relevant metadata in a Java class. This metadata-bearing Java class BookProviderMetaData is shown in Listing 3-24. Some key elements of this metadata class are highlighted.

Listing 3-24. *Defining Metadata for Your Database: The BookProviderMetaData Class*

```
public class BookProviderMetaData
{
    public static final String AUTHORITY = "com.androidbook.provider.BookProvider";

    public static final String DATABASE_NAME = "book.db";
    public static final int DATABASE_VERSION = 1;
    public static final String BOOKS_TABLE_NAME = "books";

    private BookProviderMetaData() {}
```

```java
//inner class describing BookTable
public static final class BookTableMetaData implements BaseColumns
{
    private BookTableMetaData() {}
    public static final String TABLE_NAME = "books";

    //uri and MIME type definitions
    public static final Uri CONTENT_URI =
                    Uri.parse("content://" + AUTHORITY + "/books");

    public static final String CONTENT_TYPE =
                    "vnd.android.cursor.dir/vnd.androidbook.book";

    public static final String CONTENT_ITEM_TYPE =
                    "vnd.android.cursor.item/vnd.androidbook.book";

    public static final String DEFAULT_SORT_ORDER = "modified DESC";

    //Additional Columns start here.
    //string type
    public static final String BOOK_NAME = "name";

    //string type
    public static final String BOOK_ISBN = "isbn";

    //string type
    public static final String BOOK_AUTHOR = "author";

    //Integer from System.currentTimeMillis()
    public static final String CREATED_DATE = "created";

    //Integer from System.currentTimeMillis()
    public static final String MODIFIED_DATE = "modified";
}
}
```

This BookProviderMetaData class starts by defining its authority to be com.androidbook. provider.BookProvider. We are going to use this string to register the provider in the Android manifest file. This string forms the front part of the URIs intended for this provider.

This class then proceeds to define its one table (books) as an inner BookTableMetaData class. The BookTableMetaData class then defines a URI for identifying a collection of books. Given the authority in the previous paragraph, the URI for a collection of books will look like this:

```
content://com.androidbook.provider.BookProvider/books
```

This URI is indicated by the constant

```
BookProviderMetaData.BookTableMetaData.CONTENT_URI
```

The BookTableMetaData class then proceeds to define the MIME types for a collection of books and a single book. The provider implementation will use these constants to return the MIME types for the incoming URIs.

BookTableMetaData then defines the set of columns: name, isbn, author, created (creation date), and modified (last-updated date).

■**Note** You should point out your columns' data types through comments in the code.

The metadata class BookTableMetaData also inherits from the BaseColumns class that provides the standard _id field, which represents the row ID. With these metadata definitions in hand, we're ready to tackle the provider implementation.

Extending ContentProvider

Implementing our BookProvider sample content provider involves extending the ContentProvider class and overriding onCreate() to create the database and then implement the query, insert, update, delete, and getType methods. This section covers the setup and creation of the database, while the following sections deal with each of the individual methods: query, insert, update, delete, and getType.

A query method requires the set of columns it needs to return. This is similar to a select clause that requires column names along with their as counterparts (sometimes called synonyms). Android uses a map object that it calls a projection map to represent these column names and their synonyms. We will need to set up this map so we can use it later in the query-method implementation. In the code for the provider implementation (see Listing 3-25), you will see this done up front.

Most of the methods we'll be implementing take a URI as an input. The provider implementation needs a mechanism to distinguish one URI from the other; Android uses a class called UriMatcher for this work. So we need to set up this object with all our URI variations. You will see this code in Listing 3-25 after the segment that creates a projection map. We'll further explain the UriMatcher class in the section "Using UriMatcher to Figure Out the URIs," but for now, know that the code shown here allows the content provider to identify one URI vs. the other.

And finally, the code in Listing 3-25 overrides the onCreate() method to facilitate the database creation. We have demarcated the code with highlighted comments to reflect the three areas we have talked about here:

- Setting up a column projection

- Setting up the UriMatcher

- Creating the database

Listing 3-25. *Implementing the BookProvider Content Provider*

```java
public class BookProvider extends ContentProvider
{
    //Create a Projection Map for Columns
    //Projection maps are similar to "as" construct in an sql
    //statement whereby you can rename the
    //columns.
    private static HashMap<String, String> sBooksProjectionMap;
    static
    {
        sBooksProjectionMap = new HashMap<String, String>();
        sBooksProjectionMap.put(BookTableMetaData._ID, BookTableMetaData._ID);

        //name, isbn, author
        sBooksProjectionMap.put(BookTableMetaData.BOOK_NAME
                                        , BookTableMetaData.BOOK_NAME);
        sBooksProjectionMap.put(BookTableMetaData.BOOK_ISBN
                                        , BookTableMetaData.BOOK_ISBN);
        sBooksProjectionMap.put(BookTableMetaData.BOOK_AUTHOR
                                        , BookTableMetaData.BOOK_AUTHOR);

        //created date, modified date
        sBooksProjectionMap.put(BookTableMetaData.CREATED_DATE
                                        , BookTableMetaData.CREATED_DATE);
        sBooksProjectionMap.put(BookTableMetaData.MODIFIED_DATE
                                        , BookTableMetaData.MODIFIED_DATE);
    }

    //Provide a mechanism to identify all the incoming uri patterns.
    private static final UriMatcher sUriMatcher;
    private static final int INCOMING_BOOK_COLLECTION_URI_INDICATOR = 1;
    private static final int INCOMING_SINGLE_BOOK_URI_INDICATOR = 2;
    static {
        sUriMatcher = new UriMatcher(UriMatcher.NO_MATCH);
        sUriMatcher.addURI(BookProviderMetaData.AUTHORITY
                            , "books"
                            , INCOMING_BOOK_COLLECTION_URI_INDICATOR);

        sUriMatcher.addURI(BookProviderMetaData.AUTHORITY
                            , "books/#",
                            INCOMING_SINGLE_BOOK_URI_INDICATOR);

    }
```

// Deal with OnCreate call back

```
    private DatabaseHelper mOpenHelper;

    @Override
    public boolean onCreate() {
        mOpenHelper = new DatabaseHelper(getContext());
        return true;
    }

    private static class DatabaseHelper extends SQLiteOpenHelper {

        DatabaseHelper(Context context) {
            super(context, BookProviderMetaData.DATABASE_NAME, null
                    , BookProviderMetaData.DATABASE_VERSION);
        }
```

//Create the database

```
        @Override
        public void onCreate(SQLiteDatabase db) {
            db.execSQL("CREATE TABLE " + BookTableMetaData.TABLE_NAME + " ("
                    + BookProviderMetaData.BookTableMetaData._ID
                    + " INTEGER PRIMARY KEY,"
                    + BookTableMetaData.BOOK_NAME + " TEXT,"
                    + BookTableMetaData.BOOK_ISBN + " TEXT,"
                    + BookTableMetaData.BOOK_AUTHOR + " TEXT,"
                    + BookTableMetaData.CREATED_DATE + " INTEGER,"
                    + BookTableMetaData.MODIFIED_DATE + " INTEGER"
                    + ");");
        }
```

//Deal with version changes

```
        @Override
        public void onUpgrade(SQLiteDatabase db, int oldVersion, int newVersion) {
            Log.w(TAG, "Upgrading database from version " + oldVersion + " to "
                    + newVersion + ", which will destroy all old data");
            db.execSQL("DROP TABLE IF EXISTS " + BookTableMetaData.TABLE_NAME);
            onCreate(db);
        }
    }
}
```

Fulfilling MIME-type Contracts

The BookProvider content provider must also implement the getType() method to return a MIME type for a given URI. This method, like many other methods of a content provider, is overloaded with respect to the incoming URI. As a result, the first responsibility of the getType() method is to distinguish the type of the URI. Is it a collection of books, or a single book?

As we pointed out in the previous section, we will use the UriMatcher to decipher this URI type. Depending on this URI, the BookTableMetaData class has defined the MIME-type constants to return for each URI. Without further ado, we present the complete code for the getType() method implementation in Listing 3-26.

Listing 3-26. *The getType() Method Implementation*

```
@Override
public String getType(Uri uri) {
    switch (sUriMatcher.match(uri)) {
    case INCOMING_BOOK_COLLECTION_URI_INDICATOR:
        return BookTableMetaData.CONTENT_TYPE;

    case INCOMING_SINGLE_BOOK_URI_INDICATOR:
        return BookTableMetaData.CONTENT_ITEM_TYPE;

    default:
        throw new IllegalArgumentException("Unknown URI " + uri);
    }
}
```

Implementing the Query Method

The query method in a content provider is responsible for returning a collection of rows depending on an incoming URI and a where clause.

Like the other methods, the query method uses UriMatcher to identify the URI type. If the URI type is a single-item type, the method retrieves the book ID from the incoming URI like this:

1. It extracts the path segments using getPathSegments().

2. It indexes into the URI to get the first path segment, which happens to be the book ID.

The query method then uses the projections that we created in Listing 3-25 to identify the return columns. In the end, query returns the cursor to the caller. Throughout this process, the query method uses the SQLiteQueryBuilder object to formulate and execute the query (see Listing 3-27).

Listing 3-27. *The query() Method Implementation*

```
@Override
public Cursor query(Uri uri, String[] projection, String selection
                            , String[] selectionArgs, String sortOrder)
{
    SQLiteQueryBuilder qb = new SQLiteQueryBuilder();

     switch (sUriMatcher.match(uri))
     {
         case INCOMING_BOOK_COLLECTION_URI_INDICATOR:
         qb.setTables(BookTableMetaData.TABLE_NAME);
         qb.setProjectionMap(sBooksProjectionMap);
         break;
```

```
        case INCOMING_SINGLE_BOOK_URI_INDICATOR:
        qb.setTables(BookTableMetaData.TABLE_NAME);
        qb.setProjectionMap(sBooksProjectionMap);
        qb.appendWhere(BookTableMetaData._ID + "="
                                        + uri.getPathSegments().get(1));
        break;

        default:
        throw new IllegalArgumentException("Unknown URI " + uri);
    }

    // If no sort order is specified use the default
    String orderBy;
    if (TextUtils.isEmpty(sortOrder)) {
        orderBy = BookTableMetaData.DEFAULT_SORT_ORDER;
    } else {
        orderBy = sortOrder;
    }

    // Get the database and run the query
    SQLiteDatabase db =
            mOpenHelper.getReadableDatabase();
    Cursor c = qb.query(db, projection, selection,
                        selectionArgs, null, null, orderBy);
    int i = c.getCount();

    // Tell the cursor what uri to watch,
    // so it knows when its source data changes
    c.setNotificationUri(getContext().getContentResolver(), uri);
    return c;
}
```

Implementing an Insert Method

The insert method in a content provider is responsible for inserting a record into the underlying database and then returning a URI that points to the newly created record.

Like the other methods, insert uses UriMatcher to identify the URI type. The code first checks whether the URI indicates the proper collection-type URI. If not, the code throws an exception (see Listing 3-28).

The code then validates the optional and mandatory column parameters. The code can substitute default values for some columns if they are missing.

Next, the code uses a SQLiteDatabase object to insert the new record and returns the newly inserted ID. In the end, the code constructs the new URI using the returned ID from the database.

Listing 3-28. *The insert() Method Implementation*

```java
@Override
public Uri insert(Uri uri, ContentValues values) {
    // Validate the requested uri
    if (sUriMatcher.match(uri) != INCOMING_BOOK_COLLECTION_URI_INDICATOR) {
        throw new IllegalArgumentException("Unknown URI " + uri);
    }

    Long now = Long.valueOf(System.currentTimeMillis());

    //validate input fields
    // Make sure that the fields are all set
    if (values.containsKey(BookTableMetaData.CREATED_DATE) == false) {
        values.put(BookTableMetaData.CREATED_DATE, now);
    }

    if (values.containsKey(BookTableMetaData.MODIFIED_DATE) == false) {
        values.put(BookTableMetaData.MODIFIED_DATE, now);
    }

    if (values.containsKey(BookTableMetaData.BOOK_NAME) == false) {
        throw new SQLException(
            "Failed to insert row because Book Name is needed " + uri);
    }

    if (values.containsKey(BookTableMetaData.BOOK_ISBN) == false) {
        values.put(BookTableMetaData.BOOK_ISBN, "Unknown ISBN");
    }
    if (values.containsKey(BookTableMetaData.BOOK_AUTHOR) == false) {
        values.put(BookTableMetaData.BOOK_ISBN, "Unknown Author");
    }

    SQLiteDatabase db = mOpenHelper.getWritableDatabase();
    long rowId = db.insert(BookTableMetaData.TABLE_NAME
                              , BookTableMetaData.BOOK_NAME, values);
    if (rowId > 0) {
        Uri insertedBookUri = ContentUris.withAppendedId(
                              BookTableMetaData.CONTENT_URI, rowId);
        getContext().getContentResolver().notifyChange(insertedBookUri, null);
        return insertedBookUri;
    }

    throw new SQLException("Failed to insert row into " + uri);
}
```

Implementing an Update Method

The update method in a content provider is responsible for updating a record based on the column values passed in, as well as the where clause that is passed in. The update method then returns the number of rows updated in the process.

Like the other methods, update uses UriMatcher to identify the URI type. If the URI type is a collection, the where clause is passed through so it can affect as many records as possible. If the URI type is a single-record type, then the book ID is extracted from the URI and specified as an additional where clause. In the end, the code returns the number of records updated (see Listing 3-29).

Listing 3-29. *The update() Method Implementation*

```
@Override
public int update(Uri uri, ContentValues values, String where, String[] whereArgs)
{
        SQLiteDatabase db = mOpenHelper.getWritableDatabase();
        int count;
        switch (sUriMatcher.match(uri)) {
        case INCOMING_BOOK_COLLECTION_URI_INDICATOR:
            count = db.update(BookTableMetaData.TABLE_NAME,
                                                values, where, whereArgs);
            break;

        case INCOMING_SINGLE_BOOK_URI_INDICATOR:
            String rowId = uri.getPathSegments().get(1);
            count = db.update(BookTableMetaData.TABLE_NAME
                    , values
                    , BookTableMetaData._ID + "=" + rowId
                    + (!TextUtils.isEmpty(where) ? " AND (" + where + ')' : "")
                    , whereArgs);
            break;

        default:
            throw new IllegalArgumentException("Unknown URI " + uri);
        }

        getContext().getContentResolver().notifyChange(uri, null);
        return count;
    }
}
```

Implementing a Delete Method

The delete method in a content provider is responsible for deleting a record based on the where clause that is passed in. The delete method then returns the number of rows deleted in the process.

Like the other methods, delete uses UriMatcher to identify the URI type. If the URI type is a collection type, the where clause is passed through so you can delete as many records as possible. If the where clause is null, all records will be deleted. If the URI type is a single-record type, the book ID is extracted from the URI and specified as an additional where clause. In the end, the code returns the number of records deleted (see Listing 3-30).

Listing 3-30. *The delete() Method Implementation*

```
@Override
public int delete(Uri uri, String where, String[] whereArgs) {
    SQLiteDatabase db = mOpenHelper.getWritableDatabase();
    int count;
    switch (sUriMatcher.match(uri)) {
    case INCOMING_BOOK_COLLECTION_URI_INDICATOR:
        count = db.delete(BookTableMetaData.TABLE_NAME, where, whereArgs);
        break;

    case INCOMING_SINGLE_BOOK_URI_INDICATOR:
        String rowId = uri.getPathSegments().get(1);
        count = db.delete(BookTableMetaData.TABLE_NAME
          , BookTableMetaData._ID + "=" + rowId
          + (!TextUtils.isEmpty(where) ? " AND (" + where + ')' : "")
          , whereArgs);
        break;

    default:
        throw new IllegalArgumentException("Unknown URI " + uri);
    }
    getContext().getContentResolver().notifyChange(uri, null);
    return count;
}
```

Using UriMatcher to Figure Out the URIs

We've mentioned the UriMatcher class several times now; let's delve into it. Almost all methods in a content provider are overloaded with respect to the URI. For example, the same query() method is called whether you want to retrieve a single book or a list of multiple books. It is up to the method to know which type of URI is being requested. Android's UriMatcher utility class helps you identify the URI types.

Here's how it works: you tell an instance of UriMatcher what kind of URI patterns to expect. You will also associate a unique number with each pattern. Once these patterns are registered, you can then ask UriMatcher if the incoming URI matches a certain pattern.

As we've mentioned, our BookProvider content provider has two URI patterns: one for a collection of books, and one for a single book. The code in Listing 3-31 registers both these patterns using UriMatcher. It allocates 1 for a collection of books and a 2 for a single book (the URI patterns themselves are defined in the metadata for the books table).

Listing 3-31. *Registering URI Patterns with UriMatcher*

```
private static final UriMatcher sUriMatcher;
//define ids for each uri type
private static final int INCOMING_BOOK_COLLECTION_URI_INDICATOR = 1;
private static final int INCOMING_SINGLE_BOOK_URI_INDICATOR = 2;

static {
    sUriMatcher = new UriMatcher(UriMatcher.NO_MATCH);
    //Register pattern for the books
    sUriMatcher.addURI(BookProviderMetaData.AUTHORITY
                          , "books"
                          , INCOMING_BOOK_COLLECTION_URI_INDICATOR);
    //Register pattern for a single book
    sUriMatcher.addURI(BookProviderMetaData.AUTHORITY
                          , "books/#",
                          INCOMING_SINGLE_BOOK_URI_INDICATOR);

}
```

Now that this registration is in place, you can see how UriMatcher plays a part in the query-method implementation:

```
switch (sUriMatcher.match(uri)) {
    case INCOMING_BOOK_COLLECTION_URI_INDICATOR:
    case INCOMING_SINGLE_BOOK_URI_INDICATOR:
    default:
        throw new IllegalArgumentException("Unknown URI " + uri);
}
```

Notice how the match method returns the same number that was registered earlier. The constructor of UriMatcher takes an integer to use for the root URI. UriMatcher returns this number if there are neither path segments nor authorities on the URL. UriMatcher also returns NO_MATCH when the patterns don't match. You can construct a UriMatcher with no root-matching code; in that case, Android initializes UriMatcher to NO_MATCH internally. So you could have written the code in Listing 3-31 as this instead:

```
static {
    sUriMatcher = new UriMatcher();
    sUriMatcher.addURI(BookProviderMetaData.AUTHORITY
                          , "books"
                          , INCOMING_BOOK_COLLECTION_URI_INDICATOR);

    sUriMatcher.addURI(BookProviderMetaData.AUTHORITY
                          , "books/#",
                          INCOMING_SINGLE_BOOK_URI_INDICATOR);
}
```

Using Projection Maps

A content provider acts like an intermediary between an abstract set of columns and a real set of columns in a database, yet these column sets might differ. While constructing queries, you must map between the where-clause columns that a client specifies and the real database columns. You set up this *projection map* with the help of the SQLiteQueryBuilder class.

Here is what the Android SDK documentation says about the mapping method public void setProjectionMap(Map columnMap) available on the QueryBuilder class:

> *Sets the projection map for the query. The projection map maps from column names that the caller passes into query to database column names. This is useful for renaming columns as well as disambiguating column names when doing joins. For example you could map "name" to "people.name". If a projection map is set it must contain all column names the user may request, even if the key and value are the same.*

Here is how our BookProvider content provider sets up the projection map:

```
sBooksProjectionMap = new HashMap<String, String>();
sBooksProjectionMap.put(BookTableMetaData._ID, BookTableMetaData._ID);

//name, isbn, author
sBooksProjectionMap.put(BookTableMetaData.BOOK_NAME
                                        , BookTableMetaData.BOOK_NAME);
sBooksProjectionMap.put(BookTableMetaData.BOOK_ISBN
                                        , BookTableMetaData.BOOK_ISBN);
sBooksProjectionMap.put(BookTableMetaData.BOOK_AUTHOR
                                        , BookTableMetaData.BOOK_AUTHOR);

//created date, modified date
sBooksProjectionMap.put(BookTableMetaData.CREATED_DATE
                                        , BookTableMetaData.CREATED_DATE);
sBooksProjectionMap.put(BookTableMetaData.MODIFIED_DATE
                                        , BookTableMetaData.MODIFIED_DATE);
```

And then the query builder uses the variable sBooksProjectionMap like this:

```
queryBuilder.setTables(NOTES_TABLE_NAME);
queryBuilder.setProjectionMap(sNotesProjectionMap);
```

Registering the Provider

Finally, you must register the content provider in the Android.Manifest.xml file using this tag structure:

```
<provider android:name="BooksProvider"
   android:authorities=" com.androidbook.provider.BookProvider "/>
```

This concludes our discussion about content providers. In this section, you learned the nature of content URIs and MIME types, and how to use SQLite to construct your own providers that respond to URIs. Once your underlying data is exposed in this manner, any application on the Android Platform can take advantage of it. This ability to access and update data using URIs, irrespective of the process boundaries, falls right in step with the current service-centric, cloud-computing landscape that we described in Chapter 1. In the next section, we will cover intents.

Understanding Intents

Android folds multiple ideas into the concept of an *intent*. You can use intents to invoke other applications from your application. You can use intents to invoke internal or external compo-nents from your application. You can use intents to raise events so that others can respond in a manner similar to a publish-and-subscribe model. You can use intents to represent actions.

At the simplest level, an intent is an action that you can tell Android to invoke. The action Android invokes depends on what is registered for that action. Imagine you've written the fol-lowing activity:

```
public class BasicViewActivity extends Activity
{
    @Override
    public void onCreate(Bundle savedInstanceState)
    {
        super.onCreate(savedInstanceState);
        setContentView(R.layout.some-view);
    }
}//eof-class
```

Android allows you to register this activity in its manifest file, making it available for other applications to invoke. The registration looks like this:

```
<activity android:name="BasicViewActivity"
          android:label="Basic View Tests">
  <intent-filter>
    <action android:name="com.androidbook.intent.action.ShowBasicView"/>
    <category android:name="android.intent.category.DEFAULT" />
  </intent-filter>
</activity>
```

The registration here not only involves an activity, but also an action that you can use to invoke that activity. The activity designer usually chooses a name for the action and specifies that action as part of an intent-filter for this activity. As we go through the rest of the chapter, you will have a chance to learn more about these intent-filters.

Now that you have specified the activity and its registration against an action, you can use an intent to invoke this BasicViewActivity:

```
public static invokeMyApplication(Activity parentActivity)
{
    String actionName= " com.androidbook.intent.action.ShowBasicView ";
    Intent intent = new Intent(actionName);
    parentActivity.startActivity(intent);
}
```

■**Note** The general convention for an action name is `<your-package-name>`.intent.action.`YOUR_`
`ACTION_NAME`.

Available Intents in Android

Now that you have a basic understanding of intents, you can give them a test run by invoking one
of the prefabricated applications that comes with Android (see Listing 3-32). The page at http://
developer.android.com/guide/appendix/g-app-intents.html documents the available applications and the intents that invoke them. The predefined applications include the following:

- A browser application to open a browser window

- An application to call a telephone number

- An application to present a phone dialer so the user can enter the numbers and make
  the call through the UI

- A mapping application to show the map of the world at a given latitude/longitude
  coordinate

- A detailed mapping application that can show Google street views

Listing 3-32. *Exercising Android's Prefabricated Applications*

```
public class IntentsUtils
{
    public static void invokeWebBrowser(Activity activity)
    {
        Intent intent = new Intent(Intent.ACTION_VIEW);
        intent.setData(Uri.parse("http://www.google.com"));
        activity.startActivity(intent);
    }
    public static void invokeWebSearch(Activity activity)
    {
        Intent intent = new Intent(Intent.ACTION_WEB_SEARCH);
        intent.setData(Uri.parse("http://www.google.com"));
        activity.startActivity(intent);
    }
    public static void dial(Activity activity)
    {
        Intent intent = new Intent(Intent.ACTION_DIAL);
        activity.startActivity(intent);
    }
```

```java
   public static void call(Activity activity)
   {
      Intent intent = new Intent(Intent.ACTION_CALL);
      intent.setData(Uri.parse("tel:555-555-5555"));
      activity.startActivity(intent);
   }
   public static void showMapAtLatLong(Activity activity)
   {
      Intent intent = new Intent(Intent.ACTION_VIEW);
      //geo:lat,long?z=zoomlevel&q=question-string
      intent.setData(Uri.parse("geo:0,0?z=4&q=business+near+city"));
      activity.startActivity(intent);
   }

   public static void tryOneOfThese(Activity activity)
   {
      IntentsUtils.call(activity);
   }
}
```

You will be able to exercise this code as long you have a simple activity with a simple view (like the one in the previous section) and a menu item to invoke tryOneOfThese(activity). Creating a simple menu is easy (see Listing 3-33).

Listing 3-33. *A Test Harness to Create a Simple Menu*

```java
public class HelloWorld extends Activity
{
   public void onCreate(Bundle savedInstanceState)   {
      super.onCreate(savedInstanceState);

      TextView tv = new TextView(this);
      tv.setText("Hello, Android. Say hello");
      setContentView(tv);
      registerMenu(this.getTextView());
   }
   @Override
   public boolean onCreateOptionsMenu(Menu menu)    {
      super.onCreateOptionsMenu(menu);
      int base=Menu.FIRST; // value is 1
      MenuItem item1 = menu.add(base,base,base,"Test");
      return true;
   }

   @Override
   public boolean onOptionsItemSelected(MenuItem item)   {
      if (item.getItemId() == 1)       {
         IntentUtils.tryOneOfThese(this);
      }
```

```
    else {
      return super.onOptionsItemSelected(item);
    }
    return true;
  }
}
```

■**Note** See Chapter 2 for instructions on how to make an Android project out of these files, as well as how to compile and run it. You can also read the early parts of Chapter 5 to see more sample code relating to menus.

Intents and Data URIs

So far we've covered the simplest of the intents, where all we need is the name of an action. The ACTION_DIAL activity in Listing 3-32 is one of these. So to invoke the dialer, all we need is the dialer's action and nothing else:

```
public static void dial(Activity activity)
{
    Intent intent = new Intent(Intent.ACTION_DIAL);
    activity.startActivity(intent);
}
```

Unlike ACTION_DIAL, the intent ACTION_CALL that is used to make a call to a given phone number takes an additional parameter called Data. This parameter points to a URI, which in turn points to the phone number:

```
public static void call(Activity activity)
{
    Intent intent = new Intent(Intent.ACTION_CALL);
    intent.setData(Uri.parse("tel:555-555-5555"));
    activity.startActivity(intent);
}
```

The action portion of an intent is a string or a string constant, usually prefixed by the Java package name. The data portion is always a string representing a URI. The format of this URI could be specific to each activity that is invoked by that action. In this case, the CALL action decides what kind of data URI it would expect. From the URI it extracts the telephone number.

■**Note** The invoked activity can also use the URI as a pointer to a data source, and extract the data from the data source and use that data instead. This would be the case for media such as audio, video, and images.

Generic Actions

The actions `Intent.ACTION_CALL` and `Intent.ACTION_DIAL` could easily lead us to the wrong assumption that there is a one-to-one relationship between an action and what it invokes. To disprove this, let us extract a counterexample from the `IntentUtils` code in Listing 3-32:

```
public static void invokeWebBrowser(Activity activity)
{
    Intent intent = new Intent(Intent.ACTION_VIEW);
    intent.setData(Uri.parse("http://www.google.com"));
    activity.startActivity(intent);
}
```

Note that the action is simply stated as `ACTION_VIEW`. How does Android know which activity to invoke in response to such a generic action name? In these cases, Android relies more heavily on the nature of the URI. Android looks at the scheme of the URI, which happens to be `http`, and questions all the registered activities to see which ones understand this scheme. Out of these, it inquires which ones can handle the `VIEW` and then invokes that activity. For this to work, the browser activity should have registered a `VIEW` intent against the data scheme of `http`. That intent declaration might look like this in the manifest file:

```
<activity…..>
    <intent-filter>
          <action android:name="android.intent.action.VIEW" />
        <data android:scheme="http"/>
        <data android:scheme="https"/>
    </intent-filter>
</activity>
```

You can learn more about the data options by looking at the XML definition for the data element at `http://code.google.com/android/reference/android/R.styleable.html#AndroidManifestData`. The child elements or attributes of data include these:

```
host
mimeType
path
pathPattern
pathPrefix
port
scheme
```

`mimeType` is one attribute you'll see used often. For example, the following intent-filter for the activity that displays a list of notes indicates the MIME type as a directory of notes:

```
<intent-filter>
    <action android:name="android.intent.action.VIEW" />
    <data android:mimeType="vnd.android.cursor.dir/vnd.google.note" />
</intent-filter>
```

The screen that displays a single note, on the other hand, declares its intent-filter using a MIME type indicating a single note item:

```
<intent-filter>
   <action android:name="android.intent.action.VIEW" />
   <data android:mimeType="vnd.android.cursor.item/vnd.google.note" />
</intent-filter>
```

Using Extra Information

In addition to its primary attributes of action and data, an intent can include additional attributes called *extras*. An extra can provide more information to the component that receives the intent. The extra data is in the form of key/value pairs: the key name should start with the package name, and the value name can be any fundamental data type or arbitrary object as long as it implements the android.os.Parcelable interface. This extra information is represented by an Android class called android.os.Bundle.

The following two methods on an Intent class provide access to the extra Bundle:

```
//Get the Bundle from an Intent
Bundle extraBundle = intent.getExtras();

// Place a bundle in an intent
Bundle anotherBundle = new Bundle();

//populate the bundle with key/value pairs
…..
//set the bundle on the Intent
intent.putExtras(anotherBundle);
```

getExtras is straightforward: it returns the Bundle that the intent has. putExtras checks whether the intent currently has a bundle. If the intent already has a bundle, putExtras transfers the additional keys and values from the new bundle to the existing bundle. If the bundle doesn't exist, putExtras will create one and copy the key/value pairs from the new bundle to the created bundle.

■**Note** putExtras replicates the incoming bundle rather than referencing it. So if you were to change the incoming bundle, you wouldn't be changing the bundle inside the intent.

You can use a number of methods to add fundamental types to the bundle. Here are some of the methods that add simple data types to the extra data:

```
putExtra(String name, boolean value);
putExtra(String name, int value);
putExtra(String name, double value);
putExtra(String name, String value);
```

And here are some not-so-simple extras:

```
//simple array support
putExtra(String name, int[] values);
putExtra(String name, float[] values);

//Serializable objects
putExtra(String name, Serializable value);

//Parcelable support
putExtra(String name, Parcelable value);

//Add another bundle at a given key
//Bundles in bundles
putExtra(String name, Bundle value);

//Add bundles from another intent
//copy of bundles
putExtra(String name, Intent anotherIntent);

//Explicit Array List support
putIntegerArrayListExtra(String name, ArrayList arrayList);
putParcelableArrayListExtra(String name, ArrayList arrayList);
putStringArrayListExtra(String name, ArrayList arrayList);
```

On the receiving side, equivalent methods starting with get retrieve information from the extra bundle based on key names.

The Intent class defines extra key strings that go with certain actions. You can discover a number of these extra-information key constants at http://code.google.com/android/reference/android/content/Intent.html#EXTRA_ALARM_COUNT.

Let us consider a couple of example extras that involve sending e-mails:

EXTRA_EMAIL: You will use this string key to hold a set of e-mail addresses. The value of the key is android.intent.extra.EMAIL. It should point to a string array of textual e-mail addresses.

EXTRA_SUBJECT: You will use this key to hold the subject of an e-mail message. The value of the key is android.intent.extra.SUBJECT. The key should point to a string of subject.

Using Components to Directly Invoke an Activity

You've seen a couple of ways to start an activity using intents. You saw an explicit action start an activity, and you saw a generic action start an activity with the help of a data URI. Android also provides a more direct way to start an activity: you can specify the activity's ComponentName, which is an abstraction around an object's package name and class name. There are a number of methods available on the Intent class to specify a component:

```
setComponent(ComponentName name);
setClassName(String packageName, String classNameInThatPackage);
setClassName(Context context, String classNameInThatContext);
setClass(Context context, Class classObjectInThatContext);
```

Ultimately, they are all shortcuts for calling one method:

```
setComponent(ComponentName name);
```

ComponentName wraps a package name and a class name together. For example, the following code invokes the contacts activity that ships with the emulator:

```
Intent intent = new Intent();
intent.setComponent(new ComponentName(
    "com.android.contacts"
    ,"com.android.contacts.DialtactsContactsEntryActivity");
startActivity(intent)
```

Notice that the package name and the class name are fully qualified, and are used in turn to construct the ComponentName before passing to the Intent class.

You can also use the class name directly without constructing a ComponentName. Consider the BasicViewActivity code snippet again:

```
public class BasicViewActivity extends Activity
{
    @Override
    public void onCreate(Bundle savedInstanceState)
    {
        super.onCreate(savedInstanceState);
        setContentView(R.layout.some-view);
    }
}//eof-class
```

Given this, you can use the following code to start this activity:

```
Intent directIntent = new Intent(activity, BasicViewActivity.class);
activity.start(directIntent);
```

If you want any type of intent to start an activity, however, you should register the activity in the Android.Manifest.xml file like this:

```
        <activity android:name="BasicViewActivity"
                  android:label="Test Activity">
```

No intent-filters are necessary for invoking an activity directly through its class name or component name.

Best Practice for Component Designers

If you look at the design for the contacts application in Android, you will notice some patterns for designing with intents. To make intents known to the clients of this application, the contacts application defines them in three classes in a package called android.provider. contacts. These three classes are as follows:

```
contacts.Intents
contacts.Intents.Insert //nested class
contacts.Intents.UI //nested class
```

The top-level class contacts.Intents defines the primary intents that the contacts application will respond to and the events that the app generates as it does its work.

The nested class contacts.Intents.Insert defines the supporting intents and other constants to insert new records. The contacts.Intents.UI nested class defines a number of ways to invoke the UI. The intents also clarify the extra information needed to invoke them, including key names and their expected value types.

As you design your own content providers and activities that act upon those content providers, you might want to follow this pattern for making intents explicit by defining constants for them in interfaces or classes.

Understanding Intent Categories

You can classify activities into categories so you can search for them based on a category name. For example, during startup Android looks for activities whose category (also known as a tag) is marked as CATEGORY_LAUNCHER. It then picks up these activity names and icons and places them on the home screen to launch.

Another example: Android looks for an activity tagged as CATEGORY_HOME to show the home screen during startup. Similarly, CATEGORY_GADGET marks an activity as suitable for embedding or reuse inside another activity.

The format of the string for a category like CATEGORY_LAUNCHER follows the category definition convention:

```
android.intent.category.LAUNCHER
```

You will need to know these text strings for category definitions because activities register their categories in the AndroidManifest.xml file as part of their activity-filter definitions. Here is an example:

```
    <activity android:name=".HelloWorld"
            android:label="@string/app_name">
        <intent-filter>
            <action android:name="android.intent.action.MAIN" />
            <category android:name="android.intent.category.LAUNCHER" />
        </intent-filter>
    </activity>
```

■**Note** Activities might have certain capabilities that restrict them or enable them, such as whether you can embed them in a parent activity. These types of activity characteristics are declared through categories.

Let us take a quick look at some predefined Android categories and how you use them (see Table 3-2).

Table 3-2. *Activity Categories and Their Descriptions*

Category Name	Description
CATEGORY_DEFAULT	An activity can declare itself as a DEFAULT activity to operate on a certain aspect of data such as type, scheme, and so on.
CATEGORY_BROWSABLE	An activity can declare itself as BROWSABLE by promising the browser that it will not violate browser-security considerations when started.
CATEGORY_TAB	An activity of this type is embeddable in a tabbed parent activity.
CATEGORY_ALTERNATIVE	An activity can declare itself as an ALTERNATIVE activity for a certain type of data that you are viewing. These items normally show up as part of the options menu when you are looking at that document. For example, print view is considered an alternative to regular view.
CATEGORY_SELECTED_ALTERNATIVE	An activity can declare itself as an ALTERNATIVE activity for a certain type of data. This is similar to listing a series of possible editors for a text document or an HTML document.
CATEGORY_LAUNCHER	Assigning this category to an activity will allow it to be listed on the launcher screen.
CATEGORY_HOME	An activity of this type will be the home screen. Typically, there should be only one activity of this type. If there are more, the system will prompt you to pick one.
CATEGORY_PREFERENCE	This activity identifies an activity as a preference activity, so it will be shown as part of the preferences screen.
CATEGORY_GADGET	An activity of this type is embeddable in a parent activity.
CATEGORY_TEST	A test activity.
CATEGORY_EMBED	This category has been superseded by the GADGET category, but it's been kept for backward compatibility.

You can read the details of these activity categories at the following Android SDK URL for the Intent class: http://code.google.com/android/reference/android/content/Intent. html#CATEGORY_ALTERNATIVE.

When you use an intent to start an activity, you can specify the kind of activity to choose by specifying a category. Or you can search for activities that match a certain category. Here is an example to retrieve a set of main activities that match the category of CATEGORY_SAMPLE_CODE:

```
Intent mainIntent = new Intent(Intent.ACTION_MAIN, null);
mainIntent.addCategory(Intent.CATEGORY_SAMPLE_CODE);
PackageManager pm = getPackageManager();
List<ResolveInfo> list = pm.queryIntentActivities(mainIntent, 0);
```

PackageManager is a key class that allows you to discover activities that match certain intents without invoking them. You can cycle through the received activities and invoke them as you see fit, based on the ResolveInfo API.

Following the same logic, you can also get a list of all launchable applications by populating an intent with a category of CATEGORY_LAUNCHER:

```
//Get me all launchable applications
Intent mainIntent = new Intent(Intent.ACTION_MAIN, null);
mainIntent.addCategory(Intent.CATEGORY_LAUNCHER);
List mApps = getPackageManager().queryIntentActivities(mainIntent, 0);
```

In fact, we can do better. Let's start an activity based on the preceding intent category CATEGORY_LAUNCHER:

```
public static void invokeAMainApp(Activity activity)
{
    Intent mainIntent = new Intent(Intent.ACTION_MAIN, null);
    mainIntent.addCategory(Intent.CATEGORY_LAUNCHER);
    activity.startActivity(mainIntent);
}
```

More than one activity will match the intent, so which activity will Android pick? To resolve this, Android presents a "Complete action using" dialog that lists all the possible activities so that you can choose one to run.

Here is another example of using an intent to go to a home page:

```
//Go to home screen
Intent mainIntent = new Intent(Intent.ACTION_MAIN, null);
mainIntent.addCategory(Intent.CATEGORY_HOME);
startActivity(mainIntent);
```

If you don't want to use Android's default home page, you can write your own and declare that activity to be of category HOME. In that case, the preceding code will give you an option to open your home activity because more than one home activity is registered now:

```
//Replace the home screen with yours
<intent-filter>
    <action android:value="android.intent.action.MAIN" />
    <category android:value="android.intent.category.HOME"/>
    <category android:value="android.intent.category.DEFAULT" />
</intent-filter>
```

The Rules for Resolving Intents to Their Components

So far, we have discussed a number of aspects about intents. To recap, we talked about actions, data URIs, extra data, and finally categories. Given these aspects, Android uses the following algorithm to resolve the intents to activities.

At the top of the hierarchy, with an air of exclusivity, is the component name attached to an intent. If this is set, then every other aspect or attribute of the intent is ignored and that component is chosen for execution.

Android then looks at the action attribute of the intent. If the intent indicates an action, then the target activity must list that action as part of its intent-filter. If no other attributes are specified, then Android invokes this activity. If there are multiple activities, Android will present the activity chooser.

Android then looks at the data portion of the intent. If the intent specifies a data URI, the type is retrieved from this URI via ContentProvider.getType() if it is not already supplied in the intent. The target activity must indicate through an intent-filter that it can handle data of this type. If the data URI is not a content URI or the data type is not specified, then the URI scheme is taken into account. The target activity then should indicate that it could handle the URIs of this type of scheme.

Android then looks at the category. Android will only pick activities matching that category. As a result, if the intent category is specified, then the target activity should declare this category in its intent-filter.

Exercising the ACTION_PICK

So far we have exercised intents or actions that mainly invoke another activity without expecting any results back. Now let's look at an action that is a bit more involved in that it returns a value after being invoked. ACTION_PICK is one such generic action.

The idea of ACTION_PICK is to start an activity that displays a list of items. The activity then should allow a user to pick one item from that list. Once the user picks the item, the activity should return the URI of the picked item to the caller. This allows reuse of the UI's functionality to select items of a certain type.

You should indicate the collection of items to choose from using a MIME type that points to an Android content cursor. The actual MIME type of this URI should look similar to the following:

vnd.android.cursor.dir/vnd.google.note

It is the responsibility of the activity to retrieve the data from the content provider based on the URI. This is also the reason that data should be encapsulated into content providers where possible.

For all actions that return data like this, we cannot use startActivity() because startActivity() does not return any result. startActivity() cannot return a result because it opens the new activity as a modal dialog in a separate thread and leaves the main thread for attending events. In other words, startActivity() is an asynchronous call with no callbacks to indicate what happened in the invoked activity. But if you want to return data, you can use a variation on startActivity() called startActivityForResult(), which comes with a callback.

Let us look at the signature of the `startActivityForResult()` method from the `Activity` class:

```
public void startActivityForResult(Intent intent, int requestCode)
```

This method launches an activity from which you would like a result. When this activity exits, the source activity's `onActivityResult()` method will be called with the given `requestCode`. The signature of this callback method is

```
protected void onActivityResult(int requestCode, int resultCode, Intent data)
```

The `requestCode` is what you passed in to the `startActivityForResult()` method. The `resultCode` can be `RESULT_OK`, `RESULT_CANCELED`, or a custom code. The custom codes should start at `RESULT_FIRST_USER`. The `Intent` parameter contains any additional data that the invoked activity wants to return. In the case of `ACTION_PICK`, the returned data in the intent points to the data URI of a single item (see Listing 3-34).

Listing 3-34. *Returning Data After Invoking an Action*

```
public static void invokePick(Activity activity)
{
  Intent pickIntent = new Intent(Intent.ACTION_PICK);
  int requestCode = 1;
  pickIntent.setData(Uri.parse(
    "content://com.google.provider.NotePad/notes"));
  activity.startActivityForResult(pickIntent, requestCode);
}

protected void onActivityResult(int requestCode
    ,int resultCode
    ,Intent outputIntent)
{
  super.onActivityResult(requestCode, resultCode, outputIntent);
  parseResult(this, requestCode, resultCode, outputIntent);
}
public static void parseResult(Activity activity
    , int requestCode
    , int resultCode
    , Intent outputIntent)
{
    if (requestCode != 1)
    {
    Log.d("Test", "Some one else called this. not us");
            return;
    }
    if (resultCode != Activity.RESULT_OK)
    {
      Log.d("Result code is not ok:" + resultCode);
            return;
    }
```

```
    Log.d("Test", "Result code is ok:" + resultCode);
    Uri selectedUri = outputIntent.getData();
    Log.d("Test", "The output uri:" + selectedUri.toString());

    //Proceed to display the note
    outputIntent.setAction(Intent.VIEW);
    startActivity(outputIntent);
}
```

The constants RESULT_OK, RESULT_CANCEL, and RESULT_FIRST_USER are all defined in the Activity class. The numerical values of these constants are

```
RESULT_OK = -1;
RESULT_CANCEL = 0;
RESULT_FIRST_USER = 1;
```

To make this work, the implementer should have code that explicitly addresses the needs of a PICK. Let's look at how this is done in the Google sample Notepad application. When the item is selected in the list of items, the intent that invoked the activity is checked to see whether it's a PICK intent. If it is, the data URI is set in a new intent and returned through setResult():

```
@Override
protected void onListItemClick(ListView l, View v, int position, long id) {
    Uri uri = ContentUris.withAppendedId(getIntent().getData(), id);

    String action = getIntent().getAction();
    if (Intent.ACTION_PICK.equals(action) ||
            Intent.ACTION_GET_CONTENT.equals(action))
    {
        // The caller is waiting for us to return a note selected by
        // the user.  They have clicked on one, so return it now.
        setResult(RESULT_OK, new Intent().setData(uri));
    } else {
        // Launch activity to view/edit the currently selected item
        startActivity(new Intent(Intent.ACTION_EDIT, uri));
    }
}
```

Exercising the GET_CONTENT Action

ACTION_GET_CONTENT is similar to ACTION_PICK. In the case of ACTION_PICK, you are specifying a URI that points to a collection of items such as a collection of notes. You will expect the action to pick one of the notes and return it to the caller. In the case of ACTION_GET_CONTENT, you indicate to Android that you need an item of a particular MIME type. Android searches for either activities that can create one of those items or activities that can choose from an existing set of items that satisfy that MIME type.

Using ACTION_GET_CONTENT, you can pick a note from a collection of notes supported by the Notepad application using the following code:

```
public static void invokeGetContent(Activity activity)
{
    Intent pickIntent = new Intent(Intent.ACTION_GET_CONTENT);
    int requestCode = 2;
    pickIntent.setType("vnd.android.cursor.item/vnd.google.note");
    activity.startActivityForResult(pickIntent, requestCode);
}
```

Notice how the intent type is set to the MIME type of a single note. Contrast this with the ACTION_PICK code in the following snippet, where the input is a data URI:

```
public static void invokePick(Activity activity)
{
  Intent pickIntent = new Intent(Intent.ACTION_PICK);
  int requestCode = 1;
  pickIntent.setData(Uri.parse(
    "content://com.google.provider.NotePad/notes"));
  activity.startActivityForResult(pickIntent, requestCode);
}
```

For an activity to respond to ACTION_GET_CONTENT, the activity has to register an intent-filter indicating that the activity can provide an item of that MIME type. Here is how the SDK's Notepad application accomplishes this:

```
<activity android:name="NotesList" android:label="@string/title_notes_list">
......
<intent-filter>
    <action android:name="android.intent.action.GET_CONTENT" />
    <category android:name="android.intent.category.DEFAULT" />
    <data android:mimeType="vnd.android.cursor.item/vnd.google.note" />
    </intent-filter>
…..
</activity>
```

The rest of the code for responding to onActivityResult() is identical to the previous ACTION_PICK example. If there are multiple activities that can return the same MIME type, Android will show you the chooser dialog to let you pick an activity. The default chooser might not allow you to pick a different title, however. To address this restriction, Android provides the createChooser method on the Intent class that lets you use a specialized chooser whose title can be changed. Here is an example of how to invoke such a chooser:

```
//start with your target Intent type you want to pick
Intent intent  = new Intent();
intent.setType(…);
Intent chooserIntent = Intent.createChooser(intent, "Hello use this title");
activity.startActivityForResult(chooserIntent);
```

Summary

In this chapter we covered the Android SDK's three key concepts: resources, content providers, and intents. In the section on resources, you learned how to create resources in XML files and use their resource IDs in programming. In the section about content providers, you learned how to work with URIs and MIME types, along with how to encapsulate data access in a content provider. You also learned the basics of creating and using a SQLite database, which should work well even if you use it without a content-provider abstraction. The third section showed you how to use intents to start other activities in a number of ways. Now you know how intents pave the way for plug-and-play and accomplish reuse at the UI level. With a good grasp of these three concepts, you should find it much easier to understand the Android SDK and Android UI programming in general.

CHAPTER 4

■ ■ ■

Building User Interfaces and Using Controls

Thus far, we have covered the fundamentals of Android but have not touched the user interface (UI). In this chapter, we are going to discuss user interfaces and controls. We will begin by discussing the general philosophy of UI development in Android, then we'll describe the common UI controls that ship with the Android SDK. We will also discuss layout managers and view adapters. We will conclude by discussing the Hierarchy Viewer tool—a tool used to debug and optimize Android UIs.

UI Development in Android

UI development in Android is fun. It's fun because the unattractive features in some other platforms are absent from Android. Swing, for example, has to support desktop applications as well as Java applets. Thus, the Java Foundation Classes (JFC) contains so much functionality that it's frustrating to use and difficult to navigate. JavaServer Faces (JSF) is another example. JSF, a common framework used to build web applications, is actually built on top of JavaServer Pages (JSP) and servlets. So you have to know all of the underlying frameworks before you can begin working with JSF.

Fortunately, this type of baggage carried by other platforms does not exist in Android. With Android, we have a simple framework with a limited set of out-of-the-box controls. The available screen area is generally limited. This, combined with the fact that the user usually wants to do one specific action, allows us to easily build a good user interface to deliver a good user experience.

The Android SDK ships with a host of controls that you can use to build user interfaces for your application. Similar to other SDKs, the Android SDK provides text fields, buttons, lists, grids, and so on. In addition, Android also provides a collection of controls that are appropriate for mobile devices.

At the heart of the common controls are two classes: `android.view.View` and `android.view.ViewGroup`. As the name of the first class suggests, the `View` class represents a general-purpose `View` object. The common controls in Android ultimately extend the `View` class.

ViewGroup is also a view, but contains other views too. ViewGroup is the base class for a list of layout classes. Android, like Swing, uses the concept of layouts to manage how controls are laid out within a container view. Using layouts, as we'll see, makes it easy for us to control the position and orientation of the controls in our user interfaces.

You can choose from several approaches to build user interfaces in Android. You can construct user interfaces entirely in code. You can also define user interfaces in XML. You can even combine the two—define the user interface in XML and then refer to it, and modify it, in code. To demonstrate this, we are going to build a simple user interface using each of these three approaches.

Before we get started, let's define some nomenclature. In this book and other Android literature, you will find the terms *view*, *control*, *widget*, *container*, and *layout* in discussions regarding UI development. If you are new to Android programming or UI development in general, you might not be familiar with these terms. We'll briefly describe them before we get started (see Table 4-1).

Table 4-1. *UI Nomenclature*

Term	Description
View, Widget, Control	Each of these represents a user interface element. Examples include a button, a grid, a list, a window, a dialog box, and so on. The terms "view," "widget," and "control" are used interchangeably in this chapter.
Container	This is a view used to contain other views. For example, a grid can be considered a container because it contains cells, each of which is a view.
Layout	This is an XML file used to describe a view.

Figure 4-1 shows a screenshot of the application that we are going to build. Next to the screenshot is the layout hierarchy of the controls and containers in the application.

Figure 4-1. *The user interface and layout of an activity*

We will refer to this layout hierarchy as we discuss the sample programs. For now, know that the application has one activity. The user interface for the activity is composed of three containers: a container that contains a person's name, a container that contains the address, and an outer parent container for the child containers.

The first example, Listing 4-1, demonstrates building the user interface entirely in code. To try this out, create a new Android project with an activity named **MainActivity** and then copy the code from Listing 4-1 into your MainActivity class.

Listing 4-1. *Creating a Simple User Interface Entirely in Code*

```java
package pro.android;
import android.app.Activity;
import android.os.Bundle;
import android.view.ViewGroup.LayoutParams;
import android.widget.LinearLayout;
import android.widget.TextView;
public class MainActivity extends Activity
{
    private LinearLayout nameContainer;

    private LinearLayout addressContainer;

    private LinearLayout parentContainer;


    /** Called when the activity is first created. */
    @Override
    public void onCreate(Bundle savedInstanceState)
    {
        super.onCreate(savedInstanceState);

        createNameContainer();

        createAddressContainer();

        createParentContainer();

        setContentView(parentContainer);

    }

    private void createNameContainer()
    {
        nameContainer = new LinearLayout(this);

        nameContainer.setLayoutParams(new LayoutParams(LayoutParams.FILL_PARENT,
                LayoutParams.WRAP_CONTENT));
        nameContainer.setOrientation(LinearLayout.HORIZONTAL);

        TextView nameLbl = new TextView(this);

        nameLbl.setText("Name: ");
        nameContainer.addView(nameLbl);
```

```
        TextView nameValueLbl = new TextView(this);
        nameValueLbl.setText("John Doe");

        nameContainer.addView(nameValueLbl);
    }

    private void createAddressContainer()
    {
        addressContainer = new LinearLayout(this);

        addressContainer.setLayoutParams(new LayoutParams(LayoutParams.FILL_PARENT,
                LayoutParams.WRAP_CONTENT));
        addressContainer.setOrientation(LinearLayout.VERTICAL);

        TextView addrLbl = new TextView(this);

        addrLbl.setText("Address:");

        TextView addrValueLbl = new TextView(this);

        addrValueLbl.setText("911 Hollywood Blvd");

        addressContainer.addView(addrLbl);
        addressContainer.addView(addrValueLbl);

    }

    private void createParentContainer()
    {
        parentContainer = new LinearLayout(this);

        parentContainer.setLayoutParams(new LayoutParams(LayoutParams.FILL_PARENT,
                LayoutParams.FILL_PARENT));
        parentContainer.setOrientation(LinearLayout.VERTICAL);

        parentContainer.addView(nameContainer);
        parentContainer.addView(addressContainer);
    }
}
```

As shown in Listing 4-1, the activity contains three LinearLayout objects. As we mentioned earlier, layout objects contain logic to position objects within a portion of the screen. A LinearLayout, for example, knows how to lay out controls either vertically or horizontally. Layout objects can contain any type of view—even other layouts.

The nameContainer object contains two TextView controls: one for the label Name: and the other to hold the actual name (i.e., John Doe). The addressContainer also contains two TextView controls. The difference between the two containers is that the nameContainer is laid out horizontally and the addressContainer is laid out vertically. Both of these containers live within the parentContainer, which is the root view of the activity. After the containers have been built, the activity sets the content of the view to the root view by calling setContentView(parentContainer). When it comes time to render the user interface of the activity, the root view is called to render itself. The root view then calls its children to render themselves, and the child controls call their children, and so on, until the entire user interface is rendered.

As shown in Listing 4-1, we have several LinearLayout controls. In fact, two of them are laid out vertically and one is laid out horizontally. The nameContainer is laid out horizontally. This means the two TextView controls appear side by side horizontally. The addressContainer is laid out vertically, which means that the two TextView controls are stacked one on top of the other. The parentContainer is also laid out vertically, which is why the nameContainer appears above the addressContainer. Note a subtle difference between the two vertically laid-out containers: addressContainer and parentContainer. parentContainer is set to take up the entire width and height of the screen:

```
parentContainer.setLayoutParams(new LayoutParams(LayoutParams.FILL_PARENT,
    LayoutParams.FILL_PARENT));
```

And addressContainer wraps its content vertically:

```
addressContainer.setLayoutParams(new LayoutParams(LayoutParams.FILL_PARENT,
    LayoutParams.WRAP_CONTENT));
```

Now let's build the same user interface in XML (see Listing 4-2). Recall from Chapter 3 that XML layout files are stored under the resources (/res/) directory within a folder called layout. To try out this example, create an XML file named test.xml and place it under the layout folder. Create a new activity and override its onCreate() method. In the onCreate() method, call the base class's onCreate() method and then call setContentView(R.layout.test).

Listing 4-2. *Creating a User Interface Entirely in XML*

```
<?xml version="1.0" encoding="utf-8"?>
<LinearLayout xmlns:android="http://schemas.android.com/apk/res/android"
    android:orientation="vertical" android:layout_width="fill_parent"
    android:layout_height="fill_parent">
    <!-- NAME CONTAINER -->
    <LinearLayout xmlns:android="http://schemas.android.com/apk/res/android"
        android:orientation="horizontal" android:layout_width="fill_parent"
        android:layout_height="wrap_content">

        <TextView  android:layout_width="wrap_content"
        android:layout_height="wrap_content" android:text="Name:" />

        <TextView android:layout_width="wrap_content"
        android:layout_height="wrap_content" android:text="John Doe" />

    </LinearLayout>
```

```
<!-- ADDRESS CONTAINER -->
<LinearLayout xmlns:android="http://schemas.android.com/apk/res/android"
    android:orientation="vertical" android:layout_width="fill_parent"
    android:layout_height="wrap_content">

    <TextView android:layout_width="fill_parent"
    android:layout_height="wrap_content" android:text="Address:" />

    <TextView android:layout_width="fill_parent"
    android:layout_height="wrap_content" android:text="911 Hollywood Blvd." />
</LinearLayout>

</LinearLayout>
```

The XML snippet shown in Listing 4-2, combined with a call to setContentView(R.layout.test), will render the same user interface. The XML file is self-explanatory, but note that we have three container views defined. The first LinearLayout is the equivalent of our parent container. This container sets its orientation to vertical by setting the corresponding property like this: android:orientation="vertical". The parent container contains two LinearLayout containers, which represent the nameContainer and addressContainer.

Listing 4-2 is a contrived example. Notably, its doesn't make any sense to hard-code the values of the TextView controls in the XML layout. Ideally, we should design our user interfaces in XML and then reference the controls from code. This approach enables us to bind dynamic data to the controls defined at design time. In fact, this is the recommended approach.

Listing 4-3 shows the same user interface with slightly different XML. This XML assigns IDs to the TextView controls so that we can refer to them in code.

Listing 4-3. *Creating a User Interface in XML with IDs*

```
<?xml version="1.0" encoding="utf-8"?>
<LinearLayout xmlns:android="http://schemas.android.com/apk/res/android"
    android:orientation="vertical" android:layout_width="fill_parent"
    android:layout_height="fill_parent">
    <!-- NAME CONTAINER -->
    <LinearLayout xmlns:android="http://schemas.android.com/apk/res/android"
        android:orientation="horizontal" android:layout_width="fill_parent"
        android:layout_height="wrap_content">

        <TextView android:id="@+id/nameText" android:layout_width="wrap_content"
        android:layout_height="wrap_content" android:text="@+string/name_text" />

        <TextView android:id="@+id/nameValueText"
android:layout_width="wrap_content"
        android:layout_height="wrap_content" />

    </LinearLayout>
```

```xml
<!-- ADDRESS CONTAINER -->
<LinearLayout xmlns:android="http://schemas.android.com/apk/res/android"
    android:orientation="vertical" android:layout_width="fill_parent"
    android:layout_height="wrap_content">

        <TextView android:id="@+id/addrText" android:layout_width="fill_parent"
        android:layout_height="wrap_content" android:text="@+string/addr_text" />

        <TextView android:id="@+id/addrValueText"
android:layout_width="fill_parent"
        android:layout_height="wrap_content" />
    </LinearLayout>

</LinearLayout>
```

The code in Listing 4-4 demonstrates how you can obtain references to the controls defined in the XML to set their properties.

Listing 4-4. *Referring to Controls in Resources at Runtime*

```java
    setContentView(R.layout.main);

TextView nameValue = (TextView)findViewById(R.id.nameValueText);
 nameValue.setText("John Doe");
 TextView addrValue = (TextView)findViewById(R.id.addrValueText);
 addrValue.setText("911 Hollywood Blvd.");
```

The code in Listing 4-4 is straightforward, but note that we load the resource (by calling setContentView(R.layout.main)) before calling findViewById()—we cannot get references to views if they have not been loaded yet.

Understanding Android's Common Controls

We will now start our discussion of the common controls in the Android SDK. We'll start with text controls and then discuss buttons, check boxes, radio buttons, lists, grids, date and time controls, and a map-view control. We will also talk about layout controls. Finally, we will conclude the chapter by showing you how to write your own custom controls.

Text Controls

Text controls are likely to be the first type of control that you'll work with in Android. Android has a complete, but not overwhelming, set of text controls. In this section, we are going to discuss the TextView, EditText, AutoCompleteTextView, and MultiCompleteTextView controls. Figure 4-2 shows the controls in action.

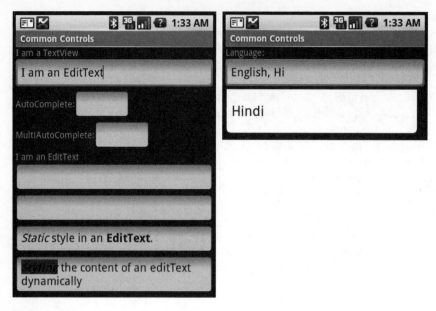

Figure 4-2. *Text controls in Android*

TextView

The TextView control knows how to display text but does not allow editing. This might lead you to conclude that the control is essentially a dummy label. Not true. The TextView control has a few interesting properties that make it very handy. If you know that the content of the TextView is going to contain a web URL, for example, you can set the autoLink property to web and the control will find and highlight the URL. Moreover, when the user clicks the TextView, the system will take care of launching the browser with the URL.

Actually, a more interesting use of TextView comes via the android.text.util.Linkify class (see Listing 4-5).

Listing 4-5. *Using the Linkify Class with a TextView*

```
TextView tv =(TextView)this.findViewById(R.id.cctvex);
tv.setText("Please visit my website, http://www.sayedhashimi.com
or email me at sayed@sayedhashimi.com.");
Linkify.addLinks(tv, Linkify.ALL);
```

As shown, you can pass a TextView to the Linkify class to find and add links to the content of the TextView. In our example, we call the addLinks() method of Linkify, passing the TextView and a mask indicating what types of links that Linkify should look for. Linkify can create links for text that looks like a phone number, an e-mail address, a web URL, or a map address. Passing Linkify.ALL tells the class to "linkify" all of these link types. Clicking a link will cause the default intent to be called for that action. For example, clicking a web URL will launch the browser with the URL. Clicking a phone number will launch the phone dialer, and so on. The Linkify class can perform this work right out of the box. You can also have the class linkify other content (such as a name) by giving it a regular expression along with the content-provider URI.

EditText

The EditText control is a subclass of TextView. As suggested by the name, the EditText control allows for text editing. EditText is not as powerful as the text-editing controls that you find in JFC, for example, but users of Android-based devices probably won't type documents—they'll type a couple paragraphs at most. Therefore, the class has limited but appropriate functionality. For example, you can set the autoText property to have the control correct common misspellings. You can use the capitalize property to have the control capitalize words, the beginning of sentences, and so on. You can set the phoneNumber property if you need to accept a phone number. You can also set the password property if you need a password field.

The default behavior of the EditText control is to display text on one line and expand as needed. In other words, if the user types past the first line, another line will appear, and so on. You can, however, force the user to a single line by setting the singleLine property to true. In this case, the user will have to continue typing on the same line.

Software programming for mobile devices is all about helping the user make a decision quickly. Thus, a common task is to highlight or style a portion of the EditText's content. You can do this statically or dynamically. Statically, you can apply markup directly to the strings in your string resources (<string name="styledText"><i>Static</i> style in an <b>EditText</b>. </string>) and then reference it in your XML or from code. Note that you can use only the following HTML tags with string resources: <i>, <b>, and <u>.

Styling an EditText control's content programmatically requires a little additional work but allows for much more flexibility (see Listing 4-6).

Listing 4-6. *Applying Styles to the Content of an EditText Dynamically*

```
EditText et =(EditText)this.findViewById(R.id.cctvex5);
et.setText("Styling the content of an editText dynamically");
Spannable spn = et.getText();
spn.setSpan(new BackgroundColorSpan(Color.RED), 0, 7,
Spannable.SPAN_EXCLUSIVE_EXCLUSIVE);
spn.setSpan(new StyleSpan(android.graphics.Typeface.BOLD_ITALIC)
, 0, 7, Spannable.SPAN_EXCLUSIVE_EXCLUSIVE);
```

As shown in Listing 4-6, you can get the content of the EditText (as a Spannable object) and then set styles to portions of the text. The code in the listing sets the text styling to bold and italics and sets the background to red. Of course, you are not limited to bold, italics, and underline as before.

AutoCompleteTextView

The AutoCompleteTextView control is a TextView with auto-complete functionality. In other words, as the user types in the TextView, the control can display suggestions for the user to select. Listing 4-7 demonstrates the AutoCompleteTextView control.

Listing 4-7. *Using an AutoCompleteTextView Control*

```
AutoCompleteTextView actv = (AutoCompleteTextView) this.findViewById(R.id.ccactv);

ArrayAdapter<String> aa = new ArrayAdapter<String>(this,
                android.R.layout.simple_dropdown_item_1line,
new String[] {"English", "Hebrew", "Hindi", "Spanish", "German","Greek" });

actv.setAdapter(aa);
```

The AutoCompleteTextView control shown in Listing 4-7 suggests a language to the user. For example, if the user types **en**, the control suggests English. If the user types **gr**, the control recommends Greek, and so on.

If you have used a suggestion control, or a similar auto-complete control, then you know that controls like this have two parts: a text-view control and a control that displays the suggestion(s). That's the general concept. To use a control like this, you have to create the control, create the list of suggestions, tell the control the list of suggestions, and possibly tell the control how to display the suggestions. Alternatively, you could create a second control for the suggestions and then associate the two controls.

Android has made this simple, as is evident from Listing 4-7. To use an AutoCompleteTextView, you can define the control in your layout file and then reference it in your activity. You then create an adapter class that holds the suggestions and define the ID of the control that will show the suggestion (in this case, a simple list item). In Listing 4-7, the second parameter to the ArrayAdapter tells the adapter to use a simple list item to show the suggestion. The final step is to associate the adapter with the AutoCompleteTextView, which you do using the setAdapter() method.

MultiAutoCompleteTextView

If you have played with the AutoCompleteTextView control, then you know that the control offers suggestions only for the *entire* text in the text view. In other words, if you type a sentence, you don't get suggestions for each word. That's where MultiAutoCompleteTextView comes in. You can use the MultiAutoCompleteTextView to provide suggestions as the user types. For example, Figure 4-2 shows that the user typed the word **English** followed by a comma, and then **Hi**, at which point the control suggested **Hindi**. If the user were to continue, the control would offer additional suggestions.

Using the MultiAutoCompleteTextView is like using the AutoCompleteTextView. The difference is that you have to tell the control where to start suggesting again. For example, in Figure 4-2, you can see that the control can offer suggestions at the beginning of the sentence and after it sees a comma. The MultiAutoCompleteTextView control requires that you give it a tokenizer that can parse the sentence and tell it whether to start suggesting again. Listing 4-8 demonstrates using the MultiAutoCompleteTextView control.

Listing 4-8. *Using the MultiAutoCompleteTextView Control*

```
MultiAutoCompleteTextView mactv = (MultiAutoCompleteTextView) this
                .findViewById(R.id.ccmactv);
ArrayAdapter<String> aa2 = new ArrayAdapter<String>(this,
                android.R.layout.simple_dropdown_item_1line,
new String[] {"English", "Hebrew", "Hindi", "Spanish", "German","Greek" });

mactv.setAdapter(aa2);

mactv.setTokenizer(new MultiAutoCompleteTextView.CommaTokenizer());
```

The only significant difference between Listing 4-7 and Listing 4-8 is the use of MultiAutoCompleteTextView and the call to the setTokenizer() method.

Button Controls

Buttons are common in any widget toolkit, and Android is no exception. Android offers the typical set of buttons as well as a few extras. In this section, we will discuss three types of button controls: the basic button, the image button, and the toggle button. Figure 4-3 shows a UI with these controls. The button at the top is the basic button, the middle button is an image button, and the last one is a toggle button.

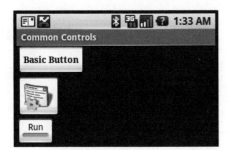

Figure 4-3. *Android button controls*

Let's get started with the basic button.

The Button Control

The basic button class in Android is android.widget.Button. There's not much to this type of button, other than how you use it to handle click events (see Listing 4-9).

Listing 4-9. *Handling Click Events on a Button*

```
<Button android:id="@+id/ccbtn1"
    android:text="@+string/basicBtnLabel"
    android:typeface="serif" android:textStyle="bold"
android:layout_width="fill_parent"
    android:layout_height="wrap_content" />
```

```
Button btn = (Button)this.findViewById(R.id.ccbtn1);
btn.setOnClickListener(new OnClickListener()
{
    public void onClick(View v)
    {
        Intent intent = getButtonIntent();
        intent.setAction("some intent data");
         setResult(RESULT_OK, intent);
         finish();
    }
});
```

Listing 4-9 shows how to register for a button-click event. You register for the on-click event by calling the setOnClickListener method with an OnClickListener. In Listing 4-9, an anonymous listener is created on the fly to handle click events for btn. When the button is clicked, the OnClick method of the listener is called.

The ImageButton Control

Android provides an image button via android.widget.ImageButton. Using an image button is similar to using the basic button (see Listing 4-10).

Listing 4-10. *Using an ImageButton*

```
<ImageButton android:id="@+id/imageBtn"
    android:layout_width="wrap_content"
    android:layout_height="wrap_content"
/>

ImageButton btn = (ImageButton)this.findViewById(R.id.imageBtn);
btn.setImageResource(R.drawable.icon);
```

You can set the button's image dynamically by calling setImageResource or modifying the XML layout file (by setting the android:src property to the image ID), as shown in Listing 4-11.

Listing 4-11. *Setting the ImageButton Image via XML*

```
<ImageButton android:id="@+id/imageBtn" android:src="@drawable/btnImage"
    android:layout_width="wrap_content"
    android:layout_height="wrap_content"
/>
```

The ToggleButton Control

The ToggleButton, like a check box or a radio button, is a two-state button. This button can be in either the On state or the Off state. As shown in Figure 4-3, the ToggleButton's default behavior is to show a green bar when in the On state, and a grayed-out bar when in the Off state. Moreover, the default behavior also sets the button's text to "On" when it's in the On state and "Off" when it's in the Off state.

Listing 4-12 shows an example.

Listing 4-12. *The Android ToggleButton*

```
<ToggleButton android:id="@+id/cctglBtn" android:layout_
width="wrap_content" android:layout_height="wrap_content"
android:text="Toggle Button"/>
```

You can modify the text for the ToggleButton if "On"/"Off" is not appropriate for your application. For example, if you have a background process that you want to start and stop via a ToggleButton, you could set the button's text to "Run" and "Stop" by using android:textOn and android:textOff properties (see Listing 4-13).

Listing 4-13. *Setting the ToggleButton's Label*

```
<ToggleButton android:id="@+id/cctglBtn"
              android:layout_width="wrap_content"
              android:layout_height="wrap_content"
android:textOn="Run" android:textOff="Stop"
android:text="Toggle Button"/>
```

The CheckBox Control

A check-box control plays a part in virtually all widget toolkits. HTML, JFC, and JSF all support the concept of a check box. The check-box control is a two-state button that allows the user to toggle its state.

In Android, you can create a check box by creating an instance of android.widget. CheckBox. See Listing 4-14 and Figure 4-4.

Listing 4-14. *Creating Check Boxes*

```
<LinearLayout xmlns:android="http://schemas.android.com/apk/res/android"
        android:orientation="vertical" android:layout_width="fill_parent"
        android:layout_height="fill_parent">

<CheckBox android:text="Chicken"
android:layout_width="wrap_content" android:layout_height="wrap_content" />

<CheckBox android:text="Fish"
android:layout_width="wrap_content" android:layout_height="wrap_content" />

<CheckBox android:text="Steak"
android:layout_width="wrap_content" android:layout_height="wrap_content" />

</LinearLayout>
```

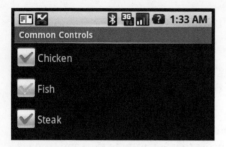

Figure 4-4. *Using the CheckBox control*

You manage the state of a check box by calling setChecked() or toggle(). You can obtain the state by calling isChecked().

If you need to implement specific logic when a check box is checked or unchecked, you can register for the on-checked event by calling setOnCheckedChangeListener() with an implementation of the OnCheckedChangeListener interface. You'll then have to implement the onCheckedChanged() method, which will be called when the check box is checked or unchecked.

The RadioButton Control

Radio-button controls are an integral part of any UI toolkit. A radio button gives the user several choices and forces her to select a single item. To enforce this single-selection model, radio buttons generally belong to a group and each group is forced to have only one item selected at a time.

To create a group of radio buttons in Android, first create a RadioGroup and then populate the group with radio buttons. Listing 4-15 and Figure 4-5 show an example.

Listing 4-15. *Using Android Radio-Button Widgets*

```
<LinearLayout xmlns:android="http://schemas.android.com/apk/res/android"
        android:orientation="vertical" android:layout_width="fill_parent"
        android:layout_height="fill_parent">

<RadioGroup android:layout_width="wrap_content"
        android:layout_height="wrap_content">

<RadioButton     android:id="@+id/chRBtn"
        android:text="Chicken" android:layout_width="wrap_content"
        android:layout_height="wrap_content"/>

<RadioButton  android:id="@+id/fishRBtn" android:text="Fish"
        android:layout_width="wrap_content"
        android:layout_height="wrap_content"/>

<RadioButton android:id="@+id/stkRBtn" android:text="Steak"
        android:layout_width="wrap_content"
        android:layout_height="wrap_content"/>
```

```
</RadioGroup>
```

```
</LinearLayout>
```

In Android, you implement a radio group using `android.widget.RadioGroup` and a radio button using `android.widget.RadioButton`.

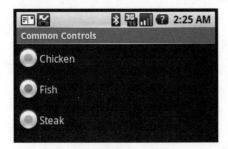

Figure 4-5. *Using radio buttons*

Note that the radio buttons within the radio group are, by default, unchecked to begin with. To set one of the radio buttons to the checked state, you can obtain a reference to the radio button programmatically and call `setChecked()`:

```
RadioButton rbtn = (RadioButton)this.findViewById(R.id.stkRBtn);
rbtn.setChecked(true);
```

You can also use the `toggle()` method to toggle the state of the radio button. As with the `CheckBox` control, you will be notified of on-checked or on-unchecked events if you call the `setOnCheckedChangeListener()` with an implementation of the `OnCheckedChangeListener` interface.

Realize that `RadioGroup` can also contain views other than the radio button. For example, Listing 4-16 adds a `TextView` after the last radio button. Also note that a radio button lies outside the radio group.

Listing 4-16. *A Radio Group with More Than Just Radio Buttons*

```
<LinearLayout xmlns:android="http://schemas.android.com/apk/res/android"
        android:orientation="vertical"
        android:layout_width="fill_parent"
        android:layout_height="fill_parent">

<RadioButton android:id="@+id/anotherRadBtn"
        android:text="Outside"
        android:layout_width="wrap_content"
        android:layout_height="wrap_content"/>
<RadioGroup android:id="@+id/rdGrp"
        android:layout_width="wrap_content"
        android:layout_height="wrap_content">
```

```
<RadioButton android:id="@+id/chRBtn"
        android:text="Chicken"
        android:layout_width="wrap_content"
        android:layout_height="wrap_content"/>
<RadioButton android:id="@+id/fishRBtn"
        android:text="Fish"
        android:layout_width="wrap_content"
        android:layout_height="wrap_content"/>
<RadioButton android:id="@+id/stkRBtn"
        android:text="Steak"
        android:layout_width="wrap_content"
        android:layout_height="wrap_content"/>

<TextView android:text="My Favorite"
        android:layout_width="wrap_content"
        android:layout_height="wrap_content"/>
</RadioGroup>

</LinearLayout>
```

Listing 4-16 shows that you can have non-RadioButton controls inside a radio group. Moreover, you should know that the radio group can enforce single-selection only on the radio buttons within its own container. That is, the radio button with ID anotherRadBtn will not be affected by the radio group shown in Listing 4-16 because it is not one of the group's children.

Also know that you can manipulate the RadioGroup programmatically. For example, you can obtain a reference to a radio group programmatically and add a radio button (or other type of control):

```
RadioGroup rdgrp = (RadioGroup)findViewById(R.id.rdGrp);
RadioButton newRadioBtn = new RadioButton(this);
newRadioBtn.setText("Pork");
rdgrp.addView(newRadioBtn);
```

List Controls

The Android SDK offers several list controls. Figure 4-6 shows a ListView control that we'll discuss in this section.

The ListView control displays a list of items vertically. You generally use a ListView by writing a new activity that extends android.app.ListActivity. ListActivity contains a ListView, and you set the data for the ListView by calling the setListAdapter method. Listing 4-17 demonstrates this.

Figure 4-6. *Using the ListView control*

Listing 4-17. *Adding Items to a ListView*

```xml
<?xml version="1.0" encoding="utf-8"?>
<LinearLayout xmlns:android="http://schemas.android.com/apk/res/android"
    android:orientation="horizontal"
    android:layout_width="wrap_content"
    android:layout_height="wrap_content">

<CheckBox xmlns:android="http://schemas.android.com/apk/res/android"
    android:id="@+id/row_chbox"
    android:layout_width="wrap_content"
    android:layout_height="wrap_content"
/>

<TextView android:id="@+id/row_tv" android:layout_width="wrap_content"
    android:layout_height="wrap_content"
/>
</LinearLayout>
```

```java
public class ListDemoActivity extends ListActivity
{
    private SimpleCursorAdapter adapter;
```

```
@Override
protected void onCreate(Bundle savedInstanceState)
{
    super.onCreate(savedInstanceState);
    Cursor c = getContentResolver().query(People.CONTENT_URI,
null, null, null, null);
    startManagingCursor(c);
    String[] cols = new String[]{People.NAME};
    int[] names = new int[]{R.id.row_tv};
    adapter = new SimpleCursorAdapter(this,R.layout.lists,c,cols,names);
    this.setListAdapter(adapter);
    }
}
```

Listing 4-17 creates a `ListView` control populated with the list of contacts on the device. To the right of each contact is a check-box control. As we stated earlier, the usage pattern is to extend `ListActivity` and then set the list's adapter by calling `setListAdapter` on the activity. In our example, we query the device for the list of contacts and then create a projection to select only the names of the contacts—a projection defines the columns that we are interested in. We then map a name to a `TextView` control. Finally, we create a cursor adapter and set the list's adapter. The adapter class has the smarts to take the rows in the data source and pull out the name of each contact to populate the user interface.

You'll notice that the `onCreate` method does not set the content view of the activity. Instead, because the base class `ListActivity` contains a `ListView` already, it just needs to provide the data for the `ListView`. If you want additional controls outside the `ListView`, you can override the `ListView` referenced in `ListActivity` in your layout file and add the desired controls. For example, you could add a button below the `ListView` in the UI to submit an action on the selected items, as shown in Figure 4-7.

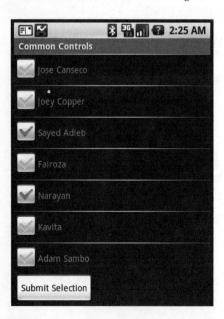

Figure 4-7. *An additional button that lets the user submit the selected item(s)*

The layout XML file for this example is broken up into two files. The first contains the user interface definition of the activity—the ListView and the button (see Figure 4-7 and Listing 4-18).

Listing 4-18. *Overriding the ListView Referenced by ListActivity*

```xml
<?xml version="1.0" encoding="utf-8"?>
<LinearLayout xmlns:android="http://schemas.android.com/apk/res/android"
    android:orientation="vertical"
    android:layout_width="fill_parent"
    android:layout_height="wrap_content">


    <LinearLayout xmlns:android="http://schemas.android.com/apk/res/android"
        android:orientation="vertical"
        android:layout_width="fill_parent"
        android:layout_height="wrap_content">

    <ListView android:id="@android:id/list"
            android:layout_width="fill_parent"
            android:layout_height="0dip"
            android:layout_weight="1"
            android:stackFromBottom="true"
            android:transcriptMode="normal"/>

    </LinearLayout>

    <LinearLayout xmlns:android="http://schemas.android.com/apk/res/android"
        android:orientation="vertical"
        android:layout_width="fill_parent"
        android:layout_height="wrap_content">

    <Button android:layout_width="wrap_content"
        android:layout_height="wrap_content" android:text="Submit Selection" />

    </LinearLayout>
</LinearLayout>
```

The second file contains the definition of the items in the list, which is the same as the definition in Listing 4-17. The activity implementation would then look like Listing 4-19.

Listing 4-19. *Setting the Content View of the ListActivity*

```java
public class ListDemoActivity extends ListActivity
{
    private SimpleCursorAdapter adapter;

    @Override
    protected void onCreate(Bundle savedInstanceState)
    {
        super.onCreate(savedInstanceState);

        setContentView(R.layout.lists);

        Cursor c = getContentResolver().query(People.CONTENT_URI,
null, null, null, null);
        startManagingCursor(c);

        String[] cols = new String[]{People.NAME};
        int[] names = new int[]{R.id.row_tv};
        adapter = new SimpleCursorAdapter(this,R.layout.list_item,c,cols,names);
        this.setListAdapter(adapter);
    }
}
```

Listing 4-19 shows that the activity calls setContentView to set the user interface for the activity. It also sets the layout file for the items in the list, when it creates the adapter (we'll talk more about adapters in the "Understanding Adapters" section toward the end of this chapter).

Grid Controls

Most widget toolkits offer one or more grid-based controls. Android has a GridView control that can display data in the form of a grid. Note that although we use the term "data" here, the contents of the grid can be text, images, and so on.

The GridView control displays information in a grid. The usage pattern for the GridView is to define the grid in the XML layout (see Listing 4-20), and then bind the data to the grid using an android.widget.ListAdapter.

Listing 4-20. *Definition of a GridView in an XML Layout and Associated Java Code*

```xml
<GridView xmlns:android="http://schemas.android.com/apk/res/android"
android:id="@+id/dataGrid"
    android:layout_width="fill_parent"
    android:layout_height="fill_parent"
    android:padding="10px"
    android:verticalSpacing="10px"

    android:horizontalSpacing="10px"
    android:numColumns="auto_fit"
    android:columnWidth="100px"
    android:stretchMode="columnWidth"
```

```
        android:gravity="center"
        />


    protected void onCreate(Bundle savedInstanceState) {
            super.onCreate(savedInstanceState);


            setContentView(R.layout.gridview);
            GridView gv = (GridView)this.findViewById(R.id.dataGrid);

            Cursor c = getContentResolver().query(People.CONTENT_URI,
  null, null, null, null);
            startManagingCursor(c);

            String[] cols = new String[]{People.NAME};
            int[] names = new int[]{R.id.grid_entry};

SimpleCursorAdapter adapter = new SimpleCursorAdapter(
                this,R.layout.grid_item,c,cols,names);

            gv.setAdapter(adapter);

    }
```

Listing 4-20 defines a simple GridView in an XML layout. The grid is then loaded into the activity's content view. The generated UI is shown in Figure 4-8.

Figure 4-8. *A GridView populated with contact information*

The grid shown in Figure 4-8 displays the names of the contacts on the device. We have decided to show a TextView with the contact names, but you could easily generate a grid filled with images and the like.

The interesting thing about the GridView is that the adapter used by the grid is a ListAdapter. Lists are generally one-dimensional whereas grids are two-dimensional. What we can conclude, then, is that the grid actually displays list-oriented data. In fact, if you call getSelection(), you get back an integer representing the index of the selected item. Likewise, to set a selection in the grid, you call setSelection() with the index of the item you want selected.

Date and Time Controls

Date and time controls are quite common in many widget toolkits. Android offers several date- and time-based controls, some of which we'll discuss in this section. Specifically, we are going to introduce the DatePicker, the TimePicker, the AnalogClock, and the DigitalClock controls.

The DatePicker and TimePicker Controls

As the names suggest, you use the DatePicker control to select a date and the TimePicker control to pick a time. Listing 4-21 and Figure 4-9 show examples of these controls.

Listing 4-21. *The DatePicker and TimePicker Controls in XML*

```xml
<LinearLayout xmlns:android="http://schemas.android.com/apk/res/android"
        android:orientation="vertical"
        android:layout_width="fill_parent"
        android:layout_height="fill_parent">

    <DatePicker android:id="@+id/datePicker"
    android:layout_width="wrap_content" android:layout_height="wrap_content" />

    <TimePicker android:id="@+id/timePicker"
    android:layout_width="wrap_content" android:layout_height="wrap_content" />

</LinearLayout>
```

Figure 4-9. *The DatePicker and TimePicker UIs*

If you look at the XML layout, you can see that defining these controls is quite easy. The user interface, however, looks a bit overdone. Both controls seem a bit oversized, but for a mobile device, you can't argue with the look and feel.

As with any other control in the Android toolkit, you can access the controls programmatically to initialize them or to retrieve data from them. For example, you can initialize these controls as shown in Listing 4-22.

Listing 4-22. *Initializing the DatePicker and TimePicker with Date and Time, Respectively*

```
protected void onCreate(Bundle savedInstanceState) {
    super.onCreate(savedInstanceState);

    setContentView(R.layout.datetime);

    DatePicker dp = (DatePicker)this.findViewById(R.id.datePicker);
    dp.init(2008, 11, 10, null);

    TimePicker tp = (TimePicker)this.findViewById(R.id.timePicker);
    tp.setIs24HourView(true);
    tp.setCurrentHour(new Integer(10));
    tp.setCurrentMinute(new Integer(10));
}
```

Listing 4-22 sets the date on the DatePicker to November 10, 2008. Similarly, the number of hours and minutes is set to 10. Note also that the control supports 24-hour view.

Finally, note that Android offers versions of these controls as modal windows, such as DatePickerDialog and TimePickerDialog. These controls are useful if you want to display the control to the user and force the user to make a selection.

The AnalogClock and DigitalClock Controls

Android also offers an AnalogClock and a DigitalClock (see Figure 4-10).

Figure 4-10. *Using the AnalogClock and DigitalClock*

As shown, the analog clock in Android is a two-handed clock, one hand for the hour indicator and the other hand for the minute indicator. The digital clock supports seconds in addition to hours and minutes.

These two controls are not that interesting because they don't let you modify the date or time. In other words, they are merely clocks whose only capability is to display the current time. Thus, if you want to change the date or time, you'll need to stick to the DatePicker/ TimePicker or DatePickerDialog/TimePickerDialog.

Other Interesting Controls in Android

The controls that we have discussed so far are fundamental to any Android application. In addition to these, Android also offers a few other interesting controls. We'll briefly introduce these other controls in this section.

The MapView Control

The com.google.android.maps.MapView control can display a map. You can instantiate this control either via XML layout or code, but the activity that uses it must extend MapActivity. MapActivity takes care of multithreading requests to load a map, perform caching, and so on.

Listing 4-23 shows an example instantiation of a MapView.

Listing 4-23. *Creating a MapView Control via XML Layout*

```
<LinearLayout xmlns:android="http://schemas.android.com/apk/res/android"
        android:orientation="vertical" android:layout_width="fill_parent"
        android:layout_height="fill_parent">

    <com.google.android.maps.MapView
        android:layout_width="fill_parent"
        android:layout_height="fill_parent"
        android:enabled="true"
        android:clickable="true"
        android:apiKey="myAPIKey"
        />

</LinearLayout>
```

As shown, the interesting thing about using the MapView is that you'll have to first obtain a mapping-API key. To get a key, you'll have to register with Google at

```
http://code.google.com/android/toolbox/apis/mapkey.html
```

After you obtain an API key, you can then instantiate a MapView either programmatically or via XML. In XML, you set the android:apiKey property. In code, you'll have to pass the key to the MapView constructor. Note that we'll discuss the MapView control in detail in Chapter 7, when we discuss location-based services.

The Gallery Control

The Gallery control is a horizontally scrollable list control that always focuses at the center of the list. This control generally functions as a photo gallery in touch mode. You can instantiate a Gallery either via XML layout or code:

```
<Gallery
    android:id="@+id/galleryCtrl"
    android:layout_width="fill_parent"
    android:layout_height="wrap_content"
/>
```

Using the Gallery control is similar to using a list control. That is to say, you get a reference to the gallery, then call the setAdapter() method to populate data, then register for on-selected events.

This concludes our discussion of the Android control set. As we mentioned in the beginning of the chapter, building user interfaces in Android requires you to master two things: the control set and the layout managers. In the next section, we are going to discuss the Android layout managers.

Understanding Layout Managers

Like Swing, Android offers a collection of view classes that act as containers for views. These container classes are called layouts (or layout managers), and each implements a specific strategy to manage the size and position of its children. For example, the LinearLayout class lays out its children either horizontally or vertically, one after the other.

The layout managers that ship with the Android SDK are defined in Table 4-2.

Table 4-2. *Android Layout Managers*

Layout Manager	Description
LinearLayout	Organizes its children either horizontally or vertically.
TableLayout	Organizes its children in tabular form.
RelativeLayout	Organizes its children relative to one another or to the parent.
AbsoluteLayout	Positions children based on exact coordinates.
FrameLayout	Allows you to dynamically change the control(s) in the layout.

We will discuss these layout managers in the sections that follow.

The LinearLayout Layout Manager

The LinearLayout is the most popular layout. This layout manager organizes its children either horizontally or vertically based on the value of the orientation property. Listing 4-24 shows a LinearLayout with horizontal configuration.

Listing 4-24. *A LinearLayout with Horizontal Configuration*

```
<LinearLayout xmlns:android="http://schemas.android.com/apk/res/android"
    android:orientation="horizontal"
    android:layout_width="fill_parent"
    android:layout_height="wrap_content">

    <!-- add children here-->
</LinearLayout>
```

You can create a vertically oriented LinearLayout by setting the value of orientation to vertical.

Understanding Weight and Gravity

The orientation attribute is the first important attribute recognized by the LinearLayout layout manager. Other important properties that can affect size and position of child controls include *weight* and *gravity*. You use weight to assign size importance to a control relative to the other controls in the container. Suppose a container has three controls: one has a weight of 1 (the highest possible value), while the others have a weight of 0. In this case, the control whose weight equals 1 will consume the empty space in the container. Gravity is essentially alignment. For example, if you want to align a label's text to the right, you would set its gravity to right.

Note Layout managers extend android.widget.ViewGroup, as do many control-based container classes such as ListView. Although the layout managers and control-based containers extend the same class, the layout-manager classes strictly deal with the sizing and position of controls and not user interaction with child controls. For example, compare the LinearLayout to the ListView control. On the screen, they look similar in that both can organize children vertically. But the ListView control provides APIs for the user to make selections, while the LinearLayout does not. In other words, the control-based container (ListView) supports user interaction with the items in the container, whereas the layout manager (LinearLayout) addresses sizing and positioning only.

Now let's look at an example involving the weight and gravity properties (see Figure 4-11).

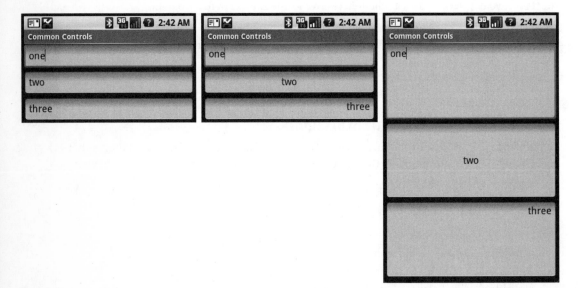

Figure 4-11. *Using the LinearLayout layout manager*

Figure 4-11 shows three user interfaces that utilize LinearLayout, with different weight and gravity settings. The UI on the left uses the default settings for weight and gravity. The XML layout for this first user interface is shown in Listing 4-25.

Listing 4-25. *Three Text Fields Arranged Vertically in a LinearLayout, Using Default Values for Weight and Gravity*

```
<LinearLayout xmlns:android="http://schemas.android.com/apk/res/android"
    android:orientation="vertical" android:layout_width="fill_parent"
    android:layout_height="fill_parent">

    <EditText android:layout_width="fill_parent"
        android:layout_height="wrap_content"
        android:text="one"/>
    <EditText android:layout_width="fill_parent"
        android:layout_height="wrap_content"
        android:text="two"/>
    <EditText android:layout_width="fill_parent"
        android:layout_height="wrap_content"
        android:text="three"/>
</LinearLayout>
```

The user interface in the center of Figure 4-11 uses the default value for weight but sets android:gravity for the controls in the container to left, center, and right, respectively. The last example sets the android:layout_weight attribute of the center component to 1.0 and leaves the others to the default value of 0.0 (see Listing 4-26). By setting the weight attribute to 1.0 for the middle component and leaving the weight attributes for the other two components at 0.0, we are specifying that the center component should take up all the remaining white space in the container and that the other two components should remain at their ideal size.

Similarly, if you want two of the three controls in the container to share the remaining white space among them, you would set the weight to 1.0 for those two and leave the third one at 0.0. Finally, if you want the three components to share the space equally, you'd set all of their weight values to 1.0. Doing this would expand each text field equally.

Listing 4-26. *LinearLayout with Weight Configurations*

```
<LinearLayout xmlns:android="http://schemas.android.com/apk/res/android"
    android:orientation="vertical" android:layout_width="fill_parent"
    android:layout_height="fill_parent">

    <EditText android:layout_width="fill_parent" android:layout_weight="1.0"
    android:layout_height="wrap_content" android:text="one"
    android:gravity="left"/>

    <EditText android:layout_width="fill_parent"
    android:layout_height="wrap_content" android:text="two"
    android:gravity="center" android:layout_weight="1.0"/>
```

```
    <EditText android:layout_width="fill_parent" android:layout_weight="1.0"
    android:layout_height="wrap_content" android:text="three"
    android:gravity="right"
    />
</LinearLayout>
```

android:gravity vs. android:layout_gravity

Note that Android defines two similar gravity attributes: android:gravity and android: layout_gravity. Here's the difference: android:gravity is a setting used by the view, whereas android:layout_gravity is used by the container (android.view.ViewGroup). For example, you can set android:gravity to center to have the text in the EditText centered within the control. Similarly, you can align an EditText to the far right of a LinearLayout (the container) by setting android:layout_gravity="right". See Figure 4-12 and Listing 4-27.

Figure 4-12. *Applying gravity settings*

Listing 4-27. *Understanding the Difference Between android:gravity and android:layout_gravity*

```
<LinearLayout xmlns:android="http://schemas.android.com/apk/res/android"
    android:orientation="vertical" android:layout_width="fill_parent"
    android:layout_height="fill_parent">

    <EditText android:layout_width="wrap_content" android:gravity="center"
    android:layout_height="wrap_content" android:text="one"
 android:layout_gravity="right"/>
</LinearLayout>
```

As shown in Figure 4-12, the text is centered within the EditText and the EditText itself is aligned to the right of the LinearLayout.

The TableLayout Layout Manager

The TableLayout layout manager is an extension of LinearLayout. This layout manager structures its child controls into rows and columns. Listing 4-28 shows an example.

Listing 4-28. *A Simple TableLayout*

```
<TableLayout xmlns:android="http://schemas.android.com/apk/res/android"
        android:layout_width="fill_parent"
        android:layout_height="fill_parent">

    <TableRow>
        <TextView android:layout_width="wrap_content"
        android:layout_height="wrap_content" android:text="First Name:"/>

        <EditText android:layout_width="wrap_content"
        android:layout_height="wrap_content" android:text="Barack"/>

    </TableRow>

    <TableRow>
        <TextView android:layout_width="wrap_content"
        android:layout_height="wrap_content" android:text="Last Name:"/>

        <EditText android:layout_width="wrap_content"
        android:layout_height="wrap_content" android:text="Obama"/>

    </TableRow>

</TableLayout>
```

To use a TableLayout, you create an instance of TableLayout and then place TableRow elements within it. TableRow elements then contain the controls of the table. The user interface for Listing 4-28 is shown in Figure 4-13.

Figure 4-13. *The TableLayout layout manager*

Because the contents of a TableLayout are defined by rows as opposed to columns, Android determines the number of columns in the table by finding the row with the most cells. For example, Listing 4-29 creates a table with two rows where one row has two cells and the other has three cells (see Figure 4-14). In this case, Android creates a table with two rows and three columns.

Listing 4-29. *An Irregular Table Definition*

```
<TableLayout xmlns:android="http://schemas.android.com/apk/res/android"
        android:layout_width="fill_parent"
        android:layout_height="fill_parent">

    <TableRow>
        <TextView android:layout_width="wrap_content"
        android:layout_height="wrap_content" android:text="First Name:"/>

        <EditText android:layout_width="wrap_content"
        android:layout_height="wrap_content" android:text="Barack"/>

    </TableRow>

    <TableRow>
        <TextView android:layout_width="wrap_content"
        android:layout_height="wrap_content" android:text="Last Name:"/>

        <EditText android:layout_width="wrap_content"
        android:layout_height="wrap_content" android:text="Hussein"/>

        <EditText android:layout_width="wrap_content"
        android:layout_height="wrap_content" android:text="Obama"/>

    </TableRow>

</TableLayout>
```

Figure 4-14. *An irregular TableLayout*

Realize that we have a table with two rows, each of which has three columns. The last column of the first row is an empty cell.

In Listings 4-28 and 4-29, we populated the TableLayout with TableRow elements. Although this is the usual pattern, you can place any android.widget.View as a child of the table. For example, Listing 4-30 creates a table where the first row is an EditText (also see Figure 4-15).

Listing 4-30. *Using an EditText Instead of a TableRow*

```
<TableLayout xmlns:android="http://schemas.android.com/apk/res/android"
        android:layout_width="fill_parent"
        android:layout_height="fill_parent"
        android:stretchColumns="0,1,2">

<EditText
    android:text="Full Name:"/>

    <TableRow>
        <TextView android:layout_width="wrap_content"
        android:layout_height="wrap_content" android:text="Barack"/>

        <TextView android:layout_width="wrap_content"
        android:layout_height="wrap_content" android:text="Hussein"/>

        <TextView android:layout_width="wrap_content"
        android:layout_height="wrap_content" android:text="Obama"/>

    </TableRow>

</TableLayout>
```

Figure 4-15. *An EditText as a child of a TableLayout*

The user interface for Listing 4-30 is shown in Figure 4-15. Notice that the EditText takes up the entire width of the screen, even though we have not specified this in the XML layout. That's because children of TableLayout always span the entire row. In other words, children of TableLayout cannot specify android:layout_width="wrap_content"—they are forced to accept fill_parent. They can, however, set android:layout_height.

Because the content of a table is not always known at design time, TableLayout offers several attributes that can help you control the layout of a table. For example, Listing 4-30 sets the android:stretchColumns property on the TableLayout to "0,1,2". This gives a hint to the TableLayout that columns 0, 1, and 2 can be stretched if required, based on the contents of the table.

Similarly, you can set android:shrinkColumns to wrap the content of a column or columns if other columns require more space. You can also set android:collapseColumns to make columns invisible. Note that columns are identified with a zero-based indexing scheme.

TableLayout also offers android:layout_span. You can use this property to have a cell span multiple columns. This field is similar to the HTML colspan property.

At times, you might also need to provide spacing within the contents of a cell or a control. The Android SDK supports this via android:padding and its siblings. android:padding lets you control the space between a view's outer boundary and its content (see Listing 4-31).

Listing 4-31. *Using android:padding*

```
<LinearLayout xmlns:android="http://schemas.android.com/apk/res/android"
    android:orientation="vertical" android:layout_width="fill_parent"
    android:layout_height="fill_parent">

    <EditText android:layout_width="wrap_content"
    android:layout_height="wrap_content" android:text="one"
    android:padding="40px" />
</LinearLayout>
```

Listing 4-31 sets the padding to 40px. This creates 40 pixels of white space between the EditText control's outer boundary and the text displayed within it. Figure 4-16 shows the same EditText with two different padding values. The UI on the left does not set any padding, while the one on the right sets android:padding="40px".

Figure 4-16. *Utilizing padding*

android:padding sets the padding for all sides: left, right, top, and bottom. You can control the padding for each side by using android:leftPadding, android:rightPadding, android:topPadding, and android:bottomPadding.

Android also defines android:layout_margin, which is similar to android:padding. In fact, android:padding/android:layout_margin is analogous to android:gravity/android:layout_gravity. That is, one is for a view, while the other is for a container.

Finally, the padding value is always set as a dimension type. Android supports the following dimension types:

- *Pixels*: Defined as px. This dimension represents physical pixels on the screen.

- *Inches*: Defined as in.

- *Millimeters*: Defined as mm.

- *Device-independent pixels*: Defined as dip or dp. This dimension type uses a 160-dp screen as a frame of reference, and then maps that to the actual screen. For example, a screen with a 160-pixel width would map 1 dip to 1 pixel.

- *Scaled pixels*: Defined as sp. Generally used with font types. This dimension type will take the user's preferences and font size into account to determine actual size.

Note that the preceding dimension types are not specific to padding—any Android field that accepts a dimension value (such as android:layout_width or android:layout_height) can accept these types.

The RelativeLayout Layout Manager

Another interesting layout manager is the RelativeLayout. As the name suggests, this layout manager implements a policy where the controls in the container are laid out relative to either the container or another control in the container. Listing 4-32 and Figure 4-17 show an example.

Listing 4-32. *Using a RelativeLayout Layout Manager*

```
<RelativeLayout xmlns:android="http://schemas.android.com/apk/res/android"
        android:layout_width="fill_parent"
        android:layout_height="wrap_content">

<TextView android:id="@+id/userNameLbl"
        android:layout_width="fill_parent"
        android:layout_height="wrap_content"
        android:text="Username: "
        android:layout_alignParentTop="true" />

<EditText android:id="@+id/userNameText"
        android:layout_width="fill_parent"
        android:layout_height="wrap_content"
    android:layout_below="@id/userNameLbl" />

<TextView android:id="@+id/pwdLbl"
        android:layout_width="fill_parent"
        android:layout_height="wrap_content"
        android:layout_below="@id/userNameText"
          android:text="Password: " />

<EditText android:id="@+id/pwdText"
        android:layout_width="fill_parent"
        android:layout_height="wrap_content"
    android:layout_below="@id/pwdLbl"
    />

<TextView android:id="@+id/pwdHintLbl"
        android:layout_width="fill_parent"
        android:layout_height="wrap_content"
        android:layout_below="@id/pwdText"
          android:text="Password Criteria... " />
```

```
<TextView android:id="@+id/disclaimerLbl"
        android:layout_width="fill_parent"
        android:layout_height="wrap_content"
        android:layout_alignParentBottom="true"
          android:text="Use at your own risk... " />

</RelativeLayout>
```

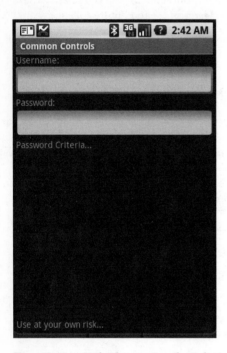

Figure 4-17. *A UI laid out using the RelativeLayout layout manager*

As shown, the user interface looks like a simple login form. The username label is pinned to the top of the container because we set android:layout_alignParentTop to true. Similarly, the username input field is positioned below the username label because we set android:layout_below. The password label appears below the username label, the password input field appears below the password label, and the disclaimer label is pinned to the bottom of the container because we set android:layout_alignParentBottom to true.

Working with RelativeLayout is fun due to its simplicity. In fact, once you start using it, it'll become your favorite layout manager—you'll find yourself going back to it over and over again.

The AbsoluteLayout Layout Manager

The layout managers discussed thus far implement specific but very different strategies for laying out the contents of a container. Android also offers a layout manager that allows you to specify the exact position for the controls in the container. This layout manager is called AbsoluteLayout (see Listing 4-33).

Listing 4-33. *An XML Layout Using AbsoluteLayout*

```
<AbsoluteLayout
android:layout_width="fill_parent"
android:layout_height="fill_parent"
xmlns:android="http://schemas.android.com/apk/res/android"
>

<TextView
android:layout_width="wrap_content"
android:layout_height="wrap_content"
android:text="Username:"
android:layout_x="50px"
android:layout_y="50px" />


<EditText
android:layout_width="wrap_content"
android:layout_height="wrap_content"
android:layout_x="160px"
android:layout_y="50px" />

<TextView
android:layout_width="wrap_content"
android:layout_height="wrap_content"
android:text="Password:"
android:layout_x="50px"
android:layout_y="100px" />


<EditText
android:layout_width="wrap_content"
android:layout_height="wrap_content"
android:layout_x="160px"
android:layout_y="100px" />

</AbsoluteLayout>
```

The user interface generated from the layout in Listing 4-33 is shown in Figure 4-18.

Figure 4-18. *A UI that uses the AbsoluteLayout layout manager*

The user interface shown in Figure 4-18 is a familiar UI—we have used this in several of our previous examples. The difference is obviously in the XML layout. As shown in Listing 4-33, we define two TextView instances along with two EditText fields. But in this example we've specified the x-y coordinates of the controls, whereas we didn't do that in the previous examples.

Note that the screen-coordinate system used in Android defines (0,0) as the top-left corner of the screen. As you move to the right, the x coordinate increases. Similarly, as you move down, the y coordinate increases.

In our examples thus far, we have generated user interfaces with the XML layouts. Although this is the recommended approach, you don't have to do it this way. In fact, most of the time you'll have to mix XML layout with Java code to create UIs. AbsoluteLayout is a good candidate for this approach because you can dynamically calculate the location of controls. Listing 4-34 shows how you can position an image using AbsoluteLayout.

Listing 4-34. *Using the AbsoluteLayout Programmatically*

```java
public void onCreate(Bundle icicle)
{
        super.onCreate(icicle);
        ImageView img = new ImageView(this);
        imgsetImageResource(R.drawable.myimage);

        AbsoluteLayout al = new AbsoluteLayout(this);

        mContentView.addView(img,
            new AbsoluteLayout.LayoutParams(
            50,  // width
                50,  //height
                0,   //left
                    0);  //top

        setContentView(al);
}
```

Listing 4-34 loads an image from the drawable resource folder and then positions it at (50,50). It then sets the content view of the activity to an AbsoluteLayout.

The FrameLayout Layout Manager

The layout managers that we've discussed implement various layout strategies. In other words, each one has a specific way that it positions and orients its children on the screen. With these layout managers, you can have many controls on the screen at one time, each taking up a portion of the screen. Android also offers a layout manager that is mainly used to display a single item. This layout manager is called the FrameLayout layout manager. You mainly use this utility layout class to dynamically display a single view, but you can populate it with many items, setting one to visible while the others are nonvisible. Listing 4-35 demonstrates using a FrameLayout.

Listing 4-35. *Populating a FrameLayout*

```xml
<?xml version="1.0" encoding="utf-8"?>
<FrameLayout xmlns:android="http://schemas.android.com/apk/res/android"
    android:id="@+id/frmLayout"
    android:layout_width="fill_parent"
    android:layout_height="fill_parent">

    <ImageView
      android:id="@+id/oneImgView" android:src="@drawable/one"
      android:scaleType="fitCenter"
      android:layout_width="fill_parent"
      android:layout_height="fill_parent"/>
    <ImageView
      android:id="@+id/twoImgView" android:src="@drawable/two"
      android:scaleType="fitCenter"
      android:layout_width="fill_parent"
      android:layout_height="fill_parent"
      android:visibility="gone" />

</FrameLayout>

@Override
protected void onCreate(Bundle savedInstanceState) {
    super.onCreate(savedInstanceState);

    setContentView(R.layout.frame);


    ImageView one = (ImageView)this.findViewById(R.id.oneImgView);
    ImageView two = (ImageView)this.findViewById(R.id.twoImgView);

    one.setOnClickListener(new OnClickListener(){

        @Override
        public void onClick(View view) {
            ImageView two = (ImageView)FramelayoutActivity.this.
```

```
findViewById(R.id.twoImgView);

            two.setVisibility(View.VISIBLE);

            view.setVisibility(View.GONE);
        }});

    two.setOnClickListener(new OnClickListener(){

        @Override
        public void onClick(View view) {
            ImageView one = (ImageView)FramelayoutActivity.
this.findViewById(R.id.oneImgView);

            one.setVisibility(View.VISIBLE);

            view.setVisibility(View.GONE);
        }});
}
```

Listing 4-35 shows the layout file as well as the onCreate() method of the activity. The idea of the demonstration is to load two ImageView objects in the FrameLayout, with only one of the ImageView objects visible at a time. In the UI, when the user clicks the visible image, we hide one image and show the other one.

Look at Listing 4-35 more closely now, starting with the layout. You can see that we define a FrameLayout with two ImageView objects (an ImageView is a control that knows how to display images). Notice that the second ImageView's visibility is set to gone, making the control invisible. Now look at the onCreate() method. In the onCreate() method, we register listeners to click events on the ImageView objects. In the click handler, we hide one ImageView and show the other one.

As we said earlier, you generally use the FrameLayout when you need to dynamically set the content of a view to a single control. Although this is the general practice, the control will accept many children, as we demonstrated. Listing 4-35 adds two controls to the layout but has one of the controls visible at a time. The FrameLayout, however, does not force you to have only one control visible at a time. If you add many controls to the layout, the FrameLayout will simply stack the controls, one on top of the other, with the last one on top. This can create an interesting UI. For example, Figure 4-19 shows a FrameLayout with two ImageView objects that are visible. You can see that the controls are stacked, and that the top one is partially covering the image behind it.

Another interesting aspect of the FrameLayout is that if you add more than one control to the layout, the size of the layout is computed as the size of the largest item in the container. In Figure 4-19, the top image is actually much smaller than the image behind it, but because the size of the layout is computed based on the largest control, the image on top is stretched.

Also note that if you put many controls inside a FrameLayout with one or more of them invisible to start, you might want to consider using setConsiderGoneChildrenWhenMeasuring(). Because the largest child dictates the layout size, you'll have a problem if the largest child is invisible to begin with. That is, when it becomes visible, it will be only partially visible. To ensure that all items get rendered properly, call setConsiderGoneChildrenWhenMeasuring() and pass it a boolean value of true.

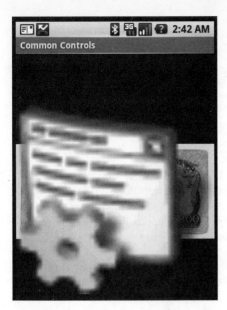

Figure 4-19. *A FrameLayout with two ImageView objects*

Customizing Layout for Various Screen Configurations

By now you know very well that Android offers a host of layout managers that help you build user interfaces. If you've played around with the layout managers that we've discussed, then you know that you can combine the layout managers in various ways to obtain the look and feel that you want. Even with all the layout managers, building UIs—and getting them right— can be a challenge. This is especially true for mobile devices. Users and manufacturers of mobile devices are getting more and more sophisticated, and that makes the developer's job even more challenging.

One of the challenges is building a UI for an application that displays in various screen configurations. For example, what would your UI look like if your application were displayed in portrait vs. landscape? If you haven't run into this yet, your mind is probably racing right now, wondering how to deal with this common scenario. Interestingly, and thankfully, Android provides some support for this use case.

Here's how it works: Android will find and load layouts from specific folders based on the configuration of the device. A device can be in one of three configurations: portrait, landscape, or square. To provide different layouts for the various configurations, you have to create specific folders for each configuration from which Android will load the appropriate layout. As you know, the default layout folder is located at res/layout. To support the portrait display, create a folder called res/layout-port. For landscape, create a folder called res/layout-land. And for square, create one called res/layout-square.

A good question at this point is, "With these three folders, do I need the default layout folder (res/layout)?" Generally, yes. Realize that Android's resource-resolution logic looks in the configuration-specific directory first. If Android doesn't find a resource there, it goes to the default layout directory. Therefore, you can place default-layout definitions in res/layout and the customized versions in the configuration-specific folders.

Note that the Android SDK does not offer any APIs for you to programmatically specify which configuration to load—the system simply selects the folder based on the configuration of the device. Also realize that the layout is not the only resource that is configuration-driven. The entire contents of the res folder can have variations for each configuration. For example, to have different drawables loaded per configuration, create folders for drawable-port, drawable-land, and drawable-square.

Understanding Adapters

Adapters have several responsibilities, as we'll see, but generally speaking, they make binding data to a control easier and more flexible. Adapters in Android are employed for widgets that extend android.widget.AdapterView. Classes that extend AdapterView include ListView, GridView, Spinner, and Gallery (see Figure 4-20). AdapterView itself actually extends android. widget.ViewGroup, which means that ListView, GridView, and so on are container controls. In other words, they display a collection of child controls.

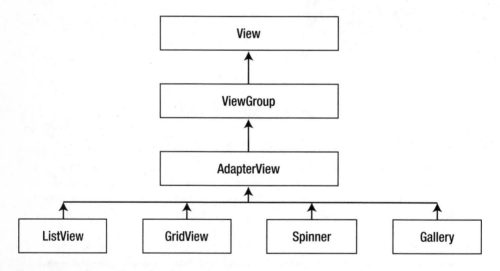

Figure 4-20. *AdapterView class hierarchy*

The purpose of an adapter is to provide the child views for the container. It takes the data and metadata about the view to construct each child view. Let's see how this works by examining the SimpleCursorAdapter.

Getting to Know SimpleCursorAdapter

The SimpleCursorAdapter, which we've used many times already, is depicted in Figure 4-21.

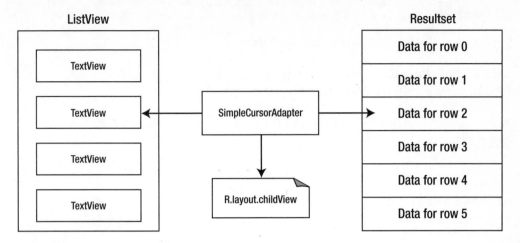

Figure 4-21. *The SimpleCursorAdapter*

The constructor of SimpleCursorAdapter looks like this: SimpleCursorAdapter(Context context, int layout, Cursor c, String[] from, int[] to). This adapter converts a row in the cursor to a child view for the container control. The definition of the child view is defined in an XML resource (layout parameter). Note that because a row in the cursor might have many columns, you tell the SimpleCursorAdapter which columns you want to select from the row by specifying an array of column names (using the from parameter).

Similarly, because each column you select is mapped to a TextView, you must specify the IDs in the to parameter. There's a one-to-one mapping between the column that you select and a TextView that displays the data in the column, so the from and to parameters must be the same size.

Figure 4-21 reveals some flexibility in using adapters. Because the container control operates on an adapter, you can substitute various types of adapters based on your data and child view. For example, if you are not going to populate an AdapterView from the database, you don't have to use the SimpleCursorAdapter. You can opt for an even "simpler" adapter—the ArrayAdapter.

Getting to Know ArrayAdapter

The ArrayAdapter is the simplest of the adapters in Android. It specifically targets list controls and assumes that TextView controls represent the list items (the child views). Creating a new ArrayAdapter generally looks like this:

```
ArrayAdapter<String> adapter = new ArrayAdapter<String>(
this,android.R.layout.simple_list_item_1,
new string[]{"sayed","satya"});
```

The constructor in the preceding code creates an ArrayAdapter where the TextView controls' data is represented by strings. Note that android.R.layout.simple_list_item_1 points to a TextView defined by the Android SDK.

ArrayAdapter provides a handy method that you can use, if the data for the list comes from a resource file. Listing 4-36 shows an example.

Listing 4-36. *Creating an ArrayAdapter from a String-Resource File*

```
Spinner s2 = (Spinner) findViewById(R.id.spinner2);

adapter = ArrayAdapter.createFromResource(this,
R.array.planets,android.R.layout.simple_spinner_item);

adapter.setDropDownViewResource(android.R.layout.simple_spinner_dropdown_item);

s2.setAdapter(adapter);


<string-array name="planets">
    <item>Mercury</item>
    <item>Venus</item>
    <item>Earth</item>
    <item>Mars</item>
    <item>Jupiter</item>
    <item>Saturn</item>
    <item>Uranus</item>
    <item>Neptune</item>
    <item>Pluto</item>
</string-array>
```

Listing 4-36 shows that ArrayAdapter has a utility method called createFromResource() that can create an ArrayAdapter whose data source is defined in a string-resource file. Using this method allows you not only to externalize the contents of the list to an XML file, but also to use localized versions.

Creating Custom Adapters

Adapters in Android are easy to use, but they have some limitations. To address this, Android provides an abstract class called BaseAdapter that you can extend if you need a custom adapter. The adapters that ship with the SDK all extend this base adapter. Thus, if you are looking to extend an adapter, you could consider the following adapters:

- ArrayAdapter<T>: This is an adapter on top of a generic array of arbitrary objects. It's meant to be used with a ListView.

- CursorAdapter: This adapter, also meant to be used in a ListView, provides data to the list via a cursor.

- SimpleAdapter: As the name suggests, this adapter is a simple adapter. The SimpleAdapter is generally used to populate a list with static data (possibly from resources).

- ResourceCursorAdapter: This adapter extends CursorAdapter and knows how to create views from resources.

- SimpleCursorAdapter: This adapter extends ResourceCursorAdapter and creates TextView/ImageView views from the columns in the cursor. The views are defined in resources.

This concludes our discussion about building UIs. In the next section, we are going to introduce you to the Hierarchy Viewer tool. This tool will help you debug and optimize your user interfaces.

Debugging and Optimizing Layouts with the Hierarchy Viewer

The Android SDK ships with a host of tools that you can use to make your development life a lot easier. Because we are on the topic of user interface development, it makes sense for us to discuss the Hierarchy Viewer tool. This tool, shown in Figure 4-22, allows you to debug your user interfaces from a layout perspective.

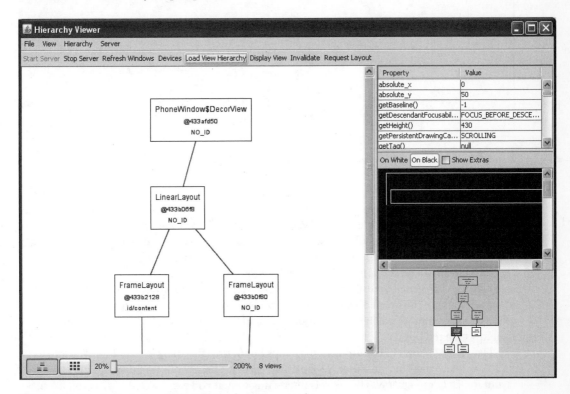

Figure 4-22. *The layout view of the Hierarchy Viewer tool*

As shown in Figure 4-22, the Hierarchy Viewer shows the hierarchy of views in the form of a tree. The idea is this: you load a layout into the tool and then inspect the layout to (1) determine possible layout problems, and/or (2) try to optimize the layout so that you minimize the number of views (for performance reasons).

To debug your UIs, run your application in the emulator and browse to the UI that you want to debug. Then go to the Android SDK /tools directory to start the Hierarchy Viewer tool. On a Windows installation, you'll see a batch file called hierarchyviewer.bat in the /tools directory. When you run the batch file, you'll see the Hierarchy Viewer's Devices screen (see Figure 4-23).

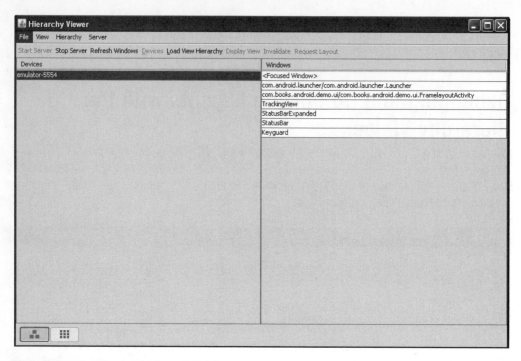

Figure 4-23. *The Hierarchy Viewer's Devices screen*

The Devices screen's left pane displays the set of devices (emulators, in this case) running on the machine. When you select a device, the list of windows in the selected device appears in the right pane. To view the hierarchy of views for a particular window, select that window from the right pane (typically the fully qualified name of your activity prefixed with the application's package name). To load the layout, click the "Load View Hierarchy" button.

In the view-hierarchy screen, you'll see the window's hierarchy of views in the left pane (see Figure 4-22). When you select a view element in the left pane, you can see the properties of that element in the properties view to the right and you can see the location of the view, relative to the other views, in the wire-frame pane to the right. The selected view will be highlighted with a red border.

Figure 4-22 shows two buttons in the status bar of the Hierarchy Viewer tool. The left button displays the Tree view that we explained earlier. The right button displays the current layout in Pixel Perfect view. This view is interesting in that you get a pixel-by-pixel representation of your layouts.

Summary

At this point, you should have a good overview of the controls that are available in the Android SDK. You should also be familiar with Android's layout managers, as well as its adapters. Given a potential screen requirement, you should be able to quickly identify the controls and layout managers that you'll use to build the screen.

In the next chapter, we'll take user interface development further—we are going to discuss menus and dialogs.

CHAPTER 5

■■■

Working with Menus and Dialogs

In Chapter 3 we introduced you to resources, content providers, and intents—the foundations of the Android SDK. Then we covered UI controls and layouts in Chapter 4. Now we'll show you how to work with Android menus and dialogs.

The Android SDK offers extensive support for menus and dialogs. You'll learn to work with several of the menu types that Android supports, including regular menus, submenus, context menus, icon menus, secondary menus, and alternative menus. The Android SDK also allows you to load menus from XML files and generates resource IDs for each of the loaded menu items. We will cover these XML menu resources as well.

Dialogs in Android are asynchronous, which provides flexibility. But if you are accustomed to the Microsoft Windows environment where dialogs are synchronous, you might find asynchronous dialogs a bit hard to use. After giving you the basics of creating and using these Android dialogs, we will provide an abstraction that will make it easier to use them.

Understanding Android Menus

Whether you've worked with Swing in Java, with WPF (Windows Presentation Foundation) in Windows, or with any other UI framework, you've no doubt worked with menus. In addition to providing comprehensive support for menus, Android presents some new patterns such as XML menus and alternative menus.

We will start this chapter by describing the basic classes involved in the Android menu framework. In the process, you will learn how to create menus and menu items, and how to respond to menu items. The key class in Android menu support is `android.view.Menu`. Every activity in Android is associated with a menu object of this type, which can contain a number of menu items and submenus. Menu items are represented by `android.view.MenuItem` and submenus are represented by `android.view.SubMenu`. These relationships are graphically represented in Figure 5-1. Strictly speaking, this is not a class diagram, but a structural diagram designed to help you visualize the relationships between the various menu-related classes and functions.

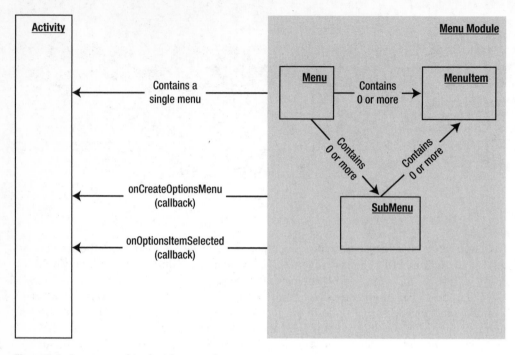

Figure 5-1. *Structure of Android menu classes*

You can group menu items together by assigning each one a group ID, which is merely an attribute. Multiple menu items that carry the same group ID are considered part of the same group. In addition to carrying a group ID, a menu item also carries a name (title), a menu-item ID, and a sort-order ID (or number). You use the sort-order IDs to specify the order of menu items within a menu. For example, if one menu item carries a sort-order number of 4 and another menu item carries a sort-order number of 6, then the first menu item will appear above the second menu item in the menu.

Some of these order-number ranges are reserved for certain kinds of menus. Secondary menu items, which are considered less important than others, start at 0x30000 and are defined by the constant Menu.CATEGORY_SECONDARY. Other types of menu categories—such as system menus, alternative menus, and container menus—have different order-number ranges. System menu items start at 0x20000 and are defined by the constant Menu.CATEGORY_SYSTEM. Alternative menu items start at 0x40000 and are defined by the constant Menu.CATEGORY_ALTERNATIVE. Container menu items start at 0x10000 and are defined by the constant Menu.CATEGORY_CONTAINER. By looking at the values for these constants, you can see the order in which they'll appear in the menu. (We'll discuss these various types of menu items in the "Working with Other Menu Types" section.)

Figure 5-1 also shows two callback methods that you can use to create and respond to menu items: onCreateOptionsMenu and onOptionsItemSelected. We will cover these in the next few subsections.

Creating a Menu

In the Android SDK, you don't need to create a menu object from scratch. Because an activity is associated with a single menu, Android creates this single menu and passes it to the onCreateOptionsMenu callback method. (As the name of the method indicates, menus in Android are also known as *options menus*.) This method allows you to populate the menu with a set of menu items (see Listing 5-1).

Listing 5-1. *Signature for the onCreateOptionsMenu Method*

```
@Override
public boolean onCreateOptionsMenu(Menu menu)
{
    // populate menu items
    …..
    ...return true;
}
```

Once the menu items are populated, the code should return true to make the menu visible. If this method returns false, the menu becomes invisible. The code in Listing 5-2 shows how to add three menu items using a single group ID along with incremental menu-item IDs and sort-order IDs.

Listing 5-2. *Adding Menu Items*

```
@Override
public boolean onCreateOptionsMenu(Menu menu)
{
    //call the base class to include system menus
    super.onCreateOptionsMenu(menu);

    menu.add(0                       // Group
                    ,1                       // item id
                    ,0                       //order
                    ,"append"); // title

    menu.add(0,2,1,"item2");
    menu.add(0,3,2,"clear");

    //It is important to return true to see the menu
    return true;
}
```

You should also call the base-class implementation of this method to give the system an opportunity to populate the menu with system menu items. To keep these system menu items separate from other kinds of menu items, Android adds them starting at 0x20000. (As we mentioned before, the constant Menu.CATEGORY_SYSTEM defines the starting ID for these system menu items.)

The first parameter required for adding a menu item is the group ID (an integer). The second parameter is the menu-item ID, which is sent back to the callback function when that menu item is chosen. The third argument represents the sort-order ID.

The last argument is the name or title of the menu item. Instead of free text, you can use a string resource through the R.java constants file. The group ID, menu-item ID, and sort-order ID are all optional; you can use Menu.NONE if you don't want specify any of those.

Now we'll show you how to work with menu groups. Listing 5-3 shows how you would add two groups of menus: Group 1 and Group 2.

Listing 5-3. *Using Group IDs to Create Menu Groups*

```
@Override
public boolean onCreateOptionsMenu(Menu menu)
{
    //Group 1
    int group1 = 1;
    menu.add(group1,1,1,"g1.item1");
    menu.add(group1,2,2,"g1.item2");

    //Group 2
    int group2 = 2;
    menu.add(group2,3,3,"g2.item1");
    menu.add(group2,4,4,"g2.item2");

    return true; // it is important to return true
}
```

Notice how the menu-item IDs and the sort-order IDs are independent of the groups. So what good is a group, then? You can manipulate a group's menu items using these methods:

```
removeGroup(id)
setGroupCheckable(id, checkable, exclusive)
setGroupEnabled(id,boolean enabled)
setGroupVisible(id,visible)
```

removeGroup removes all menu items from that group, given the group ID. You can enable or disable menu items in a given group using the setGroupEnabled method. Similarly, you can control the visibility of a group of menu items using setGroupVisible.

setGroupCheckable is more interesting. You can use this method to show a check mark on a menu item when that menu item is selected. When applied to a group, it will enable this functionality for all menu items within that group. If this method's exclusive flag is set, then only one menu item within that group is allowed to go into a checked state. The other menu items will remain unchecked.

Responding to Menu Items

There are multiple ways of responding to menu-item clicks in Android. You can use the onOptionsItemSelected method, you can use listeners, or you can use intents. We will cover each of these techniques in this section.

Responding to Menu Items Through onOptionsItemSelected

When a menu item is clicked, Android calls the onOptionsItemSelected callback method on the Activity class (see Listing 5-4).

Listing 5-4. *Signature and Body of the onOptionsItemSelected Method*

```
@Override
public boolean onOptionsItemSelected(MenuItem item)
{
    switch(item.getItemId()) {
        .....
    }
    //for items handled
    return true;

    //for the rest
    ...return super.onOptionsItemSelected(item);
}
```

The key pattern here is to examine the menu-item ID through the getItemId() method of the MenuItem class and do what's necessary. If onOptionsItemSelected() handles a menu item, it returns true. The menu event will not be further propagated. For the menu-item call-backs that onOptionsItemSelected() doesn't deal with, onOptionsItemSelected() should call the parent method through super.onOptionsItemSelected. The default implementation of the onOptionsItemSelected() method returns false so that the "normal" processing can take place. Normal processing includes alternative means of invoking responses for a menu click.

Responding to Menu Items Through Listeners

You usually respond to menus by overriding onOptionsItemSelected; this is the recommended technique for better performance. However, a menu item allows you to register a listener that could be used as a callback.

This approach is a two-step process. In the first step, you implement the OnMenuClickListener interface. Then you take an instance of this implementation and pass it to the menu item. When the menu item is clicked, the menu item will call the onMenuItemClick() method of the OnMenuClickListener interface (see Listing 5-5).

Listing 5-5. *Using a Listener as a Callback for a Menu-Item Click*

```
//Step 1
public class MyResponse implements OnMenuClickListener
{
    //some local variable to work on
    //...
    //Some constructors
    @override
    boolean onMenuItemClick(MenuItem item)
```

```
    {
        //do your thing
        return true;
    }
}

//Step 2
MyResponse myResponse = new MyResponse(...);
menuItem.setOnMenuItemClickListener(myResponse);
...
```

The onMenuItemClick method is called when the menu item has been invoked. This code executes right when the menu item is clicked, even before the onOptionsItemSelected method is called. If onMenuItemClick returns true, no other callbacks will be executed—including the onOptionsItemSelected callback method. This means that the listener code takes precedence over the onOptionsItemSelected method.

Using an Intent to Respond to Menu Items

You can also associate a menu item with an intent by using the MenuItem's method setIntent(intent). By default, a menu item has no intent associated with it. But when an intent *is* associated with a menu item, and nothing else handles the menu item, then the default behavior is to invoke the intent using startActivity(intent). For this to work, all the handlers—especially the onOptionsItemSelected method—should call the parent class's onOptionsItemSelected() method for those items that are not handled. Or you could look at it this way: the system gives onOptionsItemSelected an opportunity to handle menu items first (followed by the listener, of course).

If you don't override the onOptionsItemSelected method, then the base class in the Android framework will do what's necessary to invoke the intent on the menu item. But if you do override this method and you're not interested in this menu item, then you must call the parent method, which in turn facilitates the intent invocation. So here's the bottom line: either don't override the onOptionsItemSelected method, or override it and invoke the parent for the menu items that you are not handling.

Creating a Test Harness for Testing Menus

Congratulations. You have learned how to create menus and how to respond to them through various callbacks. Now we'll show you a sample activity to exercise these menu APIs that you have learned so far.

The goal of this exercise is to create a simple activity with a text view in it. The text view will act like the output of a debugger. As we show and invoke menus, we will write out the invoked menu-item name and menu-item ID to this text view. The finished Menus application will look like the one shown in Figure 5-2.

Figure 5-2 shows two things of interest: the menu and the text view. The menu appears at the bottom. You will not see it, though, when you start the application; you must click the Menu button on the emulator or the device in order to see the menu. The second point of interest is the text view that lists the debug messages near the top of the screen. As you click through the available menu items, the test harness logs the menu-item names in the text view. If you click the "clear" menu item, the program clears the text view.

Figure 5-2. *Sample Menus application*

■Note Figure 5-2 does not necessarily represent the beginning state of the sample application. We have presented it here to illustrate the menu types that we'll cover in this chapter.

Follow these steps to implement the test harness:

1. Create an XML layout file that contains the text view.

2. Create an `Activity` class that hosts the layout defined in step 1.

3. Set up the menu.

4. Add some regular menu items to the menu.

5. Add some secondary menu items to the menu.

6. Respond to the menu items.

7. Modify the `AndroidManifest.xml` file to show the application's proper title.

We will cover each of these steps in the following sections and provide the necessary source code to assemble the test harness.

Creating an XML Layout

Step 1 involves creating a simple XML layout file with a text view in it (see Listing 5-6). You could load this file into an activity during its startup.

Listing 5-6. *XML Layout File for the Test Harness*

```xml
<?xml version="1.0" encoding="utf-8"?>
<LinearLayout xmlns:android="http://schemas.android.com/apk/res/android"
    android:orientation="vertical"
    android:layout_width="fill_parent"
    android:layout_height="fill_parent"
    >
<TextView android:id="@+id/textViewId"
    android:layout_width="fill_parent"
    android:layout_height="wrap_content"
    android:text="Debugging Scratch Pad"
    />
</LinearLayout>
```

Creating an Activity

Step 2 dictates that you create an activity, which is also a simple process. Assuming that the layout file in step 1 is available at \res\layout\main.xml, you can use that file through its resource ID to populate the activity's view (see Listing 5-7).

Listing 5-7. *Menu Test Harness Activity Class*

```java
public class SampleMenusActivity extends Activity {

    //Initialize this in onCreateOptions
    Menu myMenu = null;

    @Override
    public void onCreate(Bundle savedInstanceState) {
        super.onCreate(savedInstanceState);

        setContentView(R.layout.main);
    }
```

For brevity, we have not included the import statements. In Eclipse, you can automatically populate the import statements by pulling up the context menu in the editor and selecting Source ➤ Organize Imports.

Setting Up the Menu

Now that you have a view and an activity, you can move on to step 3: overriding the onCreateOptionsMenu and setting up the menu programmatically (see Listing 5-8).

Listing 5-8. *Setting Up the Menu Programatically*

```
@Override
public boolean onCreateOptionsMenu(Menu menu)
{
    //call the parent to attach any system level menus
    super.onCreateOptionsMenu(menu);

    this.myMenu = menu;

    //add a few normal menus
    addRegularMenuItems(menu);

    //add a few secondary menus
    add5SecondaryMenuItems(menu);

    //it must return true to show the menu
    //if it is false menu won't show
    return true;
}
```

The code in Listing 5-8 first calls the parent onCreateOptionsMenu to give the parent an opportunity to add any system-level menus. Note that in releases 1.0, 1.1, and 1.5 of the Android SDK, this method does not add new menu items. The code then remembers the Menu object in order to manipulate it later for demonstration purposes. After that, the code proceeds to add a few regular menu items and a few secondary menu items.

Adding Regular Menu Items

Now for step 4: adding a few regular menu items to the menu. The code for addRegularMenuItems appears in Listing 5-9.

Listing 5-9. *The addRegularMenuItems Function*

```
private void addRegularMenuItems(Menu menu)
{
    int base=Menu.FIRST; // value is 1

    menu.add(base,base,base,"append");
    menu.add(base,base+1,base+1,"item 2");
    menu.add(base,base+2,base+2,"clear");

    menu.add(base,base+3,base+3,"hide secondary");
    menu.add(base,base+4,base+4,"show secondary");

    menu.add(base,base+5,base+5,"enable secondary");
    menu.add(base,base+6,base+6,"disable secondary");

    menu.add(base,base+7,base+7,"check secondary");
    menu.add(base,base+8,base+8,"uncheck secondary");
}
```

The Menu class defines a few convenience constants, one of which is Menu.FIRST. You can use this as a baseline number for menu IDs and other menu-related sequential numbers. Notice how you can peg the group ID at base and increment only the sort-order ID and menu-item ID. In addition, the code adds a few specific menu items such as "hide secondary," "enable secondary," and others to demonstrate some of the menu concepts.

Adding Secondary Menu Items

Let us now add a few secondary menu items to perform step 5 (see Listing 5-10). Secondary menu items, as mentioned earlier, start at 0x30000 and are defined by the constant Menu.CATEGORY_SECONDARY. Their sort-order IDs are higher than regular menu items, so they appear after the regular menu items in a menu. Note that the sort order is the only thing that distinguishes a secondary menu item from a regular menu item. In all other aspects, a secondary menu item works and behaves like any other menu item.

Listing 5-10. *Adding Secondary Menu Items*

```
private void add5SecondaryMenuItems(Menu menu)
{
    //Secondary items are shown just like everything else
    int base=Menu.CATEGORY_SECONDARY;

    menu.add(base,base+1,base+1,"sec. item 1");
    menu.add(base,base+2,base+2,"sec. item 2");
    menu.add(base,base+3,base+3,"sec. item 3");
    menu.add(base,base+3,base+3,"sec. item 4");
    menu.add(base,base+4,base+4,"sec. item 5");
}
```

Responding to Menu-Item Clicks

Now that the menus are set up, we move on to step 6: responding to them. When a menu item is clicked, Android calls the onOptionsItemSelected callback method of the Activity class by passing a reference to the clicked menu item. You then use the getItemId() method on the MenuItem to see which item it is.

It is not uncommon to see either a switch statement or a series of if and else statements calling various functions in response to menu items. Listing 5-11 shows this standard pattern of responding to menu items in the onOptionsItemSelected callback method. (You will learn a slightly better way of doing the same thing in the "Loading Menus Through XML Files" section, where you will have symbolic names for these menu-item IDs.)

Listing 5-11. *Responding to Menu-Item Clicks*

```
@Override
public boolean onOptionsItemSelected(MenuItem item)      {
    if (item.getItemId() == 1)         {
        appendText("\nhello");
    }
```

```java
    else if (item.getItemId() == 2)        {
       appendText("\nitem2");
    }
    else if (item.getItemId() == 3)        {
       emptyText();
    }
    else if (item.getItemId() == 4)        {
       //hide secondary
       this.appendMenuItemText(item);
       this.myMenu.setGroupVisible(Menu.CATEGORY_SECONDARY,false);
    }
    else if (item.getItemId() == 5)        {
       //show secondary
       this.appendMenuItemText(item);
       this.myMenu.setGroupVisible(Menu.CATEGORY_SECONDARY,true);
    }
    else if (item.getItemId() == 6)        {
       //enable secondary
       this.appendMenuItemText(item);
       this.myMenu.setGroupEnabled(Menu.CATEGORY_SECONDARY,true);
    }
    else if (item.getItemId() == 7)        {
       //disable secondary
       this.appendMenuItemText(item);
       this.myMenu.setGroupEnabled(Menu.CATEGORY_SECONDARY,false);
    }
    else if (item.getItemId() == 8)        {
       //check secondary
       this.appendMenuItemText(item);
       myMenu.setGroupCheckable(Menu.CATEGORY_SECONDARY,true,false);
    }
    else if (item.getItemId() == 9)        {
       //uncheck secondary
       this.appendMenuItemText(item);
       myMenu.setGroupCheckable(Menu.CATEGORY_SECONDARY,false,false);
    }
    else        {
       this.appendMenuItemText(item);
    }
    //should return true if the menu item
    //is handled
    return true;
 }
```

Listing 5-11 also exercises operations on menus at the group level; calls to these methods are highlighted in bold. The code also logs the details about the clicked menu item to the TextView. Listing 5-12 shows some utility functions to write to the TextView. Notice an additional method on a MenuItem to get its title.

Listing 5-12. *Utility Functions to Write to the Debug TextView*

```
//Given a string of text append it to the TextView
    private void appendText(String text)    {
        TextView tv = (TextView)this.findViewById(R.id.textViewId);
        tv.setText(tv.getText() + text);
    }


//Given a menu item append its title to the TextView
    private void appendMenuItemText(MenuItem menuItem)    {
        String title = menuItem.getTitle().toString();
        TextView tv = (TextView)this.findViewById(R.id.textViewId);
        tv.setText(tv.getText() + "\n" + title);
    }
//Empty the TextView of its contents
    private void emptyText()    {
        TextView tv = (TextView)this.findViewById(R.id.textViewId);
        tv.setText("");
    }
```

Tweaking the AndroidManifest.xml File

Your final step in the process to create the test harness is to update the application's
AndroidManifest.xml file. This file, which is automatically created for you when you create a
new project, is available in your project's root directory.

> This is the place where you register the Activity class (such as SampleMenusActivity) and
where you specify a title for the activity. We called this activity "Sample Menus Application," as
shown in Figure 5-2. See this entry highlighted in Listing 5-13.

Listing 5-13. *The AndroidManifest.xml File for the Test Harness*

```xml
<?xml version="1.0" encoding="utf-8"?>
<manifest xmlns:android="http://schemas.android.com/apk/res/android"
     package="your-package-name-goes-here "
     android:versionCode="1"
     android:versionName="1.0.0">
    <application android:icon="@drawable/icon" android:label="Sample Menus">
        <activity android:name=".SampleMenusActivity"
                   android:label="Sample Menus Application">
            <intent-filter>
                <action android:name="android.intent.action.MAIN" />
                <category android:name="android.intent.category.LAUNCHER" />
            </intent-filter>
        </activity>
    </application>
</manifest>
```

Using the code we've provided, you should be able to quickly construct this test harness for experimenting with menus. We showed you how to create a simple activity initialized with a text view, and then how to populate and respond to menus. Most menus follow this basic yet functional pattern. You can use Figure 5-2 as a guide for what kind of UI to expect when you are done with the exercise. But as we pointed out, what you see might not exactly match the figure because we haven't yet shown you how to add the icon menus. Your UI might differ even after you add the icon menus, because your images might differ from the images we used.

Working with Other Menu Types

So far we've covered some the of the simpler, although quite functional, menu types. As you walk through the SDK, you will see that Android also supports icon menus, submenus, context menus, and alternative menus. Out of these, alternative menus are unique to Android. We will cover all of these menu types in this section.

Expanded Menus

Recall from Figure 5-2 that the sample application displays a menu item called "More" at the bottom-right corner of the menu. We didn't show you how to add this menu item in any of the sample code, so where does it come from?

If an application has more menu items than it can display on the main screen, Android shows the "More" menu item to allow the user to see the rest. This menu, called an *expanded menu*, shows up automatically when there are too many menu items to display in the limited amount of space. But the expanded menu has a limitation: it cannot accommodate icons. Users who click "More" will see a resultant menu that omits icons.

Working with Icon Menus

Now that we've hinted at icon menus, let's talk about them in more detail. Android supports not only text, but also images or icons as part of its menu repertoire. You can use icons to represent your menu items instead of and in addition to text. But note a few limitations when it comes to using icon menus. First, as you saw in the previous paragraph, you can't use icon menus for expanded menus. Second, icon menu items do not support menu-item check marks. Third, if the text in an icon menu item is too long, it will be truncated after a certain number of characters depending on the size of the display. (This last limitation applies to text-based menu items also.)

Creating an icon menu item is straightforward. You create a regular text-based menu item as before, then you use the setIcon method on the MenuItem class to set the image. You'll need to use the image's resource ID, so you must generate it first by placing the image or icon in the /res/drawable directory. For example, if the icon's file name is balloons, then the resource ID will be R.drawable.balloons.

Here is some sample code that demonstrates this:

```
//add a menu item and remember it so that you can use it
//subsequently to set the icon on it.
MenuItem item8 = menu.add(base,base+8,base+8,"uncheck secondary");
item8.setIcon(R.drawable.balloons);
```

As you add menu items to the menu, you rarely need to keep a local variable returned by the menu.add method. But in this case, you need to remember the returned object so you can add the icon to the menu item. The code in this example also demonstrates that the type returned by the menu.add method is MenuItem.

The icon will show as long as the menu item is displayed on the main application screen. If it's displayed as part of the expanded menu, the icon will not show. The menu item displaying an image of balloons in Figure 5-2 is an example of an icon menu item.

Working with Submenus

Let's take a look at Android's submenus now. Figure 5-1 points out the structural relationship of a SubMenu to a Menu and a MenuItem. A Menu object can have multiple SubMenu objects. Each SubMenu object is added to the Menu object through a call to the Menu.addSubMenu method (see Listing 5-14). You add menu items to a submenu the same way that you add menu items to a menu. This is because SubMenu is also derived from a Menu object. However, you cannot add additional submenus to a submenu.

Listing 5-14. *Adding Submenus*

```
private void addSubMenu(Menu menu)
{
    //Secondary items are shown just like everything else
    int base=Menu.FIRST + 100;
    SubMenu sm = menu.addSubMenu(base,base+1,Menu.NONE,"submenu");
    sm.add(base,base+2,base+2,"sub item1");
    sm.add(base,base+3,base+3, "sub item2");
    sm.add(base,base+4,base+4, "sub item3");

     //submenu item icons are not supported
    item1.setIcon(R.drawable.icon48x48_2);

    //the following is ok however
    sm.setIcon(R.drawable.icon48x48_1);

    //This will result in a runtime exception
     //sm.addSubMenu("try this");
}
```

■**Note** A SubMenu, as a subclass of the Menu object, continues to carry the addSubMenu method. The compiler won't complain if you add a submenu to another submenu, but you'll get a runtime exception if you try to do it.

The Android SDK documentation also suggests that submenus do not support icon menu items. When you add an icon to a menu item and then add that menu item to a submenu, the menu item will ignore that icon, even if you don't see a compile-time or runtime error. However, the submenu itself can have an icon.

Provisioning for System Menus

Most Windows applications come with menus such as File, Edit, View, Open, Close, and Exit. These menus are called system menus. The Android SDK suggests that the system could insert a similar set of menus when an options menu is created. However, releases 1.0, 1.1, and 1.5 of the Android SDK do not populate any of these menus as part of the menu-creation process. It is conceivable that these system menus might be implemented in a subsequent release. The documentation suggests that programmers make provisions in their code so that they can accommodate these system menus when they become available. You do this by calling the onCreateOptionsMenu method of the parent, which allows the system to add system menus to a group identified by the constant CATEGORY_SYSTEM.

Working with Context Menus

Users of desktop programs are no doubt familiar with context menus. In Windows applications, for example, you can access a context menu by right-clicking a UI element. Android supports the same idea of context menus through an action called a *long click*. A long click is a mouse click held down slightly longer than usual on any Android view.

On handheld devices such as cell phones, mouse clicks are implemented in a number of ways, depending on the navigation mechanism. If your phone has a wheel to move the cursor, a press of the wheel would serve as the mouse click. Or if the device has a touch pad, then a tap or a press would be equivalent to a mouse click. Or you might have a set of arrow buttons for movement and a selection button in the middle; clicking that button would be equivalent to clicking the mouse. Regardless of how a mouse click is implemented on your device, if you hold the mouse click a bit longer you will realize the long click.

A context menu differs structurally from the standard options menu that we've been discussing (see Figure 5-3). Context menus have some nuances that options menus don't have.

Figure 5-3 shows that a context menu is represented as a ContextMenu class in the Android menu architecture. Just like a Menu, a ContextMenu can contain a number of menu items. You will use the same set of Menu methods to add menu items to the context menu. The biggest difference between a Menu and a ContextMenu boils down to the ownership of the menu in question. An activity owns a regular options menu, whereas a view owns a context menu. This is to be expected because the long clicks that activate context menus apply to the *view* being clicked. So an activity can have only one options menu but many context menus. Because an activity can contain multiple views, and each view can have its own context menu, an activity can have as many context menus as there are views.

Although a context menu is owned by a view, the method to populate context menus resides in the Activity class. This method is called activity.onCreateContextMenu(), and its role resembles that of the activity.onCreateOptionsMenu() method. This callback method also carries with it the view for which the context menu items are to be populated.

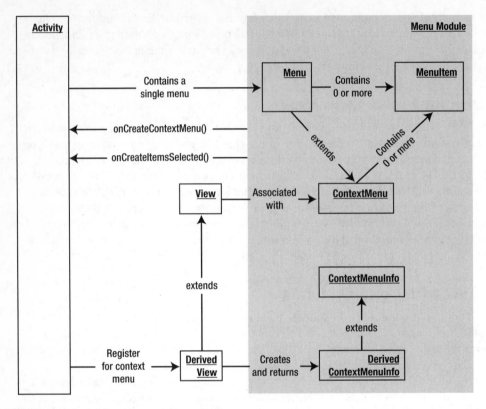

Figure 5-3. *Activities, views, and context menus*

There is one more notable wrinkle to the context menu. Whereas the onCreateOptionsMenu() method is automatically called for every activity, this is not the case with onCreateContextMenu(). A view in an activity does not *have* to own a context menu. You can have three views in your activity, for example, but perhaps you want to enable context menus for only one view and not the others. If you want a particular view to own a context menu, you must register that view with its activity specifically for the purpose of owning a context menu. You do this through the activity.registerForContextMenu(view) method, which we'll discuss in the section "Registering a View for a Context Menu."

Now note the ContextMenuInfo class shown in Figure 5-3. An object of this type is passed to the onCreateContextMenu method. This is one way for the view to pass additional information to this method. For a view to do this, it needs to override the getContextViewInfo() method and return a derived class of ContextMenuInfo with additional methods to represent the additional information. You might want to look at the source code for android.view.View to fully understand this interaction.

■**Note** Per the Android SDK documentation, context menus do not support shortcuts, icons, or submenus.

Now that you know the general structure of the context menus, let's look at some sample code that demonstrates each of the steps to implement a context menu:

1. Register a view for a context menu in an activity's onCreate() method.

2. Populate the context menu using onCreateContextMenu(). You must complete step 1 before this callback method is invoked by Android.

3. Respond to context-menu clicks.

Registering a View for a Context Menu

The first step in implementing a context menu is registering a view for the context menu in an activity's onCreate() method. If you were to use the menu test harness introduced in this chapter, you could register the TextView for a context menu in that test harness by using the code in Listing 5-15. You will first find the TextView and then call registerForContextMenu on the activity using the TextView as an argument. This will set up the TextView for context menus.

Listing 5-15. *Registering a TextView for a Context Menu*

```
@Override
public void onCreate(Bundle savedInstanceState) {
    super.onCreate(savedInstanceState);
    setContentView(R.layout.main);

    TextView tv = (TextView)this.findViewById(R.id.textViewId);
    registerForContextMenu(this.getTextView());
}
```

Populating a Context Menu

Once a view like the TextView in this example is registered for context menus, Android will call the onCreateContextMenu() method with this view as the argument. This is where you can populate the context menu items for that context menu. The onCreateContextMenu() callback method provides three arguments to work with.

The first argument is a preconstructed ContextMenu object, the second is the view (such as the TextView) that generated the callback, and the third is the ContextMenuInfo class that we covered briefly while discussing Figure 5-3. For a lot of simple cases, you can just ignore the ContextMenuInfo object. However, some views might pass extra information through this object. In those cases, you will need to cast the ContextMenuInfo class to a subclass and then use the additional methods to retrieve the additional information.

Some examples of classes derived from ContextMenuInfo include AdapterContextMenuInfo and ExpandableContextMenuInfo. Views that are tied to database cursors in Android use the AdapterContextMenuInfo class to pass the row ID within that view for which the context menu is being displayed. In a sense, you can use this class to further clarify the object underneath the mouse click, even within a given view.

Listing 5-16 demonstrates the onCreateContextMenu() method.

Listing 5-16. *The onCreateContextMenu() Method*

```
@Override
public void onCreateContextMenu(ContextMenu menu, View v, ContextMenuInfo menuInfo)
{
        menu.setHeaderTitle("Sample Context Menu");
        menu.add(200, 200, 200, "item1");
}
```

Responding to Context Menu Items

The third step in our implementation of a context menu is responding to context-menu clicks. The mechanism of responding to context menus is similar to the mechanism of responding to options menus. Android provides a callback method similar to onOptionsItemSelected() called onContextItemSelected(). This method, like its counterpart, is also available on the Activity class. Listing 5-17 demonstrates onContextItemSelected().

Listing 5-17. *Responding to Context Menus*
```
@Override

public boolean onContextItemSelected(MenuItem item)

{

        if (item.itemId() = some-menu-item-id)

        {

                //handle this menu item

                return true;

        }

… other exception processing

}
```

Working with Alternative Menus

So far you have learned to create and work with menus, submenus, and context menus. Android introduces a new concept called *alternative menus*, which allow alternative menu items to be part of menus, submenus, and context menus. Alternative menus allow multiple applications on Android to use one another. These alternative menus are part of the Android interapplication communication or usage framework.

Specifically, alternative menus allow one application to include menus from another application. When the alternative menus are chosen, the target application or activity will be launched with a URL to the data needed by that activity. The invoked activity will then use the data URL from the intent that is passed. To understand alternative menus well, you must first understand content providers, content URIs, content MIME types, and intents (see Chapter 3).

The general idea here is this: imagine you are writing a screen to display some data. Most likely, this screen will be an activity. On this activity, you will have an options menu that allows you to manipulate or work with the data in a number of ways. Also assume for a moment that you are working with a document or a note that is identified by a URI and a corresponding MIME type. What you want to do as a programmer is anticipate that the device will eventually contain more programs that will know how to work with this data or display this data. You want to give this new set of programs an opportunity to display their menu items as part of the menu that you are constructing for this activity.

To attach alternative menu items to a menu, follow these steps while setting up the menu in the onCreateOptionsMenu method:

1. Create an intent whose data URI is set to the data URI that you are showing at the moment.

2. Set the category of the intent as CATEGORY_ALTERNATIVE.

3. Search for activities that allow operations on data supported by this type of URI.

4. Add intents that can invoke those activities as menu items to the menu.

These steps tell us a lot about the nature of Android applications, so we'll examine each one. As we know now, attaching the alternative menu items to the menu happens in the onCreateOptionsMenu method:

```
@Override public boolean onCreateOptionsMenu(Menu menu)
{
}
```

Let us now figure out what code makes up this function. We first need to know the URI for the data we might be working on in this activity. You can get the URI like this:

```
this.getIntent().getData()
```

This works because the Activity class has a method called getIntent() that returns the data URI for which this activity is invoked. This invoked activity might be the main activity invoked by the main menu; in that case, it might not have an intent and the getIntent() method will return null. In your code, you will have to guard against this situation.

Our goal now is to find out what other programs know how to work with this kind of data. We do this search using an intent as an argument. Here's the code to construct that intent:

```
Intent criteriaIntent = new Intent(null, getIntent().getData());
intent.addCategory(Intent.CATEGORY_ALTERNATIVE);
```

Once we construct the intent, we will also add a category of actions that we are interested in. Specifically, we are interested only in activities that can be invoked as part of an alternative menu. We are ready now to tell the Menu object to search for matching activities and add them as menu options (see Listing 5-18).

Listing 5-18. *Populating a Menu with Alternative Menu Items*

```
// Search for, and populate the menu with matching Activities.
menu.addIntentOptions(
    Menu.CATEGORY_ALTERNATIVE,    // Group
    Menu.CATEGORY_ALTERNATIVE,    // Any unique IDs we might care to add.
    Menu.CATEGORY_ALTERNATIVE,    // order
    getComponentName(),           // Name of the class displaying
                                  //the menu--here, it's this class.
    null,                         // No specifics.
    criteriaIntent,               // Previously created intent that
                                  // describes our requirements.
    0,                            // No flags.
    null);                        // returned menu items
```

Before going through this code line by line, we'll explain what we mean by the term *matching activities*. A *matching activity* is an activity that's capable of handling a URI that it has been given. Activities typically register this information in their manifest files using URIs, actions, and categories. Android provides a mechanism that lets you use an Intent object to look for the matching activities given these attributes.

Now let's look closely at Listing 5-18. The method addIntentOptions on the Menu class is responsible for looking up the activities that match an intent's URI and category attributes. Then the method adds these activities to the menu under the right group with the appropriate menu-item IDs and sort-order IDs. The first three arguments deal with this aspect of the method's responsibility. In Listing 5-18, we start off with the Menu.CATEGORY_ALTERNATIVE as the group under which the new menu items will be added. We also use this same constant as the starting point for the menu-item IDs and sort-order IDs.

The next argument points to the fully qualified component name of the activity that this menu is part of. The code uses a helper method called getComponentName(); we will leave it as an exercise for the reader to get a component name from the class and package names. This component name is needed because when a new menu item is added, that menu item will need to invoke the target activity. To do that, the system needs the source activity that started the target activity. The next argument is an array of intents that you want to use as a filter on the returned intents.

The next argument points to criteriaIntent, which we just constructed. This is the search criteria we are going after. The argument after that is a flag such as Menu.FLAG_APPEND_TO_GROUP to indicate whether to append to the set of existing menu items in this group or replace them. The default value is 0, which indicates that the menu items in the menu group should be replaced.

The last argument in Listing 5-18 is an array of menu items that are added. You could use these added menu-item references if you want to manipulate them in some manner after adding them.

All of this is well and good. But a few questions remain unanswered. For example, what will be the names of the added menu items? The Android documentation is quite silent about this. So we snooped around the source code to see what this function is actually doing behind the scenes.

As it turns out, the Menu class is only an interface, so we can't see any implementation source code for it. (Refer to Chapter 1 to see how to get to Android's source code.) The class that implements the Menu interface is called MenuBuilder. Listing 5-19 shows the source code of a relevant method, addIntentOptions, from the MenuBuilder class. (We're providing the code for your reference; we won't explain it line by line.)

Listing 5-19. *MenuBuilder.addIntentOptions Method*

```
public int addIntentOptions(int group, int id, int categoryOrder,
                            ComponentName caller,
                            Intent[] specifics,
                            Intent intent, int flags,
                            MenuItem[] outSpecificItems)
{
    PackageManager pm = mContext.getPackageManager();
    final List<ResolveInfo> lri =
            pm.queryIntentActivityOptions(caller, specifics, intent, 0);
    final int N = lri != null ? lri.size() : 0;

    if ((flags & FLAG_APPEND_TO_GROUP) == 0) {
        removeGroup(group);
    }

    for (int i=0; i<N; i++) {
        final ResolveInfo ri = lri.get(i);
        Intent rintent = new Intent(
            ri.specificIndex < 0 ? intent : specifics[ri.specificIndex]);
        rintent.setComponent(new ComponentName(
                ri.activityInfo.applicationInfo.packageName,
                ri.activityInfo.name));
        final MenuItem item = add(group, id, categoryOrder, ri.loadLabel(pm));
        item.setIntent(rintent);
        if (outSpecificItems != null && ri.specificIndex >= 0) {
            outSpecificItems[ri.specificIndex] = item;
        }
    }
    return N;
}
```

Note the line in Listing 5-19 highlighted in bold; this portion of the code constructs a menu item. The code delegates the work of figuring out a menu title to the ResolveInfo class. The source code of the ResolveInfo class shows us that the intent-filter that declared this intent should have a title associated with it. Here is an example:

```
<intent-filter android:label="Menu Title ">
    …….
    <category android:name="android.intent.category.ALTERNATE" />
    <data android:mimeType="some type data" />
</intent-filter>
```

The label value of the intent-filter ends up serving as the menu name. You can go through the Android Notepad example to see this behavior.

Working with Menus in Response to Changing Data

So far we've talked about static menus; you set them up once, and they don't change dynamically according to what's onscreen. If you want to create dynamic menus, use the onPrepareOptionsMenu method that Android provides. This method resembles onCreateOptionsMenu except that it gets called every time a menu is invoked. You should use onPrepareOptionsMenu, for example, if you want to disable some menus or menu groups based on the data you are displaying. You might want to keep this in mind as you design your menu functionality.

We need to cover one more important aspect of menus before moving on to dialogs. Android supports the creation of menus using XML files. The next high-level topic is dedicated to exploring this XML menu support in Android.

Loading Menus Through XML Files

Up until this point, we've created all our menus programmatically. This is not the most convenient way to create menus because for every menu you have to provide several IDs and define constants for each of those IDs. You'll no doubt find this tedious.

Instead, you can define menus through XML files; you can do this in Android because menus are also resources. The XML approach to menu creation offers several advantages, such as the ability to name the menus, order them automatically, give them IDs, and so on. You can also get localization support for the menu text.

Follow these steps to work with XML-based menus:

1. Define an XML file with menu tags.

2. Place the file in the /res/menu subdirectory. The name of the file is arbitrary, and you can have as many files as you want. Android automatically generates a resource ID for this menu file.

3. Use the resource ID for the menu file to load the XML file into the menu.

4. Respond to the menu items using the resource IDs generated for each menu item.

We will talk about each of these steps and provide corresponding code snippets in the following sections.

Structure of an XML Menu Resource File

First we'll look at an XML file with menu definitions (see Listing 5-20). All menu files start with the same high-level menu tag followed by a series of group tags. This group tag corresponds to the menu-item group we talked about at the beginning of the chapter. You can specify an ID for the group using the @+id approach. Each menu group will have a series of menu items with their menu-item IDs tied to symbolic names. You can refer to the Android SDK documentation for all the possible arguments for these XML tags.

Listing 5-20. *An XML File with Menu Definitions*

```xml
<menu xmlns:android="http://schemas.android.com/apk/res/android">
    <!-- This group uses the default category. -->
    <group android:id="@+id/menuGroup_Main">
        <item android:id="@+id/menu_testPick"
            android:orderInCategory="5"
            android:title="Test Pick" />
        <item android:id="@+id/menu_testGetContent"
            android:orderInCategory="5"
            android:title="Test Get Content" />
        <item android:id="@+id/menu_clear"
            android:orderInCategory="10"
            android:title="clear" />
        <item android:id="@+id/menu_dial"
            android:orderInCategory="7"
            android:title="dial" />
        <item android:id="@+id/menu_test"
            android:orderInCategory="4"
            android:title="@+string/test" />
        <item android:id="@+id/menu_show_browser"
            android:orderInCategory="5"
            android:title="show browser" />
    </group>
</menu>
```

The menu XML file in Listing 5-20 has one group. Based on the resource ID definition `@+id/menuGroup_main`, this group will be automatically assigned a resource ID called `menuGroup_main` in the `R.java` resource ID file. Similarly, all the child menu items are allocated menu-item IDs based on their symbolic resource ID definitions in this XML file.

Inflating XML Menu Resource Files

Let us assume that the name of this XML file is `my_menu.xml`. You will need to place this file in the `/res/menu` subdirectory. Placing the file in `/res/menu` automatically generates a resource ID called `Resource.menu.my_menu`.

Now let's look at how you can use this menu resource ID to populate the options menu. Android provides a class called `android.view.MenuInflater` to populate `Menu` objects from XML files. We will use an instance of this `MenuInflater` to make use of the `Resource.menu.my_menu` resource ID to populate a menu object:

```java
@Override
public boolean onCreateOptionsMenu(Menu menu)
{
    MenuInflater inflater = getMenuInflater(); //from activity
    inflater.inflate(R.menu.menu1, menu);
}
```

In this code, we first get the `MenuInflater` from the `Activity` class and then tell it to inflate the menu XML file into the menu directly.

Responding to XML-Based Menu Items

You haven't yet seen the specific advantage of this approach—it becomes apparent when you start responding to the menu items. You respond to XML menu items the way you respond to menus created programmatically, but with a small difference. As before, you handle the menu items in the `onOptionsItemSelected` callback method. But this time, you will have some help from Android's resources (see Chapter 3 for details on resources). As we mentioned in the section "Structure of an XML Menu Resource File," Android not only generates a resource ID for the XML file, but also generates the necessary menu-item IDs to help you distinguish between the menu items. This is an advantage in terms of responding to the menu items because you don't have to explicitly create and manage their menu-item IDs.

To further elaborate on this, in the case of XML menus you don't have to define constants for these IDs and you don't have to worry about their uniqueness because resource ID generation takes care of that. The following code illustrates this:

```
private void onOptionsItemSelected (MenuItem item)
{
    this.appendMenuItemText(item);
    if (item.getItemId() == R.id.menu_clear)
    {
        this.emptyText();
    }
    else if (item.getItemId() == R.id.menu_dial)
    {
        this.dial();
    }
    else if (item.getItemId() == R.id.menu_testPick)
    {
        IntentsUtils.invokePick(this);
    }
    else if (item.getItemId() == R.id.menu_testGetContent)
    {
        IntentsUtils.invokeGetContent(this);
    }
    else if (item.getItemId() == R.id.menu_show_browser)
    {
            IntentsUtils.tryOneOfThese(this);
    }
}
```

Notice how the menu-item names from the XML menu resource file have automatically generated menu-item IDs in the `R.id` space.

A Brief Introduction to Additional XML Menu Tags

As you construct your XML files, you will need to know the various XML tags that are possible.
You can quickly get this information by examining the API demos that come with the Android
SDK. These Android API demos include a series of menus that help you explore all aspects of
Android programming. If you look at the /res/menu subdirectory, you will find a number of
XML menu samples. We'll briefly cover some key tags here.

Group Category Tag

In an XML file, you can specify the category of a group by using the menuCategory tag:

```
<group android:id="@+id/some_group_id "
      android:menuCategory="secondary">
```

Checkable Behavior Tags

You can use the checkableBehavior tag to control checkable behavior at a group level:

```
<group android:id="@+id/noncheckable_group"
      android:checkableBehavior="none">
```

You can use the checked tag to control checkable behavior at an item level:

```
<item android:id=".."
     android:title="…"
     android:checked="true" />
```

Tags to Simulate a Submenu

A submenu is represented as a menu element under a menu item:

```
<item android:title="All without group">
     <menu>
               <item…>
     </menu>
</item>
```

Menu Icon Tag

You can use the icon tag to associate an image with a menu item:

```
<item android:id=".. "
      android:icon="@drawable/some-file" />
```

Menu Enabling/Disabling Tag

You can enable and disable a menu item using the enabled tag:

```
<item android:id=".. "
        android:enabled="true"
        android:icon="@drawable/some-file" />
```

Menu Item Shortcuts

You can set a shortcut for a menu item using the alphabeticShortcut tag:

```
<item android:id="… "
       android:alphabeticShortcut="a"

   …

   </item>
```

Menu Visibility

You can control a menu item's visibility using the visible flag:

```
<item android:id="… "
       android:visible="true"

   …

</item>
```

By now, we have covered options menus, submenus, icon menus, context menus, and alternative menus. We also covered the means and advantages of using XML menus. Now let's turn our attention to Android's support for dialogs.

Using Dialogs in Android

If you are coming from a desktop environment, you might need to think differently when you work with Android dialogs. The primary difference is that the dialogs in Android are asynchronous. This asynchronicity is a bit counterintuitive; it's as if the front of your brain is having a conversation with someone, while the back of your brain is thinking about something else. However, the "split-brain" model isn't that bad when it comes to computers. This asynchronous approach does increase the handheld's responsiveness.

Not only are Android dialogs asynchronous, but they are also *managed*; that is, they are reused between multiple invocations. This design arose from the need to optimize memory and performance as dialogs are created, shown, and dismantled.

In the following sections we will cover these aspects of Android dialogs in depth. We'll review the need for basic dialogs such as alert dialogs, and show you how to create and use them. We will then show you how to work with *prompt* dialogs—dialogs that ask the user for input and return that input to the program. We will also show you how to load your own view layouts into dialogs.

We will then address the managed nature of Android dialogs by exploring the protocol to create dialogs using callback functions in an activity. Finally, we will take the managed-dialog protocol that Android uses and abstract it out to make the asynchronous managed dialogs as seamless as possible. This abstraction might prove helpful to you in itself, and it will also give us an opportunity to explain the behind-the-scenes dialog architecture.

Designing an Alert Dialog

We will begin our exploration with alert dialogs. Alert dialogs commonly contain simple messages about validating forms or debugging. Consider the following debug example that you often find in HTML pages:

```
if (validate(field1) == false)
{
  //indicate that formatting is not valid through an alert dialog
  showAlert("What you have entered in field1 doesn't match required format");
  //set focus to the field
  //..and continue
}
```

You would likely program this dialog in JavaScript through the `alert` function, which displays a simple synchronous dialog box containing a message and an OK button. After the user clicks the OK button, the flow of the program continues. This dialog is considered modal as well as synchronous because the next line of code will not be executed until the `alert` function returns.

This type of alert dialog proves useful for debugging. But Android offers no such direct function or dialog. Instead, it supports an alert-dialog builder, a general-purpose facility for constructing and working with alert dialogs. So you can build an alert dialog yourself using the `android.app.AlertDialog.Builder` class. You can use this builder class to construct dialogs that allow users to perform the following tasks:

- Read a message and respond with Yes or No

- Pick an item from a list

- Pick multiple items from a list

- View the progress of an application

- Choose an option from a set of options

- Respond to a prompt before continuing the program

We will show you how to build one of these dialogs and invoke that dialog from a menu item. This approach, which applies to any of these dialogs, consists of these steps:

1. Construct a `Builder` object.

2. Set parameters for the display such as the number of buttons, the list of items, and so on.

3. Set the callback methods for the buttons.

4. Tell the `Builder` to build the dialog. The type of dialog that's built depends on what you've set on the `Builder` object.

5. Use `dialog.show()` to show the dialog.

Listing 5-21 shows the code that implements these steps.

Listing 5-21. *Building and Displaying an Alert Dialog*

```
public class Alerts
{
    public static void showAlert(String message, Context ctx)
    {
        //Create a builder
        AlertDialog.Builder builder = new AlertDialog.Builder(ctx);
        builder.setTitle("Alert Window");

        //add buttons and listener
        PromptListener pl = new EmptyListener();
        builder.setPositiveButton("OK", pl);

        //Create the dialog
        AlertDialog ad = builder.create();

        //show
        ad.show();
    }
}

public class EmptyListener
implements android.content.DialogInterface.OnClickListener {
    public void onClick(DialogInterface v, int buttonId)
    {
    }
}
```

You can invoke the code in Listing 5-21 by creating a menu item in your test harness and responding to it using this code:

```
if (item.getItemId() == R.id.menu_simple_alert)
{
    Alerts.showAlert("Simple Sample Alert", this);
}
```

The result will look like the screen shown in Figure 5-4.

The code for this simple alert dialog is straightforward (see Listing 5-21 and the code snippet that appears after it). Even the listener part is easy to understand. Essentially, we have nothing to perform when the button is clicked. We just created an empty listener to register against the OK button. The only odd part is that you don't do a new to create the dialog; instead, you set parameters and ask the alert-dialog builder to create it.

Figure 5-4. *A simple alert dialog*

Designing a Prompt Dialog

Now that you've successfully created a simple alert dialog, let's tackle an alert dialog that's a little more complex: the *prompt* dialog. Another JavaScript staple, the prompt dialog shows the user a hint or question and asks for input via an edit box. The prompt dialog returns that string to the program so it can continue. This will be a good example to study because it features a number of facilities provided by the `Builder` class and also allows us to examine the synchronous, asynchronous, modal, and nonmodal nature of Android dialogs.

Here are the steps you need to take in order to create a prompt dialog:

1. Come up with a layout view for your prompt dialog.

2. Load the layout into a `View` class.

3. Construct a `Builder` object.

4. Set the view in the `Builder` object.

5. Set the buttons along with their callbacks to capture the entered text.

6. Create the dialog using the alert-dialog builder.

7. Show the dialog.

Now we'll show you the code for each step.

XML Layout File for the Prompt Dialog

When we show the prompt dialog, we need to show a prompt TextView followed by an edit box where a user can type a reply. Listing 5-22 contains the XML layout file for the prompt dialog. If you call this file prompt_layout.xml, then you need to place it in the /res/layout subdirectory to produce a resource ID called R.layout.prompt_layout.

Listing 5-22. *The prompt_layout.xml File*

```xml
<LinearLayout xmlns:android="http://schemas.android.com/apk/res/android"
    android:layout_width="fill_parent"
    android:layout_height="wrap_content"
    android:orientation="vertical">

    <TextView
        android:id="@+id/promptmessage"
        android:layout_height="wrap_content"
        android:layout_width="wrap_content"
        android:layout_marginLeft="20dip"
        android:layout_marginRight="20dip"
        android:text="Your text goes here"
        android:gravity="left"
        android:textAppearance="?android:attr/textAppearanceMedium" />

    <EditText
        android:id="@+id/editText_prompt"
        android:layout_height="wrap_content"
        android:layout_width="fill_parent"
        android:layout_marginLeft="20dip"
        android:layout_marginRight="20dip"
        android:scrollHorizontally="true"
        android:autoText="false"
        android:capitalize="none"
        android:gravity="fill_horizontal"
        android:textAppearance="?android:attr/textAppearanceMedium" />

</LinearLayout>
```

Setting Up an Alert-Dialog Builder with a User View

Let's combine steps 2 through 4 from our instructions to create a prompt dialog: loading the XML view and setting it up in the alert-dialog builder. Android provides a class called android.view.LayoutInflater to create a View object from an XML layout definition file. We will use an instance of the LayoutInflater to populate the view for our dialog based on the XML layout file (see Listing 5-23).

Listing 5-23. *Inflating a Layout into a Dialog*

```
LayoutInflater li = LayoutInflater.from(ctx);
View view = li.inflate(R.layout.promptdialog, null);

//get a builder and set the view
AlertDialog.Builder builder = new AlertDialog.Builder(ctx);
builder.setTitle("Prompt");
builder.setView(view);
```

In Listing 5-23, we get the LayoutInflater using the static method LayoutInflater. from(ctx) and then use the LayoutInflater object to inflate the XML to create a View object. We then configure an alert-dialog builder with a title and the view that we just created.

Setting Up Buttons and Listeners

We now move on to step 5: setting up buttons. You need to provide OK and Cancel buttons so the user can respond to the prompt. If the user clicks Cancel, then the program doesn't need to read any text for the prompt. If the user clicks OK, the program gets the value from the text and passes it back to the activity.

To set up these buttons, you need a listener to respond to these callbacks. We will give you the code for the listener in the "Prompt Dialog Listener" section, but first examine the button setup in Listing 5-24.

Listing 5-24. *Setting Up OK and Cancel Buttons*

```
//add buttons and listener
PromptListener pl = new PromptListener(view,ctx);
builder.setPositiveButton("OK", pl);
builder.setNegativeButton("Cancel", pl);
```

The code in Listing 5-24 assumes that the name of the listener class is PromptListener. We have registered this listener against each button.

Creating and Showing the Prompt Dialog

Finally, we finish up with steps 6 and 7: creating and showing the prompt dialog. That's easy to do once you have the alert-dialog builder (see Listing 5-25).

Listing 5-25. *Telling the Alert-Dialog Builder to Create the Dialog*

```
//get the dialog
AlertDialog ad = builder.create();
ad.show();

//return the prompt
return pl.getPromptReply();
```

The last line uses the listener to return the reply for the prompt. Now, as promised, we'll show you the code for the PromptListener class.

Prompt Dialog Listener

The prompt dialog interacts with an activity through a listener callback class called
PromptListener. The class has one callback method called onClick, and the button ID that is
passed to onClick identifies what type of button is clicked. The rest of the code is easy to follow
(see Listing 5-26). When the user enters text and clicks the OK button, the value of the text is
transferred to the promptReply field. Otherwise, the value stays null.

Listing 5-26. *PromptListener, the Listener Callback Class*

```java
public class PromptListener
implements android.content.DialogInterface.OnClickListener
{
    // local variable to return the prompt reply value
    private String promptReply = null;

    //Keep a variable for the view to retrieve the prompt value
    View promptDialogView = null;

    //Take in the view in the constructor
    public PromptListener(View inDialogView)   {
        promptDialogView = inDialogView;
    }

//Call back method from dialogs
    public void onClick(DialogInterface v, int buttonId)   {
        if (buttonId == DialogInterface.BUTTON1)       {
            //ok button
            promptReply = getPromptText();
        }
        else     {
            //cancel button
            promptValue = null;
        }
    }

    //Just an access method for what is in the edit box
    private String getPromptText()   {
        EditText et =  (EditText)
        promptDialogView.findViewById(R.id.promptEditTextControlId);
        return et.getText().toString();
    }
    public String getPromptReply() { return promptReply; }
}
```

Putting It All Together

Now that we have explained each piece of code that goes into a prompt dialog, we'll present it in one place so you can use it to test the dialog (see Listing 5-27). We have excluded the PromptListener class because it appears separately in Listing 5-26.

Listing 5-27. *Code to Test the Prompt Dialog*

```
public class Alerts
{
    public static String prompt(String message, Context ctx)
    {
        //load some kind of a view
        LayoutInflater li = LayoutInflater.from(ctx);
        View view = li.inflate(R.layout.promptdialog, null);

        //get a builder and set the view
        AlertDialog.Builder builder = new AlertDialog.Builder(ctx);
        builder.setTitle("Prompt");
        builder.setView(view);

        //add buttons and listener
        PromptListener pl = new PromptListener(view,ctx);
        builder.setPositiveButton("OK", pl);
        builder.setNegativeButton("Cancel", pl);

        //get the dialog
        AlertDialog ad = builder.create();

        //show
        ad.show();

        return pl.getPromptReply();
    }
}
```

You can invoke the code in Listing 5-27 by creating a menu item in the test harness described at the beginning of this chapter and responding to that menu item using this code:

```
if (item.getItemId() == R.id.menu_simple_alert)
{
    String  reply = Alerts.showPrompt("Your text goes here", this);
}
```

The result should look like the screen shown in Figure 5-5.

Figure 5-5. *A simple prompt dialog*

After writing all this code, however, you will notice that the prompt dialog always returns null even if the user enters text into it. As it turns out, in the following code

```
ad.show() //dialog.show
return pl.getPromptReply(); // listener.getpromptReply()
```

the show() method will invoke the dialog asynchronously. This means the getPromptReply() method gets called for the prompt value before the user has time to enter text and click the OK button. This fallacy takes us to the heart of the nature of Android dialogs.

Nature of Dialogs in Android

As we've mentioned, displaying dialogs in Android is an asynchronous process. Once a dialog is shown, the main thread that invoked the dialog returns and continues to process the rest of the code. This doesn't mean that the dialog isn't *modal*. The dialog is still modal. The mouse clicks apply only to the dialog, while the parent activity goes back to its message loop.

On some windowing systems, modal dialogs behave a bit differently. The caller is blocked until the user provides a response through the dialog. (This block can be a virtual block instead of a real block.) On the Windows operating system, the message-dispatching thread starts dispatching to the dialog and suspends dispatching to the parent window. When the dialog closes, the thread returns to the parent window. This makes the call synchronous.

Such an approach might not work for a handheld device, where unexpected events on the device are more frequent and the main thread needs to respond to those events. To accomplish this level of responsiveness, Android returns the main thread to its message loop right away.

The implication of this model is that you cannot have a simple dialog where you ask for a response and wait for it before moving on. In fact, your programming model for dialogs must differ in its incorporation of callbacks.

Rearchitecting the Prompt Dialog

Let us revisit the problematic code in the previous prompt-dialog implementation:

```
if (item.getItemId() == R.id.menu_simple_alert)
{
    String  reply = Alerts.showPrompt("Your text goes here", this);
}
```

As we have proved through the discussion, the value of the string variable reply will be null, because the prompt dialog initiated by Alerts.showPrompt() is incapable of returning a value on the same thread. The only way you can accomplish this is to have the activity implement the callback method directly and not rely on the PromptListener class. Get this done in the Activity class by implementing the OnClickListener:

```
public class SampleActivity extends Activity
implements android.content.DialogInterface.OnClickListener
{
…… other code

if (item.getItemId() == R.id.menu_simple_alert)
{
    Alerts.showPrompt("Your text goes here", this);
}
…..
public void onClick(DialogInterface v, int buttonId)
{
        //figure out a way here to read the reply string from the dialog
}
```

As you can see from this onClick callback method, you can correctly read the variables from the instantiated dialog because the user will have closed the dialog by the time this method is called.

It is perfectly legitimate to use dialogs this way. However, Android provides a supplemental mechanism to optimize performance by introducing *managed dialogs*—dialogs that are reused between multiple invocations. You'll still need to use callbacks when you work with managed dialogs, though. In fact, everything you've learned in implementing the prompt dialog will help you work with managed dialogs and understand the motivation behind them.

Working with Managed Dialogs

Android follows a managed-dialog protocol to promote the reuse of previously created dialog instances rather than create new dialogs in response to actions. In this section, we will talk about the details of the managed-dialog protocol and show you how to implement the alert dialog as a managed dialog. However, in our view, the managed-dialog protocol makes using dialogs tedious. We will subsequently develop a small framework to abstract out most of this protocol to make it easier to work with managed dialogs.

Understanding the Managed-Dialog Protocol

The primary goal of the managed-dialog protocol is to reuse a dialog if it's invoked a second time. It is similar to using object pools in Java. The managed-dialog protocol consists of these steps:

1. Assign a unique ID to each dialog you want to create and use. Suppose one of the dialogs is tagged as 1.

2. Tell Android to show a dialog called 1.

3. Android checks whether the current activity already has a dialog tagged as 1. If the dialog exists, Android shows it without re-creating it. Android calls the onPrepareDialog() function before showing the dialog, for cleanup purposes.

4. If the dialog doesn't exist, Android calls the onCreateDialog method by passing the dialog ID (1, in this case).

5. You, as the programmer, need to override the onCreateDialog method. You must create the dialog using the alert-dialog builder and return it. But before creating the dialog, your code needs to determine which dialog ID needs to be created. You'll need a switch statement to figure this out.

6. Android shows the dialog.

7. The dialog calls the callbacks when its buttons are clicked.

Let's now use this protocol to reimplement our nonmanaged alert dialog as a managed alert dialog.

Recasting the Nonmanaged Dialog as a Managed Dialog

We will follow each of the steps laid out to reimplement the alert dialog. Let's start by defining a unique ID for this dialog in the context of a given activity:

```
//unique dialog id
private static final int DIALOG_ALERT_ID = 1;
```

That is simple enough. We have just created an ID to represent a dialog to orchestrate the callbacks. This ID will allow us to do the following in response to a menu item:

```
 if (item.getItemId() == R.id.menu_simple_alert)
{
     showDialog(this.DIALOG_ALERT_ID);
}
```

The Android SDK method showDialog triggers a call to the onCreateDialog() method. Android is smart enough not to call onCreateDialog() multiple times. When this method is called, we need to create the dialog and return it to Android. Android then keeps the created dialog internally for reuse purposes. Here is the sample code to create the dialog based on a unique ID:

```
@Override
protected Dialog onCreateDialog(int id) {
    switch (id) {
        case DIALOG_ALERT_ID:
            return createAlertDialog();
    }
    return null;
}

private Dialog createAlertDialog()
{
    AlertDialog.Builder builder = new AlertDialog.Builder(this);
    builder.setTitle("Alert");
    builder.setMessage("some message");
    EmptyOnClickListener emptyListener = new EmptyOnClickListener();
    builder.setPositiveButton("Ok", emptyListener );
    AlertDialog ad = builder.create();
    return ad;
}
```

Notice how onCreateDialog() has to figure out the incoming ID to identify a matching dialog. createAlertDialog() itself is kept in a separate function and parallels the alert-dialog creation described in the previous sections. This code also uses the same EmptyOnClickListener that was used when we worked with the alert dialog.

Because the dialog is created only once, you need a mechanism if you want to change something in the dialog every time you show it. You do this through the onPrepareDialog() callback method:

```
@Override
protected void onPrepareDialog(int id, Dialog dialog) {
    switch (id) {
    case DIALOG_ALERT_ID:
        prepareAlertDialog(dialog);
    }
}

private void prepareAlertDialog(Dialog d)    {
    AlertDialog ad = (AlertDialog)d;
    //change something about this dialog
}
```

With this code in place, showDialog(1) will work. Even if you were to invoke this method multiple times, your onCreateMethod will get called only once. You can follow the same protocol to redo the prompt dialog.

So responding to dialog callbacks is work, but the managed-dialog protocol adds even more work. After looking at the managed-dialog protocol, we got the idea to abstract out the protocol and rearrange it in such a way that it accomplishes two goals:

- Moving the dialog identification and creation out of the activity class
- Concentrating the dialog creation and response in a dedicated dialog class

In the next subsection, we will go through the design of this framework and then use it to re-create both the alert and prompt dialogs.

Simplifying the Managed-Dialog Protocol

As you've probably noticed, working with managed alert dialogs can become quite messy and can pollute the mainline code. If we abstract out this protocol into a simpler protocol, the new protocol could look like this:

1. Create an instance of a dialog you want by using new and keeping it as a local variable. Call this dialog1.

2. Show the dialog using dialog1.show().

3. Implement one method in the activity called dialogFinished().

4. In the dialogFinished() method, read attributes from dialog1 such as dialog1. getValue1().

Under this scheme, showing a managed alert dialog will look like this:

```
….class MyActivity ….
{
    //new dialog
    ManagedAlertDialog  mad = new ManagedAlertDialog("message", …, .. );

    ….some menu method
    if (item.getItemId() == R.id.menu_simple_alert)
    {
        //show dialog
        mad.show();
    }
    …..
    //access the mad dialog for internals if you want
    dialogFinsihed()
    {
        ….
        //use values from dialog
        mad.getA();
        mad.getB();
    }
}
```

We would like to think this is a far simpler model to work with dialogs. You don't have to remember IDs, you don't have to pollute the mainline code with dialog creation, and you can use derived dialog objects directly to access values.

The principle of this abstraction is as follows. As a first step, we abstract out the creation of a dialog and the preparation of that dialog into a class that identifies a base dialog. We call this interface IDialogProtocol. This dialog also has a show() method on it directly. These dialogs are collected and kept in a registry in the base class for an activity, and they use their IDs as keys. The base activity will de-multiplex the onCreate, onPrepare, and onClick calls based on their IDs and reroute them to the dialog class. This architecture is further illustrated in Figure 5-6.

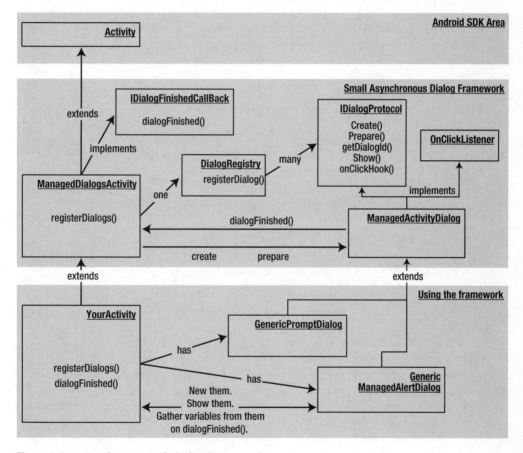

Figure 5-6. *A simple managed-dialog framework*

Listing 5-28 illustrates the utility of this framework.

Listing 5-28. *The Abstraction of the Managed-Dialog Protocol*

```
public class MainActivity extends ManagedDialogsActivity
{
    //dialog 1
    private GenericManagedAlertDialog gmad =
        new GenericManagedAlertDialog(this,1,"InitialValue");

    //dialog 2
    private GenericPromptDialog gmpd =
        new GenericPromptDialog(this,2,"InitialValue");

    //menu items to start the dialogs
    else if (item.getItemId() == R.id.menu_simple_alert)
    {
        gmad.show();
    }
    else if (item.getItemId() == R.id.menu_simple_prompt)
    {
        gmpd.show();
    }

    //dealing with call backs
    public void dialogFinished(ManagedActivityDialog dialog, int buttonId)
    {
        if (dialog.getDialogId() == gmpd.getDialogId())
        {
            String replyString = gmpd.getReplyString();
        }
    }
}
```

To make use of this framework, you start by extending ManagedDialogsActivity. Then you instantiate the dialogs you need, each of which derives from ManagedActivityDialog. In a menu-item response, you can simply do a show() on these dialogs. The dialogs themselves take the necessary parameters up front in order to be created and shown. Although we are passing a dialog ID, we don't need to remember those IDs anymore. You could even abstract these IDs out completely if you'd like.

Now we'll explore each of the classes shown in Figure 5-6.

IDialogProtocol

The IDialogProtocol interface defines what it means to be a managed dialog. Responsibilities of a managed dialog include creating the dialog and preparing it every time it is shown. It also makes sense to delegate the show functionality to the dialog itself. A dialog also must recognize button clicks and call the respective parent of the dialog closure. The following interface code represents these ideas as a set of functions:

```
public interface IDialogProtocol
{
    public Dialog create();
    public void prepare(Dialog dialog);
    public int getDialogId();
    public void show();
    public void onClickHook(int buttonId);
}
```

ManagedActivityDialog

The abstract class ManagedActivityDialog provides the common implementation for all the dialog classes wanting to implement the IDialogProtocol interface. It leaves the create and prepare functions to be overridden by the base classes, but provides implementations for the rest of the IDialogProtocol methods. ManagedActivityDialog also informs the parent activity that the dialog has finished after responding to a button-click event. It uses the template-hook pattern and allows the derived classes to specialize the hook method onClickHook. This class is also responsible for redirecting the show() method to the parent activity, thereby providing a more natural implementation for show(). You should use the ManagedActivityDialog class as the base class for all your new dialogs (see Listing 5-29).

Listing 5-29. *The ManagedActivityDialog Class*

```
public abstract class ManagedActivityDialog implements IDialogProtocol
    ,android.content.DialogInterface.OnClickListener

{
    private ManagedDialogsActivity mActivity;
    private int mDialogId;
    public ManagedActivityDialog(ManagedDialogsActivity a, int dialogId)
    {
        mActivity = a;
        mDialogId = dialogId;
    }
    public int getDialogId()
    {
        return mDialogId;
    }
    public void show()
    {
        mActivity.showDialog(mDialogId);
    }
    public void onClick(DialogInterface v, int buttonId)
    {
        onClickHook(buttonId);
        this.mActivity.dialogFinished(this, buttonId);
    }
}
}
```

DialogRegistry

The DialogRegistry class is responsible for two things. It keeps a mapping between the dialog IDs and the actual dialog (factory) instances. It also translates the generic onCreate and onPrepare calls to the specific dialogs using the ID-to-object mapping. The ManagedDialogsActivity uses the DialogRegistry class as a repository to register new dialogs (see Listing 5-30).

Listing 5-30. *The DialogRegistry Class*

```
public class DialogRegistry
{
    SparseArray<IDialogProtocol> idsToDialogs
                                                   = new SparseArray();

    public void registerDialog(IDialogProtocol dialog)
    {
        idsToDialogs.put(dialog.getDialogId(),dialog);
    }

    public Dialog create(int id)
    {
        IDialogProtocol dp = idsToDialogs.get(id);
        if (dp == null) return null;

        return dp.create();
    }
    public void prepare(Dialog dialog, int id)
    {
        IDialogProtocol dp = idsToDialogs.get(id);
        if (dp == null)
        {
            throw new RuntimeException("Dialog id is not registered:" + id);
        }
        dp.prepare(dialog);
    }
}
```

ManagedDialogsActivity

The ManagedDialogsActivity class acts as a base class for your activities that support managed dialogs. It keeps a single instance of DialogRegistry to keep track of the managed dialogs identified by the IDialogProtocol interface. It allows the derived activities to register their dialogs through the registerDialogs() function. As shown in Figure 5-6, it is also responsible for transferring the create and prepare semantics to the respective dialog instance by locating that dialog instance in the dialog registry. Finally, it provides the callback method dialogFinished for each dialog in the dialog registry (see Listing 5-31).

Listing 5-31. *The ManagedDialogsActivity Class*

```java
public class ManagedDialogsActivity extends Activity
            implements IDialogFinishedCallBack
{
   //A registry for managed dialogs
    private DialogRegistry dr = new DialogRegistry();

   public void onCreate(Bundle savedInstanceState) {
       super.onCreate(savedInstanceState);
       this.registerDialogs();
   }

   protected void registerDialogs()
   {
       // does nothing
       // have the derived classes override this method
       // to register their dialogs
       // example:
       // registerDialog(this.DIALOG_ALERT_ID_3, gmad);

   }
   public void registerDialog(IDialogProtocol dialog)
   {
       this.dr.registerDialog(dialog);
   }

   @Override
   protected Dialog onCreateDialog(int id) {
             return this.dr.create(id);
   }
   @Override
   protected void onPrepareDialog(int id, Dialog dialog) {
             this.dr.prepare(dialog, id);
   }

   public void dialogFinished(ManagedActivityDialog dialog, int buttonId)
   {
       //nothing to do
       //have derived classes override this
   }
}
```

IDialogFinishedCallBack

The IDialogFinishedCallBack interface allows the ManagedActivityDialog class to tell the parent activity that the dialog has finished and that the parent activity can call methods on the dialog to retrieve parameters. Usually a ManagedDialogsActivity implements this interface and acts as a parent activity to the ManagedActivityDialog (see Listing 5-32).

Listing 5-32. *The IDialogFinishedCallBack Interface*

```
public interface IDialogFinishedCallBack
{
    public static int OK_BUTTON = -1;
    public static int CANCEL_BUTTON = -2;
    public void dialogFinished(ManagedActivityDialog dialog, int buttonId);
}
```

GenericManagedAlertDialog

GenericManagedAlertDialog is the alert-dialog implementation; it extends
ManagedActivityDialog. This class is responsible for creating the actual alert dialog
using the alert-dialog builder. It also carries all the information it needs as local variables.
Because GenericManagedAlertDialog implements a simple alert dialog, it does nothing in
the onClickHook method. The key thing to note is that when you use this approach,
GenericManagedAlertDialog encapsulates all pertinent information in one place (see
Listing 5-33). That keeps the mainline code in the activity squeaky-clean.

Listing 5-33. *The GenericManagedAlertDialog Class*

```
public class GenericManagedAlertDialog extends ManagedActivityDialog
{
    private String alertMessage = null;
    private Context ctx = null;
    public GenericManagedAlertDialog(ManagedDialogsActivity inActivity,
                            int dialogId,
                            String initialMessage)
    {
        super(inActivity,dialogId);
        alertMessage = initialMessage;
        ctx = inActivity;
    }
    public Dialog create()
    {
        AlertDialog.Builder builder = new AlertDialog.Builder(ctx);
        builder.setTitle("Alert");
        builder.setMessage(alertMessage);
        builder.setPositiveButton("Ok", this );
        AlertDialog ad = builder.create();
        return ad;
    }

    public void prepare(Dialog dialog)
    {
        AlertDialog ad = (AlertDialog)dialog;
        ad.setMessage(alertMessage);
    }
```

```
   public void setAlertMessage(String inAlertMessage)
   {
      alertMessage = inAlertMessage;
   }
   public void onClickHook(int buttonId)
   {
      //nothing to do
      //no local variables to set
   }
}
```

GenericPromptDialog

The GenericPromptDialog class encapsulates all the needs of a prompt dialog by extending the ManagedActivityDialog class and providing the necessary create and prepare methods (see Listing 5-34). You can also see that it saves the reply text in a local variable so that the parent activity can get to it in the dialogFinished callback method.

Listing 5-34. *The GenericPromptDialog Class*

```
public class GenericPromptDialog extends ManagedActivityDialog
{
   private String mPromptMessage = null;
   private View promptView = null;
   String promptValue = null;

   private Context ctx = null;
   public GenericPromptDialog(ManagedDialogsActivity inActivity,
         int dialogId,
         String promptMessage)
   {
      super(inActivity,dialogId);
      mPromptMessage = promptMessage;
      ctx = inActivity;
   }
   public Dialog create()
   {
       LayoutInflater li = LayoutInflater.from(ctx);
       promptView = li.inflate(R.layout.promptdialog, null);
       AlertDialog.Builder builder = new AlertDialog.Builder(ctx);
       builder.setTitle("prompt");
       builder.setView(promptView);
       builder.setPositiveButton("OK", this);
       builder.setNegativeButton("Cancel", this);
       AlertDialog ad = builder.create();
       return ad;
   }
```

```java
    public void prepare(Dialog dialog)
    {
        //nothing for now
    }
    public void onClickHook(int buttonId)
    {
        if (buttonId == DialogInterface.BUTTON1)
        {
            //ok button
            String promptValue = getEnteredText();
        }
    }
    private String getEnteredText()
    {
        EditText et =
            (EditText)
            promptView.findViewById(R.id.editText_prompt);
        String enteredText = et.getText().toString();
        Log.d("xx",enteredText);
        return enteredText;
    }
}
```

Summary

You now have a thorough understanding of Android menus and dialogs, which are key components of UI programming. You learned how to work with the various kinds of menus available in Android, including submenus, icon menus, context menus, and alternative menus. You also saw how to work with menus more effectively by using XML menu resources.

We presented a test harness for the menus, which you'll find useful not only for testing menus but also for testing other programs you end up writing. Menus provide a simple way to invoke and test new functionality.

You also saw that dialogs present a special challenge in Android. We showed you the implications of asynchronous dialogs and presented an abstraction to simplify the managed dialogs.

The knowledge you gained in this chapter and in the previous chapter on UI controls should give you a good foundation for writing your own complex UI programs. This foundation should also serve you well in preparation for the next chapter on animation.

CHAPTER 6

■■■

Unveiling 2D Animation

The previous chapters should've given you a solid introduction to UI programming in Android. In this chapter, we would like to further strengthen your ability to create intuitive and appealing applications on the Android Platform by covering the animation capabilities of the Android SDK. If our experience is any guide, we assert that animation brings a lot of fun to the staid, unanimated world of programming.

Animation is a process by which an object on a screen changes its color, position, size, or orientation over time. Android supports three types of animation: *frame-by-frame animation*, which occurs when a series of frames is drawn one after the other at regular intervals; *layout animation*, in which you animate views inside a container view such as lists and tables; and *view animation*, in which you animate any general-purpose view. The latter two types fall into the category of *tweening animation*, which involves the drawings in between the key drawings. You accomplish this kind of animation by changing the intermediate values at regular intervals and redrawing the surface. We will cover each type of animation using working examples and in-depth analysis.

Frame-by-frame animation is the simplest of the three animation types, so we'll cover that one in this chapter's first section. We'll show you how it works, how to tell a story using it, and how to use the `AnimationDrawable` class to execute the frames at a certain refresh rate. We will present an example, with screenshots and code, in which you'll animate an image of a ball moving along the circumference of a circle.

In the second section we'll cover layout animation, which is more involved than frame-by-frame animation but still easier than view animation. We will talk about scale animation (changing size), translate animation (changing position), rotate animation (changing orientation), and alpha animation (changing a color gradient). We will show you how to declare these animations in an XML file and associate the animation IDs with a container view such as a list box. As an example, you'll apply a variety of animation transformations to a series of text items in a list box. We will also cover interpolators, which define an animation's rate of change, and animation sets, which contain an aggregated set of individual animations.

In the last section on view animation, we will cover animating a view by changing the transformation matrices. You'll need a good understanding of transformation matrices to grasp the material in this section, so we'll provide several examples to illustrate their behavior. Android also introduces the idea of a `Camera` to simulate 3D-like viewing capabilities by projecting a 2D view moving in 3D space. This section will illustrate both of these ideas by taking a `ListView` and rotating it in 3D space.

Frame-by-Frame Animation

Frame-by-frame animation is the simple process of showing a series of images in succession at quick intervals so that the end effect is that of an object moving. This is how movie or film projectors work. We'll explore an example in which we'll design an image and save that image as a number of distinct images, where each one differs from the other slightly. Then we will take the collection of those images and run them through the sample code to simulate animation.

Planning for Frame-by-Frame Animation

Before you start writing code, you first need to plan the animation sequence using a series of drawings. As an example of this planning exercise, Figure 6-1 shows a set of same-sized circles with a colored ball on each of the circles placed at a different position. You can take a series of these pictures showing the circle at the same size and position but the colored ball at different points along the circle's border. Once you save seven or eight of these frames, you can use animation to show that the colored ball is moving around the circle.

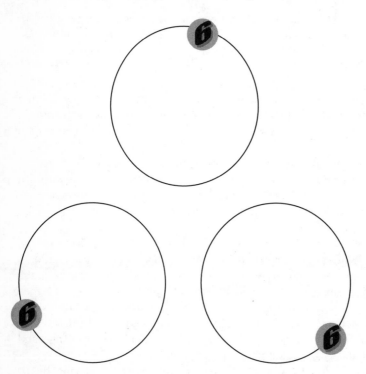

Figure 6-1. *Designing your animation before coding it*

Give the image a base name of colored-ball. Then you can store eight of these images in the /res/drawable subdirectory so that you can access them using their resource IDs. The name of each image will have the pattern colored-ball-N, where N is the digit representing the image number. When you are finished with the animation, you want it to look like Figure 6-2.

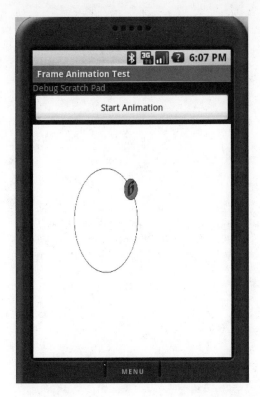

Figure 6-2. *Frame-by-frame animation test harness*

The primary area in this activity is used by the animation view. We have included a button to start and stop the animation to observe its behavior. We have also included a debug scratch pad at the top, so you can write any significant events to it as you experiment with this program.

Creating the Activity

Start by creating the basic XML layout file for our test-animation activity screen (see Listing 6-1).

Listing 6-1. *XML Layout File for the Animation Test Harness*

```
<?xml version="1.0" encoding="utf-8"?>
<!-filename: /res/layout/frame_animations_layout.xml -->
<LinearLayout xmlns:android="http://schemas.android.com/apk/res/android"
    android:orientation="vertical"
    android:layout_width="fill_parent"
    android:layout_height="fill_parent"
    >
<TextView android:id="@+id/textViewId1"
    android:layout_width="fill_parent"
    android:layout_height="wrap_content"
    android:text="Debug Scratch Pad"
    />
```

```xml
<Button
    android:id="@+id/startFAButtonId"
    android:layout_width="fill_parent"
    android:layout_height="wrap_content"
    android:text="Start Animation"
/>
<ImageView
        android:id="@+id/animationImage"
        android:layout_width="fill_parent"
        android:layout_height="wrap_content"
        />
</LinearLayout>
```

The first control is the debug-scratch text control, which is a simple TextView. You then add a button to start and stop the animation. The last view is the ImageView, where you will play the animation. Once you have the layout, create an activity to load this view (see Listing 6-2).

Listing 6-2. *Activity to Load the ImageView*

```java
public class FrameAnimationActivity extends Activity
{
    @Override
    public void onCreate(Bundle savedInstanceState)
    {
        super.onCreate(savedInstanceState);
        setContentView(R.layout.frame_animations_layout);
    }
}
```

You will be able to run this activity from any menu item you might have in your current application by executing the following code:

```java
Intent intent = new Intent(inActivity,FrameAnimationActivity.class);
inActivity.startActivity(intent);
```

At this point, you will see an activity that looks like the one in Figure 6-3.

Figure 6-3. *Frame-by-frame animation activity*

Adding Animation to the Activity

Now that you have the activity and layout in place, we'll show you how to add animation to this sample. In Android, you accomplish frame-by-frame animation through a class in the graphics package called `AnimationDrawable`. This class can take a list of `Drawable` resources (like images) and render them at specified intervals. This class is really a thin wrapper around the animation support provided by the basic `Drawable` class.

The `Drawable` class enables animation by asking its container or view to invoke a `Runnable` class that essentially redraws the `Drawable` using a different set of parameters. Note that you don't need to know these internal implementation details to use the `AnimationDrawable` class. But if your needs are more complex, you can look at the `AnimationDrawable` source code for guidance in writing your own animation protocols.

To make use of the `AnimationDrawable` class, start with a set of `Drawable` resources placed in the `/res/drawable` subdirectory. You will then construct an XML file that defines the list of frames (see Listing 6-3).

Listing 6-3. *XML File Defining the List of Frames to be Animated*

```
<animation-list xmlns:android="http://schemas.android.com/apk/res/android"
        android:oneshot="false">
    <item android:drawable="@drawable/colored-ball1" android:duration="50" />
    <item android:drawable="@drawable/colored-ball2" android:duration="50" />
    <item android:drawable="@drawable/colored-ball3" android:duration="50" />
    <item android:drawable="@drawable/colored-ball4" android:duration="50" />
    <item android:drawable="@drawable/colored-ball5" android:duration="50" />
    <item android:drawable="@drawable/colored-ball6" android:duration="50" />
    <item android:drawable="@drawable/colored-ball7" android:duration="50" />
    <item android:drawable="@drawable/colored-ball8" android:duration="50" />
</animation-list>
```

Each frame points to one of the colored-ball images you have assembled through their resource IDs. The animation-list tag essentially gets converted into an AnimationDrawable object representing the collection of images. You will then need to set this Drawable as a background resource for our ImageView in the sample. Assuming that the file name for this XML file is frame_animation.xml and that it resides in the /res/drawable subdirectory, you can use the following code to set the AnimationDrawable as the background of the ImageView:

```
view.setBackGroundResource(Resource.drawable.frame_animation);
```

With this code, Android realizes that the resource ID Resource.drawable.frame_animation is an XML resource and accordingly constructs a suitable AnimationDrawable Java object for it before setting it as the background. Once this is set, you can access this AnimationDrawable object by doing a get on the view object like this:

```
Object  backgroundObject = view.getBackground();
AnimationDrawable ad = (AnimationDrawable)backgroundObject;
```

Once you have the AnimationDrawable, you can use the start() and stop() methods of this object to start and stop the animation. Here are two other important methods on this object:

```
setOneShot();
addFrame(drawable, duration);
```

The setOneShot() method runs the animation once and then stops. The addFrame() method adds a new frame using a Drawable object and sets its display duration. The functionality of the addFrame() method resembles that of the XML tag android:drawable.

Put this all together to get the complete code for our frame-by-frame animation test harness (see Listing 6-4).

Listing 6-4. *Complete Code for the Frame-by-Frame Animation Test Harness*

```
public class FrameAnimationActivity extends Activity {
    @Override
    public void onCreate(Bundle savedInstanceState)
    {
        super.onCreate(savedInstanceState);
        setContentView(R.layout.frame_animations_layout);
        this.setupButton();
    }

    private void setupButton()
    {
        Button b = (Button)this.findViewById(R.id.startFAButtonId);
        b.setOnClickListener(
            new Button.OnClickListener(){
                public void onClick(View v)
                {
                    parentButtonClicked(v);
                }
            });
    }
    private void parentButtonClicked(View v)
    {
        animate();
    }
    private void animate()
    {
        ImageView imgView = (ImageView)findViewById(R.id.imageView);
        imgView.setVisibility(ImageView.VISIBLE);
        imgView.setBackgroundResource(R.drawable.frame_animation);

        AnimationDrawable frameAnimation =
            (AnimationDrawable) imgView.getBackground();

        if (frameAnimation.isRunning())
        {
            frameAnimation.stop();
        }
        else
        {
            frameAnimation.stop();
            frameAnimation.start();
        }
    }
}//eof-class
```

The animate() method locates the ImageView in the current activity and sets its background to the AnimationDrawable identified by the resource R.drawable.frame_animation. The code then retrieves this object and performs the animation. The start/stop button is set up such that if the animation is running, clicking the button will stop it; if the animation is in a stopped state, clicking the button will start it.

As a note, if you set the OneShot parameter of the animation list to true, then the animation will stop after executing once. However, there is no clear-cut way to know when that happens. Although the animation ends when it plays the last picture, you have no callback telling you when it finishes. Because of this, there isn't a direct way to invoke another action in response to the completed animation.

That drawback aside, you can bring great visual effects to bear by drawing a number of images in succession through the simple process of frame-by-frame animation.

Layout Animation

As you have seen, frame-by-frame animation is a quick and dirty way to add visual effects to your Android applications. Layout animation is almost as simple. You'll use layout animation with the ListView and GridView, which are the two most commonly used controls in Android. Specifically, you'll use layout animation to add visual effects to the way each item in a ListView or GridView is displayed. In fact, you can use this type of animation on all controls derived from a ViewGroup.

As we pointed out at the beginning of this chapter, layout animation works by applying *tweening* principles to each view that is part of the layout being animated. Tweening is a process in which a number of the view's properties are changed at regular intervals. Every view in Android has a matrix that maps the view to the screen. By changing this matrix in a number of ways, you can accomplish scaling, rotation, and movement (translation) of the view. By changing the transparency of the view from 0 to 1, for example, you can accomplish what is called an *alpha* animation.

In this section, we will offer a simple test harness to learn, test, and experiment with layout-animation capabilities. We will show you how to attach a tweening animation to a ListView. We will also introduce and explain the idea of interpolators and their role in animation. The SDK documentation on interpolators is a bit vague, so we will clarify interpolator behavior by showing you relevant source code. We will also cover something called a LayoutAnimationController that mediates between an animation and a ViewGroup.

Basic Tweening Animation Types

Before we design the test harness to apply the various tweening animations, we'll give you some detail on the basic types of tweening animation:

- *Scale animation*: You use this type of animation to make a view smaller or larger either on the x axis or on the y axis. You can also specify the pivot point around which you want the animation to take place.

- *Rotate animation*: You use this to rotate a view around a pivot point by a certain number of degrees.

- *Translate animation*: You use this to move a view along the x axis or the y axis.

- *Alpha animation*: You use this to change the transparency of a view.

All of the parameter values associated with these animations have a from and a to flavor because you must specify the starting values and ending values for when the animation starts and ends. Each animation also allows duration as an argument and a time interpolator as an argument. We'll cover interpolators at the end of this section on layout animation, but for now, know that interpolators determine the rate of change of the animated argument during animation.

You'll define these animations as XML files in the /res/anim subdirectory. You will see this amply illustrated in the test harness, but Listing 6-5 shows a quick sample to cement your understanding of how these animations are described.

Listing 6-5. *A Scale Animation Defined in an XML File at /res/anim/scale.xml*

```
<set xmlns:android="http://schemas.android.com/apk/res/android"
android:interpolator="@android:anim/accelerate_interpolator">
    <scale
        android:fromXScale="1"
        android:toXScale="1"
        android:fromYScale="0.1"
        android:toYScale="1.0"
        android:duration="500"
        android:pivotX="50%"
        android:pivotY="50%"
        android:startOffset="100" />
</set>
```

Once you have this file, you can associate this animation with a layout; this means that each view in the layout will go through this animation. The test harness goes through this process in much more detail, as you'll see shortly.

This is a good place to point out that each of these animations is represented as a Java class in the android.view.animation package. The Java documentation for each of these classes describes not only their Java methods, but also the allowed XML arguments for each type of animation.

Now that you have enough background on animation types to understand layout animation, let's proceed to the design of the layout-animation test harness.

Planning the Layout-Animation Test Harness

You can test all the layout-animation concepts we've covered using a simple ListView set in an activity. Once you have a ListView, you can attach an animation to it so that each list item will go through that animation.

Assume you have a scale animation that makes a view grow from 0 to its original size on the y axis. You can attach that animation to a ListView. When this happens, the ListView will animate each item in that list using this animation. You can set some additional parameters that extend the basic animation, such as animating the list from top to bottom or from bottom to top. You specify these parameters through an intermediate class that acts as a mediator between the individual animation and the list.

You can define both the individual animation and the mediator in XML files in the /res/anim subdirectory. Once you have the mediator XML file, you can use that file as an input to the ListView in its own XML layout definition. This will become clear to you when you see the code listings we'll provide in the rest of this section. Once you have this basic setup working, you can start altering the individual animations to see how they impact the ListView display.

Our examples will cover scale animation, translate animation, rotate animation, alpha animation, and a combination of translate and alpha animation. If this high-level plan seems a bit vague, just hang tight; by the end of this section, you will know what we are talking about.

Before we embark on this exercise, you should see what the ListView will look like after the animation completes (see Figure 6-4).

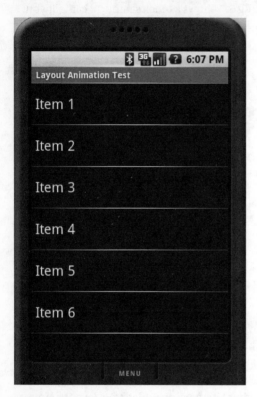

Figure 6-4. *The end result of animating the ListView*

Creating the Activity and the ListView

Start by creating an XML layout for the ListView in Figure 6-4 so you can load that layout in a basic activity. Listing 6-6 contains a simple layout with a ListView in it. You will need to place this file in the /res/layout subdirectory. Assuming the file name is list_layout.xml, your complete file will reside in /res/layout/list_layout.xml.

Listing 6-6. *XML Layout File Defining the ListView*

```xml
<?xml version="1.0" encoding="utf-8"?>
<!-- filename: /res/layout/list_layout.xml -->
<LinearLayout xmlns:android="http://schemas.android.com/apk/res/android"
    android:orientation="vertical"
    android:layout_width="fill_parent"
    android:layout_height="fill_parent"
    >

    <ListView
        android:id="@+id/list_view_id"
        android:layout_width="fill_parent"
        android:layout_height="fill_parent"
        />
</LinearLayout>
```

Listing 6-6 shows a simple LinearLayout with a single ListView in it. However, we should mention one point about the ListView definition. If you happen to work through the Notepad examples and other Android examples, you'll see that the ID for a ListView is usually specified as @android:id/list. As we discussed in Chapter 3, the resource reference @android:id/list points to an ID that is predefined in the android namespace. The question is, when do we use this android:id vs. our own ID such as @+id/list_view_id?

You will need to use @android:id/list only if the activity is a ListActivity. A ListActivity assumes that a ListView identified by this predetermined ID is available for loading. In this case, you're using a general-purpose activity rather than a ListActivity, and you are going to explicitly populate the ListView yourself. As a result, there are no restrictions on the kind of ID you can allocate to represent this ListView. However, you do have the option of also using @android:id/list because it doesn't conflict with anything as there is no ListActivity in sight.

This surely is a digression, but it's worth noting as you create your own ListViews outside a ListActivity. Now that you have the layout needed for the activity, you can write the code for the activity to load this layout file so you can generate your UI (see Listing 6-7).

Listing 6-7. *Code for the Layout-Animation Activity*

```java
public class LayoutAnimationActivity extends Activity
{
    @Override
    public void onCreate(Bundle savedInstanceState)
    {
        super.onCreate(savedInstanceState);
        setContentView(R.layout.list_layout);
        setupListView();
    }
}
```

```
private void setupListView()
{
      String[] listItems = new String[] {
            "Item 1", "Item 2", "Item 3",
            "Item 4", "Item 5", "Item 6",
      };

      ArrayAdapter listItemAdapter =
            new ArrayAdapter(this
                  ,android.R.layout.simple_list_item_1
                  ,listItems);
      ListView lv = (ListView)this.findViewById(R.id.list_view_id);
      lv.setAdapter(listItemAdapter);
}
}
```

Some of this code in Listing 6-7 is obvious, and some is not. The first part of the code simply loads the view based on the generated layout ID R.layout.list_layout. Our goal is to take the ListView from this layout and populate it with six text items. These text items are loaded up into an array. You'll need to set a data adapter into a ListView so that the ListView can show those items.

To create the necessary adapter, you will need to specify how each item will be laid out when the list is displayed. You specify the layout by using a predefined layout in the base Android framework. In this example, this layout is specified as

```
android.R.layout.simple_list_item_1
```

The other possible view layouts for these items include

```
simple_list_item_2
simple_list_item_checked
simple_list_item_multiple_choice
simple_list_item_single_choice
```

You can refer to the Android documentation to see how each of these layouts look and behave. You can now invoke this activity from any menu item in your application using the following code:

```
Intent intent = new Intent(inActivity,LayoutAnimationActivity.class);
inActivity.startActivity(intent);
```

However, as with any other activity invocation, you will need to register the LayoutAnimationActivity in the AndroidManifest.xml file for the preceding intent invocation to work. Here is the code for it:

```
<activity android:name=". LayoutAnimationActivity"
      android:label="View Animation Test Activity"/>
```

Animating the ListView

Now that you have the test harness ready (see Listings 6-6 and 6-7), you'll learn how to apply scale animation to this ListView. Take a look at how this scale animation is defined in an XML file (see Listing 6-8).

Listing 6-8. *Defining Scale Animation in an XML File*

```
<set xmlns:android="http://schemas.android.com/apk/res/android"
android:interpolator="@android:anim/accelerate_interpolator">
    <scale
            android:fromXScale="1"
            android:toXScale="1"
            android:fromYScale="0.1"
            android:toYScale="1.0"
            android:duration="500"
            android:pivotX="50%"
            android:pivotY="50%"
            android:startOffset="100" />
</set>
```

These animation-definition files reside in the /res/anim subdirectory. Let's break down these XML attributes into plain English. The from and to scales point to the starting and ending magnification factors. Here, the magnification starts at 1 and stays at 1 on the x axis. This means the list items will not grow or shrink on the x axis. On the y axis, however, the magnification starts at 0.1 and grows to 1.0. In other words, the object being animated starts at one-tenth of its normal size and then grows to reach its normal size. The scaling operation will take 500 milliseconds to complete. The center of action is halfway (50%) between x and y. The startOffset value refers to the number of milliseconds to wait before starting the animation.

The parent node of scale animation points to an animation set that could allow more than one animation to be in effect. We will cover one of those examples as well. But for now, there is only one animation in this set.

Name this file scale.xml and place it in the /res/anim subdirectory. You are not yet ready to set this animation XML as an argument to the ListView; the ListView first requires another XML file that acts as a mediator between itself and the animation set. The XML file that describes that mediation is shown in Listing 6-9.

Listing 6-9. *Definition for a Layout-Controller XML File*

```
<layoutAnimation xmlns:android="http://schemas.android.com/apk/res/android"
        android:delay="30%"
        android:animationOrder="reverse"
        android:animation="@anim/scale" />
```

You will also need to place this XML file in the /res/anim subdirectory. For our example, assume that the file name is list_layout_controller. Once you look at this definition, you can see why this intermediate file is necessary. This XML file specifies that the animation in the list should proceed in reverse, and that the animation for each item should start with a 30 percent delay with respect to the total animation duration. This XML file also refers to the individual animation file, scale.xml. Also notice that instead of the file name, the code uses the resource reference @anim/scale.

Now that you have the necessary XML input files, we'll show you how to update the ListView XML definition to include this animation XML as an argument. First, review the XML files you have so far:

```
// individual scale animation
/res/anim/scale.xml

// the animation mediator file
/res/anim/list_layout_controller.xml

// the activity view layout file
/res/layout/list_layout.xml
```

With these files in place, you need to modify the XML layout file list_layout.xml to have the ListView point to the list_layout_controller.xml file (see Listing 6-10).

Listing 6-10. *The Updated Code for the list_layout.xml File*

```
<?xml version="1.0" encoding="utf-8"?>
<LinearLayout xmlns:android="http://schemas.android.com/apk/res/android"
    android:orientation="vertical"
    android:layout_width="fill_parent"
    android:layout_height="fill_parent"
    >
    <ListView
        android:id="@+id/list_view_id"
        android:persistentDrawingCache="animation|scrolling"
        android:layout_width="fill_parent"
        android:layout_height="fill_parent"
        android:layoutAnimation="@anim/list_layout_controller" />
        />
</LinearLayout>
```

The changed lines are highlighted in bold. android:layoutAnimation is the key tag, which points to the mediating XML file that defines the layout controller using the XML tag layoutAnimation (see Listing 6-9). The layoutAnimation tag, in turn, points to the individual animation, which in this case is the scale animation defined in scale.xml. Android also recommends setting the persistentDrawingCache tag to optimize for animation and scrolling. Refer to the Android SDK documentation for more details on this tag.

When you update the list_layout.xml file as shown in Listing 6-10, Eclipse's ADT plug-in will automatically recompile the package taking this change into account. If you were to run the application now, you would see the scale animation take effect on the individual items. We have set the duration to 500 milliseconds so that you can observe the scale change clearly as each item is drawn.

Now you're in a position to experiment with different animation types. You'll try alpha animation next. To do this, create a file called /res/anim/alpha.xml and populate it with the content from Listing 6-11.

Listing 6-11. *The alpha.xml File to Test Alpha Animation*

```
<alpha xmlns:android="http://schemas.android.com/apk/res/android"
       android:interpolator="@android:anim/accelerate_interpolator"
       android:fromAlpha="0.0" android:toAlpha="1.0" android:duration="1000" />
```

Alpha animation is responsible for controlling the fading of color. In this example, you are asking the alpha animation to go from invisible to full color in 1000 milliseconds, or 1 second. Make sure the duration is 1 second or longer; otherwise, the color change is hard to notice.

Every time you want to change the animation of an individual item like this, you will need to change the mediator XML file (see Listing 6-9) to point to this new animation file. Here is how to change the animation from scale animation to alpha animation:

```
<layoutAnimation xmlns:android="http://schemas.android.com/apk/res/android"
       android:delay="30%"
       android:animationOrder="reverse"
       android:animation="@anim/alpha" />
```

The changed line in the layoutAnimation XML file is highlighted. Let us now try an animation that combines a change in position with a change in color gradient. Listing 6-12 shows the sample XML for this animation.

Listing 6-12. *Combining Translate and Alpha Animations Through an Animation Set*

```
<set xmlns:android="http://schemas.android.com/apk/res/android"
android:interpolator="@android:anim/accelerate_interpolator">
    <translate android:fromYDelta="-100%" android:toYDelta="0"
android:duration="500" />
    <alpha android:fromAlpha="0.0" android:toAlpha="1.0"
android:duration="500" />
</set>
```

Notice how we have specified two animations in the animation set. The translate animation will move the text from top to bottom in its currently allocated display space. The alpha animation will change the color gradient from invisible to visible as the text item descends into its slot. The duration setting of 500 will allow the user to perceive the change in a comfortable fashion. Of course, you will have to change the layoutAnimation mediator XML file again with a reference to this file name. Assuming the file name for this combined animation is /res/anim/translate-alpha.xml, your layoutAnimation XML file will look like this:

```
<layoutAnimation xmlns:android="http://schemas.android.com/apk/res/android"
       android:delay="30%"
       android:animationOrder="reverse"
       android:animation="@anim/translate-alpha" />
```

Let us see now how to use rotate animation (see Listing 6-13).

Listing 6-13. *Rotate Animation XML File*

```
<rotate xmlns:android="http://schemas.android.com/apk/res/android"
        android:interpolator="@android:anim/accelerate_interpolator"
        android:fromDegrees="0.0"
      android:toDegrees="360"
      android:pivotX="50%"
      android:pivotY="50%"
      android:duration="500" />
```

The code in Listing 6-13 will spin each text item in the list one full circle around the midpoint of the text item. The duration of 500 milliseconds is a good amount of time for the user to perceive the rotation. As before, to see this effect you must change the layout-controller XML file and the ListView XML layout file and then rerun the application.

Now we've covered the basic concepts in layout animation, where we start with a simple animation file and associate it with a ListView through an intermediate layoutAnimation XML file. That's all you need to do to see the animated effects. However, we need to talk about one more thing with regard to layout animation: interpolators.

Using Interpolators

Interpolators tell an animation how a certain property, such as a color gradient, changes over time: Will it change in a linear fashion, or in an exponential fashion? Will it start quickly, but slow down toward the end? Consider the alpha animation that we introduced in Listing 6-11:

```
<alpha xmlns:android="http://schemas.android.com/apk/res/android"
       android:interpolator="@android:anim/accelerate_interpolator"
       android:fromAlpha="0.0" android:toAlpha="1.0" android:duration="1000" />
```

The animation identifies the interpolator it wants to use—the accelerate_interpolator, in this case. There is a corresponding Java object that defines this interpolator. Also, note that we've specified this interpolator as a resource reference. This means there must be a file corresponding to the anim/accelerate_interpolator that describes what this Java object looks like and what additional parameters it might take. That indeed is the case. Look at the XML file definition for @android:anim/accelerate_interpolator:

```
<accelerateInterpolator
  xmlns:android="http://schemas.android.com/apk/res/android"
  factor="1" />
```

You can see this XML file in the following subdirectory within the Android package:

```
/res/anim/accelerate_interpolator.xml
```

The accelerateInterpolator XML tag corresponds to a Java object with this name:

```
android.view.animation.AccelerateInterpolator
```

You can look up the Java documentation for this class to see what XML tags are available. This interpolator's goal is to provide a multiplication factor given a time interval based on a hyperbolic curve. The source code for the interpolator illustrates this:

```
public float getInterpolation(float input)
{
    if (mFactor == 1.0f)
    {
        return (float)(input * input);
    }
    else
    {
        return (float)Math.pow(input, 2 * mFactor);
    }
}
```

Every interpolator implements this getInterpolation method differently. In this case, if the interpolator is set up so that the factor is 1.0, it will return the square of the factor. Otherwise, it will return a power of the input that is further scaled by the factor. So if the factor is 1.5, then you will see a cubic function instead of a square function.

The supported interpolators include

```
AccelerateDecelerateInterpolator
AccelerateInterpolator
CycleInterpolator
DecelerateInterpolator
LinearInterpolator
```

You can find the behavior of these interpolators described at the following URL:

```
http://code.google.com/android/reference/android/view/animation/package-summary.html
```

The Java documentation for each of these classes also points out the XML tags available to control them.

This concludes our section on layout animation. We will now move to the third section on view animation, in which we'll discuss animating a view programmatically.

View Animation

Now that you're familiar with frame-by-frame animation and layout animation, you're ready to tackle view animation—the most complex of the three animation types. View animation allows you to animate any arbitrary view by manipulating the transformation matrix that is in place for displaying the view.

We will start this section by giving you a brief introduction to view animation. We will then show you the code for a test harness to experiment with view animation, followed by a few view-animation examples. Then we'll explain how you can use the Camera object in association with view animation. (This Camera has nothing to do with the physical camera on the device; it's purely a graphics concept.) Finally, we'll give you an in-depth look at working with transformation matrices.

Understanding View Animation

When a view is displayed on a presentation surface in Android, it goes through a transformation matrix. In graphics applications, you use transformation matrices to transform a view in some way. The process involves taking the input set of pixel coordinates and color combinations and translating them into a new set of pixel coordinates and color combinations. At the end of a transformation, you will see an altered picture in terms of size, position, orientation, or color.

You can achieve all of these transformations mathematically by taking the input set of coordinates and multiplying them in some manner using a transformation matrix to arrive at a new set of coordinates. By changing the transformation matrix, you can impact how a view will look. A matrix that *doesn't* change the view when you multiply by it is called an *identity matrix*. You typically start with an identity matrix and apply a series of transformations involving size, position, and orientation. You then take the final matrix and use that matrix to draw the view.

Android exposes the transformation matrix for a view by allowing you to register an animation object with that view. The animation object will have a callback that lets it obtain the current matrix for a view and change it in some manner to arrive at a new view. We will go through this process in this section.

Let's start by planning an example for animating a view. You'll begin with an activity where you'll place a ListView with a few items, similar to the way you began the example in the "Layout Animation" section. You will then create a button at the top of the screen to start the ListView animation when clicked (see Figure 6-5). Both the button and the ListView appear, but nothing has been animated yet. You'll use the button to trigger the animation.

Figure 6-5. *The view-animation activity*

When you click the Start Animation button in this example, you want the view to start small in the middle of the screen and gradually become bigger until it consumes all the space that is allocated for it. We'll show you how to write the code to make this happen. Listing 6-14 shows the XML layout file that you can use for the activity.

Listing 6-14. *XML Layout File for the View-Animation Activity*

```xml
<?xml version="1.0" encoding="utf-8"?>
<!-- This file is at /res/layout/list_layout.xml -->
<LinearLayout xmlns:android="http://schemas.android.com/apk/res/android"
    android:orientation="vertical"
    android:layout_width="fill_parent"
    android:layout_height="fill_parent"
    >
<Button
    android:id="@+id/btn_animate"
    android:layout_width="fill_parent"
    android:layout_height="wrap_content"
    android:text="Start Animation"
/>
<ListView
    android:id="@+id/list_view_id"
    android:persistentDrawingCache="animation|scrolling"
    android:layout_width="fill_parent"
    android:layout_height="fill_parent"
 />
</LinearLayout>
```

Notice that the file location and the file name are embedded at the top of the XML file for your reference. This layout has two parts: the first is the button named btn_animate to animate a view, and the second is the ListView, which is named list_view_id.

Now that you have the layout for the activity, you can create the activity to show the view and set up the Start Animation button (see Listing 6-15).

Listing 6-15. *Code for the View-Animation Activity, Before Animation*

```java
public class ViewAnimationActivity extends Activity {

    @Override
    public void onCreate(Bundle savedInstanceState)
    {
        super.onCreate(savedInstanceState);
        setContentView(R.layout.list_layout);
        setupListView();
        this.setupButton();
    }
```

```
    private void setupListView()
    {
        String[] listItems = new String[] {
                "Item 1", "Item 2", "Item 3",
                "Item 4", "Item 5", "Item 6",
        };

        ArrayAdapter listItemAdapter =
            new ArrayAdapter(this
                    ,android.R.layout.simple_list_item_1
                    ,listItems);
        ListView lv = (ListView)this.findViewById(R.id.list_view_id);
        lv.setAdapter(listItemAdapter);
    }
    private void setupButton()
    {
        Button b = (Button)this.findViewById(R.id.btn_animate);
        b.setOnClickListener(
            new Button.OnClickListener(){
              public void onClick(View v)
              {
                  //animateListView();
              }
            });
    }
}
```

The code for the view-animation activity in Listing 6-15 closely resembles the code for the layout-animation activity in Listing 6-7. We have similarly loaded the view and set up the ListView to contain six text items. We've set up the button in such a way that it would call animateListView() when clicked. But for now, comment out that part until you get this basic example running.

You can invoke this activity as soon as you register it in the AndroidManifest.xml file:

```
<activity android:name=".ViewAnimationActivity"
        android:label="View Animation Test Activity">
```

Once this registration is in place, you can invoke this view-animation activity from any menu item in your application by executing the following code:

```
Intent intent = new Intent(this, ViewAnimationActivity.class);
startActivity(intent);
```

When you run this program, you will see the UI as laid out in Figure 6-5.

Adding Animation

Our aim in this example is to add animation to the ListView shown in Figure 6-5. To do that, you need a class that derives from android.view.animation.Animation. You then need to override the applyTransformation method to modify the transformation matrix. Call this derived class ViewAnimation. Once you have the ViewAnimation class, you can do something like this on the ListView class:

```
ListView lv = (ListView)this.findViewById(R.id.list_view_id);
lv.startAnimation(new ViewAnimation());
```

Let us go ahead and show you the source code for ViewAnimation and discuss the kind of animation we want to accomplish (see Listing 6-16).

Listing 6-16. *Code for the ViewAnimation Class*

```
public class ViewAnimation extends Animation
{
    public ViewAnimation2(){}

    @Override
    public void initialize(int width, int height, int parentWidth,
                                              int parentHeight)
    {
        super.initialize(width, height, parentWidth, parentHeight);
        setDuration(2500);
        setFillAfter(true);
        setInterpolator(new LinearInterpolator());
    }
    @Override
    protected void applyTransformation(float interpolatedTime, Transformation t)
    {
        final Matrix matrix = t.getMatrix();
        matrix.setScale(interpolatedTime, interpolatedTime);
    }
}
```

The initialize method is a callback method that tells us about the dimensions of the view. This is also a place to initialize any animation parameters you might have. In this example, we have set the duration to be 2500 milliseconds (2.5 seconds). We have also specified that we want the animation effect to remain intact after the animation completes by setting FillAfter to true. Plus, we've indicated that the interpolator is a linear interpolator, meaning that the animation changes in a gradual manner from start to finish. All of these properties come from the base android.view.animation.Animation class.

The main part of the animation occurs in the applyTransformation method. The Android framework will call this method again and again to simulate animation. Every time Android calls the method, interpolatedTime has a different value. This parameter changes from 0 to 1 depending on where you are in the 2.5-second duration that you set during initialization. When interpolatedTime is 1, you are at the end of the animation.

Our goal, then, is to change the transformation matrix that is available through the transformation object called t in the applyTransformation method. You will first get the matrix and change something about it. When the view gets painted, the new matrix will take effect. You can find the kinds of methods available on the Matrix object by looking up the API documentation for android.graphics.Matrix:

http://code.google.com/android/reference/android/graphics/Matrix.html

In Listing 6-16, here is the code that changes the matrix:

```
matrix.setScale(interpolatedTime, interpolatedTime);
```

The setScale method takes two parameters: the scaling factor in the x direction and the scaling factor in the y direction. Because the interpolatedTime goes between 0 and 1, you can use that value directly as the scaling factor. So when you start the animation, the scaling factor is 0 in both x and y directions. Halfway through the animation, this value will be 0.5 in both x and y directions. At the end of the animation, the view will be at its full size because the scaling factor will be 1 in both x and y directions. The end result of this animation is that the ListView starts out tiny and grows into full size.

Listing 6-17 shows the complete source code for the ViewAnimationActivity that includes the animation.

Listing 6-17. *Code for the View-Animation Activity, Including Animation*

```
public class ViewAnimationActivity extends Activity {

    @Override
    public void onCreate(Bundle savedInstanceState)
    {
        super.onCreate(savedInstanceState);
        setContentView(R.layout.list_layout);
        setupListView();
        this.setupButton();
    }
    private void setupListView()
    {
        String[] listItems = new String[] {
                "Item 1", "Item 2", "Item 3",
                "Item 4", "Item 5", "Item 6",
        };

        ArrayAdapter listItemAdapter =
            new ArrayAdapter(this
                    ,android.R.layout.simple_list_item_1
                    ,listItems);
        ListView lv = (ListView)this.findViewById(R.id.list_view_id);
        lv.setAdapter(listItemAdapter);
    }
```

```
private void setupButton()
{
    Button b = (Button)this.findViewById(R.id.btn_animate);
    b.setOnClickListener(
        new Button.OnClickListener(){
          public void onClick(View v)
          {
              animateListView();
          }
        });
}
private void animateListView()
{
    ListView lv = (ListView)this.findViewById(R.id.list_view_id);
    lv.startAnimation(new ViewAnimation());
}
}
```

When you run the code in Listing 6-17, you will notice something odd. Instead of uni-formly growing larger from the middle of the screen, the ListView grows larger from the top-left corner. The reason is that the origin for the matrix operations is at the top-left cor-ner. To get the desired effect, you first have to move the whole view so that the view's center matches the animation center (top-left). Then you apply the matrix and move the view back to the previous center.

Here's the code for doing this:

```
final Matrix matrix = t.getMatrix();
matrix.setScale(interpolatedTime, interpolatedTime);
matrix.preTranslate(-centerX, -centerY);
matrix.postTranslate(centerX, centerY);
```

The preTranslate and postTranslate methods set up a matrix before the scale operation and after the scale operation. This is equivalent to making three matrix transformations in tan-dem. The code

```
matrix.setScale(interpolatedTime, interpolatedTime);
matrix.preTranslate(-centerX, -centerY);
matrix.postTranslate(centerX, centerY);
```

is equivalent to

```
move to a different center
scale it
move to the original center
```

Here is the code for the transformation method that will give us the desired effect:

```
protected void applyTransformation(float interpolatedTime, Transformation t)
{
        final Matrix matrix = t.getMatrix();
        matrix.setScale(interpolatedTime, interpolatedTime);
        matrix.preTranslate(-centerX, -centerY);
        matrix.postTranslate(centerX, centerY);
}
```

You will see this pattern of pre and post applied again and again. You can also accomplish this result using other methods on the Matrix class, but this technique is the most common—plus, it's succinct. We will, however, cover these other methods toward the end of this section.

More important, the Matrix class allows you not only to scale a view, but also to move it around through translate methods and change its orientation through rotate methods. You can experiment with these methods and see what the resulting animation looks like. In fact, the animations presented in the preceding "Layout Animation" section are all implemented internally using the methods on this Matrix class.

Using Camera to Provide Depth Perception in 2D

The graphics package in Android provides another animation-related—or more accurately, transformation-related—class called Camera. You can use this class to provide depth perception by projecting a 2D image moving in 3D space onto a 2D surface. For example, you can take our ListView and move it back from the screen by 10 pixels along the z axis and rotate it by 30 degrees around the y axis. Here is an example of manipulating the matrix using a Camera:

```
...
Camera camera = new Camera();
..
protected void applyTransformation(float interpolatedTime, Transformation t)
{
    final Matrix matrix = t.getMatrix();
    camera.save();
    camera.translate(0.0f, 0.0f, (1300 - 1300.0f * interpolatedTime));
    camera.rotateY(360 * interpolatedTime);
    camera.getMatrix(matrix);

    matrix.preTranslate(-centerX, -centerY);
    matrix.postTranslate(centerX, centerY);
    camera.restore();
}
```

This code animates the ListView by first placing the view 1300 pixels back on the z axis and then bringing it back to the plane where the z coordinate is 0. While doing this, the code also rotates the view from 0 degrees to 360 degrees around the y axis. Let's see how the code relates to this behavior by looking at the following method:

```
camera.translate(0.0f, 0.0f, (1300 - 1300.0f * interpolatedTime));
```

This method tells the camera object to translate the view such that when interpolatedTime is 0 (at the beginning of the animation), the z value will be 1300. As the animation progresses, the z value will get smaller and smaller until the end, when the interpolatedTime becomes 1 and the z value becomes 0.

The method camera.rotateY(360 * interpolatedTime) takes advantage of 3D rotation around an axis by the camera. At the beginning of the animation, this value will be 0. At the end of the animation, it will be 360.

The method camera.getMatrix(matrix) takes the operations performed on the Camera so far and imposes those operations on the matrix that is passed in. Once the code does that, the matrix has the translations it needs to get the end effect of having a Camera. Now the Camera is out of the picture (no pun intended) because the matrix has all the operations embedded in it. Then you do the pre and post on the matrix to shift the center and bring it back. At the end, you set the Camera to its original state that was saved earlier.

When you plug this code into our example, you will see the ListView arriving from the center of the view in a spinning manner toward the front of the screen, as we intended when we planned our animation.

As part of our discussion about view animation, we showed you how to animate any view by extending an Animation class and then applying it to a view. In addition to letting you manipulate matrices (both directly and through a Camera class), the Animation class lets you detect various stages in an animation. We will cover this in the next subsection.

Exploring the AnimationListener Class

Android uses a listener interface called AnimationListener to monitor animation events (see Listing 6-18). You can listen to these animation events by implementing the AnimationListener interface and setting that implementation against the Animation class implementation.

Listing 6-18. *An Implementation of the AnimationListener Interface*

```
public class ViewAnimationListener
implements Animation.AnimationListener {

    private ViewAnimationListener(){}

    public void onAnimationStart(Animation animation)
    {
        Log.d("Animation Example", "onAnimationStart");
    }
    public void onAnimationEnd(Animation animation)
    {
        Log.d("Animation Example", "onAnimationEnd");
    }
    public void onAnimationRepeat(Animation animation)
    {
        Log.d("Animation Example", "onAnimationRepeat");
    }
}
```

The ViewAnimationListener class just logs messages. You can update the animateListView method in the view-animation example (see Listing 6-17) to take the animation listener into account:

```
private void animateListView()
{
    ListView lv = (ListView)this.findViewById(R.id.list_view_id);
    ViewAnimation animation = new ViewAnimation();
    animation.setAnimationListener(new ViewAnimationListener()):
    lv.startAnimation(animation);
}
```

Some Notes on Transformation Matrices

As you have seen in this chapter, matrices are key to transforming views and animations. We will now briefly explore some key methods of the Matrix class. These are the primary operations on a matrix:

```
matrix.reset();
matrix.setScale();
matrix.setTranslate()
matrix.setRotate();
matrix.setSkew();
```

The first operation resets a matrix to an identity matrix, which causes no change to the view when applied. setScale is responsible for changing size, setTranslate is responsible for changing position to simulate movement, and setRotate is responsible for changing orientation. setSkew is responsible for distorting a view.

You can concatenate matrices or multiply them together to compound the effect of individual transformations. Consider the following example, where m1, m2, and m3 are identity matrices:

```
m1.setScale();
m2.setTranlate()
m3.concat(m1,m2)
```

Transforming a view by m1 and then transforming the resulting view with m2 is equivalent to transforming the same view by m3. Note that set methods replace the previous transformations, and that m3.concat(m1,m2) is different from m3.concat(m2,m1).

You have already seen the pattern used by preTranslate and postTranslate methods to affect matrix transformation. In fact, pre and post methods are not unique to translate, and you have versions of pre and post for every one of the set transformation methods. Ultimately, a preTranslate such as m1.preTranslate(m2) is equivalent to

```
m1.concat(m2,m1)
```

In a similar manner, the method m1.postTranslate(m2) is equivalent to

```
m1.concat(m1,m2)
```

By extension, the code

```
matrix.setScale(interpolatedTime, interpolatedTime);
matrix.preTranslate(-centerX, -centerY);
matrix.postTranslate(centerX, centerY);
```

is equivalent to

```
Matrix matrixPreTranslate = new Matrix();
matrixPreTranslate.setTranslate(-centerX, -centerY);

Matrix matrixPostTranslate = new Matrix();
matrixPostTranslate.setTranslate(cetnerX, centerY);

matrix.concat(matrixPreTranslate,matrix);
matrix.postTranslate(matrix,matrixpostTranslate);
```

Summary

In this chapter, we showed you a fun way to enhance your UI programs by extending them with animation capabilities. We covered all major types of animation supported by Android, including frame-by-frame animation, layout animation, and view animation. We also covered supplemental animation concepts such as interpolators and transformation matrices.

Now that you have this background, we encourage you to go through the API samples that come with the Android SDK to examine the sample XML definitions for a variety of animations. We will also return to animation briefly in Chapters 10 and 13, when you'll see how to draw and animate using OpenGL.

But now we will turn our attention to services in Android. We'll cover location-based services and security in Chapter 7, and HTTP-related services in Chapter 8.

■■■

CHAPTER 7

Exploring Security and Location-Based Services

In this chapter, we are going to talk about Android's application-security model and location-based services. Although the two topics are disparate, you need to understand security prior to working with location-based services.

The first part of the chapter discusses security, which is a fundamental part of the Android Platform. In Android, security spans all phases of the application lifecycle—from design-time policy considerations to runtime boundary checks. You'll learn Android's security architecture and understand how to design secure applications.

The second part of the chapter concerns location-based services. Location-based services comprise one of the more exciting pieces of the Android SDK. This portion of the SDK provides APIs to let application developers display and manipulate maps, obtain real-time device-location information, and take advantage of other exciting features. After you read this section of the book, you'll definitely be convinced that Android is truly amazing.

Let's get started with the Android security model.

Understanding the Android Security Model

Security in Android spans the deployment and execution of the application. With respect to deployment, Android applications have to be signed with a digital signature in order for you to install them onto a device. With respect to execution, Android runs each application within a separate process, each of which has a unique and permanent user ID (assigned at install time). This places a boundary around the process and prevents one application from having direct access to another's data. Moreover, Android defines a declarative permission model that protects sensitive features (such as the contact list).

In the next several sections, we are going to discuss these topics. But before we get started, let's provide an overview of some of the security concepts that we'll refer to later.

Overview of Security Concepts

As we said earlier, Android requires that applications be signed with a digital certificate. One of the benefits of this requirement is that an application cannot be updated with a version that was not published by the original author. If we publish an application, for example, then you cannot update our application with your version (unless, of course, you somehow obtain our certificate and the password associated with it). That said, what does it mean for an application to be signed? And what is the process of signing an application?

You sign an application with a digital certificate. A digital certificate is an artifact that contains information about you, such as your company name, address, and so on. A few important attributes of a digital certificate include its signature and public/private key. A public/private key is also called a key pair. Note that although you use digital certificates here to sign .apk files, you can also use them for other purposes (such as encrypted communication). You can obtain a digital certificate from a trusted certificate authority (CA) and/or generate one yourself using tools such as the keytool, which we'll discuss shortly. Digital certificates are stored in keystores. A keystore contains a list of digital certificates, each of which has an alias that you can use to refer to it in the keystore.

Signing an Android application requires three things: a digital certificate, an .apk file, and a utility that knows how to apply the signature of the digital certificate to the .apk file. As you'll see, we use a free utility that is part of the Java Runtime Environment (JRE) distribution called the *keytool*. This utility is a command-line tool that knows how to sign a .jar file with a digital certificate.

Now let's move on and talk about how you can sign an .apk file with a digital certificate.

Signing Applications for Deployment

In order to install an Android application onto a device, you first need to sign the Android package (.apk file) with the digital signature of a certificate. The certificate, however, can be self-signed—you do not need to purchase a certificate from a certificate authority such as VeriSign.

Signing your application for deployment involves two steps. The first step is to generate a certificate using the keytool (or similar tool). The second step involves using the *jarsigner* tool (or similar tool) to sign the .apk file with the signature of the generated certificate. Note that during development, the ADT plug-in for Eclipse takes care of signing your .apk file before deploying onto the emulator. Moreover, the default certificate used for signing during development cannot be used for production deployment onto a real device.

Generating a Self-Signed Certificate Using the Keytool

The keytool utility manages a database of private keys and their corresponding X.509 certificates (a standard for digital certificates). This utility ships with the JRE and resides under the JRE bin directory.

In this section, we'll show you how to generate a keystore with a single entry, which you'll later use to sign an Android .apk file. To generate a keystore entry, do the following:

1. Create a folder to hold the keystore at `c:\android\release\`.

2. Open a command window to the JRE bin directory and execute the keytool utility with the parameters shown in Listing 7-1.

Listing 7-1. *Generating a Keystore Entry Using the Keytool*

```
keytool -genkey -v -keystore c:\android\release\release.keystore
-alias androidbook -storepass paxxword -keypass paxxword -keyalg RSA
-validity 14000
```

All of the arguments passed to the keytool are summarized in Table 7-1.

Table 7-1. *Arguments Passed to the Keytool*

Argument	Description
genkey	Tells the keytool to generate a public/private key pair.
v	Tells the keytool to emit verbose output during key generation.
keystore	Path to the keystore database (in this case, a file).
alias	A unique name for the keystore entry. The alias is used later to refer to the keystore entry.
storepass	The password for the keystore.
keypass	The password used to access the private key.
keyalg	The algorithm.
validity	The validity period.

The keytool will prompt you for the passwords listed in Table 7-1 if you do not provide them on the command line. The command in Listing 7-1 will generate a keystore database at `c:\android\release\`. The database will be a file named `release.keystore`. The `validity` of the entry will be 14,000 days (or approximately 38 years)—which is a long time from now. You should understand the reason for this. The Android documentation recommends that you specify a validity period long enough to surpass the entire lifespan of the application, which will include many updates to the application. It recommends that the validity be at least 25 years. Moreover, if you plan to publish the application on Android Market (`http://www.android.com/market/`), your certificate will need to be valid through October 22, 2033.

Going back to the keytool, the argument `alias` is a unique name given to the entry in the keystore database; you can later use this name to refer to the entry. When you run the keytool command in Listing 7-1, keytool will ask you a few questions (see Figure 7-1) and then generate the keystore database and entry.

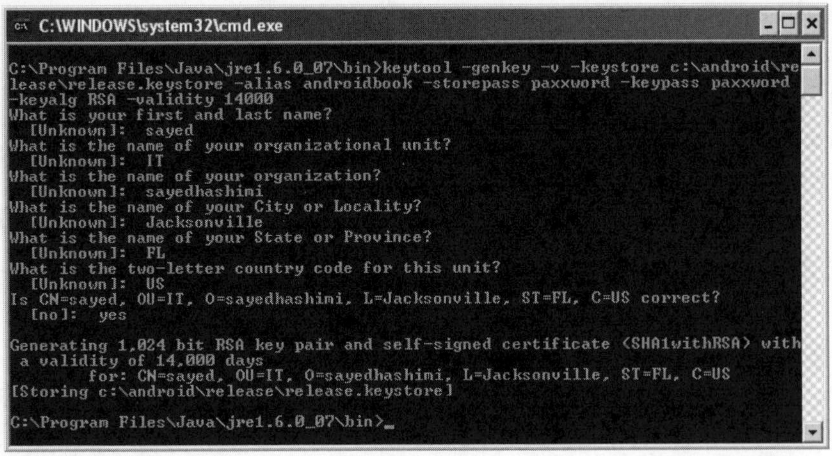

Figure 7-1. *Additional questions asked by the keytool*

Now you have a digital certificate that you can use to sign your .apk file. To sign an .apk file with the certificate, you use the jarsigner tool. Here's how to do that.

Using the Jarsigner Tool to Sign the .apk File

The keytool in the previous section created a digital certificate, which is one of the parameters to the jarsigner tool. The other parameter for the jarsigner is the actual Android package to be signed. To generate an Android package, you need to use the "Export Unsigned Application Package" utility in the ADT plug-in for Eclipse. You access the utility by right-clicking an Android project in Eclipse, selecting Android Tools, and then selecting "Export Unsigned Application Package." Running the "Export Unsigned Application Package" utility will generate an .apk file that will not be signed with the debug certificate. To see how this works, run the "Export Unsigned Application Package" utility on one of your Android projects and store the generated .apk file at c:\android\release\myapp.apk.

With the .apk file and the keystore entry, run the jarsigner tool to sign the .apk file (see Listing 7-2).

Listing 7-2. *Using Jarsigner to Sign the .apk File*

```
jarsigner -keystore c:\android\release\release.keystore -storepass paxxword
-keypass paxxword  c:\android\release\myapp.apk androidbook
```

To sign the .apk file, you pass the location of the keystore, the keystore password, the private-key password, the path to the .apk file, and the alias for the keystore entry. The jarsigner will then sign the .apk file with the signature from the keystore entry. Note that the jarsigner tool is an executable that ships with the JDK, in the bin directory—it is not packaged with the JRE. To run the jarsigner tool, you will need to either open a command window to the JDK bin directory or ensure that your JDK bin directory is on the system path.

As we pointed out earlier, Android requires that an application be signed with a digital signature to prevent a malicious programmer from updating your application with his version. For this to work, Android requires that updates to an application be signed with the same signature as the original. If you sign the application with a different signature, Android treats them as two different applications.

Once you have signed an .apk file, you can install it onto the emulator manually using the adb tool. As an exercise, start the emulator and open a command window to the Android SDK `tools` directory. Then run the adb tool with the `install` command:

```
adb install "PATH TO APK FILE GOES HERE"
```

Now let's see how signing affects the process of updating an application.

Installing Updates to an Application and Signing

Earlier we mentioned that a certificate has an expiration date and that Google recommends you set expiration dates far into the future, to account for a lot of application updates. That said, what happens if the certificate does expire? Would Android still run the application? Fortunately, yes—Android tests the certificate's expiration only at install time. Once your application is installed, it will continue to run even if the certificate expires.

But what about updates? Unfortunately, you will not be able to update the application. In other words, as Google suggests, you need to make sure the life of the certificate is long enough to support the entire life of the application. If a certificate does expire, Android will not install an update to the application. The only choice left will be for you to create another application—an application with a different package name—and sign it with a new certificate. So as you can see, it is critical for you to consider the expiration date of the certificate when you generate it.

Now that you understand security with respect to deployment and installation, let's move on to runtime security in Android.

Performing Runtime Security Checks

Runtime security in Android happens at the process level and at the operation level. At the process level, Android prevents one application from directly accessing another application's data. It does this by running each application within a different process and under a unique and permanent user ID. At the operational level, Android defines a list of protected features and resources. In order for your application to access this information, you have to add one or more permission requests to your `AndroidManifest.xml` file. You can also define custom permissions with your application.

In the sections that follow, we will talk about process-boundary security and how to declare and use predefined permissions. We will also discuss creating custom permissions and enforcing them within your application. Let's start by dissecting Android security at the process boundary.

Understanding Security at the Process Boundary

Unlike your desktop environment where most of the applications run under the same user ID, each Android application generally runs under its own unique ID. By running each application under a different ID, Android creates an isolation boundary around each process. This prevents one application from directly accessing another application's data.

Although each process has a boundary around it, data sharing between applications is obviously possible, but has to be explicit. In other words, to get data from another application, you have to go through the components of that application. For example, you can query a content provider of another application, you can invoke an activity in another application, or—as you'll see in Chapter 8—you can communicate with a service of another application. All of these facilities provide methods for you to share information between applications, but they do so in an explicit manner because you don't access the underlying database, files, and so on.

Android's security at the process boundary is clear and simple. Things get interesting when we start talking about protecting resources (such as contact data), features (such as the device's camera), and our own components. To provide this protection, Android defines a permission scheme. Let's dissect that now.

Declaring and Using Permissions

Android defines a permission scheme meant to protect resources and features on the device. For example, applications, by default, cannot access the contacts list, make phone calls, and so on. To protect the user from malicious applications, Android requires applications to request permissions if they need to use a protected feature or resource. As you'll see shortly, permission requests go in the manifest file. At install time, the APK installer either grants or denies the requested permissions based on the signature of the .apk file and/or feedback from the user. If a permission is not granted, any attempt to execute or access the associated feature will result in a permission failure.

Table 7-2 shows some commonly used features and the permissions they require. Note that you are not yet familiar with all the features listed in Table 7-2, but you will see them later (either in this chapter or subsequent chapters).

Table 7-2. *Features and Resources, and the Permissions They Require*

Feature/Resource	Required Permission	Description
Camera	android.permission.CAMERA	Enables you to access the device's camera.
Internet	android.permission.INTERNET	Enables you to make a network connection.
User's Contact Data	android.permission.READ_CONTACTS android.permission.WRITE_CONTACTS	Enables you to read from or write to the user's contact data.
User's Calendar Data	android.permission.READ_CALENDAR android.permission.WRITE_CALENDAR	Enables you to read from or write to the user's calendar data.
Record Audio	android.permission.RECORD_AUDIO	Enables you to record audio.
GPS Location Information	android.permission.ACCESS_FINE_LOCATION	Enables you to access fine-grained location information. This includes GPS location information.
WiFi Location Information	android.permission.ACCESS_COARSE_LOCATION	Enables you to access coarse-grained location information. This includes WiFi location information.
Battery Information	android.permission.BATTERY_STATS	Enables you to obtain battery-state information.
Bluetooth	android.permission.BLUETOOTH	Enables you to connect to paired Bluetooth devices.

For a complete list of permissions, see `http://developer.android.com/reference/android/Manifest.permission.html`.

Application developers can request permissions by adding entries to the `AndroidManifest.xml` file. For example, Listing 7-3 asks to access the camera on the device, to read the list of contacts, and to read the calendar.

Listing 7-3. *Permissions in AndroidManifest.xml*

```
<manifest xmlns:android="http://schemas.android.com/apk/res/android"
    package="com.android.app.permApp" >
    <uses-permission android:name="android.permission.CAMERA" />
    <uses-permission android:name="android.permission.READ_CONTACTS"/>
    <uses-permission android:name="android.permission.READ_CALENDAR" />
</manifest>
```

Note that you can either hand-code permissions in the `AndroidManifest.xml` file or use the manifest editor. The manifest editor is wired up to launch when you open (double-click) the manifest file. The manifest editor contains a drop-down list that has all of the permissions preloaded to prevent you from making a mistake. As shown in Figure 7-2, you can access the permissions list by selecting the Permissions tab in the manifest editor.

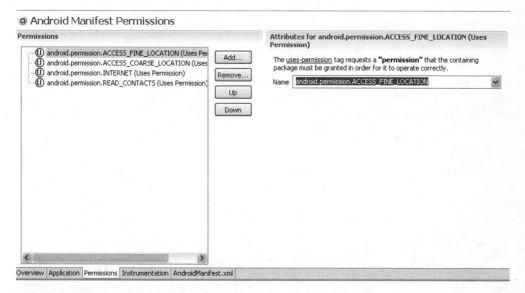

Figure 7-2. *The Android manifest editor tool in Eclipse*

You now know that Android defines a set of permissions that protects a set of features and resources. Similarly, you can define, and enforce, custom permissions with your application. Let's see how that works.

Understanding and Using Custom Permissions

Android allows you to define custom permissions with your application. For example, if you wanted to prevent certain users from starting one of the activities in your application, you could do that by defining a custom permission. To use custom permissions, you first declare them in your AndroidManifest.xml file. Once you've defined a permission, you can then refer to it as part of your component definition. We'll show you how this works.

Let's create an application containing an activity that not everyone is allowed to start. Instead, to start the activity, a user must have a specific permission. Once you have the application with a privileged activity, you can then write a client that knows how to call the activity.

First create the project with the custom permission and activity. Open the Eclipse IDE and select New ➤ New Project ➤ Android Project. This will open the "New Android Project" dialog box. Enter **CustomPermission** as the project name, select the "Create new project in workspace" radio button, and mark the "Use default location" check box. Enter **com.cust.perm** as the package name, **CustPermMainActivity** as the activity name, and **Custom Permission** as the application name. Click the Finish button to create the project. The generated project will have the activity you just created, which will serve as the default (main) activity. Let's also create a so-called *privileged activity*—an activity that requires a special permission. In the Eclipse IDE, go to the com.cust.perm package, create a class named **PrivActivity**, and copy the code shown in Listing 7-4.

Listing 7-4. *The PrivActivity Class*

```
package com.cust.perm;

import android.app.Activity;
import android.os.Bundle;
import android.view.ViewGroup.LayoutParams;
import android.widget.LinearLayout;
import android.widget.TextView;


public class PrivActivity extends Activity
{

    @Override
    public void onCreate(Bundle savedInstanceState) {
        super.onCreate(savedInstanceState);
        LinearLayout view = new LinearLayout(this);

        view.setLayoutParams(new LayoutParams(
                LayoutParams.FILL_PARENT, LayoutParams.WRAP_CONTENT));
        view.setOrientation(LinearLayout.HORIZONTAL);
```

```
TextView nameLbl = new TextView(this);

nameLbl.setText("Hello from PrivActivity");
view.addView(nameLbl);

setContentView(view);

    }
}
```

As you can see, `PrivActivity` does not do anything miraculous. This is obviously intentional because we want to protect this activity with a permission and then call it from a client. If the client succeeds, then you'll see the text "Hello from PrivActivity" on the screen. Now that you have an activity you want to protect, you can create the permission for it.

To create a custom permission, you have to define it in the `AndroidManifest.xml` file. The easiest way to do this is to use the manifest editor. Double-click the `AndroidManifest.xml` file and then select the Permissions tab. In the Permissions window, click the Add button, choose Permission, and then click the OK button. The manifest editor will create an empty new permission for you. Populate the new permission by setting its attributes as shown in Figure 7-3.

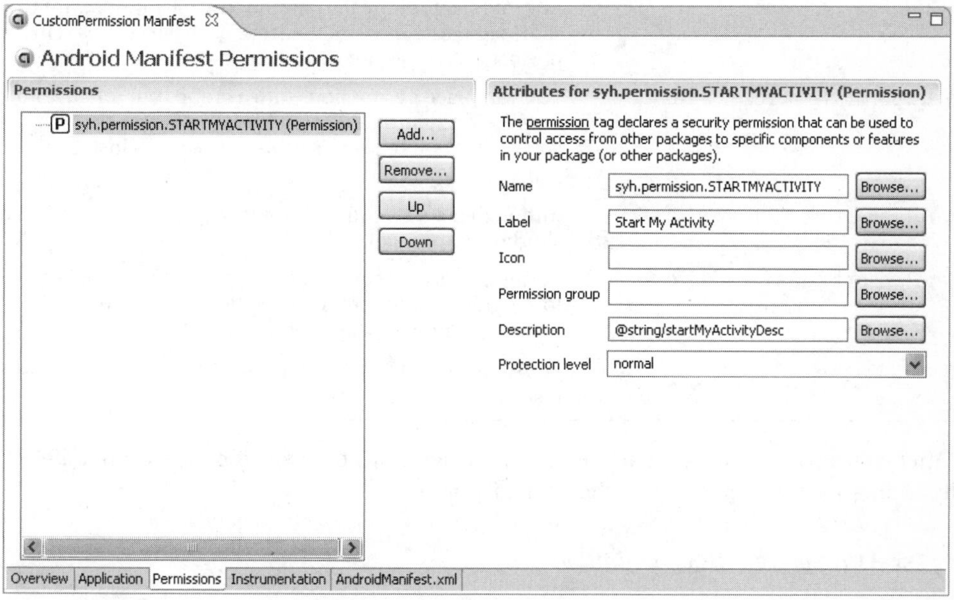

Figure 7-3. *Declaring a custom permission using the manifest editor*

As shown in Figure 7-3, a permission has a name, a label, an icon, a permission group, a description, and a protection level. Table 7-3 defines these properties.

Table 7-3. *Attributes of a Permission*

Attribute	Required?	Description
android:name	Yes	Name of the permission. You should generally follow the Android naming scheme (*.permission.*).
android:protectionLevel	Yes	Defines the "potential for risk" associated with the permission. Must be one of the following values: normal dangerous signature signatureOrSystem Depending on the protection level, the system might take a different action when determining whether to grant the permission or not. normal signals that the permission is low-risk and will not harm the system, the user, or other applications. dangerous signals that the permission is high-risk, and that the system will likely require input from the user before granting this permission. signature tells Android that the permission should be granted only to applications that have been signed with the same digital signature as the application that declared the permission. signatureOrSystem tells Android to grant the permission to applications with the same signature or to the Android package classes. This protection level is not to be used at this time.
android:permissionGroup	No	You can place permissions into a group, but for custom permissions you should avoid setting this property. If you really want to set this property, use this instead: android.permission-group.SYSTEM_TOOLS.
android:label	No	Although it's not required, use this property to provide a short description of the permission.
android:description	No	Although it's not required, you should use this property to provide a more useful description of what the permission is for and what it protects.
android:icon	No	Permissions can be associated with an icon out of your resources (such as @drawable/myicon).

After you add the permission in Figure 7-3, the manifest editor will modify your manifest file by adding a permission entry, as shown in Listing 7-5.

Listing 7-5. *A Custom Permission Definition*

```
<permission
android:protectionLevel="normal"
android:name="syh.permission.STARTMYACTIVITY "
android:label="Start My Activity"
android:description="@string/startMyActivityDesc"></permission>
```

Now you have a custom permission. Next, you want to tell the system that the PrivActivity activity should be launched only by applications that have the syh.permission.STARTMYACTIVITY permission. You can set a required permission on an activity by adding the android:permission attribute to the activity definition in the AndroidManifest.xml file. For you to be able to launch the activity, you'll also need an intent-filter to the activity. Update your AndroidManifest.xml file with the content from Listing 7-6.

Listing 7-6. *The AndroidManifest.xml File for the Custom-Permission Project*

```xml
<?xml version="1.0" encoding="utf-8"?>
<manifest xmlns:android="http://schemas.android.com/apk/res/android"
      package="com.cust.perm"
      android:versionCode="1"
      android:versionName="1.0.0">
    <application android:icon="@drawable/icon" android:label="@string/app_name">
        <activity android:name=".CustPermMainActivity"
                  android:label="@string/app_name">
            <intent-filter>
                <action android:name="android.intent.action.MAIN" />
                <category android:name="android.intent.category.LAUNCHER" />
            </intent-filter>
        </activity>
    <activity android:name="PrivActivity"
android:permission="syh.permission.STARTMYACTIVITY">
        <intent-filter>
                <action android:name="android.intent.action.MAIN" />
                <category android:name="android.intent.category.LAUNCHER" />
        </intent-filter>
    </activity>
</application>

<permission
android:protectionLevel="normal"
android:label="Start My Activity"
android:description="@string/startMyActivityDesc"
android:name="syh.permission.STARTMYACTIVITY"></permission>


</manifest>
```

Now run the project in the emulator. Although the main activity does not do anything, you just want the application installed on the emulator before you write a client for the privileged activity. Also, Listing 7-6 assumes that you have added a string constant named startMyActivityDesc to your string resources. To ensure compilation of Listing 7-6, add the following string resource to the res/values/strings.xml file:

```xml
<string name="startMyActivityDesc">Allows starting my activity</string>
```

Let's write a client for the activity. In the Eclipse IDE, click New ➤ Project ➤ Android Project. Enter **ClientOfCustomPermission** as the project name, select the "Create new project in workspace" radio button, and mark the "Use default location" check box. Set the package name to **com.client.cust.perm**, the activity name to **ClientCustPermMainActivity**, and the application name to **Client Of Custom Permission**. Click the Finish button to create the project.

Next, you want to write an activity that displays a button you can click to call the privileged activity. Copy the layout shown in Listing 7-7 to the main.xml file in the project you just created.

Listing 7-7. *Main.xml File for the Client Project*

```xml
<?xml version="1.0" encoding="utf-8"?>
<LinearLayout xmlns:android="http://schemas.android.com/apk/res/android"
    android:orientation="vertical"
    android:layout_width="fill_parent"
    android:layout_height="fill_parent"
    >
    <Button android:id="@+id/btn"
    android:text="Launch PrivActivity"
    android:layout_width="wrap_content"
    android:layout_height="wrap_content" />
</LinearLayout>
```

As you can see, the XML layout file defines a single button whose text reads "Launch PrivActivity." Now let's write an activity that will handle the button-click event and launch the privileged activity. Copy the code from Listing 7-8 to your ClientCustPermMainActivity class.

Listing 7-8. *The Modified ClientCustPermMainActivity Activity*

```java
package com.client.cust.perm;

import android.app.Activity;
import android.content.Intent;
import android.os.Bundle;
import android.view.View;
import android.view.View.OnClickListener;
import android.widget.Button;

public class ClientCustPermMainActivity extends Activity {
    @Override
    public void onCreate(Bundle savedInstanceState) {
        super.onCreate(savedInstanceState);
        setContentView(R.layout.main);

        Button btn = (Button)findViewById(R.id.btn);
        btn.setOnClickListener(new OnClickListener(){

            @Override
            public void onClick(View arg0) {
```

```
        Intent intent = new Intent();

        intent.setClassName("com.cust.perm","com.cust.perm.PrivActivity");
        startActivity(intent);
    }});

}
}
```

As shown in Listing 7-8, you obtain a reference to the button defined in the main.xml file and then wire up the on-click listener. When the button is invoked, you create a new intent, and then set the class name of the activity you want to launch. In this case, you want to launch the com.cust.perm.PrivActivity in the com.cust.perm package.

The only thing missing at this point is to add a uses-permission entry into the manifest file to tell the Android runtime that you need the syh.permission.STARTMYACTIVITY to run. Replace your client project's manifest file with that shown in Listing 7-9.

Listing 7-9. *The Client Manifest File*

```
<?xml version="1.0" encoding="utf-8"?>
<manifest xmlns:android="http://schemas.android.com/apk/res/android"
    package="com.client.cust.perm"
    android:versionCode="1"
    android:versionName="1.0.0">
    <application android:icon="@drawable/icon" android:label="@string/app_name">
        <activity android:name=".ClientCustPermMainActivity"
                android:label="@string/app_name">
            <intent-filter>
                <action android:name="android.intent.action.MAIN" />
                <category android:name="android.intent.category.LAUNCHER" />
            </intent-filter>
        </activity>

</application>

<uses-permission android:name="syh.permission.STARTMYACTIVITY"></uses-permission>

</manifest>
```

As shown in Listing 7-9, we added a uses-permission entry to request the custom permission required to start the PrivActivity we implemented in the custom-permission project.

With that, you should be able to deploy the client project to the emulator and then select the "Launch PrivActivity" button. When the button is invoked, you should see the text "Hello from PrivActivity."

After you successfully call the privileged activity, remove the uses-permission entry from your client project's manifest file and redeploy the project to the emulator. Once it's deployed, confirm that you get a permission denial when you invoke the button to launch the privileged activity. Note that LogCat will display a permission-denial exception.

Now you know how custom permissions work in Android. Obviously, custom permissions are not limited to activities. In fact, you can apply both predefined and custom permissions to Android's other types of components as well.

Working with Location-Based Services

The location-based services facility in Android sits on two pillars: the mapping APIs and the location APIs. Each of these APIs is isolated with respect to its own package. For example, the mapping package is com.google.android.maps and the location package is android.location. The mapping APIs in Android provide facilities for you to display a map and manipulate it. For example, you can zoom and pan, you can change the map mode (from satellite view to street view, for example), you can add custom data to the map, and so on. The other end of the spectrum is Global Positioning System (GPS) data and real-time location data, both of which are handled by the location package.

In this section, we'll go through each of these packages. We'll start with the mapping APIs and show you how to use maps with your applications. As you'll see, mapping in Android boils down to using the MapView UI control and the MapActivity class in addition to the mapping APIs, which integrate with Google Maps. We will also show you how to place custom data onto the maps that you display. After talking about maps, we'll delve into location-based services, which extend the mapping concepts. We will show you how to use the Android Geocoder class and the LocationManager service. We will also touch on threading issues that surface when you use these APIs. If you are using the Android 1.5 SDK, you'll need to set the SDK Target of your Android project to Google APIs. See Chapter 12 for details.

Understanding the Mapping Package

As we mentioned, the mapping APIs comprise one of the components of Android's location-based services. The mapping package contains everything you'll need to display a map on the screen, handle user interaction with the map (such as zooming), display custom data on top of the map, and so on. The first step to working with this package is to display a map. To do that, you'll use the MapView view class. Using this class, however, requires some prep work. Specifically, before you can use the MapView, you'll need to get a *map-api key* from Google. The map-api key enables Android to interact with Google Maps services to obtain map data. Here's how to obtain a map-api key.

Obtaining a map-api Key from Google

The first thing to understand about the map-api key is that you'll need two keys: one for development with the emulator, and another for production (on the device). The reason for this is that the certificate used to obtain the map-api key will differ between development and production (as we discussed in the first part of this chapter).

For example, during development, the ADT plug-in generates the .apk file and deploys it to the emulator. Because the .apk file must be signed with a certificate, the ADT plug-in uses the debug certificate during development. For production deployment, you'll likely use a self-signed certificate to sign your .apk file. The good news is that you can obtain a map-api key for development and one for production, and swap the keys before exporting the production build.

To obtain a map-api key, you need the certificate that you'll use to sign your application. (Recall that in the development phase, the ADT plug-in uses a debug certificate to sign your application for you prior to deployment onto the emulator.) So you'll get the MD5 fingerprint of your certificate, then you'll enter it on Google's web site to generate an associated map-api key.

First you must locate your debug certificate, which is generated and maintained by Android. On a Windows XP machine, this is the path to the certificate:

```
C:\Documents and Settings\<username>\Local Settings\Application Data\
Android\debug.keystore
```

You can find the exact location using the Eclipse IDE. Go to Window ➤ Preferences ➤ Android ➤ Build. The debug certificate's location will be displayed in the "Default debug keystore" field, as shown in Figure 7-4.

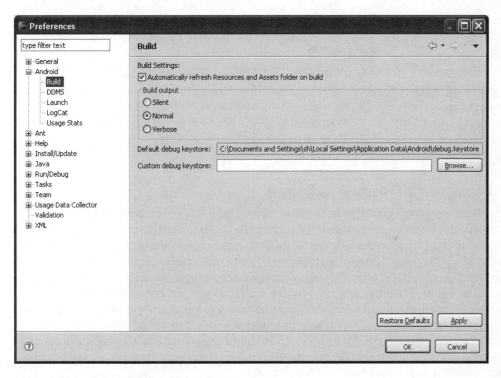

Figure 7-4. *The debug certificate's location*

To extract the MD5 fingerprint, you can run the keytool with the -list option, as shown in Listing 7-10.

Listing 7-10. *Using the Keytool to Obtain the MD5 Fingerprint of the Debug Certificate*

```
keytool -list -alias androiddebugkey -keystore
"C:\Documents and Settings\sh\
Local Settings\Application Data\Android\
debug.keystore" -storepass android -keypass android
```

Note that the `alias` of the debug store is `androiddebugkey`. Similarly, the keystore password is `android` and the private-key password is also `android`. When you run the command in Listing 7-10, the keytool provides the fingerprint (see Figure 7-5).

```
C:\WINDOWS\system32\cmd.exe                                              _ □ ×

C:\Program Files\Java\jdk1.6.0_07\bin>keytool -list -alias androiddebugkey -keys
tore "C:\Documents and Settings\sh\Local Settings\Application Data\Android\debug
.keystore" -storepass android -keypass android
androiddebugkey, Sep 26, 2008, PrivateKeyEntry,
Certificate fingerprint (MD5): 57:60:66:6F:63:E6:5F:6B:89:5F:47:3C:D1:12:F8:00

C:\Program Files\Java\jdk1.6.0_07\bin>
```

Figure 7-5. *The keytool output for the list option*

Now paste your certificate's MD5 fingerprint in the appropriate field on this Google site:

`http://code.google.com/android/maps-api-signup.html`

Then click the "Generate API Key" button to get a corresponding map-api key from the Google Maps service. The map-api key is active immediately, so you can start using it to obtain map data from Google. Note that you will need a Google account to obtain a map-api key—when you try to generate the map-api key, you will be prompted to log in to your Google account.

Now let's start playing with maps.

Understanding MapView and MapActivity

A lot of the mapping technology in Android relies on the `MapView` UI control and an extension of `android.app.Activity` called `MapActivity`. The `MapView` and `MapActivity` classes take care of the heavy lifting when it comes to displaying and manipulating a map in Android. One of the things that you'll have to remember about these two classes is that they have to work together. Specifically, in order to use a `MapView`, you need to instantiate it within a `MapActivity`. In addition, when instantiating a `MapView`, you need to supply the map-api key. If you instantiate a `MapView` using an XML layout, you need to set the `android:apiKey` property. If you create a `MapView` programmatically, you have to pass the map-api key to the `MapView` constructor. Lastly, because the underlying data for the map comes from Google Maps, your application will need permission to access the Internet. This means you need at least the following permission request in your `AndroidManifest.xml` file:

```
<uses-permission android:name="android.permission.INTERNET" />
```

In fact, whenever you use location-based services (maps, GPS, and so on), you should include three permissions in your `AndroidManifest.xml` file (see Listing 7-11).

Listing 7-11. *Minimum Required Permissions to Use Location-Based Services*

```
<uses-permission android:name="android.permission.ACCESS_FINE_LOCATION" />
<uses-permission android:name="android.permission.ACCESS_COARSE_LOCATION" />
<uses-permission android:name="android.permission.INTERNET" />
```

Recall from Table 7-2 that `android.permission.ACCESS_FINE_LOCATION` allows you to obtain "fine" location data such as GPS data. `android.permission.ACCESS_COARSE_LOCATION` allows you to obtain "coarse" location data, which includes WiFi location information.

With the prerequisites out of the way, have a look at Figure 7-6.

Figure 7-6. *A MapView control in street-view mode*

Figure 7-6 shows an application that displays a map in street-view mode. The application also demonstrates how you can zoom in, zoom out, and change the map's view mode. The XML layout is shown in Listing 7-12.

Listing 7-12. *XML Layout of MapView Demo*

```
<LinearLayout xmlns:android="http://schemas.android.com/apk/res/android"
        android:orientation="vertical" android:layout_width="fill_parent"
        android:layout_height="fill_parent">


<LinearLayout xmlns:android="http://schemas.android.com/apk/res/android"
        android:orientation="horizontal" android:layout_width="fill_parent"
        android:layout_height="wrap_content">

        <Button android:id="@+id/zoomin" android:layout_width="wrap_content"
        android:layout_height="wrap_content" android:text="+"/>

        <Button android:id="@+id/zoomout" android:layout_width="wrap_content"
        android:layout_height="wrap_content" android:text="-"/>
```

```
    <Button android:id="@+id/sat" android:layout_width="wrap_content"
        android:layout_height="wrap_content" android:text="Satellite"/>

    <Button android:id="@+id/street" android:layout_width="wrap_content"
        android:layout_height="wrap_content" android:text="Street"/>

    <Button android:id="@+id/traffic" android:layout_width="wrap_content"
        android:layout_height="wrap_content" android:text="Traffic"/>

</LinearLayout>

<com.google.android.maps.MapView android:id="@+id/mapview"
            android:layout_width="fill_parent"
            android:layout_height="wrap_content"
            android:apiKey="07vhLOusFXryRakmo2A4t8aKViWwKyGJGEDqpdg"
            />

</LinearLayout>
```

As shown in Listing 7-12, a parent LinearLayout contains a child LinearLayout and a MapView. The child LinearLayout contains the buttons shown at the top of Figure 7-6. Also note that you need to update the MapView control's android:apiKey value with the value of your own map-api key.

The code for our sample mapping application is shown in Listing 7-13.

Listing 7-13. *The MapActivity Extension Class That Loads the XML Layout*

```java
import android.os.Bundle;
import android.view.View;
import android.view.View.OnClickListener;
import android.widget.Button;

import com.google.android.maps.MapActivity;
import com.google.android.maps.MapView;
public class MapViewDemoActivity extends MapActivity
{
    private MapView mapView;
    @Override
    protected void onCreate(Bundle savedInstanceState) {
        super.onCreate(savedInstanceState);

        setContentView(R.layout.mapview);

        mapView = (MapView)findViewById(R.id.mapview);

        Button zoominBtn = (Button)findViewById(R.id.zoomin);
        Button zoomoutBtn = (Button)findViewById(R.id.zoomout);
```

```java
Button satBtn = (Button)findViewById(R.id.sat);
Button streetBtn = (Button)findViewById(R.id.street);
Button trafficBtn = (Button)findViewById(R.id.traffic);

// zoomin
zoominBtn.setOnClickListener(new OnClickListener(){

    @Override
    public void onClick(View view)
    {
        mapView.getController().zoomIn();
    }});
// zoom out
zoomoutBtn.setOnClickListener(new OnClickListener(){

    @Override
    public void onClick(View view)
    {
        mapView.getController().zoomOut();
    }});

// satellite
satBtn.setOnClickListener(new OnClickListener(){

    @Override
    public void onClick(View view)
    {
        mapView.setStreetView(false);
        mapView.setTraffic(false);
        mapView.setSatellite(true);
    }});
// street
streetBtn.setOnClickListener(new OnClickListener(){

    @Override
    public void onClick(View view)
    {
        mapView.setTraffic(false);
        mapView.setSatellite(false);
        mapView.setStreetView(true);
    }});
// traffic
trafficBtn.setOnClickListener(new OnClickListener(){
```

```
        @Override
        public void onClick(View view)
        {
            mapView.setSatellite(false);
            mapView.setStreetView(false);
            mapView.setTraffic(true);
        }});
    }

    @Override
    protected boolean isRouteDisplayed() {
        return false;
    }

}
```

As shown in Listing 7-13, displaying the `MapView` using `onCreate()` is no different from displaying any other control. That is, you set the content view of the UI to a layout file that contains the `MapView`, and that takes care of it. Suprisingly, supporting zoom features is also fairly easy. To zoom in or zoom out, you use the `MapController` class of the `MapView`. Do this by calling `mapView.getController()` and then calling the approproiate `zoomIn()` or `zoomOut()` method. Zooming this way produces a one-level zoom; users need to repeat the action to increase the amount of magnification or reduction.

You'll also find it straightforward to offer the ability to change view modes. The `MapView` supports several modes: map, street, satellite, and traffic. Map is the default mode. Street mode places a layer on top of the map that contains street information such as road names. Satellite mode shows the map in satellite view. Traffic mode shows traffic information on the map. Note that traffic mode is supported on a limited number of major highways. To change modes, you must call the appropriate setter method with `true` and set the other modes to `false`. The reason for this is that one mode can overlay another mode. For example, you can overlay satellite and street modes one on top of the other.

You'll probably agree that the amount of code required to display a map and to implement zoom and mode changes is minimal with Android (see Listing 7-13). Android's mapping capability is definitely unbeatable. It might come as a shock to some of you that the code gets even easier. Take a look at the XML layout and code shown in Listing 7-14.

Listing 7-14. *Zooming and Panning Made Easier*

```xml
<RelativeLayout xmlns:android="http://schemas.android.com/apk/res/android"
        android:orientation="vertical" android:layout_width="fill_parent"
        android:layout_height="fill_parent">

    <com.google.android.maps.MapView android:id="@+id/mapview"
            android:layout_width="fill_parent"
            android:layout_height="wrap_content"
            android:apiKey="07vhLOusFXryRakmo2A4t8aKViWwKyGJGEDqpdg"
            />
```

```xml
<LinearLayout xmlns:android="http://schemas.android.com/apk/res/android"
android:id="@+id/zoomCtrls"
           android:orientation="horizontal" android:layout_width="fill_parent"
           android:layout_height="wrap_content"
android:layout_alignParentBottom="true">

</LinearLayout>

</RelativeLayout>
```

```java
public class MapViewDemoActivity extends MapActivity
{
    private MapView mapView;
    @Override
    protected void onCreate(Bundle savedInstanceState) {
        super.onCreate(savedInstanceState);

        setContentView(R.layout.mapview);

        mapView = (MapView)findViewById(R.id.mapview);

        LinearLayout layout = (LinearLayout)findViewById(R.id.zoomCtrls);
        layout.addView(mapView.getZoomControls());

        mapView.setClickable(true);
    }

    @Override
    protected boolean isRouteDisplayed() {
        return false;
    }

}
```

The difference between Listing 7-14 and Listing 7-13 is that we changed the XML layout for our view to use RelativeLayout. We removed all the zoom controls and view-mode controls and replaced them with an empty LinearLayout oriented at the bottom of the screen. The magic in this example is in the code and not the layout. Specifically, notice that we populated the LinearLayout with mapView.getZoomControls(). This means that the MapView already has controls that allow you to zoom in and out. All you have to do is get a reference to the controls and then add it to your view (wherever you want it). Figure 7-7 shows the MapView's default zoom controls.

We are not done yet. The MapView control is very powerful. The last line in the onCreate() method of Listing 7-14 calls mapView.setClickable(true). This, in fact, enables panning of the map.

Now let's learn how to add custom data to the map.

Figure 7-7. *The MapView's built-in zoom controls*

Using Overlays

Google Maps provides a facility that allows you to place custom data on top of the map. You can see an example of this if you search for pizza restaurants in your area: Google Maps places pushpins, or balloon markers, to indicate each location. The way Google Maps provides this facility is by allowing you to add a layer on top of the map. Android provides several classes that help you to add layers to a map. The key class for this type of functionality is Overlay, but you can use an extension of this class called ItemizedOverlay. Listing 7-15 shows an example.

Listing 7-15. *Marking Up a Map Using ItemizedOverlay*

```
import java.util.ArrayList;
import java.util.List;

import android.graphics.Canvas;
import android.graphics.drawable.Drawable;
import android.os.Bundle;
import android.widget.LinearLayout;

import com.google.android.maps.GeoPoint;
import com.google.android.maps.ItemizedOverlay;
import com.google.android.maps.MapActivity;
import com.google.android.maps.MapView;
import com.google.android.maps.OverlayItem;
```

```java
public class MappingOverlayActivity extends MapActivity {
    private MapView mapView;

    @Override
    protected void onCreate(Bundle savedInstanceState) {
        super.onCreate(savedInstanceState);

        setContentView(R.layout.mapview);

        mapView = (MapView) findViewById(R.id.mapview);

        LinearLayout layout = (LinearLayout) findViewById(R.id.zoomCtrls);
        layout.addView(mapView.getZoomControls());

        mapView.setClickable(true);

        Drawable marker=getResources().getDrawable(R.drawable.mapmarker);
        marker.setBounds(0, 0, marker.getIntrinsicWidth(),
marker.getIntrinsicHeight());
        mapView.getOverlays().add(new InterestingLocations(marker));
    }

    @Override
    protected boolean isRouteDisplayed() {
        return false;

    }

    class InterestingLocations extends ItemizedOverlay {
        private List<OverlayItem> locations = new ArrayList<OverlayItem>();
        private Drawable marker;

        public InterestingLocations(Drawable marker)
        {
            super(marker);
            this.marker=marker;
            // create locations of interest
            GeoPoint disneyMagicKingdom = new
GeoPoint((int)(28.418971*1000000),(int)(-81.581436*1000000));
            GeoPoint disneySevenLagoon = new
GeoPoint((int)(28.410067*1000000),(int)(-81.583699*1000000));

            locations.add(new OverlayItem(disneyMagicKingdom ,
"Magic Kingdom", "Magic Kingdom"));
            locations.add(new OverlayItem(disneySevenLagoon ,
"Seven Lagoon", "Seven Lagoon"));

            populate();
        }
```

```
        @Override
        public void draw(Canvas canvas, MapView mapView, boolean shadow) {
            super.draw(canvas, mapView, shadow);

            boundCenterBottom(marker);
        }

        @Override
        protected OverlayItem createItem(int i) {
            return locations.get(i);
        }

        @Override
        public int size() {
            return locations.size();
        }

    }
}
```

Listing 7-15 demonstrates how you can overlay markers onto a map. The example places two markers (see Figure 7-8): one at Disney's Magic Kingdom, and another one at Disney's Seven Seas Lagoon (both near Orlando, Florida).

In order for you to add markers onto a map, you have to create and add an extension of com.google.android.maps.Overlay to the map. The Overlay class itself cannot be instantiated, so you'll have to extend it or use one of the extensions. In our example, we have implemented InterestingLocations, which extends ItemizedOverlay, which in turn extends Overlay. The Overlay class defines the contract for an overlay, and ItemizedOverlay is a handy implementation that makes it easy for you to create a list of locations that can be marked on a map.

The general usage pattern is to extend the ItemizedOverlay class and add your "items"— interesting locations—in the constructor. After you instantiate your points of interest, you call the populate() method of ItemizedOverlay. The populate() method is a utility that caches the OverlayItem(s). Internally, the class calls the size() method to determine the number of overlay items, and then enters a loop, calling createItem(i) for each item. In the createItem method, you return the already created item given the index in the array.

As you can see from Listing 7-15, you simply create the points and call populate() to show markers on a map. The Overlay contract manages the rest. To make it all work, the onCreate() method of the activity creates the InterestingLocations instance, passing in the Drawable that's used for the markers. Then onCreate()adds the InterestingLocations instance to the overlay collection (mapView.getOverlays().add()).

Another interesting aspect of Listing 7-15 is the creation of the OverlayItem(s). In order to create an OverlayItem, you need an object of type GeoPoint. The GeoPoint class represents a location by its latitude and longitude, in micro degrees. In our example, we obtained the latitude and longitude of Magic Kingdom and Seven Seas Lagoon using geocoding sites on the web. (As you'll see shortly, you can use geocoding to convert an address to a latitude/longitude pair, for example.) We then converted the latitude and longitude to micro degrees (because the APIs operate on micro degrees) by multiplying by 1,000,000 and then performing a cast to an integer.

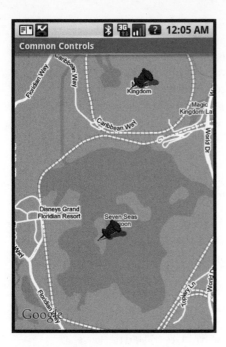

Figure 7-8. *MapView with markers*

All in all, you'll agree that placing markers on a map couldn't be easier. Or could it? We don't have a database of latitude/longitude pairs, but we're guessing that we'll need to somehow create one or more GeoPoints using a real address. That's when you can use the Geocoder, which is part of the location package that we'll discuss next.

Understanding the Location Package

The android.location package provides facilities for location-based services. In this section, we are going to discuss two important pieces of this package: the Geocoder class and the LocationManager service. We'll start with Geocoder.

Geocoding with Android

If you are going to do anything practical with maps, you'll likely have to convert an address (or location) to a latitude/longitude pair. This concept in known as *geocoding*, and the android.location.Geocoder class provides this facility. In fact, the Geocoder class provides both forward and backward conversion—it can take an address and return a latitude/longitude pair, and it can translate a latitude/longitude pair into a list of addresses. The class provides the following methods:

- List<Address> getFromLocation(double latitude, double longitude, int maxResults)

- List<Address> getFromLocationName(String locationName, int maxResults, double lowerLeftLatitude, double lowerLeftLongitude, double upperRightLatitude, double upperRightLongitude)

- List<Address> getFromLocationName(String locationName, int maxResults)

It turns out that computing an address is not an exact science, due to the various ways a location can be described. For example, the getFromLocationName() methods can take the name of a place, the physical address, an airport code, or simply a well-known name for the location. Thus, the methods provide a list of addresses and not a single address. Because the methods return a list, you are encouraged to limit the result set by providing a value for maxResults that ranges between 1 and 5. Now let's see an example.

Listing 7-16 shows the XML layout and corresponding code for the user interface shown in Figure 7-9. To run the example, you'll need to update the listing with your own map-api key.

Listing 7-16. *Working with the Android Geocoder Class*

```xml
<RelativeLayout xmlns:android="http://schemas.android.com/apk/res/android"
        android:layout_width="fill_parent"
        android:layout_height="fill_parent">

    <LinearLayout android:layout_width="fill_parent"
android:layout_alignParentBottom="true"
        android:layout_height="wrap_content" android:orientation="vertical" >

        <EditText android:layout_width="fill_parent" android:id="@+id/location"
        android:layout_height="wrap_content" android:text="White House"/>

        <Button android:id="@+id/geocodeBtn"
android:layout_width="wrap_content"
android:layout_height="wrap_content" android:text="Find Location"/>
    </LinearLayout>

    <com.google.android.maps.MapView
    android:id="@+id/geoMap" android:clickable="true"
            android:layout_width="fill_parent"
            android:layout_height="320px"
            android:apiKey="07vhLOusFXryRakmo2A4t8aKViWwKyGJGEDqpdg"
            />

</RelativeLayout>

import java.io.IOException;
import java.util.List;

import android.location.Address;
import android.location.Geocoder;
import android.os.Bundle;
import android.view.View;
import android.view.View.OnClickListener;
import android.widget.Button;
import android.widget.EditText;
```

```java
import com.google.android.maps.GeoPoint;
import com.google.android.maps.MapActivity;
import com.google.android.maps.MapView;

public class GeocodingDemoActivity extends MapActivity
{
    Geocoder geocoder = null;
    MapView mapView = null;
    @Override
    protected boolean isRouteDisplayed() {
        return false;
    }

    @Override
    protected void onCreate(Bundle icicle)
    {
        super.onCreate(icicle);

        setContentView(R.layout.geocode);
        mapView = (MapView)findViewById(R.id.geoMap);
        // lat/long of Jacksonville, FL
        int lat = (int)(30.334954*1000000);
        int lng = (int)(-81.5625*1000000);
        GeoPoint pt = new GeoPoint(lat,lng);
        mapView.getController().setZoom(10);
        mapView.getController().setCenter(pt);
        mapView.getController().animateTo(pt);
        //
        Button geoBtn =(Button)findViewById(R.id.geocodeBtn);

        geocoder = new Geocoder(this);

        //
        geoBtn.setOnClickListener(new OnClickListener(){

        @Override
        public void onClick(View arg0) {
            try {
                EditText loc = (EditText)findViewById(R.id.location);
                String locationName = loc.getText().toString();

                List<Address> addressList =
geocoder.getFromLocationName(locationName, 5);
                if(addressList!=null && addressList.size()>0)
                {
                    int lat = (int)addressList.get(0).getLatitude()*1000000;
                    int lng = (int)addressList.get(0).getLongitude()*1000000;
```

```
                    GeoPoint pt = new GeoPoint(lat,lng);
                    mapView.getController().setZoom(10);
                    mapView.getController().setCenter(pt);
                    mapView.getController().animateTo(pt);
                }
            } catch (IOException e) {
                e.printStackTrace();
            }
        }});


    }
}
```

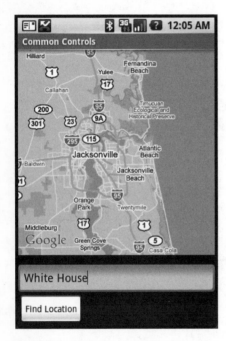

Figure 7-9. *Geocoding to a point given the location name*

To demonstrate the uses of geocoding in Android, type the name of the location, or its address, in the EditText field and then click the Find Location button. In order to find the address of a location, call the getFromLocationName() method of Geocoder. The location can be an address or a well-known name such as "White House." Geocoding can be a timely operation, so we recommend that you limit the results to five, as the Android documentation suggests. The call to getFromLocationName() returns a list of addresses. The sample application takes the list of addresses and processes the first one if any were found. Every address has a latitude and longitude, which you use to create a GeoPoint. You then get the map controller and navigate to the point. Note that before you call animateTo(), you set the zoom level to 10 and center the map to the same point. The zoom level can be set to an integer between 1 and 21, inclusive. As you move from 1 toward 21, the zoom level increases by a factor of 2.

You should understand a few points with respect to geocoding. First, a returned address is not always an exact address. Obviously, because the returned list of addresses depends on the accuracy of the input, you need to make every effort to provide an accurate location name to the Geocoder. Second, whenever possible, set the maxResults parameter to a value between 1 and 5. Lastly, you should seriously consider doing the geocoding operation in a different thread from the UI thread. There are two reasons for this. The first is obvious: the operation is time-consuming and you don't want the UI to hang while you do the geocoding. The second reason is that with a mobile device, you always need to assume that the network connection can be lost and that the connection is weak. Therefore, you need to handle input/output (I/O) exceptions and timeouts appropriately. Once you have computed the addresses, you can then post the results to the UI thread. Let's investigate this a bit more.

Geocoding with Background Threads

Using background threads to handle time-consuming operations is very common. The general pattern is to handle a UI event (such as a button click) to initiate a timely operation. From the event handler, you create a new thread to execute the work and start the thread. The UI thread then returns to the user interface to handle interaction with the user, while the background thread works. After the background thread completes, a part of the UI might have to be updated or the user might have to be notified. The background thread does not update the UI directly; instead, the background thread notifies the UI thread to update itself. Listing 7-17 demonstrates this idea using geocoding.

Listing 7-17. *Geocoding in a Separate Thread*

```
import java.io.IOException;
import java.util.List;

import android.app.AlertDialog;
import android.app.Dialog;
import android.app.ProgressDialog;
import android.location.Address;
import android.location.Geocoder;
import android.os.Bundle;
import android.os.Handler;
import android.os.Message;
import android.view.View;
import android.view.View.OnClickListener;
import android.widget.Button;
import android.widget.EditText;

import com.google.android.maps.GeoPoint;
import com.google.android.maps.MapActivity;
import com.google.android.maps.MapView;
public class GeocodingWithThreadsDemoActivity extends MapActivity
```

```java
{
    Geocoder geocoder = null;
    MapView mapView = null;
    ProgressDialog progDialog=null;
    List<Address> addressList=null;
    @Override
    protected boolean isRouteDisplayed() {
        return false;
    }

    @Override
    protected void onCreate(Bundle icicle) {
        super.onCreate(icicle);

        setContentView(R.layout.geocode);
        mapView = (MapView)findViewById(R.id.geoMap);
        // lat/long of Jacksonville, FL
        int lat = (int)(30.334954*1000000);
        int lng = (int)(-81.5625*1000000);
        GeoPoint pt = new GeoPoint(lat,lng);
        mapView.getController().setZoom(10);
        mapView.getController().setCenter(pt);
        mapView.getController().animateTo(pt);
        //
        Button geoBtn =(Button)findViewById(R.id.geocodeBtn);

        geocoder = new Geocoder(this);

        //
        geoBtn.setOnClickListener(new OnClickListener(){

            @Override
            public void onClick(View view) {
                EditText loc = (EditText)findViewById(R.id.location);
                String locationName = loc.getText().toString();

                progDialog =
ProgressDialog.show(GeocodingWithThreadsDemoActivity.this,
"Processing...", "Finding Location...", true, false);

                findLocation(locationName);
            }});

    }

    private void findLocation(final String locationName)
    {
```

```java
        Thread thrd = new Thread()
        {
            public void run()
            {
                try {
                    // do background work
                    addressList = geocoder.getFromLocationName(locationName, 5);
                    //send message to handler to process results
                    uiCallback.sendEmptyMessage(0);

                } catch (IOException e) {
                    e.printStackTrace();
                }
            }
        };
        thrd.start();
    }
    // ui thread callback handler
    private Handler uiCallback = new Handler()
    {
        @Override
        public void handleMessage(Message msg)
        {
            progDialog.dismiss();

            if(addressList!=null && addressList.size()>0)
            {
                int lat = (int)addressList.get(0).getLatitude()*1000000;
                int lng = (int)addressList.get(0).getLongitude()*1000000;
                GeoPoint pt = new GeoPoint(lat,lng);
                mapView.getController().setZoom(10);
                mapView.getController().setCenter(pt);
                mapView.getController().animateTo(pt);

            }
            else
            {
                Dialog foundNothingDlg = new
AlertDialog.Builder(GeocodingWithThreadsDemoActivity.this)
                    .setIcon(0)
                    .setTitle("Failed to Find Location")
                    .setPositiveButton("Ok", null)
                    .setMessage("Location Not Found...")
                    .create();
                foundNothingDlg.show();
            }
        }
    };
}
```

```
// geocode.xml
<RelativeLayout xmlns:android="http://schemas.android.com/apk/res/android"
        android:layout_width="fill_parent"
        android:layout_height="fill_parent">
        <LinearLayout android:layout_width="fill_parent"
android:layout_alignParentBottom="true"
            android:layout_height="wrap_content" android:orientation="vertical" >

            <EditText android:layout_width="fill_parent" android:id="@+id/location"
            android:layout_height="wrap_content" android:text="ORLANDO FLORIDA"/>

            <Button android:id="@+id/geocodeBtn"
android:layout_width="wrap_content"
android:layout_height="wrap_content" android:text="Find Location"/>
        </LinearLayout>

        <com.google.android.maps.MapView
        android:id="@+id/geoMap" android:clickable="true"
            android:layout_width="fill_parent"
            android:layout_height="320px"
            android:apiKey="PUT_MAPPING-API KEY HERE"
            />

</RelativeLayout>
```

Listing 7-17 is a modified version of the example in Listing 7-16. The difference is that now, in the onClick() method, you display a progress dialog and call findLocation() (see Figure 7-10). findLocation() then creates a new thread and calls the start() method, which ultimately results in a call to the thread's run() method. In the run() method, you use the Geocoder class to search for the location. When the search is done, you must post the message to something that knows how to interact with the UI thread, because you need to update the map. Android provides the android.os.Handler class for this purpose. From the background thread, call the uiCallback.sendEmptyMessage(0) to have the UI thread process the results from the search. The code calls the handler's callback, which looks at the addressList returned by the Geocoder. The callback then updates the map with the result or displays an alert dialog to indicate that the search returned nothing. The UI for this example is shown in Figure 7-10.

Figure 7-10. *Showing a progress window during long operations*

Understanding the LocationManager Service

The LocationManager service is one of the key services offered by the android.location package. This service provides two things: a mechanism for you to obtain the device's geographical location, and a facility for you to be notified (via an intent) when the device enters a specified geographical location.

In this section, you are going to learn how the LocationManager service works. To use the service, you must first obtain a reference to it. Listing 7-18 shows the usage pattern for the LocationManager service.

Listing 7-18. *Using the LocationManager Service*

```java
import java.util.List;

import android.app.Activity;
import android.content.Context;
import android.location.Location;
import android.location.LocationManager;
import android.os.Bundle;
public class LocationManagerDemoActivity extends Activity
{
```

```
@Override
protected void onCreate(Bundle savedInstanceState)
{
    super.onCreate(savedInstanceState);
    LocationManager locMgr =
(LocationManager)this.getSystemService(Context.LOCATION_SERVICE);
Location loc = locMgr.getLastKnownLocation(LocationManager.GPS_PROVIDER);

List<String> providerList = locMgr.getAllProviders();


}
}
```

The LocationManager service is a system-level service. System-level services are services that you obtain from the context using the service name; you don't instantiate them directly. The android.app.Activity class provides a utility method called getSystemService() that you can use to obtain a system-level service. As shown in Listing 7-18, you call getSystemService() and pass in the name of the service you want—in this case, Context.LOCATION_SERVICE.

The LocationManager service provides geographical-location details by using location providers. Currently, there are two types of location providers: GPS and Network. GPS providers use a Global Positioning System to obtain location information, whereas network providers use cell-phone towers or WiFi networks to obtain location information. The LocationManager class can provide the device's last-known location (practically the current location) via the getLastKnownLocation() method. Location information is obtained from a provider, so the method takes as a parameter the name of the provider you want to use. Valid values for provider names are LocationManager.GPS_PROVIDER and LocationManager.Network. Calling getLastKnownLocation() returns an android.location.Location instance. The Location class provides the location's latitude and longitude, the time the location was computed, and possibly the device's altitude, speed, and bearing.

Because the LocationManager operates on providers, the class provides APIs to obtain providers. For example, you can get all of the providers by calling getAllProviders(). You can obtain a specific provider by calling getProvider(), passing the name of the provider as an argument (such as LocationManager.GPS_PROVIDER).

To that end, the gotcha with using the LocationManager services occurs at development time—LocationManager needs location information and the emulator doesn't really have access to GPS or cell towers. So in order for you to develop with the LocationManager service, you (sort of) tell the emulator about your location. For example, you can ask the LocationManager to notify you if the device is near a location. To test something like this with the emulator, you would have to send the emulator periodic updates on your location; the emulator would then play that information back to the application. Listing 7-19 shows an example.

Listing 7-19. *Registering for Location Updates*

```
import android.app.Activity;
import android.content.Context;
import android.location.Location;
import android.location.LocationListener;
```

```java
import android.location.LocationManager;
import android.os.Bundle;
import android.widget.Toast;

public class LocationUpdateDemoActivity extends Activity
{
    @Override
    public void onCreate(Bundle savedInstanceState)
    {
        super.onCreate(savedInstanceState);

        LocationManager locMgr = (LocationManager)
getSystemService(Context.LOCATION_SERVICE);

        LocationListener locListener = new LocationListener()
        {

            public void  onLocationChanged(Location location)
                {
                        if (location != null)
                        {
                                Toast.makeText(getBaseContext(),
                                    "New location latitude [" +
location.getLatitude() +
                                        "] longitude [" + location.getLongitude()+"]",
                                    Toast.LENGTH_SHORT).show();
                        }
                }

            public void  onProviderDisabled(String provider)
                {
                }

            public void  onProviderEnabled(String provider)
                {
                }

            public void  onStatusChanged(String provider,
int status, Bundle extras)
                {
                }


        };
```

```
        locMgr.requestLocationUpdates(
            LocationManager.GPS_PROVIDER,
            0,
            0,
            locListener);
    }
}
```

As we said, one of the primary uses of the LocationManager service is to receive notifications of the device's location. Listing 7-19 demonstrates how you can register a listener to receive location-update events. To register a listener, you call the requestLocationUpdates() method, passing the provider type as one of the parameters. When the location changes, the LocationManager calls the onLocationChanged() method of the listener with the new Location. In Listing 7-19, our listener implementation simply shows a message in the UI to indicate the new latitude and longitude of the location. To test this in the emulator, you can use the Dalvik Debug Monitor Service (DDMS) interface that ships with the ADT plug-in for Eclipse. The DDMS UI provides a screen for you to send the emulator a new location (see Figure 7-11).

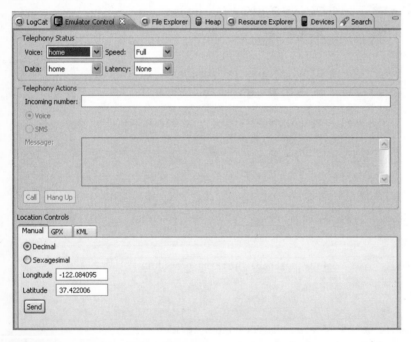

Figure 7-11. *Using the DDMS UI in Eclipse to send location data to the emulator*

As shown in Figure 7-11, the Manual tab in the DDMS user interface allows you to send a new GPS location (latitude/longitude pair) to the emulator. Sending a new location will fire the onLocationChanged() method on the listener, which will result in a message to the user conveying the new location.

You can send location data to the emulator using several other techniques, as shown in the DDMS user interface (see Figure 7-11). For example, the DDMS interface allows you to submit a GPS Exchange Format (GPX) file or a Keyhole Markup Language (KML) file. You can obtain sample GPX files from these sites:

- http://www.topografix.com/gpx_resources.asp

- http://tramper.co.nz/?view=gpxFiles

- http://www.gpxchange.com/

Similarly, you can use the following KML resources to obtain or create KML files:

- http://bbs.keyhole.com/

- http://code.google.com/apis/kml/documentation/kml_tut.html

So you can upload a GPX or KML file to the emulator and set the speed at which the emulator will play back the file (see Figure 7-12). The emulator will then send location updates to your application based on the configured speed.

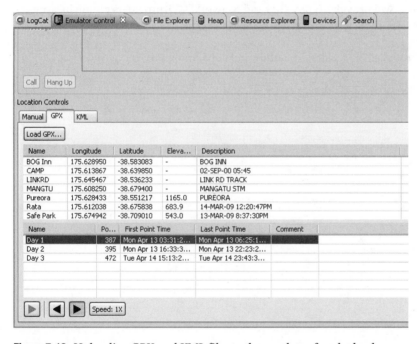

Figure 7-12. *Uploading GPX and KML files to the emulator for playback*

Summary

In this chapter, we discussed two important parts of the Android SDK: the application-security model and location-based services.

With respect to security, you learned that Android requires all applications to be signed with a digital signature. We discussed ensuring build-time security with the emulator and Eclipse, as well as signing an Android package for release. We also talked about runtime security—you learned that the Android installer requests the permissions your application needs at install time. If a particular permission is denied, then any code that attempts to access a resource protected by a permission will result in a permission exception. We also showed you how to define the permissions required by your application, as well as how to sign the .apk file for deployment.

With respect to location-based services, we talked at length about using the MapView control and the MapActivity class. We started with the basics of the map and then showed you how to utilize overlays to place markers on maps. We even showed you how to geocode and handle geocoding in background threads. The last thing we talked about was the LocationManager class, which provides detailed location information through providers. You can choose from two provider types: GPS and Network. GPS providers obtain location information using Global Positioning Systems, while network providers utilize cell towers and WiFi networks.

In the next chapter, we'll talk about building and consuming services in Android.

CHAPTER 8

Building and Consuming Services

The Android Platform provides a complete software stack. This means you get an operating system and middleware, as well as working applications (such as a phone dialer). Alongside all of this, you have an SDK that you can use to write applications for the platform. Thus far, we've seen that we can build applications that directly interact with the user through a user interface. We have not, however, discussed background services or the possibilities of building components that run in the background.

In this chapter, we are going to focus on building and consuming services in Android. First we'll discuss consuming HTTP services, then we'll discuss interprocess communication (communication between applications on the same device).

Consuming HTTP Services

Android applications and mobile applications in general are small apps with a lot of functionality. One of the ways that mobile apps deliver such rich functionality on such a small device is that they pull information from various sources. For example, the T-Mobile G1 comes with the Maps application, which provides seemingly sophisticated mapping functionality. We, however, know that the application is integrated with Google Maps and other services, which provide most of the sophistication.

That said, it is likely that the applications you write will also leverage information from other applications. A common integration strategy is to use HTTP. For example, you might have a Java servlet that provides services you want to leverage from one of your Android applications. How do you do that with Android? Interestingly, the Android SDK ships with Apache's HttpClient (`http://hc.apache.org/httpclient-3.x/`), which is universally used within the J2EE space. The Android SDK ships with a version of the HttpClient that has been modified for Android, but the APIs are very similar to the APIs in the J2EE version.

The Apache HttpClient is a comprehensive HTTP client. Although it offers full support for the HTTP protocol, you will likely utilize `HTTP GET` and `POST`. In this section, we will discuss using the HttpClient to make `HTTP GET` and `HTTP POST` calls.

Using the HttpClient for HTTP GET Requests

Here's the general pattern for using the HttpClient:

1. Create an HttpClient (or get an existing reference).

2. Instantiate a new HTTP method, such as PostMethod or GetMethod.

3. Set HTTP parameter names/values.

4. Execute the HTTP call using the HttpClient.

5. Process the HTTP response.

Listing 8-1 shows how to execute an HTTP GET using the HttpClient.

■**Note** Because the code attempts to use the Internet, you will need to add android.permission. INTERNET to your manifest file when making HTTP calls using the HttpClient.

Listing 8-1. *Using the HttpClient to Get an HTTP GET request*

```
import java.io.BufferedReader;
import java.io.IOException;
import java.io.InputStreamReader;
import java.net.URI;

import org.apache.http.HttpResponse;
import org.apache.http.client.HttpClient;
import org.apache.http.client.methods.HttpGet;
import org.apache.http.impl.client.DefaultHttpClient;

public class TestHttpGet {

    public void executeHttpGet() throws Exception {
    BufferedReader in = null;
    try {
        HttpClient client = new DefaultHttpClient();
        HttpGet request = new HttpGet();
        request.setURI(new URI("http://code.google.com/android/"));
        HttpResponse response = client.execute(request);
        in = new BufferedReader
(new InputStreamReader(response.getEntity()
            .getContent()));
```

```
            StringBuffer sb = new StringBuffer("");
            String line = "";
            String NL = System.getProperty("line.separator");
            while ((line = in.readLine()) != null) {
                sb.append(line + NL);
            }
            in.close();

            String page = sb.toString();
            System.out.println(page);
        } finally {
            if (in != null) {
                try {
                    in.close();
                } catch (IOException e) {
                    e.printStackTrace();
                }
            }
        }


    }
}
```

The HttpClient provides abstractions for the various HTTP request types, such as HttpGet, HttpPost, and so on. Listing 8-1 uses the HttpClient to get the contents of the http://code. google.com/android/ URL. The actual HTTP request is executed with the call to client. execute(). After executing the request, the code reads the entire response into a string object. Note that the BufferedReader is closed in the finally block, which also closes the underlying HTTP connection.

Realize that the class in Listing 8-1 does not extend android.app.Activity. In other words, you don't need to be within the context of an activity to use HttpClient—because HttpClient is packaged with Android, you can use it from within the context of any Android component (such as an activity) or use it as part of a standalone class.

The code in Listing 8-1 executes an HTTP request without passing any HTTP parameters to the server. You can pass name/value parameters as part of the request by appending name/ value pairs to the URL, as shown in Listing 8-2.

Listing 8-2. *Adding Parameters to an HTTP GET Request*

```
HttpGet method = new HttpGet("http://somehost/WS2/Upload.aspx?one=valueGoesHere");
client.execute(method);
```

When you execute an HTTP GET, the parameters (names and values) of the request are passed as part of the URL. Passing parameters this way has some limitations. Namely, the length of a URL should be kept below 2,048 characters. Instead of using HTTP GET, you can use HTTP POST. The POST method is more flexible and passes parameters as part of the request body.

Using the HttpClient for HTTP POST Requests

Making an HTTP POST call is very similar to making an HTTP GET call (see Listing 8-3).

Listing 8-3. *Making an HTTP POST Request with the HttpClient*

```
import java.util.ArrayList;
import java.util.List;

import org.apache.http.HttpResponse;
import org.apache.http.NameValuePair;
import org.apache.http.client.HttpClient;
import org.apache.http.client.entity.UrlEncodedFormEntity;
import org.apache.http.client.methods.HttpPost;
import org.apache.http.impl.client.DefaultHttpClient;
import org.apache.http.message.BasicNameValuePair;

public class TestHttpPost
{
    public String executeHttpPost() throws Exception {
        BufferedReader in = null;
        try {
            HttpClient client = new DefaultHttpClient();
            HttpPost request = new HttpPost(
                    "http://somewebsite/WS2/Upload.aspx");

            List<NameValuePair> postParameters = new ArrayList<NameValuePair>();
            postParameters.add(new BasicNameValuePair("one", "valueGoesHere"));
            UrlEncodedFormEntity formEntity = new UrlEncodedFormEntity(
                    postParameters);

            request.setEntity(formEntity);
            HttpResponse response = client.execute(request);
            in = new BufferedReader(new InputStreamReader(response.getEntity()
                    .getContent()));

            StringBuffer sb = new StringBuffer("");
            String line = "";
            String NL = System.getProperty("line.separator");
            while ((line = in.readLine()) != null) {
                sb.append(line + NL);
            }
            in.close();

            String result = sb.toString();
            return result;
```

```
        } finally {
            if (in != null) {
                try {
                    in.close();
                } catch (IOException e) {
                    e.printStackTrace();
                }
            }
        }

    }
}
```

To make an HTTP POST call with the HttpClient, you have to call the execute method of the HttpClient with an instance of HttpPost. When making HTTP POST calls, you generally pass URL-encoded name/value form parameters as part of the HTTP request. To do this with the HttpClient, you have to create a list that contains instances of NameValuePair objects and then wrap that list with a UrlEncodedFormEntity object. The NameValuePair wraps a name/value combination and the UrlEncodedFormEntity class knows how to encode a list of NameValuePair objects suitable for HTTP calls (generally POST calls). After you create a UrlEncodedFormEntity, you can set the entity type of the HttpPost to the UrlEncodedFormEntity and then execute the request.

In Listing 8-3, we create an HttpClient and then instantiate the HttpPost with the URL of the HTTP endpoint. Next we create a list of NameValuePair objects and populate that with a single name/value parameter. We set the name of the parameter to one and the value of the parameter to valueGoesHere. We then create a UrlEncodedFormEntity instance, passing the list of NameValuePair objects to its constructor. Finally, we call the setEntity() method of the POST request and then execute the request using the HttpClient instance.

HTTP POST is actually much more powerful than this. With an HTTP POST, we can pass simple name/value parameters, as shown in Listing 8-3, as well as complex parameters such as files. HTTP POST supports another request-body format known as a "multipart POST." With this type of POST, you can send name/value parameters as before, along with arbitrary files. Unfortunately, the version of HttpClient shipped with Android does not directly support multipart POST. To do multipart POST calls, you need to get three additional Apache open source projects: Apache Commons IO, Mime4j, and HttpMime. You can download these projects from the following web sites:

- *Commons IO*: http://commons.apache.org/io/

- *Mime4j*: http://james.apache.org/mime4j/

- *HttpMime*: http://hc.apache.org/httpcomponents-client/httpmime/index.html

Alternatively, you can visit this site to download all of the required .jar files to do multipart POST with Android:

http://www.sayedhashimi.com/downloads/android/multipart-android.zip

Listing 8-4 demonstrates a multipart POST using Android.

Listing 8-4. *Making a Multipart POST Call*

```java
import java.io.ByteArrayInputStream;
import java.io.InputStream;

import org.apache.commons.io.IOUtils;
import org.apache.http.HttpResponse;
import org.apache.http.client.HttpClient;
import org.apache.http.client.methods.HttpPost;
import org.apache.http.entity.mime.MultipartEntity;
import org.apache.http.entity.mime.content.InputStreamBody;
import org.apache.http.entity.mime.content.StringBody;
import org.apache.http.impl.client.DefaultHttpClient;

import android.app.Activity;

public class TestMultipartPost extends Activity
{
    public void executeMultipartPost()throws Exception
    {

        try {
            InputStream is = this.getAssets().open("data.xml");
            HttpClient httpClient = new DefaultHttpClient();
            HttpPost postRequest =
             new HttpPost("http://192.178.10.131/WS2/Upload.aspx");

            byte[] data = IOUtils.toByteArray(is);

            InputStreamBody isb = new InputStreamBody(new
ByteArrayInputStream(data),"uploadedFile");
            StringBody sb1 = new StringBody("someTextGoesHere");
            StringBody sb2 = new StringBody("someTextGoesHere too");

            MultipartEntity multipartContent = new MultipartEntity();
            multipartContent.addPart("uploadedFile", isb);
            multipartContent.addPart("one", sb1);
            multipartContent.addPart("two", sb2);

            postRequest.setEntity(multipartContent);
            HttpResponse res =httpClient.execute(postRequest);
            res.getEntity().getContent().close();
        } catch (Throwable e)
        {
            throw e;
        }


    }
}
```

■Note The multipart example uses several .jar files that are not included as part of the Android runtime. To ensure that the .jar files will be packaged as part of your .apk file, you need to add them as external .jar files in Eclipse: right-click your project in Eclipse, select Properties, choose Java Class Path, select the Libraries tab, and then select Add External JARs.

Following these steps will make the .jar files available during compile time as well as runtime.

To execute a multipart POST, you need to create an HttpPost and call its setEntity() method with a MultipartEntity instance (rather than the UrlEncodedFormEntity we created for the name/value parameter form post). MultipartEntity represents the body of a multipart POST request. As shown, you create an instance of a MultipartEntity and then call the addPart() method with each part. Listing 8-4 adds three parts to the request: two string parts and an XML file.

Finally, if you are building an application that requires you to pass a multipart POST to a web resource, you'll likely have to debug the solution using a dummy implementation of the service on your local workstation. You can access the local machine by using localhost or IP address 127.0.0.1. With Android applications, however, you will not be able to use localhost (or 127.0.0.1) because the emulator will have its own localhost. To refer to your development workstation from the application running in the emulator, you'll have to use your workstation's IP address. On a Windows XP machine, you can obtain your IP address by running the IPConfig DOS command. You would need to modify Listing 8-4 by substituting the IP address with the IP address of your workstation.

Dealing with Exceptions

Dealing with exceptions is part of any program, but software that makes use of external services (such as HTTP services) must pay additional attention to exceptions because the potential for errors is magnified. There are several types of exceptions that you can expect while making use of HTTP services. These include transport exceptions, protocol exceptions, and timeouts. You should understand when these exceptions could occur.

Transport exceptions can occur due to a number of reasons, but the most likely scenario (with a mobile device) is poor network connectivity. Protocol exceptions are exceptions at the HTTP protocol layer. These include authentication errors, invalid cookies, and so on. You can expect to see protocol exceptions if, for example, you have to supply login credentials as part of your HTTP request but fail to do so. Timeouts, with respect to HTTP calls, come in two flavors: connection timeouts and socket timeouts. A connection timeout can occur if the HttpClient is not able to connect to the HTTP server—if, for example, the URL is not correct or the server is not available. A socket timeout can occur if the HttpClient fails to receive a response within a defined time period. In other words, the HttpClient was able to connect to the server, but the server failed to return a response within the allocated time limit.

Now that you understand the types of exceptions that might occur, how do you deal with them? Fortunately, the HttpClient is a robust framework that takes most of the burden off your shoulders. In fact, the only exception types that you'll have to worry about are the ones that you'll be able to manage easily. As we said earlier, there are three types of exceptions that you can expect: transport exceptions, protocol exceptions, and timeouts. The HttpClient takes care of transport exceptions by detecting transport issues and retrying requests (which works very well with this type of exception). Protocol exceptions are exceptions that can generally be flushed out during development. Timeouts are the ones that you'll have to deal with. A simple and effective approach to dealing with both types of timeouts—connection timeouts and socket timeouts—is to wrap the execute method of your HTTP request with a try/catch and then retry if a failure occurs. This is demonstrated in Listing 8-5.

Listing 8-5. *Implementing a Simple Retry Technique to Deal with Timeouts*

```java
import java.io.BufferedReader;
import java.io.IOException;
import java.io.InputStreamReader;
import java.net.URI;

import org.apache.http.HttpResponse;
import org.apache.http.client.HttpClient;
import org.apache.http.client.methods.HttpGet;
import org.apache.http.impl.client.DefaultHttpClient;

public class TestHttpGet {

    public String executeHttpGetWithRetry() throws Exception {
        int retry = 3;

        int count = 0;
        while (count < retry) {
            count += 1;
            try {
                String response = executeHttpGet();
                /**
                 * if we get here, that means we were successful and we can
                 * stop.
                 */
                return response;
            } catch (Exception e) {
                /**
                 * if we have exhausted our retry limit
                 */
                if (count < retry) {
                /**
                 * we have retries remaining, so log the message and go
                 * again.
                 */
                System.out.println(e.getMessage());
                } else {
                    System.out.println("could not succeed with retry...");
                    throw e;
                }
            }
        }
    }
```

```
        return null;
    }

    public String executeHttpGet() throws Exception {
        BufferedReader in = null;
        try {
            HttpClient client = new DefaultHttpClient();
            HttpGet request = new HttpGet();
            request.setURI(new URI("http://code.google.com/android/"));
            HttpResponse response = client.execute(request);
            in = new BufferedReader(new InputStreamReader(response.getEntity()
                    .getContent()));

            StringBuffer sb = new StringBuffer("");
            String line = "";
            String NL = System.getProperty("line.separator");
            while ((line = in.readLine()) != null) {
                sb.append(line + NL);
            }
            in.close();

            String result = sb.toString();
            return result;
        } finally {
            if (in != null) {
                try {
                    in.close();
                } catch (IOException e) {
                    e.printStackTrace();
                }
            }
        }


    }
}
```

The code in Listing 8-5 shows how you can implement a simple retry technique to recover from timeouts when making HTTP calls. The listing shows two methods: one that executes an HTTP GET (executeHttpGet()), and another that wraps this method with the retry logic (executeHttpGetWithRetry()). The logic is very simple. We set the number of retries we want to attempt to 3, and then we enter a while loop. Within the loop, we execute the request. Note that the request is wrapped with a try/catch block, and in the catch block we check whether we have exhausted the number of retry attempts.

When using the HttpClient as part of a real-world application, you need to pay some attention to multithreading issues that might come up. Let's delve into this now.

Addressing Multithreading Issues

The examples we've shown so far created a new HttpClient for each request. In practice, however, you should create one HttpClient for the entire application and use that for all of your HTTP communication. With one HttpClient servicing all of your HTTP requests, you should also pay attention to multithreading issues that could surface if you make multiple simultaneous requests through the same HttpClient. Fortunately, the HttpClient provides facilities that make this easy—all you have to do is create the DefaultHttpClient using a ThreadSafeClientConnManager, as shown in Listing 8-6.

Listing 8-6. *Creating an HttpClient for Multithreading Purposes*

```
// ApplicationEx.java
import org.apache.http.HttpVersion;
import org.apache.http.client.HttpClient;
import org.apache.http.conn.ClientConnectionManager;
import org.apache.http.conn.scheme.PlainSocketFactory;
import org.apache.http.conn.scheme.Scheme;
import org.apache.http.conn.scheme.SchemeRegistry;
import org.apache.http.conn.ssl.SSLSocketFactory;
import org.apache.http.impl.client.DefaultHttpClient;
import org.apache.http.impl.conn.tsccm.ThreadSafeClientConnManager;
import org.apache.http.params.BasicHttpParams;
import org.apache.http.params.HttpParams;
import org.apache.http.params.HttpProtocolParams;
import org.apache.http.protocol.HTTP;

import android.app.Application;
import android.util.Log;

public class ApplicationEx extends Application
{
    private static final String TAG = "ApplicationEx";
    private HttpClient httpClient;

    @Override
    public void onCreate()
    {
        super.onCreate();

        httpClient = createHttpClient();

    }
```

```java
    @Override
    public void onLowMemory()
    {
        super.onLowMemory();

        shutdownHttpClient();
    }

    @Override
    public void onTerminate()
    {
        super.onTerminate();
        shutdownHttpClient();
    }


    private HttpClient createHttpClient()
    {
        Log.d(TAG,"createHttpClient()...");
        HttpParams params = new BasicHttpParams();
        HttpProtocolParams.setVersion(params, HttpVersion.HTTP_1_1);
        HttpProtocolParams.setContentCharset(params, HTTP.DEFAULT_CONTENT_CHARSET);
        HttpProtocolParams.setUseExpectContinue(params, true);


        SchemeRegistry schReg = new SchemeRegistry();
        schReg.register(new Scheme("http",
      PlainSocketFactory.getSocketFactory(), 80));
        schReg.register(new Scheme("https",
      SSLSocketFactory.getSocketFactory(), 443));
        ClientConnectionManager conMgr = new
         ThreadSafeClientConnManager(params,schReg);

        return new DefaultHttpClient(conMgr, params);
    }

    public HttpClient getHttpClient() {
        return httpClient;
    }

    private void shutdownHttpClient()
    {
        if(httpClient!=null && httpClient.getConnectionManager()!=null)
        {
            httpClient.getConnectionManager().shutdown();
        }
    }
}
```

```java
// HttpActivity.java

import java.net.URI;

import org.apache.http.HttpResponse;
import org.apache.http.client.HttpClient;
import org.apache.http.client.methods.HttpGet;
import org.apache.http.util.EntityUtils;

import android.app.Activity;
import android.os.Bundle;
import android.util.Log;

public class HttpActivity extends Activity
{
    /** Called when the activity is first created. */
    @Override
    public void onCreate(Bundle savedInstanceState)
    {
        super.onCreate(savedInstanceState);

        Log.d("ServicesDemoActivity", "a debug statement");
        getHttpContent();
    }
    public void getHttpContent()
    {
        try {
            ApplicationEx app = (ApplicationEx)this.getApplication();
            HttpClient client = app.getHttpClient();
            HttpGet request = new HttpGet();
            request.setURI(new URI("http://www.google.com/"));
            HttpResponse response = client.execute(request);

            String page=EntityUtils.toString(response.getEntity());
            System.out.println(page);
        }
        catch (Exception e)
        {
            e.printStackTrace();
        }

    }

}
```

If your application needs to make more than a few HTTP calls, you should create an HttpClient that services all of your HTTP requests. One way to do this is to take advantage of the fact that each Android application has an associated application object. By default, if you don't define a custom application object, Android uses android.app.Application. Here's the interesting thing about the application object: there will always be exactly one application object for your application and all of your components can access it (using the global context object).

For example, from an activity class, you can call getApplication() to get the application object for your application. The idea here is that because the application is a singleton, and always available, we can extend that class and create our HttpClient there. We then provide an accessor method for all of the components in our application to get the HttpClient. This is what we have done in Listing 8-6. First notice that we have two classes defined in the listing (each should be placed in a separate Java file): one is our custom application object, and the other is a typical component—an activity class. In the ApplicationEx class we extend android.app.Application and then create our HttpClient in the onCreate() method. The class then provides an accessor method for components to obtain a reference to the client. In the HttpActivity class, we get a reference to the global application object and then cast that to our ApplicationEx class. We then call the getHttpClient() method and use that to make an HTTP call.

Now take a look at the createHttpClient() method of ApplicationEx. This method is responsible for creating our singleton HttpClient. Notice that when we instantiate the DefaultHttpClient(), we pass in a ClientConnectionManager. The ClientConnectionManager is responsible for managing HTTP connections for the HttpClient. Because we want to use a single HttpClient for all of the HTTP requests, we create a ThreadSafeClientConnManager.

Note that when you override or extend the default application object, you also have to modify the application node in the AndroidManifest.xml file by setting the android:name attribute like this:

```
<application android:icon="@drawable/icon"
android:label="@string/app_name"
android:name="ApplicationEx">
```

■**Note** You should also call the shutdown() method on the connection manager as demonstrated in Listing 8-6.

This concludes our discussion of using HTTP services with the HttpClient. In the sections that follow, we will turn our focus to another interesting part of the Android Platform: writing background/long-running services. Although not immediately obvious, the processes of making HTTP calls and writing Android services are linked in that you will do a lot of integration from within Android services. Take, for example, a simple mail-client application. On an Android device, this type of application will likely be composed of two pieces: one that will provide the UI to the user, and another to poll for mail messages. The polling will likely have to be done within a background service. The component that polls for new messages will be an Android service, which will in turn use the HttpClient to perform the work.

Now, let's get on with writing services.

Doing Interprocess Communication

Android supports the concept of services. Services are components that run in the background, without a user interface. You can think of these components as Windows services or Unix services. Similar to these types of services, Android services are always available but don't have to be actively doing something.

Android supports two types of services: *local services* and *remote services*. A local service is a service that is not accessible from other applications running on the device. Generally, these types of services simply support the application that is hosting the service. A remote service is accessible from other applications in addition to the application hosting the service. Remote services define themselves to clients using Android Interface Definition Language (AIDL).

Let's begin our exploration of services by writing a simple service.

Creating a Simple Service

To build a service, you extend the abstract class `android.app.Service` and put a service-configuration entry in your application's manifest file. Listing 8-7 shows an example.

Listing 8-7. *A Simple Android Service Definition*

```
import android.app.Service;
public class TestService1 extends Service
{
    private static final String TAG = "TestService1";


    @Override
    public void onCreate() {
        Log.d(TAG, "onCreate");
        super.onCreate();
    }

    @Override
    public IBinder onBind(Intent intent) {
        Log.d(TAG, "onBind");
        return null;
    }
}
// service definition entry: must go in the AndroidManifest.xml file.
<service android:name="TestService1"></service>
```

The service in Listing 8-7 isn't meant for practical use, but it serves our purpose of showing how a service is defined. To create a service, you write a class that extends `android.app.Service` and implements the `onBind()` method. You then put a service-definition entry in your `AndroidManifest.xml` file. That is how you implement a service. The next obvious question, then, is this: how do you call the service? The answer depends on the service's client and requires a bit more discussion on services.

Understanding Services in Android

We can gain more insight into the concept of a service by looking at the public methods of android.app.Service (see Listing 8-8).

Listing 8-8. *The Public Methods of a Service*

```
Application  getApplication();
abstract IBinder  onBind(Intent intent);
void onConfigurationChanged(Configuration newConfig);
void     onCreate();
void     onDestroy();
void     onLowMemory();
void     onRebind(Intent intent);
void     onStart(Intent intent, int startId);
boolean  onUnbind(Intent intent);
final void       setForeground(boolean isForeground);
final void       stopSelf();
final void       stopSelf(int startId);
final boolean    stopSelfResult(int startId);
```

The getApplication() method returns the application that implements the service. The onBind() method provides an interface for external applications running on the same device to talk to the service. onConfigurationChanged() allows the service to reconfigure itself if the device configuration changes.

The system calls onCreate() when the service is first created, but before calling onStart(). This process, which resembles the process for creating an activity, provides a way for the service to perform one-time initialization at startup. (See the "Examining the Application Lifecycle" section of Chapter 2 for details on creating an activity.) For example, if you create a background thread, do so in the onCreate() method and make sure to stop the thread in onDestroy(). The system calls onCreate(), then calls onStart(), then calls onDestroy() when the service is being shut down. The onDestroy() method provides a mechanism for the service to do final cleanup prior to going down.

Note that onStart(), onCreate(), and onDestroy() are called by the system; you should not call them directly. Moreover, if you override any of the on*() methods in your service class, be sure to call the superclass's version from yours. The various versions of stopSelf() provide a mechanism for the application to stop the service. A client can also call Context.stopService() to stop a service. We will talk about these methods and the others in the "Understanding Local Services" section.

Android supports the concept of a service for two reasons: first, to allow you to implement background tasks easily; second, to allow you to do interprocess communication between applications running on the same device. These two reasons correspond to the two types of services that Android supports: local services and remote services. An example of the first case might be a local service implemented as part of the e-mail application that we mentioned earlier. The service would poll the mail server for new messages and notify the user when new mail arrives. An example of the second case might be a router application. Suppose you have several applications running on a device and you need a service to accept messages and route them to various destinations. Rather than repeat the logic in every application, you could write a remote router service and have the applications talk to the service.

There are some important differences between local services and remote services. Specifically, if a service is strictly used by the components in the same process (to run background tasks), then the clients must start the service by calling `Context.startService()`. This type of service is a local service because its purpose is, generally, to run background tasks for the application that is hosting the service. If the service supports the `onBind()` method, it's a remote service that can be called via interprocess communication (`Context.bindService()`). We also call remote services *AIDL-supporting services* because clients communicate with the service using AIDL.

Although the interface of `android.app.Service` supports both local and remote services, it's not a good idea to provide one implementation of a service to support both types. The reason for this is that each type of service has a predefined lifecycle; mixing the two, although allowed, can cause errors.

Now we can begin a detailed examination of the two types of services. We will start by talking about local services and then discuss remote services (AIDL-supporting services). As mentioned before, local services are services that are called only by the application that hosts them. Remote services are services that support a Remote Procedure Call (RPC) mechanism. These services allow external clients, on the same device, to connect to the service and use its facilities.

■**Note** The second type of service in Android is known by several names: remote service, AIDL-supporting service, AIDL service, external service, and RPC service. These terms all refer to the same type of service— one that's meant to be accessed remotely by other applications running on the device.

Understanding Local Services

Local services are services that are started via `Context.startService()`. Once started, these types of services will continue to run until a client calls `Context.stopService()` on the service or the service itself calls `stopSelf()`. Note that when `Context.startService()` is called, the system will instantiate the service and call the service's `onStart()` method. Keep in mind that calling `Context.startService()` after the service has been started (that is, while it's running) will not result in another instance of the service, but doing so will invoke the service's `onStart()` method. Here are a couple examples of local services:

- A service to retrieve data over the network (such as the Internet) based on a timer (to either upload or download information)

- A task-executor service that lets your application's activities submit jobs and queue them for processing

Listing 8-9 demonstrates a local service by implementing a service that executes background tasks. The listing contains all of the artifacts required to create and consume the service: `BackgroundService.java`, the service itself; `MainActivity.java`, an activity class to call the service; and `main.xml`, a layout file for the activity.

Listing 8-9. *Implementing a Local Service*

```java
// BackgroundService.java

import android.app.Notification;
import android.app.NotificationManager;
import android.app.PendingIntent;
import android.app.Service;
import android.content.Intent;
import android.os.IBinder;

public class BackgroundService extends Service
{
    private NotificationManager notificationMgr;

    @Override
    public void onCreate() {
        super.onCreate();

        notificationMgr =(NotificationManager)getSystemService(
        NOTIFICATION_SERVICE);

        displayNotificationMessage("starting Background Service");

        Thread thr = new Thread(null, new ServiceWorker(), "BackgroundService");
        thr.start();

    }

    class ServiceWorker implements Runnable
    {
        public void run() {
            // do background processing here...

            // stop the service when done...
            // BackgroundService.this.stopSelf();
        }
    }

    @Override
    public void onDestroy()
    {
        displayNotificationMessage("stopping Background Service");
        super.onDestroy();

    }
```

```java
    @Override
    public void onStart(Intent intent, int startId) {
        super.onStart(intent, startId);

    }

    @Override
    public IBinder onBind(Intent intent) {
        return null;
    }

    private void displayNotificationMessage(String message)
    {

        Notification notification = new Notification(R.drawable.note,
message,System.currentTimeMillis());

        PendingIntent contentIntent =
PendingIntent.getActivity(this, 0,new Intent(this, MainActivity.class), 0);

        notification.setLatestEventInfo(this, "Background Service",message,
contentIntent);

        notificationMgr.notify(R.string.app_notification_id, notification);
    }

}

// MainActivity.java

import android.app.Activity;
import android.content.Intent;
import android.os.Bundle;
import android.util.Log;
import android.view.View;
import android.view.View.OnClickListener;
import android.widget.Button;

public class MainActivity extends Activity
{
    private static final String TAG = "MainActivity";
```

```java
    @Override
    public void onCreate(Bundle savedInstanceState)
    {
        super.onCreate(savedInstanceState);
        setContentView(R.layout.main);

        Log.d(TAG, "starting service");

        Button bindBtn = (Button)findViewById(R.id.bindBtn);
        bindBtn.setOnClickListener(new OnClickListener(){

            @Override
            public void onClick(View arg0) {
                startService(new Intent(MainActivity.this,
                        BackgroundService.class));
            }});

        Button unbindBtn = (Button)findViewById(R.id.unbindBtn);
        unbindBtn.setOnClickListener(new OnClickListener(){

            @Override
            public void onClick(View arg0) {
                stopService(new Intent(MainActivity.this,
                        BackgroundService.class));
            }});

    }
}
// main.xml (layout file for MainActivity.java)

<?xml version="1.0" encoding="utf-8"?>
<LinearLayout xmlns:android="http://schemas.android.com/apk/res/android"
    android:orientation="vertical"
    android:layout_width="fill_parent"
    android:layout_height="fill_parent"
    >
<Button  android:id="@+id/bindBtn"
    android:layout_width="wrap_content"
    android:layout_height="wrap_content"
    android:text="Bind"
    />

    <Button android:id="@+id/unbindBtn"
    android:layout_width="wrap_content"
    android:layout_height="wrap_content"
    android:text="UnBind"
    />
</LinearLayout>
```

Note that Listing 8-9 uses an activity to interface with the service, but any component in your application can use the service. This includes other services, activities, generic classes, and so on. The example creates a user interface with two buttons, labeled Bind and UnBind. Clicking the Bind button will start the service by calling startService(); clicking UnBind will stop the service by calling stopService(). Now let's talk about the meat of the example: the BackgroundService.

The BackgroundService is a typical example of a service that is used by the components of the application that is hosting the service. In other words, the application that is running the service is also the only consumer. Because the service does not support clients from outside its process, the service is a local service. And because it's a local service as opposed to a remote service, it returns null in the bind() method. Therefore, the only way to bind to this service is to call Context.startService(). The critical methods of a local service are: onCreate(), onStart(), stop*(), and onDestroy().

In the onCreate() method of the BackgroundService, we create a thread that does the service's heavy lifting. We need the application's main thread to deal with user interface activities, so we delegate the service's work to a secondary thread. Also note that we create and start the thread in onCreate() rather than onStart(). We do this because onCreate() is called only once, and we want the thread to be created only once during the life of the service. onStart() can be called more than once, so it doesn't suit our needs here. We don't do anything useful in the implementation of the thread's run method, but this would be the place to make an HTTP call, query a database, and so on.

The BackgroundService also uses the NotificationManager class to send notifications to the user when the service is started and stopped. This is one way for a local service to communicate information back to the user. To send notifications to the user, you obtain the notification manager by calling getSystemService(NOTIFICATION_SERVICE). Messages from the notification manager appear in the status bar.

To run the example, you need to create the BackgroundService.java service, the MainActivity.java activity class, and the main.xml layout file. You'll also need to create an icon named note and place it within your project's drawable folder. Plus, you need an application-level unique ID (integer) for the notification manager. You can create a unique ID by adding a dummy string constant to your string resources (a string at res/values/strings.xml). The unique ID is passed to the notification manager when you call the notify() method. In our example, we use the following:

```
<string name="app_notification_id">notification_id</string>
```

This concludes our discussion of local services. Let's dissect AIDL services—the more complicated type of service.

Understanding AIDL Services

In the previous section, we showed you how to write an Android service that is consumed by the application that hosts the service. Now we are going to show you how to build a service that can be consumed by other processes via Remote Procedure Call (RPC). As with many other RPC-based solutions, in Android you need an Interface Definition Language (IDL) to define the interface that will be exposed to clients. In the Android world, this IDL is called Android Interface Definition Language, or AIDL. To build a remote service, you do the following:

1. Write an AIDL file that defines your interface to clients. The AIDL file uses Java syntax and has an .aidl extension.

2. Add the AIDL file to your Eclipse project. The Android Eclipse plug-in will call the AIDL compiler to generate a Java interface from the AIDL file (the AIDL compiler is called as part of the build process).

3. Implement a service and return the interface from the onBind() method.

4. Add the service configuration to your AndroidManifest.xml file. The sections that follow show you how to execute each step.

Defining a Service Interface in AIDL

To demonstrate an example of a remote service, we are going to write a stock-quoter service. This service will provide a method that takes a ticker symbol and returns the stock value. To write a remote service in Android, the first step is to define the service definition in an AIDL file. Listing 8-10 shows the AIDL definition of IStockQuoteService.

Listing 8-10. *The AIDL Definition of the Stock-Quoter Service*

```
package com.syh;
interface IStockQuoteService
{
        double getQuote(String ticker);
}
```

The IStockQuoteService accepts the stock-ticker symbol as a string and returns the current stock value as a double. When you create the AIDL file, the Android Eclipse plug-in runs the AIDL compiler to process your AIDL file (as part of the build process). If your AIDL file compiles successfully, the compiler generates a Java interface suitable for RPC communication. Note that the generated file will be in the package named in your AIDL file—com.syh, in this case.

Listing 8-11 shows the generated Java file for our IStockQuoteService. Note that if you are using the Android 1.5 SDK, the generated file will be within the gen folder. See Chapter 12 for details.

Listing 8-11. *The Compiler-Generated Java File*

```
package com.syh;
import java.lang.String;
import android.os.RemoteException;
import android.os.IBinder;
import android.os.IInterface;
import android.os.Binder;
import android.os.Parcel;
/**
 *
 * @author sh
 *
 */
```

```java
public interface IStockQuoteService extends android.os.IInterface
{
/** Local-side IPC implementation stub class. */
public static abstract class Stub extends android.os.Binder
implements com.syh.IStockQuoteService
{
private static final java.lang.String DESCRIPTOR = "com.syh.IStockQuoteService";
/** Construct the stub at attach it to the interface. */
public Stub()
{
this.attachInterface(this, DESCRIPTOR);
}
/**
 * Cast an IBinder object into an IStockQuoteService interface,
 * generating a proxy if needed.
 */
public static com.syh.IStockQuoteService asInterface(android.os.IBinder obj)
{
if ((obj==null)) {
return null;
}
com.syh.IStockQuoteService in = (com.syh.IStockQuoteService)
obj.queryLocalInterface(DESCRIPTOR);
if ((in!=null)) {
return in;
}
return new com.syh.IStockQuoteService.Stub.Proxy(obj);
}
public android.os.IBinder asBinder()
{
return this;
}
public boolean onTransact(int code,
android.os.Parcel data, android.os.Parcel reply,
 int flags) throws android.os.RemoteException
{
switch (code)
{
case INTERFACE_TRANSACTION:
{
reply.writeString(DESCRIPTOR);
return true;
}
case TRANSACTION_getQuote:
{
data.enforceInterface(DESCRIPTOR);
java.lang.String _arg0;
```

```
_arg0 = data.readString();
double _result = this.getQuote(_arg0);
reply.writeNoException();
reply.writeDouble(_result);
return true;
}
}
return super.onTransact(code, data, reply, flags);
}
private static class Proxy implements com.syh.IStockQuoteService
{
private android.os.IBinder mRemote;
Proxy(android.os.IBinder remote)
{
mRemote = remote;
}
public android.os.IBinder asBinder()
{
return mRemote;
}
public java.lang.String getInterfaceDescriptor()
{
return DESCRIPTOR;
}
public double getQuote(java.lang.String ticker) throws android.os.RemoteException
{
android.os.Parcel _data = android.os.Parcel.obtain();
android.os.Parcel _reply = android.os.Parcel.obtain();
double _result;
try {
_data.writeInterfaceToken(DESCRIPTOR);
_data.writeString(ticker);
mRemote.transact(Stub.TRANSACTION_getQuote, _data, _reply, 0);
_reply.readException();
_result = _reply.readDouble();
}
finally {
_reply.recycle();
_data.recycle();
}
return _result;
}
}
static final int TRANSACTION_getQuote = (IBinder.FIRST_CALL_TRANSACTION + 0);
}
public double getQuote(java.lang.String ticker) throws android.os.RemoteException;
}
```

Note the following important points regarding the generated classes:

- The interface we defined in the AIDL file is implemented as an interface in the generated code (that is, there is an interface named IStockQuoteService).

- A static final abstract class named Stub extends android.os.Binder and implements IStockQuoteService. Note that the class is an abstract class.

- An inner class named Proxy implements the IStockQuoteService that proxies the Stub class.

- The AIDL file must reside in the package where the generated files are supposed to be (as specified in the AIDL file's package declaration).

Now let's move on and implement the AIDL interface in a service class.

Implementing an AIDL Interface

In the previous section, we defined an AIDL file for a stock-quoter service and generated the binding file. Now we are going to provide an implementation of that service. To implement the service's interface, we need to write a class that extends android.app.Service and implements the IStockQuoteService interface. To expose the service to clients, we need to provide an implementation of the onBind() method and add some configuration information to the AndroidManifest.xml file. Listing 8-12 shows an implementation of the IStockQuoteService interface.

Listing 8-12. *The IStockQuoteService Service Implementation*

```java
// StockQuoteService.java

package com.syh;

import android.app.Notification;
import android.app.NotificationManager;
import android.app.PendingIntent;
import android.app.Service;
import android.content.Intent;
import android.os.IBinder;
import android.os.RemoteException;
public class StockQuoteService extends Service
{
    private NotificationManager notificationMgr;
    public class StockQuoteServiceImpl extends IStockQuoteService.Stub
    {
        @Override
        public double getQuote(String ticker) throws RemoteException
        {
            return 20.0;
        }
    }
```

```
    }

    @Override
    public void onCreate() {
        super.onCreate();

        notificationMgr =
(NotificationManager)getSystemService(NOTIFICATION_SERVICE);

        displayNotificationMessage("onCreate() called in StockQuoteService");
    }
    @Override
    public void onDestroy()
    {
        displayNotificationMessage("onDestroy() called in StockQuoteService");
        super.onDestroy();

    }

    @Override
    public void onStart(Intent intent, int startId) {
        super.onStart(intent, startId);

    }
    @Override
    public IBinder onBind(Intent intent)
    {
        displayNotificationMessage("onBind() called in StockQuoteService");
        return new StockQuoteServiceImpl();
    }
    private void displayNotificationMessage(String message)
    {

        Notification notification =
new Notification(R.drawable.note, message,System.currentTimeMillis());

        PendingIntent contentIntent =
PendingIntent.getActivity(this, 0,new Intent(this, MainActivity.class), 0);

        notification.setLatestEventInfo(this, "StockQuoteService",message,
contentIntent);

        notificationMgr.notify(R.string.app_notification_id, notification);
    }

}
```

The StockQuoteService.java class in Listing 8-12 resembles the local BackgroundService we created earlier. The primary difference is that we now implement the onBind() method. Recall that the Stub class generated from the AIDL file was an abstract class and that it implemented the IStockQuoteService interface. In our implementation of the service, we have an inner class that extends the Stub class called StockQuoteServiceImpl. This class serves as the remote-service implementation, and an instance of this class is returned from the onBind() method. With that, we have a functional AIDL service, although external clients cannot connect to it yet.

To expose the service to clients, we need to add a service declaration in the AndroidManifest.xml file, and this time, we need an intent-filter to expose the service. Listing 8-13 shows the service declaration for the StockQuoteService.

Listing 8-13. *Manifest Declaration for the IStockQuoteService*

```
<service android:name="StockQuoteService">

<intent-filter>
                <action android:name="com.syh.IStockQuoteService" />
        </intent-filter>

</service>
```

As with all services, we define the service we want to expose with a <service> tag. For an AIDL service, we also need to add an <intent-filter> with an <action> entry for the service interface we want to expose.

With this in place, we have everything we need to deploy the service. Let's now look at how we would call the service from another application (on the same device, of course).

Calling the Service from a Client Application

When a client talks to a service, there must be a protocol or contract between the two. With Android, the contract is AIDL. So the first step in consuming a service is to take the service's AIDL file and copy it to your client project. When you copy the AIDL file to the client project, the AIDL compiler creates the same interface-definition file that was created when the service was implemented (in the service-implementation project). This exposes to the client all of the methods, parameters, and return types on the service. Let's create a new project and copy the AIDL file.

1. Create a new Android project named **ServiceClient**.

2. Create a new Java package named **com.syh**.

3. Copy the IStockQuoteService.aidl file to the package. Note that after you copy the file to the project, the AIDL compiler will generate the associated Java file.

The service interface that you regenerate serves as the contract between the client and the service. The next step is to get a reference to the service so we can call the getQuote() method. With remote services, we have to call the bindService() method rather than the startService() method. Listing 8-14 shows an activity class that acts as a client of the IStockQuoteService service. The listing also contains the layout file for the activity.

To follow along, create a layout file called `main.xml` and copy the contents of the `main.xml` section from Listing 8-14. Then create a new Java package named `com.sayed` and create an activity called `MainActivity` within the package. Finally, copy the contents of the `MainActivity` section from Listing 8-14 to your activity. Realize that the package name of the activity is not that important—you can put the activity in any package you'd like. However, the AIDL artifacts that you create are package-sensitive because the AIDL compiler generates code from the contents of the AIDL file.

Listing 8-14. *A Client of the IStockQuoteService Service*

```
package com.sayed;


import com.syh.IStockQuoteService;


import android.app.Activity;
import android.content.ComponentName;
import android.content.Context;
import android.content.Intent;
import android.content.ServiceConnection;
import android.os.Bundle;
import android.os.IBinder;
import android.os.RemoteException;
import android.util.Log;
import android.view.View;
import android.view.View.OnClickListener;
import android.widget.Button;
import android.widget.Toast;

public class MainActivity extends Activity {

    private IStockQuoteService stockService = null;
    /** Called when the activity is first created. */
    @Override
    public void onCreate(Bundle savedInstanceState) {
        super.onCreate(savedInstanceState);
        setContentView(R.layout.main);

        Button bindBtn = (Button)findViewById(R.id.bindBtn);
        bindBtn.setOnClickListener(new OnClickListener(){

            @Override
            public void onClick(View view) {
                bindService(new Intent(IStockQuoteService.class
                        .getName()),
                            serConn, Context.BIND_AUTO_CREATE);
```

```java
        }});

        Button unbindBtn = (Button)findViewById(R.id.unbindBtn);
        unbindBtn.setOnClickListener(new OnClickListener(){

            @Override
            public void onClick(View view) {
                unbindService(serConn);
            }});
    }

    private ServiceConnection serConn = new ServiceConnection() {

        @Override
        public void onServiceConnected(ComponentName name, IBinder service)
        {
            stockService = IStockQuoteService.Stub.asInterface(service);
            double val;
            try {
                val = stockService.getQuote("syh");
                Toast.makeText(MainActivity.this, "Value from service is "+val+"",
Toast.LENGTH_SHORT).show();
            } catch (RemoteException ee) {
                Log.e("MainActivity", ee.getMessage(), ee);
            }

        }

        @Override
        public void onServiceDisconnected(ComponentName name) {

        }

    };
}

// main.xml

<?xml version="1.0" encoding="utf-8"?>
<LinearLayout xmlns:android="http://schemas.android.com/apk/res/android"
    android:orientation="vertical"
    android:layout_width="fill_parent"
    android:layout_height="fill_parent"
    >
```

```
<Button  android:id="@+id/bindBtn"
    android:layout_width="wrap_content"
    android:layout_height="wrap_content"
    android:text="Bind"
    />

    <Button android:id="@+id/unbindBtn"
    android:layout_width="wrap_content"
    android:layout_height="wrap_content"
    android:text="UnBind"
    />
</LinearLayout>
```

The activity wires up the onClick listener for two buttons: Bind and UnBind. When the user clicks the Bind button, the activity calls the bindService() method. Similarly, when the user clicks UnBind, the activity calls the unbindService() method. Notice that three parameters are passed to the bindService() method: the name of the AIDL service, a ServiceConnection instance, and a flag to autocreate the service.

With an AIDL service, you need to provide an implementation of the ServiceConnection interface. This interface defines two methods: one called by the system when a connection to the service has been established, and one called when the connection to the service has been destroyed. In our activity implementation, we define a private anonymous member that implements the ServiceConnection for the IStockQuoteService. When we call the bindService() method, we pass in the reference to this member. When the connection to the service is established, we obtain a reference to the IStockQuoteService using the Stub and then call the getQuote() method.

Note that the bindService() call is an asynchronous call. It is asynchronous because the process or service might not be running and thus might have to be created or started. Because bindService() is asynchronous, the platform provides the ServiceConnection callback so we know when the service has been started and when the service is no longer available.

Now you know how to create and consume an AIDL interface. Before we move on and complicate matters further, let's review what it takes to build a simple local service vs. an AIDL service. A local service is a service that does not support onBind()—it returns null from onBind(). This type of service is accessible only to the components of the application that is hosting the service. You call local services by calling startService().

On the other hand, an AIDL service is a service that can be consumed both by components within the same process and by those that exist in other applications. This type of service defines a contract between itself and its clients in an AIDL file. The service implements the AIDL contract, and clients bind to the AIDL definition. The service implements the contract by returning an implementation of the AIDL interface from the onBind() method. Clients bind to an AIDL service by calling bindService() and they disconnect from the service by calling unbindService().

In our service examples thus far, we have strictly dealt with passing simple Java primitive types. Android services actually support passing complex types, too. This is very useful, especially for AIDL services, because you might have an open-ended number of parameters that you want to pass to a service and it's unreasonable to pass them all as simple primitives. It makes more sense to package them as complex types and then pass them to the service.

Let's see how we can pass complex types to services.

Passing Complex Types to Services

Passing complex types to and from services requires more work than passing Java primitive types. Before embarking on this work, you should get an idea of AIDL's support for nonprimitive types:

- AIDL supports String and CharSequence.

- AIDL allows you to pass other AIDL interfaces, but you need to have an import statement for each AIDL interface you reference (even if the referenced AIDL interface is in the same package).

- AIDL allows you to pass complex types that implement the android.os.Parcelable interface. You need to have an import statement in your AIDL file for these types.

- AIDL supports java.util.List and java.util.Map, with a few restrictions. The allowable data types for the items in the collection include Java primitive, String, CharSequence, or android.os.Parcelable. You do not need import statements for List or Map, but you do need them for the Parcelables.

- Nonprimitive types, other than String, require a directional indicator. Directional indicators include in, out, and inout. in means the value is set by the client, out means the value is set by the service, and inout means both the client and service set the value.

The Parcelable interface tells the Android runtime how to serialize and deserialize objects during the marshalling and unmarshalling process. Listing 8-15 shows a Person class that implements the Parcelable interface.

Listing 8-15. *Implementing the Parcelable Interface*

```
package com.syh;
import android.os.Parcel;
import android.os.Parcelable;

public class Person implements Parcelable {
    private int age;
    private String name;
    public static final Parcelable.Creator<Person> CREATOR =
new Parcelable.Creator<Person>() {
        public Person createFromParcel(Parcel in) {
            return new Person(in);
        }

        public Person[] newArray(int size) {
            return new Person[size];
        }
    };

    public Person() {
    }
```

```
    private Person(Parcel in) {
        readFromParcel(in);
    }

    @Override
    public int describeContents() {
        return 0;
    }

    @Override
    public void writeToParcel(Parcel out, int flags) {
        out.writeInt(age);
        out.writeString(name);
    }

    public void readFromParcel(Parcel in) {
        age = in.readInt();
        name = in.readString();
    }

    public int getAge() {
        return age;
    }

    public void setAge(int age) {
        this.age = age;
    }

    public String getName() {
        return name;
    }

    public void setName(String name) {
        this.name = name;
    }

}
```

The Parcelable interface defines the contract for hydration and dehydration of objects during the marshalling/unmarshalling process. Underlying the Parcelable interface is the Parcel container object. The Parcel class is a fast serialization/deserialization mechanism specially designed for interprocess communication within Android. The class provides methods that you use to flatten your members to the container and to expand the members back from the container. To properly implement an object for interprocess communication, we have to do the following:

1. Implement the `Parcelable` interface. This means that you implement `writeToParcel()` and `readFromParcel()`. The write method will write the object to the parcel and the read method will read the object from the parcel. Note that the order in which you write properties must be the same as the order in which you read them.

2. Add a `static final` property to the class with the name `CREATOR`. The property needs to implement the `android.os.Parcelable.Creator<T>` interface.

3. Provide a constructor for the `Parcelable` that knows how to create the object from the `Parcel`.

4. Define `Parcelable` classes in a file called `project.aidl` in your project's root directory. The AIDL compiler will look for this file when compiling your AIDL files. The Android Eclipse plug-in provides a tool that you can invoke to generate the `project.aidl` file. To invoke the tool, right-click your project in Eclipse and select Android Tools ➤ Create Aidl preprocess file for parcelable classes. An example of a `project.aidl` file is shown in Listing 8-16.

■**Note** Seeing `Parcelable` might have triggered the question, why is Android not using the built-in Java serialization mechanism? It turns out that the Android team came to the conclusion that the serialization in Java is far too slow to satisfy Android's interprocess-communication requirements. So the team built the `Parcelable` solution. The `Parcelable` approach requires that you explicitly serialize the members of your class, but in the end, you get a much faster serialization of your objects.

Also realize that Android provides two mechanisms that allow you to pass data to another process. The first is to pass a bundle to an activity using an intent, and the second is to pass a `Parcelable` to a service. These two mechanisms should not be confused and are not interchangeable. That is, the `Parcelable` is not meant to be passed to an activity. If you want to start an activity and pass it some data, use a bundle. `Parcelable` is meant to be used only as part of an AIDL definition.

Listing 8-16. *An Example of a project.aidl File*

```
parcelable com.syh.Person
```

As shown, the `project.aidl` file will contain an entry for each `Parcelable` in your project. In this case, we have just one `Parcelable`: `Person`. Note that the tool that generates the `project.aidl` file, which ships with the 1.0 version of the SDK, emits comments in the `project.aidl` file. If you add a `Parcelable` to your project and the project fails to compile, you will have to remove the comments from the file (leaving only the `Parcelable` entries). After you remove the comments, you will have to clean the project and rebuild it in Eclipse.

Now let's use the `Person` class in a remote service. To keep things simple, we will modify our `IStockQuoteService` to take an input parameter of type `Person`. The idea is that clients will pass a `Person` to the service to tell the service who is requesting the quote. The new `IStockQuoteService.aidl` looks like Listing 8-17.

Listing 8-17. *Passing Parcelables to Services*

```
package com.syh;
import com.syh.Person;

interface IStockQuoteService
{
    String getQuote(in String ticker,in Person requester);
}
```

The getQuote() method now accepts two parameters: the stock's ticker symbol, and a Person object to specify who is making the request. Note that we have directional indicators on the parameters because the parameters are nonprimitive types, and that we have an import statement for the Person class. Realize that the Person class is also in the same package as the service definition (com.syh).

The service implementation now looks like Listing 8-18.

Listing 8-18. *The New StockQuoteService Implementation*

```
import android.app.Notification;
import android.app.NotificationManager;
import android.app.PendingIntent;
import android.app.Service;
import android.content.Intent;
import android.os.IBinder;
import android.os.RemoteException;

public class StockQuoteService extends Service
{
    private NotificationManager notificationMgr;

    public class StockQuoteServiceImpl extends IStockQuoteService.Stub
    {

        @Override
        public String getQuote(String ticker, Person requester)
                throws RemoteException {
            return "Hello "+requester.getName()+"! Quote for "+ticker+" is 20.0";
        }

    }

    @Override
    public void onCreate() {
        super.onCreate();

        notificationMgr =
```

```
(NotificationManager)getSystemService(NOTIFICATION_SERVICE);

        displayNotificationMessage("onCreate() called in StockQuoteService");
    }
    @Override
    public void onDestroy()
    {
        displayNotificationMessage("onDestroy() called in StockQuoteService");
        super.onDestroy();

    }

    @Override
    public void onStart(Intent intent, int startId) {
        super.onStart(intent, startId);

    }
    @Override
    public IBinder onBind(Intent intent)
    {
        displayNotificationMessage("onBind() called in StockQuoteService");
        return new StockQuoteServiceImpl();
    }
    private void displayNotificationMessage(String message)
    {

        Notification notification = new Notification(R.drawable.note,
message,System.currentTimeMillis());

        PendingIntent contentIntent =
PendingIntent.getActivity(this, 0,new Intent(this, MainActivity.class), 0);

        notification.setLatestEventInfo(this, "StockQuoteService",message,
contentIntent);

        notificationMgr.notify(R.string.app_notification_id, notification);
    }

}
```

The only difference between this implementation and the previous one is that now we return the stock value as a string and not a double. The string returned to the user contains the name of the requester from the Person object, which demonstrates that we read the value sent from the client and that the Person object was passed correctly to the service.

To implement a client that passes the Person object to the service, we need to copy everything that the client needs to the client project. In our previous example, all we needed was the IStockQuoteService.aidl file. Now we also need to copy the Person.java file because the Person object is now part of the interface. After you copy the two files to the client project, you need to re-create the project.aidl file and remove the comments from it because of the bug we discussed earlier. Also note that after you remove the comments, you will need to do a clean and rebuild. Listing 8-19 shows the client code that calls the service.

Listing 8-19. *Calling the Service with a Parcelable*

```
package com.sayed;

import com.syh.IStockQuoteService;
import com.syh.Person;

import android.app.Activity;
import android.content.ComponentName;
import android.content.Context;
import android.content.Intent;
import android.content.ServiceConnection;
import android.os.Bundle;
import android.os.IBinder;
import android.os.RemoteException;
import android.util.Log;
import android.view.View;
import android.view.View.OnClickListener;
import android.widget.Button;
import android.widget.Toast;

public class MainActivity extends Activity {

    private IStockQuoteService stockService = null;
    /** Called when the activity is first created. */
    @Override
    public void onCreate(Bundle savedInstanceState) {
        super.onCreate(savedInstanceState);
        setContentView(R.layout.main);

        Button bindBtn = (Button)findViewById(R.id.bindBtn);
        bindBtn.setOnClickListener(new OnClickListener(){

            @Override
            public void onClick(View view) {
                bindService(new Intent(IStockQuoteService.class
                        .getName()),
                            serConn, Context.BIND_AUTO_CREATE);
            }

        }});

        Button unbindBtn = (Button)findViewById(R.id.unbindBtn);
        unbindBtn.setOnClickListener(new OnClickListener(){
```

```
            @Override
            public void onClick(View view) {
                unbindService(serConn);
            }});
    }

    private ServiceConnection serConn = new ServiceConnection() {

        @Override
        public void onServiceConnected(ComponentName name, IBinder service)
        {
            stockService = IStockQuoteService.Stub.asInterface(service);
            String val;
            try {
                Person person = new Person();
                person.setAge(33);
                person.setName("Sayed");
                val = stockService.getQuote("GOOG",person);
                Toast.makeText(MainActivity.this, "Value from service is: "+val+"",
Toast.LENGTH_SHORT).show();
            } catch (RemoteException ee) {
                Log.e("MainActivity", ee.getMessage(), ee);
            }

        }

        @Override
        public void onServiceDisconnected(ComponentName name) {

        }

    };
}
```

The interesting method in the client is the onServiceConnected() method. As shown, we create a new Person object and set its Age and Name properties. We then execute the service and display the result from the service call. The result looks like Figure 8-1.

```
Value from service is: Hello Sayed!
Quote for GOOG is 20.0
```

Figure 8-1. *Result from calling the service with a Parcelable*

It is also useful to see the artifacts of the service project and the client that calls it (see Figure 8-2).

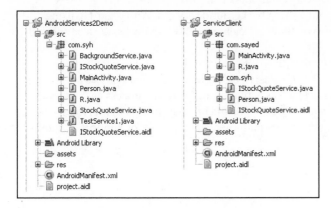

Figure 8-2. *The artifacts of the client and service*

Figure 8-2 shows the Eclipse project artifacts for the service (left) and the client (right). Note that the contract between the client and the service consists of the AIDL artifacts and the Parcelable objects exchanged between the two parties. This is the reason that we see IStockQuoteService.aidl, project.aidl, and Person.java on both sides. Because the AIDL complier generates the Java interface, stub, proxy, and so on from the AIDL artifacts, the build process creates the IStockQuoteService.java file on the client side when we copy the contract artifacts to the client project.

Now we know how to exchange complex types between services and clients. Let's briefly touch on another important aspect of calling services: synchronous vs. asynchronous service invocation.

All of the calls that you make on services are synchronous. This brings up the obvious question, do you need to implement all of your service calls in a worker thread? Not necessarily. In most other platforms, it's common for a client to use a service that is a complete black box, so the client would have to take appropriate precautions when making service calls. With Android, you will likely know what is in the service (generally because you wrote the service yourself), so you can make an informed decision. If you know that the method you are calling is doing a lot of heavy lifting, then you should consider using a secondary thread to make the call. If you are sure that the method does not have any bottlenecks, then you can safely make the call on the UI thread. If you conclude that it's best to make the service call within a worker thread, you can create the thread from the onServiceConnected() method of ServiceConnection and then call the service. You can then communicate the result to the UI thread.

Summary

This chapter was all about services. We talked about consuming external HTTP services using the Apache HttpClient and about writing background services. With regard to using the HttpClient, we showed you how to do HTTP GET calls and HTTP POST calls. We also showed you how to do multipart POSTs.

The second part of the chapter dealt with writing services in Android. Specifically, we talked about writing local services and remote services. We said that local services are services that are consumed by the components (such as activities) in the same process as the service. Remote services are services whose clients are outside the process hosting the services.

In the next chapter, we are going to discuss multimedia and telephony support in Android.

■ ■ ■

CHAPTER 9

Using the Media Framework and Telephony APIs

Now we are going to explore two very interesting portions of the Android SDK: media and telephony. In our media discussion in the first part of the chapter, we will show you how to play audio and video. We will also talk about recording audio—we discuss recording video in Chapter 12. In our telephony discussion in the second part of the chapter, we will show you how to send and receive Short Message Service (SMS) messages. We will also touch on several other interesting aspects of the telephony APIs in Android.

Let's begin by talking about the media APIs.

Using the Media APIs

Android supports playing audio and video content under the `android.media` package. In this section, we are going to explore the media APIs from this package.

At the heart of the `android.media` package is the `android.media.MediaPlayer` class. The `MediaPlayer` class is responsible for playing both audio and video content. The content for this class can come from these sources:

- *Web*: You can play content from the web via a URL.

- *.apk file*: You can play content that is packaged as part of your .apk file. You can package the media content as a resource or as an asset (within the `assets` folder).

- *Secure Digital (SD) card*: You can play content that resides on the device's SD card.

To get started, we'll show you how to build a simple application that plays an MP3 file located on the web (see Figure 9-1). After that, we will talk about using the `setDataSource()` method of the `MediaPlayer` class to play content from the .apk file or the SD card. We will conclude our media discussion by talking about some of the shortfalls of the media APIs.

Figure 9-1 shows the user interface for our first example. This application will demonstrate some of the fundamental uses of the `MediaPlayer` class, such as starting, pausing, and restarting the media file. Look at the layout for the application's user interface.

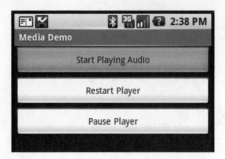

Figure 9-1. *The user interface for the media application*

The user interface consists of a LinearLayout with three buttons (see Listing 9-1): one to start the player, one to pause the player, and one to restart the player. The code and layout file for the application is shown in Listing 9-1.

Listing 9-1. *The Layout and Code for the Media Application*

```xml
<?xml version="1.0" encoding="utf-8"?>
<LinearLayout xmlns:android="http://schemas.android.com/apk/res/android"
    android:orientation="vertical"
    android:layout_width="fill_parent"
    android:layout_height="fill_parent"
    >
<Button android:id="@+id/startPlayerBtn"
    android:layout_width="fill_parent"
    android:layout_height="wrap_content"
    android:text="Start Playing Audio"
    />

<Button android:id="@+id/restartPlayerBtn"
    android:layout_width="fill_parent"
    android:layout_height="wrap_content"
    android:text="Restart Player"
    />

<Button android:id="@+id/pausePlayerBtn"
    android:layout_width="fill_parent"
    android:layout_height="wrap_content"
    android:text="Pause Player"
    />
</LinearLayout>
```

```java
import android.app.Activity;
import android.media.MediaPlayer;
import android.os.Bundle;
import android.view.View;
import android.view.View.OnClickListener;
import android.widget.Button;

public class MainActivity extends Activity
{
    static final String AUDIO_PATH =
"http://sayedhashimi.com/downloads/android/play.mp3";

    private MediaPlayer mediaPlayer;
    private int playbackPosition=0;

    /** Called when the activity is first created. */
    @Override
    public void onCreate(Bundle savedInstanceState) {
        super.onCreate(savedInstanceState);
        setContentView(R.layout.main);

        Button startPlayerBtn = (Button)findViewById(R.id.startPlayerBtn);
        Button pausePlayerBtn = (Button)findViewById(R.id.pausePlayerBtn);
        Button restartPlayerBtn = (Button)findViewById(R.id.restartPlayerBtn);

        startPlayerBtn.setOnClickListener(new OnClickListener(){

            @Override
            public void onClick(View view)
            {
                try {
                    playAudio(AUDIO_PATH);
                } catch (Exception e) {
                    e.printStackTrace();
                }
            }});

        pausePlayerBtn.setOnClickListener(new OnClickListener(){

            @Override
            public void onClick(View view)
            {
                if(mediaPlayer!=null)
                {
                    playbackPosition = mediaPlayer.getCurrentPosition();
                    mediaPlayer.pause();
                }
            }});
```

```java
        restartPlayerBtn.setOnClickListener(new OnClickListener(){

            @Override
            public void onClick(View view)
            {
                if(mediaPlayer!=null && !mediaPlayer.isPlaying())
                {
                    mediaPlayer.start();
                    mediaPlayer.seekTo(playbackPosition);
                }
        }});
    }

    private void playAudio(String url)throws Exception
    {
        killMediaPlayer();

        mediaPlayer = new MediaPlayer();
        mediaPlayer.setDataSource(url);
        mediaPlayer.prepare();
        mediaPlayer.start();
    }

    @Override
    protected void onDestroy()
    {
    super.onDestroy();

    killMediaPlayer();
    }
    private void killMediaPlayer()
    {
        if(mediaPlayer!=null)
        {
            try
            {
                mediaPlayer.release();
            }
            catch(Exception e)
            {
                e.printStackTrace();
            }
        }
    }
}
```

The code in Listing 9-1 shows that the MainActivity class contains three members: a final string that points to the URL of the MP3 file, a MediaPlayer instance, and an integer member called playbackPosition. You can see from the onCreate() method that the code wires up the click listeners for the three buttons. In the button-click handler for the Start Playing Audio button, the playAudio() method is called. In the playAudio() method, a new instance of the MediaPlayer is created and the data source of the player is set to the URL of the MP3 file. The prepare() method of the player is then called to prepare the media player for playback, and then the start() method is called to start playback.

Now look at the button-click handlers for the Pause Player and Restart Player buttons. You can see that when the Pause Player button is selected, you get the current position of the player by calling getCurrentPosition(). You then pause the player by calling pause(). When the player has to be restarted, you call start() and then call seekTo(), passing in the position obtained from getCurrentPosition(). Realize that in this scenario you are playing an MP3 file from a web address. Therefore, you will need to add android.permission.INTERNET to your manifest file.

The MediaPlayer class also contains a stop() method. Note that if you stop the player by calling stop(), you need to call prepare() before calling start() again. Conversely, if you call pause(), you can call start() again without having to prepare the player. Also, be sure to call the release() method of the media player once you are done using it. In this example, you do this as part of the killMediaPlayer() method.

The example in Listing 9-1 shows you how to play an audio file located on the web. The MediaPlayer class also supports playing media local to your .apk file. Listing 9-2 shows how to reference and play back a file from the /res folder of your .apk file.

Listing 9-2. *Using the MediaPlayer to Play Back a File Local to Your Application*

```
private void playLocalAudio()throws Exception
{
    mediaPlayer = MediaPlayer.create(this, R.raw.music_file);
    mediaPlayer.start();
}
```

If you need to include an audio or video file with your application, you should place the file in the /res/raw folder. You can then get a MediaPlayer instance for the resource by passing in the resource ID of the media file; you do this by calling the static create() method, as shown in Listing 9-2. Note that the MediaPlayer class also provides static create() methods that you can use to get a MediaPlayer rather than instantiating one yourself. For example, in Listing 9-2 you call the create() method, but you could instead call the constructor MediaPlayer(Context context,int resourceId). Using the static create() methods is preferable because they hide the creation of the MediaPlayer. However, as you will see shortly, at times you will not have a choice between these two options—you will have to instantiate the default constructor because media content cannot be located via a resource ID or a URL.

Understanding the setDataSource Method

In Listing 9-2, we called the create() method to load the audio file from a raw resource. With this approach, you don't need to call setDataSource(). Alternatively, if you instantiate the MediaPlayer yourself using the default constructor, or if your media content is not accessible through a resource ID or a URL, you'll need to call setDataSource().

The setDataSource() method has overloaded versions that you can use to customize the data source for your specific needs. For example, Listing 9-3 shows how you can load an audio file from a raw resource using a FileDescriptor.

Listing 9-3. *Setting the MediaPlayer's Data Source Using a FileDescriptor*

```
private void playLocalAudio_UsingDescriptor() throws Exception {

    AssetFileDescriptor fileDesc = getResources().openRawResourceFd(
            R.raw.music_file);
    if (fileDesc != null) {

        mediaPlayer = new MediaPlayer();
        mediaPlayer.setDataSource(fileDesc.getFileDescriptor(), fileDesc
                .getStartOffset(), fileDesc.getLength());

        fileDesc.close();

        mediaPlayer.prepare();
        mediaPlayer.start();
    }
}
```

The code in Listing 9-3 assumes that it's within the context of an activity. As shown, you call the getResources() method to get the application's resources and then use the openRawResourceFd() method to get a file descriptor for an audio file within the /res/raw folder. You then call the setDataSource() method using the AssetFileDescriptor, the starting position to begin playback, and the ending position. You can also use this version of setDataSource() if you want to play back a specific portion of an audio file. If you always want to play the entire file, you can call the simpler version of setDataSource(FileDescriptor desc), which does not require the initial offset and length.

Using one of the setDataSource() methods with the FileDescriptor can also be handy if you want to feed a media file located within your application's /data directory. For security reasons, the media player does not have access to an application's /data directory, but your application can open the file and then feed the (opened) FileDescriptor to setDataSource(). Realize that the application's /data directory resides in the set of files and folders under /data/data/APP_PACKAGE_NAME/. You can get access to this directory by calling the appropriate method from the Context class, rather than hard-coding the path. For example, you can call getFilesDir() on Context to get the current application's files directory. Currently, this path looks like the following: /data/data/APP_PACKAGE_NAME/files. Similarly, you can call getCacheDir() to get the application's cache directory. Your application will have read and write permission on the contents of these folders, so you can create files dynamically and feed them to the player.

Observe that an application's /data directory differs greatly from its /res/raw folder. The /raw folder is physically part of the .apk file, and it's static—that is, you cannot modify the .apk file dynamically. The contents of the /data directory, on the other hand, are dynamic.

Finally, if you use FileDescriptor, as shown in Listing 9-3, be sure to close the handle after calling setDataSource().

This concludes our discussion about playing audio content, so we'll now turn our attention to playing video. As you'll see, referencing video content is similar to referencing audio content. But we have not yet talked about playing content from the device's SD card, so we'll delve into that along the way.

Playing Video Content

In this section, we are going to discuss video playback using the Android SDK. Specifically, we will discuss playing a video from a web server and playing one from an SD card. As you can imagine, video playback is a bit more involved than audio playback. Fortunately, the Android SDK provides some additional abstractions that address most of the heavy lifting.

Let's get started by playing video content from a web server.

Video Playback from a Web Server

As we said, playing video requires more effort than playing audio. To take some of the pain away, Android provides a specialized view control called `android.widget.VideoView` that encapsulates creating and initializing the `MediaPlayer`. To play video, you create a `VideoView` widget and set that as the content of the UI. You then set the path or URI of the video and fire the `start()` method. Listing 9-4 demonstrates video playback in Android.

Listing 9-4. *Playing a Video Using the Media APIs*

```xml
<?xml version="1.0" encoding="utf-8"?>
<AbsoluteLayout
 android:layout_width="fill_parent" android:layout_height="fill_parent"
 xmlns:android="http://schemas.android.com/apk/res/android">
    <VideoView
        android:id="@+id/videoView"
        android:layout_width="200px"
        android:layout_height="200px"
        android:layout_x="10px"
        android:layout_y="10px" />


</AbsoluteLayout>
```
```java
@Override
protected void onCreate(Bundle savedInstanceState) {
        super.onCreate(savedInstanceState);
        this.setContentView(R.layout.video);

        videoView = (VideoView)this.findViewById(R.id.videoView);
        MediaController mc = new MediaController(this);
        videoView.setMediaController(mc);
        videoView.setVideoURI(Uri.parse(
"http://sayedhashimi.com/downloads/android/movie.mp4"));
        //videoView.setVideoURI(Uri.parse("file:///sdcard/movie.mp4"));
        videoView.requestFocus();
    }
```

The example in Listing 9-4 demonstrates video playback of a file located on the web at `http://sayedhashimi.com/downloads/android/movie.mp4`, which means the application running the code will need to request the `android.permission.INTERNET` permission. All of the playback functionality is hidden behind the `VideoView` class. In fact, all you have to do is feed the video content to the video player. The user interface of the application is shown in Figure 9-2.

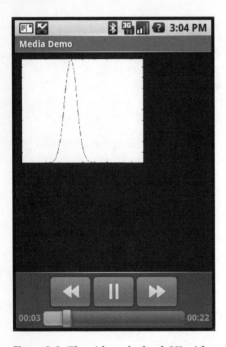

Figure 9-2. *The video-playback UI with media controls enabled*

As shown in Figure 9-2 and Listing 9-4, you can enable the `VideoView` with a media controller. You can set the `VideoView`'s media controller by calling `setMediaController()` to enable the play, pause, and seek-to controls. If you want to manipulate the video programmatically, you can call the `start()`, `pause()`, `stopPlayback()`, and `seekTo()` methods.

As we mentioned, the example in Listing 9-4 plays a video file from a web server. You can also play local files. For example, a common use case requires video playback of a file located on the SD card. We'll discuss this use case next.

Video Playback from the SD Card

Playing back video from the SD card requires little code, but it does require some prep work with regard to creating and configuring the emulator with the SD card. By default, the Android 1.1 emulator is not enabled with an SD card, so you first need to create an SD-card image and configure the emulator to use the SD card. After the card is created and the emulator is made aware of it, you can then use the Android tools within Eclipse to push the video file (or any other file) to the SD card. After the file has been loaded onto the card, you can run the video sample to play the video file at `/sdcard/movie.mp4`, for example. To configure an SD card for the Android 1.5 emulator, see Chapter 12.

Now let's create the SD-card image. The Android tools bundle contains a utility called mksdcard that can create an SD-card image. Actually, the utility creates a formatted file that is used as an SD card. To use this utility, first create a folder for the image file at c:\Android\ sdcard\, for example. Then open a command line to the Android SDK /tools directory and run the following command:

```
mksdcard 256M c:\Android\sdcard\sdcard.img
```

The command creates an SD-card image at c:\Android\sdcard\ with a file name of sdcard.img. The size of the SD card will be 256MB. After you create the SD-card image, you need to point the emulator to the image. You do this by passing a command-line argument to the emulator, as shown in Figure 9-3.

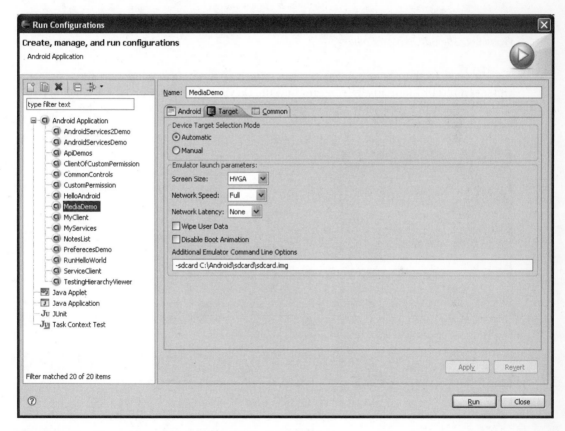

Figure 9-3. *Passing command-line arguments to the emulator*

In Eclipse, open the release/debug configuration that you want to run (select Run ➤ Run Configurations…). Select the "Android Application" node from the left pane and choose a project to show its release/debug configuration in the right pane. Select the Target tab and set the "Additional Emulator Command Line Options" field to

```
-sdcard c:\Android\sdcard\sdcard.img
```

Note that the value of the -sdcard argument is the physical path to the SD-card image on your workstation. Before you can run the video sample from the SD card, you need to upload a video file to the SD card. You can do that by using the File Explorer tool. Start the emulator after you set the -sdcard command-line option and wait until the emulator initializes. Then open Eclipse in Debug perspective. You should see the File Explorer view as shown in Figure 9-4.

Name	Size	Date	Time	Permissions	Info
⊞ 🗀 data		2008-09-22	20:44	drwxrwx--x	
⊟ 🗀 sdcard		1970-01-01	00:00	d---rwxrwx	
⊞ 🗀 download		2008-11-26	23:55	d---rwxrwx	
📄 movie.mp4	466888	2009-03-28	15:02	----rw-rw-	
📄 recordoutput.3gpp	5572	2008-12-31	18:47	----rw-rw-	
⊞ 🗀 system		2008-09-22	20:41	drwxr-xr-x	

LogCat | Emulator Control | File Explorer ⊠ | Heap | Resource Explorer | Devices | Search

Pull a file from the device

Figure 9-4. *The File Explorer view*

If the File Explorer is not shown, you can bring it up by going to Window ➤ Show View ➤ Other ➤ Android. Alternatively, you can show the Dalvik Debug Monitor Service (DDMS) perspective by going to Window ➤ Open Perspective ➤ Other ➤ DDMS, which will show all of the views shown in Figure 9-5.

Figure 9-5. *Enabling Android views*

To push a file onto the SD card, select the sdcard folder in the File Explorer and choose the button with the right-facing arrow (at the top-right corner). This launches a dialog box that lets you select a file. Select the movie file that you want to upload to the SD card. In our example, we assume that the file is located at the root of the SD card and that it's named movie.mp4 (see Listing 9-3). After the file is uploaded, you should be able to run the video sample in Listing 9-3 using the SD-card video file. The only change you'll need to make to Listing 9-3 is to update the setVideoURI() method with a file URL rather than an HTTP URL:

```
videoView.setVideoURI(Uri.parse("file:///sdcard/movie.mp4"));
```

Realize that if the File Explorer displays an empty view, you either don't have the emulator running or the project that you are running in the emulator is not selected under the Devices tab shown in Figure 9-4.

Finally, note that there are two ways to feed video content to VideoView: setVideoPath() or setVideoURI(). setVideoPath() takes a physical path, whereas setVideoURI() accepts a URL.

Understanding the MediaPlayer Oddities

In general, the MediaPlayer is very systematic, so you need to call operations in a specific order to initialize a media player properly and prepare it for playback. This list summarizes some of the oddities of using the media APIs:

- Once you set the data source of a MediaPlayer, you cannot dynamically change it to another one—you'll have to create a new MediaPlayer or call the reset() method to reinitialize the state of the player.

- After you call prepare(), you can call getCurrentPosition(), getDuration(), and isPlaying() to get the current state of the player. You can also call the setLooping() and setVolume() methods after the call to prepare().

- After you call start(), you can call pause(), stop(), and seekTo().

- Every MediaPlayer creates a new thread, so be sure to call the release() method when you are done with the media player. The VideoView takes care of this in the case of video playback, but you'll have to do it manually if you decide to use MediaPlayer instead of VideoView.

Now let's explore recording media.

Exploring Audio Recording

The Android media framework supports recording audio and video. You record media using the android.media.MediaRecorder class. In this section, we'll show you how to build an application that records audio content and then plays the content back. (We discuss video recording in Chapter 12.) The user interface of the application is shown in Figure 9-6.

Figure 9-6. *The user interface of the audio-recorder example*

As shown in Figure 9-6, the application contains four buttons: two to control recording, and two to start and stop playback of the recorded content. Listing 9-5 shows the layout file and activity class for the UI.

Listing 9-5. *Media Recording and Playback in Android*

```
// record.xml
<?xml version="1.0" encoding="utf-8"?>
<LinearLayout xmlns:android="http://schemas.android.com/apk/res/android"
    android:orientation="vertical"
    android:layout_width="fill_parent"
    android:layout_height="fill_parent"
    >
    <Button android:id="@+id/bgnBtn" android:layout_width="fill_parent"
    android:layout_height="wrap_content" android:text="Begin Recording"/>

        <Button android:id="@+id/stpBtn" android:layout_width="fill_parent"
    android:layout_height="wrap_content" android:text="Stop Recording"/>

        <Button android:id=
"@+id/playRecordingBtn" android:layout_width="fill_parent"
    android:layout_height="wrap_content" android:text="Play Recording"/>

        <Button android:id=
"@+id/stpPlayingRecordingBtn" android:layout_width="fill_parent"
    android:layout_height="wrap_content" android:text="Stop Playing Recording"/>

    </LinearLayout>
// RecorderActivity.java
import android.app.Activity;
import android.media.MediaPlayer;
import android.media.MediaRecorder;
import android.os.Bundle;
import android.view.View;
import android.view.View.OnClickListener;
import android.widget.Button;
public class RecorderActivity extends Activity {
    private MediaPlayer mediaPlayer;
    private MediaRecorder recorder;
    private static final String OUTPUT_FILE= "/sdcard/recordoutput.3gpp";

    @Override
    protected void onCreate(Bundle savedInstanceState) {
        super.onCreate(savedInstanceState);

        setContentView(R.layout.record);
```

```
    Button startBtn = (Button) findViewById(R.id.bgnBtn);

    Button endBtn = (Button) findViewById(R.id.stpBtn);

    Button playRecordingBtn = (Button) findViewById(R.id.playRecordingBtn);

    Button stpPlayingRecordingBtn =
(Button) findViewById(R.id.stpPlayingRecordingBtn);

    startBtn.setOnClickListener(new OnClickListener() {

        @Override
        public void onClick(View view) {
            try {
                beginRecording();
            } catch (Exception e) {
                e.printStackTrace();
            }
        }
    });

    endBtn.setOnClickListener(new OnClickListener() {

        @Override
        public void onClick(View view) {
            try {
                stopRecording();
            } catch (Exception e) {
                e.printStackTrace();
            }
        }
    });

    playRecordingBtn.setOnClickListener(new OnClickListener() {

        @Override
        public void onClick(View view) {
            try {
                playRecording();
            } catch (Exception e) {
                e.printStackTrace();
            }
        }
    });

    stpPlayingRecordingBtn.setOnClickListener(new OnClickListener() {
```

```java
            @Override
            public void onClick(View view) {
                try {
                    stopPlayingRecording();
                } catch (Exception e) {
                    e.printStackTrace();
                }
            }
        });
    }

    private void beginRecording() throws Exception {
        killMediaRecorder();

        File outFile = new File(OUTPUT_FILE);

        if(outFile.exists())
        {
            outFile.delete();
        }
        recorder = new MediaRecorder();
        recorder.setAudioSource(MediaRecorder.AudioSource.MIC);
        recorder.setOutputFormat(MediaRecorder.OutputFormat.THREE_GPP);
        recorder.setAudioEncoder(MediaRecorder.AudioEncoder.AMR_NB);
        recorder.setOutputFile(OUTPUT_FILE);
        recorder.prepare();
        recorder.start();

    }

    private void stopRecording() throws Exception {
        if (recorder != null) {
            recorder.stop();
        }
    }

    private void killMediaRecorder() {
        if (recorder != null) {
            recorder.release();
        }
    }
```

```
    private void killMediaPlayer() {
        if (mediaPlayer != null) {
            try {
                mediaPlayer.release();
            } catch (Exception e) {
                e.printStackTrace();
            }
        }
    }

    private void playRecording() throws Exception {
        killMediaPlayer();

        mediaPlayer = new MediaPlayer();
        mediaPlayer.setDataSource(OUTPUT_FILE);

        mediaPlayer.prepare();
        mediaPlayer.start();
    }
    private void stopPlayingRecording() throws Exception {
        if(mediaPlayer!=null)
        {
            mediaPlayer.stop();
        }
    }

    @Override
    protected void onDestroy() {
        super.onDestroy();

        killMediaRecorder();
        killMediaPlayer();
    }

}
```

Before we jump into to Listing 9-5, realize that in order to record audio, you'll need to add the following permission to your manifest file:

```
<uses-permission android:name="android.permission.RECORD_AUDIO" />
```

If you look at the onCreate() method in Listing 9-5, you see that the on-click event handlers are wired up for the four buttons. The beginRecording() method handles recording. To record audio, you must create an instance of MediaRecorder and set the audio source, output format, audio encoder, and output file. At this point, the only supported audio source is the microphone, and you must set the encoder to AMR_NB, which signifies the Adaptive Multi-Rate

(AMR) narrowband audio codec. The only supported output format for audio is 3rd Generation Partnership Project (3GPP). The recorded audio is written to the SD card at /sdcard/ recordoutput.3gpp. Note that Listing 9-5 assumes that you've created an SD-card image and that you've pointed the emulator to the SD card. If you have not done this, refer to the section "Video Playback from the SD Card" for details on setting this up.

Note that the current media APIs do not support streaming. For example, if you record audio, you cannot access the audio stream during the recording process (for analysis purposes, for example). Instead, you have to write the audio content to a file first and then work with it. Future releases of the Android SDK will likely support audio streaming. Finally, as we mentioned earlier, version 1.0 of the Android SDK does not support video recording. This feature will also probably be supported in a later release.

This concludes our discussion of the media APIs. We're sure you'll agree that playing media content is quite simple with Android. The MediaPlayer class and VideoView control wrap things up nicely. Recording audio is also simple. For more on the media framework, see Chapter 12.

Now we'll move on to the telephony APIs.

Using the Telephony APIs

In this section, we are going to explore Android's telephony APIs. Specifically, we will show you how to send and receive SMS messages, after which we'll explore making and receiving phone calls. We'll start with SMS.

Working with SMS

SMS stands for Short Message Service, as we mentioned earlier, but it's commonly called *text messaging*. The Android SDK supports sending and receiving text messages. We'll start by discussing various ways to send SMS messages with the SDK.

Sending SMS Messages

To send a text message from your application, you will add the <uses-permission android:name="android.permission.SEND_SMS" /> permission to your manifest file and then use the android.telephony.gsm.SmsManager class (see Listing 9-6).

Listing 9-6. *Sending SMS (Text) Messages*

```
import android.app.Activity;
import android.os.Bundle;
import android.telephony.gsm.SmsManager;
import android.view.View;
import android.view.View.OnClickListener;
import android.widget.Button;
import android.widget.EditText;
import android.widget.Toast;
public class TelephonyDemo extends Activity
```

```
{
    private static final String TAG = "TelephonyDemo";
    @Override
    protected void onCreate(Bundle savedInstanceState) {
        super.onCreate(savedInstanceState);

        setContentView(R.layout.sms);


        Button sendBtn = (Button)findViewById(R.id.sendSmsBtn);

        sendBtn.setOnClickListener(new OnClickListener(){

            @Override
            public void onClick(View view) {
                EditText addrTxt =
(EditText)TelephonyDemo.this.findViewById(R.id.addrEditText);

                EditText msgTxt =
(EditText)TelephonyDemo.this.findViewById(R.id.msgEditText);

                try {
                    sendSmsMessage(
addrTxt.getText().toString(),msgTxt.getText().toString());
                    Toast.makeText(TelephonyDemo.this, "SMS Sent",
Toast.LENGTH_LONG).show();
                } catch (Exception e) {
                    Toast.makeText(TelephonyDemo.this, "Failed to send SMS",
Toast.LENGTH_LONG).show();
                }
            }});
    }

    @Override
    protected void onDestroy() {
        super.onDestroy();
    }

    private void sendSmsMessage(String address,String message)throws Exception
    {
        SmsManager smsMgr = SmsManager.getDefault();
        smsMgr.sendTextMessage(address, null, message, null, null);
    }
}
```

```xml
<?xml version="1.0" encoding="utf-8"?>
<LinearLayout xmlns:android="http://schemas.android.com/apk/res/android"
    android:orientation="vertical"
    android:layout_width="fill_parent"
    android:layout_height="fill_parent"
    >


    <LinearLayout xmlns:android="http://schemas.android.com/apk/res/android"
     android:orientation="horizontal"
     android:layout_width="fill_parent"
     android:layout_height="wrap_content">

        <TextView    android:layout_width="wrap_content"
         android:layout_height="wrap_content" android:text="Destination Address:" />

        <EditText  android:id="@+id/addrEditText" android:layout_width="wrap_content"
         android:layout_height="wrap_content" android:text="9045551212" />


    </LinearLayout>

    <LinearLayout xmlns:android="http://schemas.android.com/apk/res/android"
     android:orientation="horizontal"
     android:layout_width="fill_parent"
     android:layout_height="wrap_content">

        <TextView     android:layout_width="wrap_content"
         android:layout_height="wrap_content" android:text="Text Message:" />

        <EditText android:id="@+id/msgEditText" android:layout_width="wrap_content"
         android:layout_height="wrap_content" android:text="hello sms" />


    </LinearLayout>

<Button android:id="@+id/sendSmsBtn"
    android:layout_width="fill_parent"
    android:layout_height="wrap_content"
    android:text="Send Text Message"
    />

</LinearLayout>
```

The example in Listing 9-6 demonstrates sending SMS text messages using the Android SDK. Looking at the layout snippet first, you can see that the user interface has two `EditText` fields: one to capture the SMS recipient's destination address (the phone number), and another to hold the text message. The user interface also has a button to send the SMS message, as shown in Figure 9-7.

Figure 9-7. *The UI for the SMS example*

The interesting part of the sample is the `sendSmsMessage()` method. The method uses the `SmsManager` class's `sendTextMessage()` method to send the SMS message. Here's the signature of `SmsManager.sendTextMessage()`:

```
sendTextMessage(String destinationAddress, String smscAddress, String textMsg,
PendingIntent sentIntent, PendingIntent deliveryIntent);
```

In this example, you populate only the destination address and the text-message parameters. You can, however, customize the method so it doesn't use the default SMS center (the address of the server on the cellular network that will dispatch the SMS message). You can also implement a customization in which pending intents are called when the message is sent and a delivery notification has been received.

All in all, sending an SMS message is about as simple as it gets with Android. Realize that, with the emulator, your SMS messages are not actually sent to their destinations. You can, however, assume success if the `sendTextMessage()` method returns without an exception. As shown in Listing 9-6, you use the `Toast` class to display a message in the UI to indicate whether the SMS message was sent successfully.

Sending SMS messages is only half the story. Now we'll show you how to monitor incoming SMS messages.

Monitoring Incoming SMS Messages

The first step in monitoring incoming SMS messages is requesting permission to receive them. Do this by adding the `<uses-permission android:name="android.permission.RECEIVE_SMS" />` permission to your manifest file. Next, you'll need to implement a monitor to listen for SMS messages. You accomplish this by implementing a `BroadcastReceiver` for the action `<action android:value="android.provider.Telephony.SMS_RECEIVED" />`. To implement the receiver, write a class that extends `android.content.BroadcastReceiver` and then register the receiver in your manifest file. Listing 9-7 demonstrates this.

Listing 9-7. *Monitoring SMS Messages*

```
<receiver android:name="MySMSMonitor">
    <intent-filter>
        <action android:name="android.provider.Telephony.SMS_RECEIVED"/>

    </intent-filter>
</receiver>


public class MySMSMonitor extends BroadcastReceiver
{
    private static final String ACTION = "android.provider.Telephony.SMS_RECEIVED";
    @Override
    public void onReceive(Context context, Intent intent)
    {
        if(intent!=null && intent.getAction()!=null &&
ACTION.compareToIgnoreCase(intent.getAction())==0)
        {
            Object[]pduArray= (Object[]) intent.getExtras().get("pdus");
            SmsMessage[] messages = new SmsMessage[pduArray.length];
            for (int i = 0; i<pduArray.length; i++) {
                    messages[i] = SmsMessage.createFromPdu ((byte[])pduArray [i]);
            }
            Log.d("MySMSMonitor","SMS Message Received.");
        }
    }
}
```

The top portion of Listing 9-7 is the manifest definition for the BroadcastReceiver to inter-cept SMS messages. The SMS monitor class is MySMSMonitor. The class implements the abstract onReceive() method, which is called by the system when an SMS message arrives. One way to test the application is to use the Emulator Control view in Eclipse. Run the application in the emulator and then go to Window ➤ Show View ➤ Other ➤ Android ➤ Emulator Control. The user interface allows you to send data to the emulator to emulate receiving an SMS message or phone call. As shown in Figure 9-8, you can send an SMS message to the emulator by populat-ing the "Incoming number" field and then selecting the SMS radio button. Then type some text in the "Message" field and click the Send button. Doing this sends an SMS message to the emulator and invokes your BroadcastReceiver's onReceive() method.

The onReceive() method will have the broadcast intent, which will contain the SmsMessage in the bundle property. You can extract the SmsMessage by calling intent.getExtras(). get("pdus"). This call returns an array of objects defined in Protocol Description Unit (PDU) mode—an industry-standard way of representing an SMS message. You can then convert the PDUs to Android SmsMessage objects, as shown in Listing 9-7. As you can see, you get the PDUs as an object array from the intent. You then construct an array of SmsMessage objects, equal to the size of the PDU array. Finally, you iterate over the PDU array, and create SmsMessage objects from the PDUs by calling SmsMessage.createFromPdu().

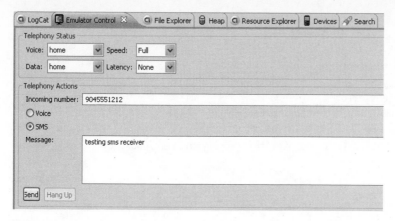

Figure 9-8. *Using the Emulator Control UI to send SMS messages to the emulator*

Now let's continue our discussion about SMS by looking at how you can work with various SMS folders.

Working with SMS Folders

Accessing the SMS inbox is another common requirement. To get started, you need to add read-SMS permission (`<uses-permission android:name="android.permission.READ_SMS"/>`) to the manifest file. Adding this permission gives you the ability to read from the SMS inbox.

To read SMS messages, you need to execute a query on the SMS inbox, as shown in Listing 9-8.

Listing 9-8. *Displaying the Messages from the SMS Inbox*

```xml
<?xml version="1.0" encoding="utf-8"?>
<LinearLayout xmlns:android="http://schemas.android.com/apk/res/android"
    android:orientation="vertical"
    android:layout_width="fill_parent"
    android:layout_height="fill_parent"
    >
    <TextView android:id="@+id/row"
    android:layout_width="fill_parent"
    android:layout_height="fill_parent"/>

</LinearLayout>
public class SMSInboxDemo extends ListActivity {

    private ListAdapter adapter;
    private static final Uri SMS_INBOX = Uri.parse("content://sms/inbox");
```

```
@Override
public void onCreate(Bundle bundle) {
    super.onCreate(bundle);
    Cursor c = getContentResolver()
            .query(SMS_INBOX, null, null, null, null);
    startManagingCursor(c);
    String[] columns = new String[] { "body" };
    int[] names = new int[] { R.id.row };
    adapter = new SimpleCursorAdapter(this, R.layout.sms_inbox, c, columns,
            names);

    setListAdapter(adapter);
}
}
```

Listing 9-8 opens the SMS inbox and creates a list in which each item contains the body portion of an SMS message. The layout portion of Listing 9-8 contains a simple TextView that will hold the body of each message in a list item. To get the list of SMS messages, you create a URI pointing to the SMS inbox (content://sms/inbox) and then execute a simple query. You then filter on the body of the SMS message and set the list adapter of the ListActivity. After executing the code from Listing 9-8, you'll see a list of SMS messages in the inbox. Make sure you generate a few SMS messages using the Emulator Control before running the code on the emulator.

Because you can access the SMS inbox, you would expect to be able to access other SMS-related folders such as the sent folder or the draft folder. The only difference between accessing the inbox and accessing the other folders is the URI you specify. For example, you can access the sent folder by executing a query against content://sms/sent. This list shows the complete list of SMS folders and the URI for each folder:

- *Inbox*: content://sms/inbox
- *Sent*: content://sms/sent
- *Draft*: content://sms/draft
- *Undelivered*: content://sms/undelivered
- *Failed*: content://sms/failed
- *All*: content://sms/all

Sending E-mail

Now that you've seen how to send SMS messages in Android, you might assume that you can access similar APIs to send e-mail. Unfortunately, Android does not provide APIs for you to send e-mail. The general consensus is that users don't want an application to start sending e-mail on their behalf. Instead, to send e-mail, you have to go through the registered e-mail application. For example, you could use ACTION_SEND to launch the e-mail application:

```
Intent emailIntent=new Intent(Intent.ACTION_SEND);

String subject = "Hi!";
String body = "hello from android....";

String extra = new String[]{"aaa@bbb.com"};
emailIntent.putExtra(Intent.EXTRA_EMAIL, extra);

emailIntent.putExtra(Intent.EXTRA_SUBJECT, subject);
emailIntent.putExtra(Intent.EXTRA_TEXT, body);
emailIntent.setType("message/rfc822");

startActivity(emailIntent);
```

This code launches the default e-mail application and allows the user to decide whether to send the e-mail or not.

Now let's talk about the telephony manager.

Working with the Telephony Manager

The telephony APIs also include the telephony manager (android.telephony.TelephonyManager), which you can use to obtain information about the telephony services on the device, get subscriber information, and register for telephony state changes. A common telephony use case requires that an application execute business logic upon incoming phone calls. So in this section, we are going to show you how to register for telephony state changes and how to detect incoming phone calls. Listing 9-9 shows the details.

Listing 9-9. *Using the Telephony Manager*

```
public class TelephonyServiceDemo extends Activity
{
    private static final String TAG="TelephonyServiceDemo";
    @Override
    protected void onCreate(Bundle savedInstanceState)
    {
        super.onCreate(savedInstanceState);

        TelephonyManager teleMgr =
(TelephonyManager)getSystemService(Context.TELEPHONY_SERVICE);
        teleMgr.listen(new MyPhoneStateListener(),
PhoneStateListener.LISTEN_CALL_STATE);
    }

    class MyPhoneStateListener extends PhoneStateListener
    {
```

```
        @Override
        public void onCallStateChanged(int state, String incomingNumber) {
            super.onCallStateChanged(state, incomingNumber);

            switch(state)
            {

                case TelephonyManager.CALL_STATE_IDLE:
                    Log.d(TAG, "call state idle...incoming number is["+
incomingNumber+"]");break;
                case TelephonyManager.CALL_STATE_RINGING:
                    Log.d(TAG, "call state ringing...incoming number is["+
incomingNumber+"]");break;
                case TelephonyManager.CALL_STATE_OFFHOOK:
                    Log.d(TAG, "call state Offhook...incoming number is["+
incomingNumber+"]");break;
                default:
                    Log.d(TAG, "call state ["+state+"]incoming number is["+
incomingNumber+"]");break;
            }
        }


    }
}
```

When working with the telephony manager, be sure to add the <uses-permission android:name="android.permission.READ_PHONE_STATE" /> permission to your manifest file so you can access phone-state information. As shown in Listing 9-9, you get notified about phone-state changes by implementing a PhoneStateListener and calling the listen() method of the TelephonyManager. When a phone call arrives, or the phone state changes, the system will call your PhoneStateListener's onCallStateChanged() method with the new state and the incoming phone number. In the case of an incoming call, you look for the CALL_STATE_RINGING state. You write a debug message to the log file in this example, but your application could implement custom business logic in its place. To emulate incoming phone calls, you can use Eclipse's Emulator Control UI, as you did with SMS messages (see Figure 9-8).

When dealing with phone-state changes, you might also need to get the subscriber's (user's) phone number. TelephonyManager.getLine1Number() will return that for you.

Summary

In this chapter, we talked about the Android media framework and the telephony APIs. With respect to media, we showed you how to play audio and video. We also showed you how to record audio. Refer to Chapter 12 for more discussion of media—video capture, intents to record audio/video, and more.

In the second part of the chapter, we talked about telephony services in Android. Specifically, we showed you how to send text messages and how to monitor incoming text messages. We also showed you how to access the various SMS folders on the device. We concluded with a discussion of the TelephonyManager class.

In the next chapter, we are going to turn our attention to 3D graphics by discussing how to use OpenGL with your Android applications.

CHAPTER 10

■ ■ ■

Programming 3D Graphics with OpenGL

In this chapter, we will talk about working with the OpenGL graphics API on the Android Platform. Specifically, we'll break down the topic into three sections. First, we'll provide an overview of OpenGL, OpenGL for Embedded Systems (OpenGL ES), and some competing standards. Second, we will explain the theory behind OpenGL and cover some of the essential OpenGL ES APIs. In the third and final section, we will give you the necessary code to build a test harness that you can use to exercise the APIs covered in the second section.

OpenGL ES is a 2D and 3D graphics API specifically for embedded systems, and Android supports it completely. The Android SDK distribution comes with a number of OpenGL ES samples to attest to this fact. However, in versions 1.0, 1.1, and 1.5 of the Android SDK, documentation on how to get started with OpenGL is minimal to nonexistent. The underlying assumption is that OpenGL ES is an open standard and that programmers can learn it from sources outside Android. A side effect of this assumption is that the few online resources that address using OpenGL with Android assume you're already familiar with OpenGL.

Here's the good news, though. In this chapter, we will help you with these minor roadblocks. With a few prerequisites, we will walk you through the creation of an OpenGL ES test harness that you can use to start drawing and experimenting with the OpenGL ES API. In the process, we will draw attention to the necessary basics of OpenGL and point you toward OpenGL resources online that will help you explore the matter further.

The way you construct this test harness, and hence the way you approach OpenGL, differs between releases 1.1 and 1.5. The approach in release 1.0 is the same as the approach in release 1.1, because the latter is a fix release for the former. We know there might be programmers out there using all three releases, so we will show you the test-harness implementation using 1.0 and 1.1 in this chapter. And we will reimplement this OpenGL test harness again in Chapter 13 using the 1.5 SDK. Even if you are programming in the 1.5 SDK, you might want to read this section to understand how the 1.5 SDK would have implemented the underlying abstraction. So, this chapter is certainly a prerequisite for Chapter 13.

By the end of this chapter, you'll be well-equipped with the ideas of drawing in three dimensions, setting up the OpenGL *camera*, and setting up the viewing volume (also called the *frustum*). We will do this by introducing almost no mathematics (unlike many OpenGL books).

■**Note** The OpenGL camera concept is similar but distinct from the Camera class in Android's graphics package, which you learned about in Chapter 6. Whereas Android's Camera object from the graphics package simulates 3D-like viewing capabilities by projecting a 2D view moving in 3D space, the OpenGL camera is a paradigm that represents a virtual viewing point. In other words, it models a real-world scene through the viewing perspective of an observer looking through a camera. You'll learn more in the subsection "Understanding the Camera and Coordinates" under "Using OpenGL ES." Both cameras are still separate from the handheld device's physical camera that you use to take pictures or shoot video.

Understanding OpenGL

OpenGL (originally called Open Graphics Library) is a 2D and 3D graphics API that was developed by Silicon Graphics Inc. (SGI) for its Unix workstations. Although SGI's version of OpenGL has been around for a long time, the first standardized spec of OpenGL emerged in 1992. Now widely adopted on all operating systems, the OpenGL standard forms the basis of much of the gaming, computer-aided design (CAD), and even virtual reality (VR) industries.

The OpenGL standard is currently being managed by an industry consortium called The Khronos Group (http://www.khronos.org), founded in 2000 by companies such as NVIDIA, Sun Microsystems, ATI Technologies, and SGI. You can learn more about the OpenGL spec at the consortium's web site:

http://www.khronos.org/opengl/

The official documentation page for OpenGL is available here:

http://www.opengl.org/documentation/

As you can see from this documentation page, you have access to many books and online resources dedicated to OpenGL. Of these, the gold standard is *OpenGL Programming Guide: The Official Guide to Learning OpenGL, Version 1.1*, also known as the "red book" of OpenGL. You can find an online version of this book here:

http://www.glprogramming.com/red/

We recommend this book highly. Unlike many other OpenGL books, this book is eminently readable. We did have some difficulty, however, unraveling the nature of *units* that are used to draw. Perhaps the authors thought it was a simpler concept than it is. We'll try to clarify the important ideas regarding what you draw and what you see in OpenGL. These ideas center on setting up the OpenGL camera and setting up a *viewing box*, also known as a *viewing volume* or *frustum*.

While we are on the subject of OpenGL, we should talk a little bit about Direct3D, which is part of Microsoft's DirectX API. It's likely that Direct3D will be the standard on Windows-based mobile devices. Moreover, because OpenGL and Direct3D are similar, you could even read books about Direct3D to get an understanding of how 3D drawing works.

This Direct3D standard, which emerged from Microsoft in 1996, is programmed using COM (Component Object Model) interfaces. In the Windows world, you use COM interfaces to communicate between different components of an application. When a component is developed and exposed through a COM interface, any development language on the Windows platform can access it, both from inside and outside the application. In the Unix world, CORBA (Common Object Request Broker Architecture) plays the role that COM plays for Windows.

OpenGL, on the other hand, uses language bindings that look similar to their C language counterparts. A language binding allows a common library to be used from many different languages such as C, C++, Visual Basic, Java, and so on.

Both the OpenGL and Direct3D standards are converging in their capabilities, but you might face a different learning curve because OpenGL is a C API whereas Direct3D is a COM interface. Plus, you'll see differences in their rendering semantics, which are the approaches used inside the library to paint (roughly) a graphic scene.

Let us now talk about OpenGL ES, the version of OpenGL geared toward the mobile platform.

OpenGL ES

The Khronos Group is also responsible for two additional standards that are tied to OpenGL: OpenGL ES, and the EGL Native Platform Graphics Interface (known simply as "EGL"). As we mentioned, OpenGL ES is a smaller version of OpenGL intended for embedded systems. While we are on the subject of embedded systems, let us point out that the Java Community Process is also developing an object-oriented abstraction for OpenGL for mobile devices called Mobile 3D Graphics API (M3G). We will briefly give you an introduction to M3G in the subsection "M3G: Another Java ME 3D Graphics Standard."

The EGL standard needs some explanation. It's essentially an enabling interface between the underlying operating system and the rendering APIs offered by OpenGL ES. Because OpenGL and OpenGL ES are general-purpose interfaces for drawing, each operating system needs to provide a standard hosting environment for OpenGL and OpenGL ES to interact with. You will get to know this need in practical terms later in the chapter, when we use the EGL APIs in our examples.

Let's come back to OpenGL ES. The target devices for OpenGL ES include cell phones, appliances, and even vehicles. Because OpenGL ES has to be much smaller than OpenGL, many convenient functions have been removed. Drawing rectangles is not directly supported in OpenGL ES, for example; you have to draw two triangles to make a rectangle.

As you start exploring Android's support for OpenGL, you'll focus primarily on OpenGL ES and its bindings to the Android OS through Java and EGL. You can find the documentation (man pages) for OpenGL ES here:

```
http://www.khronos.org/opengles/documentation/opengles1_0/html/index.html
```

We kept returning to this reference as we developed this chapter, because it identifies and explains each OpenGL ES API and describes the arguments for each. You'll find these APIs similar to Java APIs, and you'll get introduced to some of them in this chapter.

OpenGL ES and Java ME

OpenGL ES, like OpenGL, is a C-based, flat API. Because the Android SDK is a Java-based programming API, you need a Java binding to OpenGL ES. Java ME has already defined this binding through JSR 239: Java Binding for the OpenGL ES API. JSR 239 itself is based on JSR 231, which is a Java binding for OpenGL 1.5. JSR 239 could have been strictly a subset of JSR 231, but that's not the case because it must accommodate some extensions to OpenGL ES that are not in OpenGL 1.5.

You can find the documentation for JSR 239 here:

```
http://java.sun.com/javame/reference/apis/jsr239/
```

This reference will give you a sense of the APIs available in OpenGL ES. It also provides valuable information about these packages:

```
javax.microedition.khronos.egl
javax.microedition.khronos.opengles
java.nio
```

The `nio` package is necessary because the OpenGL ES implementations take only byte streams as inputs for efficiency reasons. `nio` defines a lot of utility buffers for this purpose. You will see some of these in action in the "glVertexPointer and Specifying Drawing Vertices" subsection under the main "Using OpenGL ES" section.

You can find minimal documentation of the Android SDK's support for OpenGL at this site:

```
http://developer.android.com/guide/topics/graphics/opengl.html
```

On this page, the documentation indicates that the Android implementation mostly parallels JSR 239 but warns that it might diverge from it in a few places.

M3G: Another Java ME 3D Graphics Standard

JSR 239 is merely a Java binding on a native OpenGL ES standard. As we mentioned briefly in the "OpenGL ES" subsection, Java provides another API to work with 3D graphics on mobile devices: M3G. This object-oriented standard is defined in JSR 184 and JSR 297, the latter being more recent. As per JSR 184, M3G serves as a lightweight, object-oriented, interactive 3D graphics API for mobile devices.

The object-oriented nature of M3G separates it from OpenGL ES. For details, visit the home page for JSR 184:

```
http://www.jcp.org/en/jsr/detail?id=184
```

The APIs for M3G are available in the Java package

```
javax.microedition.m3g.*;
```

M3G is a higher-level API compared to OpenGL ES, so it should be easier to learn. However, the jury is still out on how well it will perform on handhelds. As of now, Android does not support M3G.

So far, we have laid out the options available in the OpenGL space for handheld devices. We have talked about OpenGL ES and also briefly about the M3G standard. We will now focus on working with OpenGL ES on Android.

Using OpenGL ES

This section is dedicated to helping you understand the concepts behind OpenGL and the OpenGL ES API. We'll explain all the key APIs, after which you'll put them to use in the next section when you develop a test harness for OpenGL ES. First we'll discuss the basics of OpenGL and then we'll show you how Android interfaces with the OpenGL ES API.

To supplement the information from this chapter, you might want to bookmark the online resources we mentioned earlier. Here they are again:

- *OpenGL Programming Guide (the "red book")*: `http://www.glprogramming.com/red/`

- *Documentation for JSR 239 (Java Binding for the OpenGL ES API)*: `http://java.sun.com/javame/reference/apis/jsr239/`

- *The Khronos Group's OpenGL ES Reference Manual*: `http://www.khronos.org/opengles/documentation/opengles1_0/html/index.html`

■**Note** As you start using the OpenGL resources, you'll notice that some of the APIs are not available in OpenGL ES. This is where The Khronos Group's OpenGL ES Reference Manual comes in handy.

We will cover the following APIs in a fair amount of detail because they're central to understanding OpenGL and OpenGL ES:

- `glVertexPointer`
- `glDrawElements`
- `glColor`
- `glClear`
- `gluLookAt`
- `glFrustum`
- `glViewport`

As we cover these APIs, you'll learn how to

- Use the essential OpenGL ES drawing APIs
- Clear the palette
- Specify colors
- Understand the camera and coordinates
- Interact with an Android view to draw using OpenGL ES

Essential Drawing with OpenGL ES

In OpenGL, you draw in 3D space. You start out by specifying a series of points, also called vertices. Each of these points will have three values: one for the x coordinate, one for the y coordinate, and one for the z coordinate.

These points are then joined together to form a shape. You can join these points into a variety of shapes called *primitive shapes*, which include points, lines, and triangles in OpenGL ES. Note that in OpenGL, primitive shapes also include rectangles and polygons. As you work with OpenGL and OpenGL ES, you will continue to see differences whereby the latter has fewer features than the former. Here's another example: OpenGL allows you to specify each point separately, whereas OpenGL ES allows you to specify them only as a series of points in one fell swoop. However, you can often simulate OpenGL ES's missing features through other, more primitive features. For instance, you can draw a rectangle by combining two triangles.

OpenGL ES offers two primary methods to facilitate drawing:

- glVertexPointer

- glDrawElements

Note We'll use the terms "API" and "method" interchangeably when we talk about the OpenGL ES APIs.

You use glVertexPointer to specify a series of points or vertices, and you use glDrawElements to draw them using one of the primitive shapes that we pointed out earlier. We'll describe these methods in more detail, but first let's go over some nomenclature.

The names of these OpenGL and OpenGL ES APIs all begin with gl. Following gl is the method name. The method name is followed by an optional number such as 3, which points to either the number of dimensions—such as (x,y,z)—or the number of arguments. The method name is then followed by a data type such as f for float. (You can refer to any of the OpenGL online resources to learn the various data types and their corresponding letters.)

We'll tell you about one more convention. If a method takes an argument either as a byte (b) or a float (f), then the method will have two names: one ending with b, and one ending with f.

Let's now look at each of the two drawing-related methods, starting with glVertexPointer.

glVertexPointer and Specifying Drawing Vertices

The glVertexPointer method is responsible for specifying an array of points to be drawn. Each point is specified in three dimensions, so each point will have three values: x, y, and z. Here's how you can specify three points in an array:

```
float[] coords = {
    -0.5f, -0.5f, 0,   //p1: (x1,y1,z1)
     0.5f, -0.5f, 0,   //p2: (x1,y1,z1)
     0.0f,  0.5f, 0    //p3: (x1,y1,z1)
};
```

This structure is a contiguous array of floats kept in a Java-based float array. Don't worry about typing or compiling this code anywhere yet—our goal at this point is just to give you an idea of how these OpenGL ES methods work. We will give you the working examples and code when we help you develop a test harness in the last section of this chapter.

You might be wondering what units are used for the coordinates in points p1, p2, and p3. The short answer is that as you model your 3D space, these coordinate units can be anything you'd like. But subsequently, you will need to specify something called a *bounding volume* (or *bounding box*) that quantifies these coordinates. For example, you can specify the bounding box as a cube with 5-inch sides or a cube with 2-inch sides. These coordinates are also known as *world coordinates* because you are conceptualizing your world independent of the physical device's limitations. We will further explain these coordinates in the subsection "Understanding the Camera and Coordinates." For now, assume that you are using a cube that is 2 units across all its sides and centered at (x=0,y=0,z=0).

■Note The terms *bounding volume*, *bounding box*, *viewing volume*, *viewing box*, and *frustum* all refer to the same concept: the pyramid-shaped 3D volume that determines what is visible onscreen. You'll learn more in the "glFrustum and the Viewing Volume" subsection under "Understanding the Camera and Coordinates."

You can also assume that the origin is at the center of visual display. The z axis will be negative going into the display (away from you) and positive coming out of the display (toward you). x will go positive as you move right and negative as you move left. However, these coordinates will also depend on the direction from which you are viewing the scene.

To draw these points, you need to pass them to OpenGL ES through the glVertexPointer method. For efficiency reasons, however, glVertexPointer takes a native buffer that is language-agnostic rather than an array of floats. For this, you need to convert the Java-based array of floats to an acceptable C-like native buffer. You'll need to use the java.nio classes to convert the float array into the native buffer. Here's the sample code to do that:

```
jva.nio.ByteBuffer vbb = java.nio.ByteBuffer.allocateDirect(3 * 3 * 4);
vbb.order(ByteOrder.nativeOrder());
java.nio.FloatBuffer mFVertexBuffer = vbb.asFloatBuffer();
```

The byte buffer is a buffer of memory ordered into bytes. Each point has three floats because of the three axes, and each float is 4 bytes. So together you get 3 * 4 bytes for each point. Plus, a triangle has three points. So you need 3 * 3 * 4 bytes to hold all three float points of a triangle.

Once you have the points gathered into a native buffer, you can call glVertexPointer like this:

```
glVertexPointer(
                // Are we using (x,y) or (x,y,z) in each point
                3,
                // each value is a float value in the buffer
                GL10.GL_FLOAT,
                // Between two points there is no space
                0,
                // pointer to the start of the buffer
                mFVertexBuffer);
```

Let's talk about the arguments of this method. The first argument tells OpenGL ES how many dimensions there are in a point or a vertex. In this case, we specified 3 for x, y, and z. You could also specify 2 for just x and y. In that case, z would be zero. Note that this first argument is not the number of points in the buffer, but the number of dimensions used. So if you pass 20 points to draw a number of triangles, you will not pass 20 as the first argument; you would pass 2 or 3, depending on the number of dimensions used.

The second argument indicates that the coordinates need to be interpreted as floats. The third argument, called a stride, points to the number of bytes separating each point. In this case, it is zero because one point immediately follows the other. Sometimes you can add color attributes as part of the buffer after each point. If you want to do that, you'd use a stride to skip those as part of the vertex specification. The last argument is the pointer to the buffer containing the points.

Now you understand how to set up the array of points to be drawn. Next, you'll see how you'd actually draw this array of points using the glDrawElements method.

glDrawElements

Once you specify the series of points through glVertexPointer, you use the glDrawElements method to draw those points with one of the primitive shapes that OpenGL ES allows. Note that OpenGL is a state machine, meaning that it remembers the values set by one method when it invokes the next method in a cumulative manner. So you don't need to explicitly pass the points set by glVertexPointer to glDrawElements. glDrawElements will implicitly use those points. Listing 10-1 shows an example of this method with possible arguments.

Listing 10-1. *Example of glDrawElements*

```
glDrawElements(
        // type of shape
        GL10.GL_TRIANGLE_STRIP,
        // Number of indices
        3,
        // How big each index is
        GL10.GL_UNSIGNED_SHORT,
        // buffer containing the 3 indices
        mIndexBuffer);
```

The first argument indicates the type of geometrical shape to draw: GL_TRIANGLE_STRIP signifies a triangle strip. Other possible options for this argument are points only (GL_POINTS), line strips (GL_LINE_STRIP), lines only (GL_LINES), line loops (GL_LINE_LOOP), triangles only (GL_TRIANGLES), and triangle fans (GL_TRIANGLE_FAN).

The concept of a STRIP in GL_LINE_STRIP and GL_TRIANGLE_STRIP is to add new points while making use of the old ones. This way, you can avoid specifying all the points for each new object. For example, if you specify four points in an array, you can use strips to draw the first triangle out of (1,2,3) and the second one out of (2,3,4). Each new point will add a new triangle. (You can refer to the OpenGL red book for more details.) You can also vary these parameters to see how the triangles are drawn as you add new points.

The idea of a FAN in GL_TRIANGLE_FAN applies to triangles where the first point is used as a starting point for all subsequent triangles. So you're essentially making a FAN- or circle-like object with the first vertex in the middle. Suppose you have six points in your array: (1,2,3,4,5,6). With a FAN, the triangles will be drawn at (1,2,3), (1,3,4), (1,4,5), and (1,5,6). Every new point adds an extra triangle, similar to the process of extending a fan or unfolding a pack of cards.

The rest of the arguments of glDrawElements involve the method's ability to let you reuse point specification. For example, a square contains four points. Each square can be drawn as a combination of two triangles. If you want to draw two triangles to make up the square, do you have to specify six points? No. You can specify only four points and refer to them six times to draw two triangles. This process is called *indexing into the point buffer*.

Here is an example:

```
Points: (p1, p2, p3, p4)
Draw indices (p1, p2, p3,    p2,p3,p4)
```

Notice how the first triangle comprises p1,p2,p3 and the second one comprises p2,p3,p4. With this knowledge, the second argument identifies how many indices there are in the index buffer.

The third argument to glDrawElements (see Listing 10-1) points to the type of values in the index array, whether they are unsigned shorts (GL_UNSIGNED_SHORT) or unsigned bytes (GL_UNSIGNED_BYTE).

The last argument points to the index buffer. To fill up the index buffer, you need to do something similar to what you did with the vertex buffer. Start with a Java array and use the java.nio package to convert that array into a native buffer.

Here is some sample code that converts a short array of {0,1,2} into a native buffer suitable to be passed to glDrawElements:

```
//Figure out how you want to arrange your points
short[] myIndecesArray = {0,1,2};

//get a short buffer
java.nio.ShortBuffer mIndexBuffer;

//Allocate 2 bytes each for each index value
ByteBuffer ibb = ByteBuffer.allocateDirect(3 * 2);
ibb.order(ByteOrder.nativeOrder());
mIndexBuffer = ibb.asShortBuffer();

//stuff that into the buffer
for (int i=0;i<3;i++)
{
   mIndexBuffer.put(myIndecesArray[i]);
}
```

Now that you've seen mIndexBuffer at work in the preceding snippet, you can revisit Listing 10-1 and better understand what's going on.

Note Rather than create any new points, the index buffer merely indexes into the array of points indicated through the glVertexPointer. This is possible because OpenGL remembers the assets set by the previous calls in a stateful fashion.

Now we'll look at two commonly used OpenGL ES methods: glClear and glColor. We'll use each of these in our test harness.

glClear

You use the glClear method to erase the drawing surface. Using this method, you can reset not only the color, but also the depth and the type of stencils used. You specify which element to reset by the constant that you pass in: GL_COLOR_BUFFER_BIT, GL_DEPTH_BUFFER_BIT, or GL_STENCIL_BUFFER_BIT.

The color buffer is responsible for the pixels that are visible, so clearing it is equivalent to erasing the surface of any colors. The depth buffer refers to all the pixels that are visible in a 3D scene, depending on how far or close the object is.

The stencil buffer is a bit advanced to cover in this introductory chapter, except to say this: you use it to create visual effects based on some dynamic criteria, and you use glClear to erase it.

■**Note** A stencil is a drawing template that you can use to replicate a drawing many times. For example, if you are using Microsoft Office Visio, all the drawing templates that you save as *.vss files are stencils. In the noncomputer drawing world, you create a stencil by cutting out a pattern in a sheet of paper or some other flat material. Then you can paint over that sheet and remove it, creating the impression that results in a replication of that drawing.

For our purposes, you can use this code to clear the color buffer in all the examples:

```
//Clear the surface of any color
gl.glClear(gl.GL_COLOR_BUFFER_BIT);
```

Now let's talk about attaching a default color to what gets drawn.

glColor

You use glColor to set the default color for the subsequent drawing that takes place. In the following code segment, the method glColor4f sets the color to red:

```
//Set the current color
glColor4f(1.0f, 0, 0, 0.5f);
```

Recall the discussion about method nomenclature: 4f refers to the four arguments that the method takes, each of which is a float. The four arguments are components of red, green, blue, and alpha (color gradient). The starting values for each are (1,1,1,1). In this case, we have set the color to red with half a gradient (specified by the last alpha argument).

Although we have covered the basic drawing APIs, we still need to address a few things regarding the coordinates of the points that you specify in 3D space. The next subsection explains how OpenGL models a real-world scene through the viewing perspective of an observer looking through a camera.

Understanding the Camera and Coordinates

As you draw in 3D space, you ultimately must project the 3D view onto a 2D screen—similar to capturing a 3D scene using a camera in the real world. This symbolism is formally recognized in OpenGL, so many concepts in OpenGL are explained in terms of a camera.

As you will see in this subsection, the part of your drawing that becomes visible depends on the location of the camera, the direction of the camera lens, the orientation of the camera (such as upside down), the zoom level, and the size of the capturing "film."

These aspects of projecting a 3D picture onto a 2D screen are controlled by three methods in OpenGL:

- gluLookAt: Controls the direction of the camera

- glFrustum: Controls the viewing volume or zoom

- glViewport: Controls the size of the screen or the size of the camera's "film"

You won't be able to program anything in OpenGL unless you understand the implications of these three APIs. Let us elaborate on the camera symbolism further to explain how these three APIs affect what you see on an OpenGL screen. We will start with gluLookAt.

gluLookAt and the Camera Symbolism

Imagine you go on a trip to take pictures of a landscape involving flowers, trees, streams, and mountains. You get to the meadow. The scene that lies before you is equivalent to what you draw in OpenGL. You can make these drawings big, like the mountains, or small, like the flowers—as long as they are all proportional to one another. The coordinates you'll use for these drawings, as we hinted at earlier, are called *world coordinates*. Under these coordinates, you can establish a line to be four units long on the x axis by setting your points as (0,0,0) to (4,0,0).

As you are getting ready to take a picture, you find a spot to place your tripod. Then you hook up the camera to the tripod. The location of your camera—not the tripod, but the camera itself—becomes the origin of your camera in the world. So you will need to take a piece of paper and write down this location, which is called the *eye point*. If you don't specify an eye point, the camera is located at (0,0,0), which is the exact center of your screen. Usually you want to step away from the origin so that you can see the (x,y) plane that is sitting at the origin of z=0. For argument's sake, suppose you position the camera at (0,0,5). This would move the camera off your screen toward you by 5 units.

You can refer to Figure 10-1 to visualize how the camera is placed.

Once you place the camera, you start looking ahead or forward to see which portion of the scene you want to capture. You will position the camera in the direction you are looking. This far-off point that you are looking at is called a *view point* or a *look-at point*. This point specification is really a specification of the direction. So if you specify your view point as (0,0,0), then the camera is looking along the z axis toward the origin from a distance of five units, assuming the camera is positioned at (0,0,5). You can see this in Figure 10-1, where the camera is looking down the z axis.

Imagine further that there is a rectangular building at the origin. You want to look at it not in a portrait fashion, but in a landscape fashion. What do you have to do? You obviously can leave the camera in the same location and still point it toward the origin, but now you need to turn the camera by 90 degrees. This is the *orientation* of the camera, as the camera is fixed at a given eye point and looking at a specific look-at point or direction. This orientation is called the *up vector*.

The up vector simply identifies the orientation of the camera such as up, down, left, right, or at an angle. This orientation of the camera is specified using a point as well. Imagine a line from the origin—not the camera origin, but the world-coordinate origin—to this point. Whatever angle this line subtends in three dimensions at the origin is the orientation of camera.

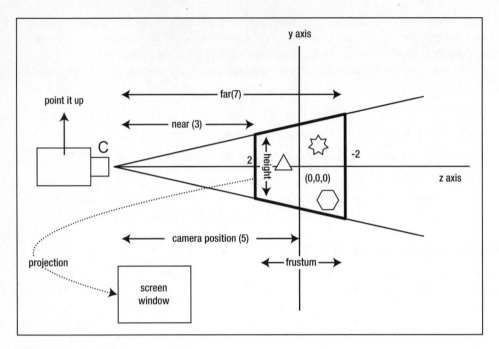

Figure 10-1. *OpenGL viewing concepts using the camera analogy*

For example, an up vector for a camera might look like (0,1,0) or even (0,15,0), both of which would have the same effect. The point (0,1,0) is a point away from the origin along the y axis going up. This means you position the camera upright. If you use (0,-1,0), you would position the camera upside down. Still, in both cases, the camera is still at the same point (0,0,5) and looking at the same origin (0,0,0). You can summarize these three coordinates like this:

- (0,0,5): Eye point (location of the camera)
- (0,0,0): Look-at point (direction the camera is pointing)
- (0,1,0): Up vector (whether the camera is up, down, or slanted)

You will use the gluLookAt method to specify these three points—the eye point, the look-at point, and the up vector:

```
gluLookAt(gl, 0,0,5,    0,0,0,    0,1,0);
```

The arguments are as follows: the first set of coordinates belongs to the eye point, the second set of coordinates belongs to the look-at point, and the third set of coordinates belongs to the up vector with respect to the origin.

Let us turn our attention now to the viewing volume.

glFrustum and the Viewing Volume

You might have noticed that none of the points describing the camera position using gluLookAt deal with size. They deal only with positioning, direction, and orientation. How can you tell the camera where to focus? How far away is the subject you are trying to capture? How wide and how tall is the subject area? You use the OpenGL method glFrustum to specify the area of the scene that you are interested in.

Think of the scene area as bounded by a box, also called the *frustum* or *viewing volume* (see the area marked by the bold border in the middle of Figure 10-1). Anything inside the box is captured, and anything outside the box is clipped and ignored. So how do you specify this viewing box? You first decide on the *near point,* or the distance between the camera and the beginning of the box. Then you can choose a *far point,* which is the distance between the camera and the end of the box. The distance between the near and far points along the z axis is the depth of the box. If you specify a near point of 50 and a far point of 200, then you will capture everything between those points and your box depth will be 150. You will also need to specify the left side of the box, the right side of the box, the top of the box, and the bottom of the box along the imaginary *ray* that joins the camera to the look-at point.

In OpenGL, you can imagine this box in one of two ways. One is called a *perspective projection,* which involves the frustum we've been talking about. This view, which simulates natural camera-like function, involves a pyramidal structure in which the far plane serves as the base and the camera serves as the apex. The near plane cuts off the "top" of the pyramid, forming the frustum between the near plane and the far plane.

The other way to imagine the box involves thinking of it as a cube. This second scenario is called *orthographic projection,* which is suited for geometrical drawings that need to preserve sizes despite the distance from the camera.

Let's see how to specify the frustum for our example:

```
//calculate aspect ratio first
float ratio = (float) w / h;

//indicate that we want a perspective projection
glMatrixMode(GL10.GL_PROJECTION);

//Specify the frustum: the viewing volume
gl.glFrustumf(
    -ratio, // Left side of the viewing box
    ratio,    // right side of the viewing box
    1,     // top of the viewing box
    -1,     // bottom of the viewing box
    3,     // how far is the front of the box from the camera
    7);    // how far is the back of the box from the camera
```

Because we set the top to 1 and bottom to -1 in the preceding code, we have set the front height of the box to 2 units. You specify the sizes for the left and right sides of the frustum by using proportional numbers, taking into account the window's aspect ratio. This is why this code uses the window height and width to figure out the proportion. The code also assumes the area of action to be between 3 and 7 units along the z axis. Anything drawn outside these coordinates, relative to the camera, won't be visible.

Because we set the camera at (0,0,5) and pointing toward (0,0,0), 3 units from the camera toward the origin will be (0,0,2) and 7 units from the camera will be (0,0,-2). This leaves the origin plane right in the middle of your 3D box.

So now you've identified how big your viewing volume is. You need to understand one more API to map these sizes to the screen: glViewport.

glViewport and Screen Size

glViewport is responsible for specifying the rectangular area on the screen onto which the viewing volume will be projected. This method takes four arguments to specify the rectangular box: the x and y coordinates of the lower-left corner, followed by the width and height. Here is an example of specifying a view as the target for this projection:

```
glViewport(0,      // lower left "x" of the rectangle on the screen
           0,                // lower left "y" of the rectangle on the screen
           width,    // width of the rectangle on the screen
           height);  // height of the rectangle on the screen
```

If your window or view size is 100 pixels in height and your frustum height is 10 units, then every logical unit of 1 translates to 10 pixels.

Congratulations. In the last few subsections, you have reached an important milestone in understanding OpenGL. Most OpenGL books take multiple chapters to bring you to this stage. This knowledge should keep you in good stead for the rest of the chapter and also for a general understanding of OpenGL on any platform.

This brings us to the next subsection, where we will explain how the standards-based OpenGL ES API is tied to Android. This is done through EGL and Android-specific concepts. We will cover this now, and then go on to the test harness.

Interfacing OpenGL ES with Android

In addition to defining OpenGL ES, The Khronos Group defines a supplemental standard called EGL that defines what it takes to use the OpenGL ES APIs on a native platform such as Android. EGL stipulates that you need to get an EGL context based on device-dependent configuration specs. Once you have this EGL context, then you can pass an Android UI object to this context to get the interface that allows you to call all the OpenGL methods. The next three subsections will cover these topics:

- Getting an EGL context

- Associating a drawing surface with OpenGL ES through the EGL context

- Disassociating the drawing surface from the EGL context and closing out the OpenGL ES resources

Getting an EGL Context

In the Android SDK distribution, the EGL API is available in the package javax.microedition. khronos.egl.EGL10. You can read more about using this package at http://java.sun.com/javame/reference/apis/jsr239/javax/microedition/khronos/egl/EGL10.html.

■**Note** Although this URL points to a web site about Java, it's relevant because Android uses the same API. All of the site's information on EGL is applicable to Android OpenGL programming as well.

Getting an EGL context involves the following steps:

1. Get an implementation of EGL10.

2. Get a display to use.

3. Initialize the display.

4. Specify a device-specific configuration to EGL.

5. Use an initialized display and a configuration to get an EGL context.

Once you have the context, you can bind the context to a window surface every time a window is created or changed, and then tear it down at the end. We will look at preparing the window surface and tearing it down in the next subsection.

But first take a look at some boilerplate code to get an EGL context (see Listing 10-2). Please note that we're providing this code for illustration purposes only; it's not meant to be compiled. You can compile the version of it that we'll use in the test harness later.

Listing 10-2. *Sample Code to Get an EGL Context*

```
//Ask for an implementation of EGL10
EGL10 mEgl = (EGL10) EGLContext.getEGL();

//get the default display
EGLDisplay mEglDisplay = mEgl.eglGetDisplay(EGL10.EGL_DEFAULT_DISPLAY);

//initialize the display
int[] version = new int[2];
mEgl.eglInitialize(mEglDisplay, version);

//config spec
int[] configSpec = {
    EGL10.EGL_DEPTH_SIZE, 0,
    EGL10.EGL_NONE
};

EGLConfig[] configs = new EGLConfig[1];
int[] num_config = new int[1];
mEgl.eglChooseConfig(mEglDisplay, configSpec, configs, 1,
    num_config);
mEglConfig = configs[0];

//Create EGL Context
mEglContext = mEgl.eglCreateContext(mEglDisplay, mEglConfig,
    EGL10.EGL_NO_CONTEXT, null);
```

The code in Listing 10-2 is pretty standard for establishing a working EGL context, except for the part where a drawing configuration could differ depending on an application. The method getEGL returns an implementation for the EGL10 interface. The rest of the methods use this EGL10 interface in an implementation-independent manner to get to the EGL context.

The method eglGetDisplay returns a default display to connect to, if an EGL_DEFAULT_ DISPLAY constant is passed in. The eglInitialize method initializes the display and returns major and minor version numbers of the OpenGL implementation.

The next method, eglChooseConfig, is more involved. This method wants you to specify the types of things that are critical to you as you draw. For example, if you want color sizes with a bit depth of 8, you might use this configuration spec:

```
int[] configAttrs = { EGL10.EGL_RED_SIZE, 8,
             EGL10.EGL_GREEN_SIZE, 8,
             EGL10.EGL_BLUE_SIZE, 8,
             EGL10.EGL_ALPHA_SIZE, EGL10.EGL_DONT_CARE,
             EGL10.EGL_DEPTH_SIZE, EGL10.EGL_DONT_CARE,
             EGL10.EGL_STENCIL_SIZE, EGL10.EGL_DONT_CARE,
             EGL10.EGL_NONE
};
```

And here's a suitable configuration spec in which the depth is zero:

```
int[] configSpec = {
    EGL10.EGL_DEPTH_SIZE, 0,
    EGL10.EGL_NONE
};
```

Refer to an OpenGL book to get a better understanding of configuration management under OpenGL. You can also check out the Android SDK OpenGL samples to get a feel for possible configurations. Based on these configuration specs, the EGL10 implementation returns a series of suitable EGLConfig references. In this case, the first configuration is chosen.

Finally, you get the needed EGL context by passing an EGLDisplay and an EGLConfig to eglCreateContext. The third argument of the eglCreateContext method indicates sharing (see Listing 10-2). Here, we've used EGL10.EGL_NO_CONTEXT as the third argument to specify that we don't want to share objects with any other context. The last argument is a set of additional attributes, which we have specified as null.

Once you have this EGL context, you can use it to associate a drawing surface with the OpenGL ES interface. This interface allows you to call the OpenGL drawing methods. In the next subsection, you'll learn how to set up this association.

Associating a Drawing Surface with OpenGL ES Through the EGL Context

All of the Android SDK's samples use a view-related class called android.view.SurfaceHolder in order to draw using OpenGL ES. This class is closely related to android.view.SurfaceView, which is a variant of a regular view class that allows drawing from a separate thread. The documentation and samples don't make it clear whether you can use any other type of view for OpenGL drawing, so we'll stick to this android.view.SurfaceHolder object. Even if subsequent releases of Android were to allow another simpler object for this purpose, you'd just need to alter the object name and the rest of the explanation should still be valid. SurfaceHolder is also the recommended class to use for high-performance drawing, so learning about it should prove helpful to you in any case.

In the "Creating and Using the OpenGL Test Harness" section, we will give you the code necessary to get a SurfaceView and then get a SurfaceHolder from that, but for now assume that you have already obtained a SurfaceView. We'll explain how you use the SurfaceHolder object through the SurfaceView to get a reference to the OpenGL ES interface (see Listing 10-3).

Listing 10-3. *Getting a Reference to the OpenGL ES Interface*

```
android.view.SurfaceHolder holder = surfaceView.getHolder();

// mEgl  points to an EGL context interface EGL10
mEglSurface = mEgl.eglCreateWindowSurface(mEglDisplay,
                                      mEglConfig, holder, null);

mEgl.eglMakeCurrent(mEglDisplay, mEglSurface, mEglSurface,
                  mEglContext);
GL gl = mEgl.getGL();
```

In the preceding "Getting an EGL Context" subsection, we showed you how to obtain a reference to the variable mEgl. You will need to create this EGL context only once for an activity and keep it for the life of that activity.

The code at the beginning of Listing 10-3 gets a SurfaceHolder object from a previously obtained SurfaceView (getting the SurfaceView itself is not shown in Listing 10-3). You then pass the SurfaceHolder object to the eglCreateWindowSurface method to bind the SurfaceView to OpenGL ES for drawing.

You then use the eglMakeCurrent method to activate the drawing. Once that's done, you use the getGL method to get a reference to the OpenGL ES interface.

After executing the code in Listing 10-3, you'll have a reference to the OpenGL ES interface, which is identified by GL. This interface contains all the standard OpenGL ES APIs.

Note that as the window surface changes, either because of resizing or other reasons, you need to disassociate and reassociate the window surface so that OpenGL ES can readjust its internal configuration in response to a changed screen environment (see Listing 10-4).

Listing 10-4. *Associating and Disassociating the Window Surface*

```
mEgl.eglMakeCurrent(mEglDisplay, EGL10.EGL_NO_SURFACE,
      EGL10.EGL_NO_SURFACE, EGL10.EGL_NO_CONTEXT);
mEgl.eglDestroySurface(mEglDisplay, mEglSurface);
```

Closing Out OpenGL at the End of the Program

In addition to disassociating the window surface, you should close out the OpenGL ES resources at the end of a program. Listing 10-5 shows the sequence you need to use; note that it includes the content from Listing 10-4 at the beginning.

Listing 10-5. *Closing Out OpenGL ES Resources*

```
//Destroy surface
mEgl.eglMakeCurrent(mEglDisplay, EGL10.EGL_NO_SURFACE,
        EGL10.EGL_NO_SURFACE,
        EGL10.EGL_NO_CONTEXT);
mEgl.eglDestroySurface(mEglDisplay, mEglSurface);

//Destroy context
mEgl.eglDestroyContext(mEglDisplay, mEglContext);

//Disassociate display
mEgl.eglTerminate(mEglDisplay);
```

Now you know all the basics necessary to start coding with OpenGL ES APIs. You learned how to position the camera, work with world coordinates, and map those coordinates to the physical screen. You know what APIs to use to draw basic figures. You also know how to initialize OpenGL ES on Android.

Because the initialization necessary to start using the OpenGL ES drawing APIs is extensive, we recommend you encapsulate this initialization code into a test harness. You can then use this test harness again and again with multiple OpenGL ES programming efforts so that you don't need to think about or repeat the initialization.

This approach is similar to the approach taken by Android in the 1.5 SDK. In this approach, we will cover how to do this within the confines of the 1.0 and 1.1 releases. In Chapter 13, we will cover how the 1.5 SDK provides almost all of this out of the box. Reimplementing this test harness using the 1.5 SDK becomes very simple. Even if you care only about 1.5, we strongly recommend that you at least read this section to understand the motivation for the test harness.

The next section will show you how to design and build this OpenGL test harness, and it will provide a few specific drawing examples that use it.

Creating and Using the OpenGL Test Harness

The OpenGL test harness that you'll develop in this section will serve as an excellent tool to learn and experiment with OpenGL programming. It will hide the OpenGL ES and Android-specific initializations through the designed encapsulation.

These processes will be encapsulated:

1. Obtaining an EGL context

2. Initializing the EGL context with a SurfaceView

3. Dealing with threading issues when working with the SurfaceView

4. Setting up the camera to provide a standard set of dimensions for your drawing

We'll base this test harness on the many OpenGL samples that ship with the Android SDK. This will allow you to integrate those samples into this framework if you need to do that. The implementation is loosely based on a Java class in the Android SDK samples (com.example. android.apis.graphics.GLSurfaceView), but we'll show you how to code it from the ground up to give it more abstraction and functionality. Here are some reasons to use the test harness rather than GLSurfaceView:

- There is no documentation on how the complex sample code works.

- GLSurfaceView is a bit difficult to follow because a number of inner classes obscure the basic idea.

- GLSurfaceView assumes that you want to animate everything you draw. For example, if you were to draw a triangle, GLSurfaceView would draw it again and again in a loop whether or not a redraw is needed.

- The GLSurfaceView abstraction works at a more basic level (mostly around SurfaceView and threading), so it doesn't encapsulate camera settings and other common OpenGL chores.

We'll help you with these issues as we create and use the test harness. We won't use any inner classes to expose the abstractions, so you'll have a clear understanding of the responsibilities of each class. And we'll provide you with a class diagram identifying each of the test-harness classes and their responsibilities (see Figure 10-2).

We'll also make animation nonessential for the test harness so that you can easily test your code for simpler cases. We'll explain every part of the code so you'll realize how it works. And once this test harness is in place, you rarely have to modify it. You'll be able to focus on your OpenGL code instead.

We will now present the test-harness design and code, as well as some snapshots of the emulator containing OpenGL drawings.

Designing the Test Harness

The classes that comprise the test harness are shown in the "OpenGL Test Harness Package" portion of Figure 10-2.

In this diagram, the view you want to draw on is represented by OpenGLTestHarness inheriting from SurfaceView. The drawing itself happens in a separate cooperating thread called OpenGLDrawingThread. This thread needs to be alive for the life of the SurfaceView. As events happen on or to the SurfaceView, it needs to inform the drawing thread of those events so that drawing can take place. As you can see from the diagram, a number of these calls are delegated to the OpenGLDrawingThread.

The thread itself needs to get an EGL context at the beginning and tear it down at the end. As the window comes into existence and changes size, the thread needs to bind and unbind the EGL context to this window. OpenGLDrawingThread uses a utility class called EglHelper to help with this work.

In the end, the test harness assumes that the variable parts of the OpenGL drawing are concentrated in a class implementing the Renderer interface. An implementation of the Renderer interface is responsible for actions such as setting the camera, positioning the camera, and setting coordinates for the viewing box (frustum).

If you agree upon a given size or volume for your viewing box, you can abstract this class out even further and leave only the drawing portion to the leaf-level implementation class. The AbstractRenderer class abstracts out these camera- and size-related operations. That leaves you to focus on the OpenGL drawing APIs.

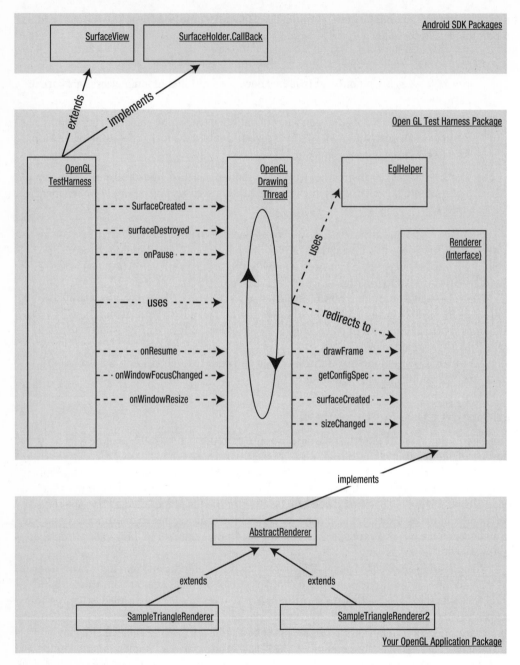

Figure 10-2. *Class diagram for the OpenGL test harness*

Consider the source code for each class in the test harness. The test harness contains the following files:

- `OpenGLTestHarnessActivity.java`: A simple activity hosting the `SurfaceView`
- `OpenGLTestHarness.java`: A `SurfaceView` tailored for OpenGL threaded drawing
- `OpenGLDrawingThread.java`: The thread responsible for drawing on the `SurfaceView`
- `EglHelper.java`: A utility class responsible for obtaining the EGL context
- `Renderer.java`: A pure interface for extending drawing code
- `AbstractRenderer.java`: A class that abstracts drawing further, leaving only the `draw` method to be abstracted; also sets up the camera and window sizes
- `SimpleTriangleRenderer.java`: A simple triangle drawing
- `SimpleTriangleRenderer2.java`: A variation of a triangle drawing using indices

The following subsections present code for each of these files. You can create your test harness by taking these classes and building them into your own project. Each source listing is followed by commentary on the important parts of the source code. For brevity, we won't include the `import` statements. In Eclipse, you can automatically populate the `import` statements by pulling up the code in the editor and selecting Source ➤ Organize Imports.

Make sure you create corresponding Java files for each class listed here before compiling. The files are presented in a logical order, but not necessarily a compilable order. You will need at least the first seven files to compile successfully; you can compile the eighth file later.

You can use the following steps to compile these files:

1. Choose a simple project you already have, such as the "Hello World!" application from Chapter 2 or the menu test harness from Chapter 5.

2. Create new classes with names that match our eight classes. Replace the body of each class with the corresponding source code from this chapter (except the package name).

3. Use Ctrl+Shift+O to resolve the imports. You might see some errors initially, but they should all disappear as soon as you have the seven or eight files in place.

4. Use a menu from the simple project in step 1 to invoke the test-harness activity. We will further explain this step after presenting all the source files.

With that, we will list each of the files now.

OpenGLTestHarnessActivity.java

`OpenGLTestHarnessActvity` is a driver class for the test harness. This is a simple Android activity that uses an implementation of the `SurfaceView` (`OpenGLTestHarness`) as its content view (see Listing 10-6).

Listing 10-6. *Code for the OpenGLTestHarnessActivity Class*

```
// filename: OpenGLTestHarnessActivity.java
public class OpenGLTestHarnessActivity extends Activity {
    private OpenGLTestHarness mTestHarness;
    @Override
    protected void onCreate(Bundle savedInstanceState) {
        super.onCreate(savedInstanceState);

        mTestHarness = new OpenGLTestHarness(this);
        mTestHarness.setRenderer(new SimpleTriangleRenderer(this));
        setContentView(mTestHarness);
    }
    @Override
    protected void onResume()    {
        super.onResume();
        mTestHarness.onResume();
    }
    @Override
    protected void onPause() {
        super.onPause();
        mTestHarness.onPause();
    }
}
```

As you come up with new OpenGL renderers, all you have to do is instantiate an OpenGLTestHarness and set it into this activity as a renderable view.

OpenGLTestHarness.java

The OpenGLTestHarness class is an implementation of the SurfaceView, and its primary responsibility is to transfer all UI events to the supporting drawing thread so the drawing thread can make the necessary decisions to draw (see Listing 10-7).

Listing 10-7. *The OpenGLTestHarness Class*

```
// filename: OpenGLTestHarness.java
public class OpenGLTestHarness extends SurfaceView
    implements SurfaceHolder.Callback
{
    public static final Semaphore sEglSemaphore = new Semaphore(1);
    public boolean mSizeChanged = true;
    public SurfaceHolder mHolder;
    private OpenGLDrawingThread mGLThread;

    public OpenGLTestHarness(Context context) {
        super(context);
        init();
    }
```

```java
public OpenGLTestHarness(Context context, AttributeSet attrs) {
    super(context, attrs);
    init();
}

private void init() {
    mHolder = getHolder();
    mHolder.addCallback(this);
    mHolder.setType(SurfaceHolder.SURFACE_TYPE_GPU);
}

public SurfaceHolder getSurfaceHolder() {
    return mHolder;
}

public void setRenderer(Renderer renderer) {
    mGLThread = new OpenGLDrawingThread(this,renderer);
    mGLThread.start();
}

public void surfaceCreated(SurfaceHolder holder) {
    mGLThread.surfaceCreated();
}

public void surfaceDestroyed(SurfaceHolder holder) {
    mGLThread.surfaceDestroyed();
}

public void surfaceChanged(SurfaceHolder holder, int format, int w, int h) {
    mGLThread.onWindowResize(w, h);
}

public void onPause() {
    mGLThread.onPause();
}

public void onResume() {
    mGLThread.onResume();
}

@Override public void onWindowFocusChanged(boolean hasFocus) {
    super.onWindowFocusChanged(hasFocus);
    mGLThread.onWindowFocusChanged(hasFocus);
}
```

```
    @Override
    protected void onDetachedFromWindow() {
        super.onDetachedFromWindow();
        mGLThread.requestExitAndWait();
    }
}
```

There is nothing significant about the boilerplate code in Listing 10-7. You use this pattern when you want another thread to draw on a SurfaceView. Now you'll look at the code for the drawing thread.

OpenGLDrawingThread.java

OpenGLDrawingThread (see Listing 10-8) is responsible for drawing OpenGL objects on the OpenGLTestHarness surface view. These two classes collaborate with each other closely.

Listing 10-8. *The OpenGLDrawingThread Class*

```
// filename: OpenGLDrawingThread.java
class OpenGLDrawingThread extends Thread
{
    private boolean mDone, mPaused, mHasFocus;
    private boolean mHasSurface, mContextLost, mSizeChanged;
    private int mWidth,mHeight;

    private Renderer mRenderer;
    private EglHelper mEglHelper;
    private OpenGLTestHarness pSv = null;

    OpenGLDrawingThread(OpenGLTestHarness sv, Renderer renderer) {
        super();
        mDone = false; mWidth = 0; mHeight = 0;
        mRenderer = renderer; mSizeChanged = false;
        setName("GLThread");
        pSv = sv;
    }

    @Override
    public void run() {
        try {
            try {
            OpenGLTestHarness.sEglSemaphore.acquire();
            } catch (InterruptedException e) {
                return;
            }
            guardedRun();
        } catch (InterruptedException e) {
            // fall thru and exit normally
```

```
        } finally {
            OpenGLTestHarness.sEglSemaphore.release();
        }
    }
    private void guardedRun() throws InterruptedException {
        mEglHelper = new EglHelper();
        int[] configSpec = mRenderer.getConfigSpec();
        mEglHelper.start(configSpec);

        GL10 gl = null;
        boolean tellRendererSurfaceCreated = true;
        boolean tellRendererSurfaceChanged = true;

        while (!mDone)
        {
            int w, h;
            boolean changed;
            boolean needStart = false;
            synchronized (this) {
                if (mPaused) {
                    Log.d("x", "Paused");
                    mEglHelper.finish();
                    needStart = true;
                }
                if(needToWait()) {
                    while (needToWait()) {
                        wait();
                        Log.d("x", "woke up from wait");
                    }
                }
                if (mDone) {
                    break;
                }
                changed = pSv.mSizeChanged;
                w = mWidth;
                h = mHeight;
                pSv.mSizeChanged = false;
                this.mSizeChanged = false;
            }
            if (needStart) {
                Log.d("x", "Need to start");
                mEglHelper.start(configSpec);
                tellRendererSurfaceCreated = true;
                changed = true;
```

```java
        }
        if (changed) {
            Log.d("x", "Change");
            gl = (GL10) mEglHelper.createSurface(pSv.mHolder);
            tellRendererSurfaceChanged = true;
        }
        if (tellRendererSurfaceCreated) {
            Log.d("x", "Render Surface created");
            mRenderer.surfaceCreated(gl);
            tellRendererSurfaceCreated = false;
        }
        if (tellRendererSurfaceChanged) {
            Log.d("x", "Render Surface changed");
            mRenderer.sizeChanged(gl, w, h);
            tellRendererSurfaceChanged = false;
        }
        if ((w > 0) && (h > 0)) {

            Log.d("x", "Drawing frame now");
            mRenderer.drawFrame(gl);
            mEglHelper.swap();
        }
      }
    }
    mEglHelper.finish();
}


private boolean needToWait() {
    return ((!mSizeChanged) || mPaused || (! mHasFocus) || (! mHasSurface)
                                || mContextLost)
        && (! mDone);
}

public void surfaceCreated() {
    synchronized(this) {
        mHasSurface = true;
        mContextLost = false;
        notify();
    }
}
public void surfaceDestroyed() {
    synchronized(this) {
        mHasSurface = false;
        notify();
    }
}
```

```
    public void onPause() {
        synchronized (this) {
            mPaused = true;
        }
    }
    public void onResume() {
        synchronized (this) {
            mPaused = false;
            notify();
        }
    }
    public void onWindowFocusChanged(boolean hasFocus) {
        synchronized (this) {
            mHasFocus = hasFocus;
            if (mHasFocus == true) {
                notify();
            }
        }
    }
    public void onWindowResize(int w, int h) {
        synchronized (this) {
            mWidth = w;
            mHeight = h;
            pSv.mSizeChanged = true;
            this.mSizeChanged = true;
            Log.d("x","window size changed. w, h:" + w + "," + h);
            if (w > 0)
            {
                notify();
            }
        }
    }
    public void requestExitAndWait()
    {
        synchronized(this) {
            mDone = true;
            notify();
        }
        try {
            join();
        } catch (InterruptedException ex) {
            Thread.currentThread().interrupt();
        }
    }
}
```

OpenGLDrawingThread is critical to understanding the interaction between OpenGL ES and the Android SDK. The OpenGLTestHarness class starts the drawing thread as soon as a renderer is set in the harness. According to the Android documentation, the first thing the run method needs to do is to wait for any previous instances to close and ensure that only one activity is running. This is because there are timing issues between onDestroy() and onCreate(). Either way, the practice is to ensure exclusive access through a semaphore.

Once the thread starts running, it will get the configSpec from the renderer and use that spec to initialize the EglHelper. EglHelper will then be used to obtain an EGL context. This is how EglHelper initializes the display and uses the display configuration to create the context based on the principles we covered in the "Getting an EGL Context" subsection.

Once the OpenGL ES interface is established through the EglHelper, the thread has to wait for a window to be created before drawing can take place. Without a window, you don't have anything to bind to the EGL context. In effect, the while loop goes into a wait mode. When a window is created or resized, the corresponding method calls from the OpenGLTestHarness SurfaceView wakes up the thread using notify. The thread will then bind the EGL context to the window and then draw. Once the drawing is complete, the thread uses the eglSwapBuffers method of EglHelper to transfer the paint buffers to the screen.

After that, the thread must return to wait mode so that it can respond to further events onscreen such as resizing, pausing, resuming, and so on. This is why the while loop needs to continue indefinitely. Pay special attention to the needToWait() function and the corresponding notify events. The needToWait() function halts the thread if the size hasn't changed, or if the surface hasn't been created, or if the focus is not there. You can enable this thread for animation if you opt *not* to check for the flag that indicates a size change. This will allow redraws even when the size doesn't change, which essentially is the basis of animation.

Now you'll see how the code for EglHelper can help you obtain the EGL context.

EglHelper.java

We have already explained the basics of what happens in the EglHelper code, such as using the configSpec, getting EGL displays, and so on. The code in Listing 10-9 reiterates those ideas, but it's more complete than the code you've seen so far.

Listing 10-9. *The EglHelper Class*

```
//filename: EglHelper.java
public class EglHelper
{
    EGL10 mEgl; EGLDisplay mEglDisplay;  EGLSurface mEglSurface;
    EGLConfig mEglConfig;   EGLContext mEglContext;
    public EglHelper(){}
    public void start(int[] configSpec)
    {
        mEgl = (EGL10) EGLContext.getEGL();
        mEglDisplay = mEgl.eglGetDisplay(EGL10.EGL_DEFAULT_DISPLAY);

        int[] version = new int[2];
        mEgl.eglInitialize(mEglDisplay, version);
```

```java
        EGLConfig[] configs = new EGLConfig[1];
        int[] num_config = new int[1];
        mEgl.eglChooseConfig(mEglDisplay, configSpec, configs, 1,
                num_config);
        mEglConfig = configs[0];

        mEglContext = mEgl.eglCreateContext(mEglDisplay, mEglConfig,
                EGL10.EGL_NO_CONTEXT, null);

        mEglSurface = null;
    }
    public GL createSurface(SurfaceHolder holder) {
        if (mEglSurface != null) {
            mEgl.eglMakeCurrent(mEglDisplay, EGL10.EGL_NO_SURFACE,
                    EGL10.EGL_NO_SURFACE, EGL10.EGL_NO_CONTEXT);
            mEgl.eglDestroySurface(mEglDisplay, mEglSurface);
        }
        mEglSurface = mEgl.eglCreateWindowSurface(mEglDisplay,
                mEglConfig, holder, null);
        mEgl.eglMakeCurrent(mEglDisplay, mEglSurface, mEglSurface,
                mEglContext);
        GL gl = mEglContext.getGL();
        return gl;
    }
    public boolean swap() {
        mEgl.eglSwapBuffers(mEglDisplay, mEglSurface);
        return mEgl.eglGetError() != EGL11.EGL_CONTEXT_LOST;
    }
    public void finish() {
        if (mEglSurface != null) {
            mEgl.eglMakeCurrent(mEglDisplay, EGL10.EGL_NO_SURFACE,
                    EGL10.EGL_NO_SURFACE,
                    EGL10.EGL_NO_CONTEXT);
            mEgl.eglDestroySurface(mEglDisplay, mEglSurface);
            mEglSurface = null;
        }
        if (mEglContext != null) {
            mEgl.eglDestroyContext(mEglDisplay, mEglContext);
            mEglContext = null;
        }
        if (mEglDisplay != null) {
            mEgl.eglTerminate(mEglDisplay);
            mEglDisplay = null;
        }
    }
}
```

Now let's take a look at the Renderer interface that needs to be implemented by your own OpenGL drawing subclasses.

Renderer.java

The Renderer interface tells the test harness what it intends to draw (see Listing 10-10). Any class that implements this protocol will be able to draw using OpenGL.

Listing 10-10. *The Methods of the Renderer Protocol*

```
//filename: Renderer.java
public interface Renderer
{
    int[]    getConfigSpec();
    void     surfaceCreated(GL10 gl);
    void     sizeChanged(GL10 gl, int width, int height);
    void     drawFrame(GL10 gl);
}
```

The getConfigSpec() method is responsible for returning the OpenGL configuration necessary to construct an EGL context. In the surfaceCreated() method, the implementer is responsible for unbinding and binding the EGL context to the surface or window. You will need to set the viewport and zoom in the sizeChanged method. drawFrame() is responsible for the actual OpenGL drawing of the model objects.

AbstractRenderer.java

The way you bind and unbind the EGL context to the surface and the way you set the viewport, camera, and so on could be common to a number of scenarios. With this in mind, we have abstracted this functionality out further by creating an abstract class to deal with these variations (see Listing 10-11).

Listing 10-11. *The AbstractRenderer Class*

```
//filename: AbstractRenderer.java
public abstract class AbstractRenderer implements Renderer
{
    public int[] getConfigSpec() {
        int[] configSpec = {
                EGL10.EGL_DEPTH_SIZE, 0,
                EGL10.EGL_NONE
        };
        return configSpec;
    }
```

```
public void surfaceCreated(GL10 gl) {
    gl.glDisable(GL10.GL_DITHER);
    gl.glHint(GL10.GL_PERSPECTIVE_CORRECTION_HINT,
            GL10.GL_FASTEST);
    gl.glClearColor(.5f, .5f, .5f, 1);
    gl.glShadeModel(GL10.GL_SMOOTH);
    gl.glEnable(GL10.GL_DEPTH_TEST);
}

public void sizeChanged(GL10 gl, int w, int h) {
    gl.glViewport(0, 0, w, h);
    float ratio = (float) w / h;
    gl.glMatrixMode(GL10.GL_PROJECTION);
    gl.glLoadIdentity();
    gl.glFrustumf(-ratio, ratio, -1, 1, 3, 7);
}

public void drawFrame(GL10 gl)
{
    gl.glDisable(GL10.GL_DITHER);
    gl.glClear(GL10.GL_COLOR_BUFFER_BIT | GL10.GL_DEPTH_BUFFER_BIT);
    gl.glMatrixMode(GL10.GL_MODELVIEW);
    gl.glLoadIdentity();
    GLU.gluLookAt(gl, 0, 0, -5, 0f, 0f, 0f, 0f, 1.0f, 0.0f);
    gl.glEnableClientState(GL10.GL_VERTEX_ARRAY);
    draw(gl);
}
protected abstract void draw(GL10 gl);
}
```

Based on our explanation of the camera symbolism, you should be able to understand this code, especially how the gluLookAt, glFrustum, and glViewport methods are used.

The aforementioned six classes complete the test harness. The next two classes exercise the test harness by drawing a simple triangle and a few variations of it. You will need at least one of these classes to be able to see something on the emulator.

SimpleTriangleRenderer.java

Now that you have the test harness built, you can use the following coordinates to draw an OpenGL triangle:

```
float[] coords = {
    -0.5f, -0.5f, 0,    //p1: (x1,y1,z1)
     0.5f, -0.5f, 0,    //p2: (x1,y1,z1)
     0.0f,  0.5f, 0     //p3: (x1,y1,z1)
};
```

Our goal in this example is to take these coordinates and tell OpenGL ES to draw them as a triangle. Based on our discussion in the "Essential Drawing with OpenGL ES" subsection under "Using OpenGL ES," you should be able to figure out how the code in Listing 10-12 accomplishes that.

Listing 10-12. *Drawing a Simple Triangle*

```java
//filename: SimpleTriangleRenderer.java
public class SimpleTriangleRenderer extends AbstractRenderer
{
    //Number of points or vertices we want to use
    private final static int VERTS = 3;

    //A raw native buffer to hold the point coordinates
    private FloatBuffer mFVertexBuffer;

    //A raw native buffer to hold indices
    //allowing a reuse of points.
    private ShortBuffer mIndexBuffer;

    public SimpleTriangleRenderer(Context context)
    {
        ByteBuffer vbb = ByteBuffer.allocateDirect(VERTS * 3 * 4);
        vbb.order(ByteOrder.nativeOrder());
        mFVertexBuffer = vbb.asFloatBuffer();

        ByteBuffer ibb = ByteBuffer.allocateDirect(VERTS * 2);
        ibb.order(ByteOrder.nativeOrder());
        mIndexBuffer = ibb.asShortBuffer();

        float[] coords = {
                -0.5f, -0.5f, 0, // (x1,y1,z1)
                 0.5f, -0.5f, 0,
                 0.0f,  0.5f, 0
        };
        for (int i = 0; i < VERTS; i++) {
            for(int j = 0; j < 3; j++) {
                mFVertexBuffer.put(coords[i*3+j]);
            }
        }
```

```
        short[] myIndecesArray = {0,1,2};
        for (int i=0;i<3;i++)
        {
            mIndexBuffer.put(myIndecesArray[i]);
        }
        mFVertexBuffer.position(0);
        mIndexBuffer.position(0);
    }

    //overridden method
    protected void draw(GL10 gl)
    {
        gl.glColor4f(1.0f, 0, 0, 0.5f);
        gl.glVertexPointer(3, GL10.GL_FLOAT, 0, mFVertexBuffer);
        gl.glDrawElements(GL10.GL_TRIANGLES, VERTS,
                GL10.GL_UNSIGNED_SHORT, mIndexBuffer);
    }
}
```

Notice how focused and sparse this code is. This level of simplicity and directness should encourage experimentation with OpenGL. The code in Listing 10-12 sets up the draw method based on the aforementioned principles for drawing a triangle. In preparation for the draw method, the code identifies the points and transports the point coordinates to a buffer. You do the same with indices for those points. Then you draw the triangle using glDrawElements.

Once you compile all this code, you can invoke the OpenGLTestHarnessActivity by using the following code segment in response to one of your menu items:

```
Intent intent = new Intent(activity,OpenGLTestHarnessActivity.class);
activity.startActivity(intent);
```

In this small code snippet, the variable activity points to the activity from which your menu item is invoked. If you are doing it in the same derived class of Activity, you can simply use the this variable.

You will also need to register this activity in the AndroidManifest.xml file for your application. Here is an example:

```
<activity android:name=".OpenGLTestHarnessActivity"
                android:label="OpenGL Test Harness"/>
```

With all of this code in place, you should see the Figure 10-3 screen in your emulator when you run the program and invoke the activity.

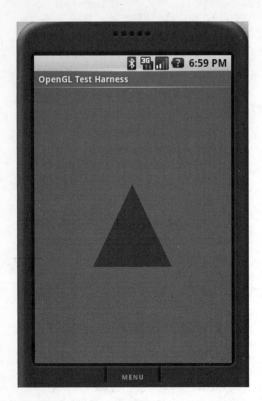

Figure 10-3. *A simple OpenGL triangle*

Changing Camera Settings

To understand the coordinates better, let us experiment with the camera-related methods and see how they affect the triangle that you drew. Remember that these are the points of our triangle: (-0.5,-0.5,0 0.5,-0.5,0   0,0.5,0). The following three camera-related methods yield the triangle as it appears in Figure 10-3:

```
//Look at the screen (origin) from 5 units away from the front of the screen
GLU.gluLookAt(gl, 0,0,5,    0,0,0,    0,1,0);

//Set the height to 2 units and depth to 4 units
gl.glFrustumf(-ratio, ratio, -1, 1, 3, 7);

//normal window stuff
gl.glViewport(0, 0, w, h);
```

Now suppose you change the camera's up vector toward the negative y direction, like this:

```
GLU.gluLookAt(gl, 0,0,5,    0,0,0,    0,-1,0);
```

If you do that, you'll see an upside-down triangle (see Figure 10-4). If you want to make this change or something like it, you can find the method in the `AbstractRenderer.java` file.

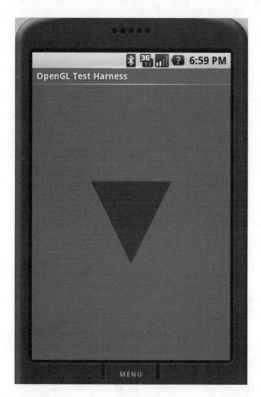

Figure 10-4. *A triangle with the camera upside down*

If you use this code to increase the viewing box's height and width by a factor of four as shown here,

```
gl.glFrustumf(-ratio * 4, ratio * 4, -1 * 4, 1 *4, 3, 7);
```

you will see the triangle shrink because the triangle stays at the same units while our viewing box has grown. This method call appears in the `AbstractRenderer.java` class (see Listing 10-11). What you see after this change is shown in Figure 10-5.

If you change the camera position so that it looks at the screen from behind, you will see your coordinates reversed in the x-y plane. You can set this up through the following code:

```
GLU.gluLookAt(gl, 0,0,-5,    0,0,0,    0,1,0);
```

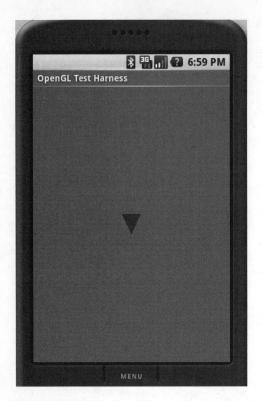

Figure 10-5. *A triangle with a viewing box that's four times bigger*

Using Indices to Add Another Triangle

Let us conclude the examples by inheriting from the AbstractRenderer class and creating another triangle simply by adding another point and using indices. Conceptually, you'll define the four points as (-1,-1,   1,-1,   0,1,   1,1). And you will ask OpenGL to draw these as (0,1,2   0,2,3). Listing 10-13 shows the code to do this. (Notice that we changed the dimensions of the triangle.)

Listing 10-13. *The SimpleTriangleRenderer2 Class*

```java
//filename: SimpleTriangleRenderer2.java
public class SimpleTriangleRenderer2 extends AbstractRenderer
{
    private final static int VERTS = 4;
    private FloatBuffer mFVertexBuffer;
    private ShortBuffer mIndexBuffer;
```

```
    public SimpleTriangleRenderer2(Context context)
    {
        ByteBuffer vbb = ByteBuffer.allocateDirect(VERTS * 3 * 4);
        vbb.order(ByteOrder.nativeOrder());
        mFVertexBuffer = vbb.asFloatBuffer();

        ByteBuffer ibb = ByteBuffer.allocateDirect(6 * 2);
        ibb.order(ByteOrder.nativeOrder());
        mIndexBuffer = ibb.asShortBuffer();

        float[] coords = {
                -1.0f, -1.0f, 0, // (x1,y1,z1)
                 1.0f, -1.0f, 0,
                 0.0f,  1.0f, 0,
                 1.0f,  1.0f, 0
        };
        for (int i = 0; i < VERTS; i++) {
            for(int j = 0; j < 3; j++) {
                mFVertexBuffer.put(coords[i*3+j]);
            }
        }
        short[] myIndecesArray = {0,1,2,    0,2,3};
        for (int i=0;i<6;i++)
        {
            mIndexBuffer.put(myIndecesArray[i]);
        }
        mFVertexBuffer.position(0);
        mIndexBuffer.position(0);
    }

    protected void draw(GL10 gl)
    {
        gl.glColor4f(1.0f, 0, 0, 0.5f);
        gl.glVertexPointer(3, GL10.GL_FLOAT, 0, mFVertexBuffer);
        gl.glDrawElements(GL10.GL_TRIANGLES, 6, GL10.GL_UNSIGNED_SHORT,
                                                    mIndexBuffer);
    }
}
```

Once the SimpleTriangleRenderer2 class is in place, you can change the code in the OpenGLTestHarnessActivity to invoke this renderer instead of the SimpleTriangleRenderer:

```
mTestHarness = new OpenGLTestHarness(this);
mTestHarness.setRenderer(new SimpleTriangleRenderer2(this));
```

The changed portion is highlighted. After you change this code, you can run the OpenGLTestHarnessActivity again to see the two triangles drawn out (see Figure 10-6).

Figure 10-6. *Two triangles with four points*

Altering this code to allow for animation is quite simple. Update the guardedRun() method in the OpenGLDrawingThread.java class so the while loop won't wait to redraw as long as the width and height are valid. This will allow continuous redraw()s even when there is no resize(). Once a draw method is called multiple times, you can use the matrix methods to rotate, scale, and move. At that point, the ideas are similar to the ones we presented in Chapter 6.

Summary

In this chapter, we covered the basics of OpenGL support in Android. We provided resources to help you learn more about OpenGL, and we explored how Android uses OpenGL ES from its SDK. You should now have enough background to work with the OpenGL samples that ship with the Android SDK. We also gave you a convenient, simplified test harness that you can use to explore OpenGL further. After experimenting with the samples and the test harness, you should be ready for advanced development with Android and OpenGL.

If you are coding in the 1.5 SDK, do read Chapters 12 and 13. Chapter 12 introduces you to the 1.5 SDK and Chapter 13 covers the simplified approach to OpenGL. However, the first two sections of this chapter are still applicable and mandatory reading even under SDK 1.5.

CHAPTER 11

Managing and Organizing Preferences

Like many other SDKs, Android supports preferences. Generally speaking, it tracks preferences for users of an application as well as the application itself. For example, a user of Microsoft Outlook might set a preference to view e-mail messages a certain way, and Microsoft Outlook itself has some default preferences that are configurable by users. But even though Android theoretically tracks preferences for both users and the application, it does not differentiate between the two. The reason for this is that Android applications run on a device that is generally not shared among several users—people don't share cell phones. So Android refers to preferences with the term *application preferences*, which encompasses both the user's preferences and the application's default preferences.

When you see Android's preferences support for the first time, you'll likely be impressed. Android offers a robust and flexible framework for dealing with preferences. It provides simple APIs that hide the reading and persisting of preferences, as well as prebuilt user interfaces that you can use to let the user make preference selections. We will explore all of these features in the sections that follow.

Exploring the Preferences Framework

Before we dig into Android's preferences framework, let's establish a scenario that would require the use of preferences and then explore how we would go about addressing it. Suppose you are writing an application that provides a facility to search for flights. Moreover, suppose that the application's default setting is to display flights based on the lowest cost, but that the user can set a preference to always sort flights by the least number of stops or by a specific airline. How would you go about doing that?

Obviously, you would have to provide a UI for the user to view the list of sort options. The list would contain radio buttons for each option, and the default (or current) selection would be preselected. To solve this problem with the Android preferences framework requires very little work. First, you would create a preferences XML file to describe the preference and then use a prebuilt activity class that knows how to show and persist preferences. Listing 11-1 shows the details.

Listing 11-1. *The Flight-Options Preferences XML File and Associated Activity Class*

```xml
<?xml version="1.0" encoding="utf-8"?>
    <PreferenceScreen
        xmlns:android="http://schemas.android.com/apk/res/android"
                android:key="flight_option_preference"
                android:title="My Preferences"
                android:summary="Set Flight Option Preferences">
            <ListPreference
                android:key="selected_flight_sort_option"
                android:title="Flight Options"
                android:summary="Set Search Options"
                android:entries="@array/flight_sort_options"
                android:entryValues="@array/flight_sort_options_values"
                android:dialogTitle="Choose Flight Options"
                android:defaultValue="@string/flight_sort_option_default_value"/>

        </PreferenceScreen>
```

```java
import android.os.Bundle;
import android.preference.PreferenceActivity;
public class FlightSortPreferencesActivity extends PreferenceActivity
{

    @Override
    protected void onCreate(Bundle savedInstanceState) {
        super.onCreate(savedInstanceState);
        addPreferencesFromResource(R.xml.flightoptions);
    }

}
```

Listing 11-1 contains an XML fragment that represents the flight-option preference setting. The listing also contains an activity class that loads the preferences XML file. Let's start with the XML. Android provides an end-to-end preferences framework. This means that the framework lets you define your preferences, display the setting(s) to the user, and persist the user's selection to the data store. You define your preferences in XML under /res/xml/. To show preferences to the user, you write an activity class that extends a predefined Android class called android.preference.PreferenceActivity, and then use the addPreferencesFromResource() method to add the resource to the activity's resource collection. The framework takes care of the rest (displaying and persisting). Note that the Android 1.5 SDK also provides a user interface that can generate preferences XML files. See Chapter 12 for details.

In this flight scenario, you create a file called `flightoptions.xml` at `/res/xml/`
`flightoptions.xml`. You then create an activity class called `FlightSortPreferencesActivity`
that extends the `android.preference.PreferenceActivity` class. Next, you call
`addPreferencesFromResource()`, passing in `R.xml.flightoptions`. Note that the preference
resource XML points to several string resources. To ensure compilation, you need to add
several string resources to your project. We will show you how to do that shortly. For now,
have a look at the UI generated by Listing 11-1 (see Figure 11-1).

Figure 11-1. *The flight-options preference UI*

Figure 11-1 contains two views. The view on the left is called a *preference screen* and the
UI on the right is a *list preference*. When the user selects "Flight Options," the "Choose Flight
Options" view appears as a modal dialog with radio buttons for each option. The user selects
an option and clicks the OK button. The framework then saves the user's selection. When the
user returns to the options screen, the view reflects the saved selection.

As we discussed, the preferences XML file and associated activity class are shown in
Listing 11-1. The code in that listing defines a `PreferenceScreen` and then creates a
`ListPreference` as a child. For the `PreferenceScreen`, you set three properties: `key`, `title`,
and `summary`. `key` is a string you can use to refer to the item programmatically (similar to how
you use `android:id`); `title` is the screen's title ("Flight Options"); and `summary` is a description
of the screen's purpose, shown below the title in a smaller font ("Set Search Options," in
this case). For the list preference, you set the `key`, `title`, and `summary`, as well as entries for
`entryValues`, `dialogTitle`, and `defaultValue`. Table 11-1 summarizes these attributes.

Table 11-1. *A Few Attributes of android.preference.ListPreference*

Attribute	Description
android:key	A name or key for the item (such as `selected_flight_sort_option`).
android:title	The title of the item.
android:summary	A short summary of the item.

android:entries	The items in the list. In our list preference, you set the entries to a string array defined in the `arrays.xml` resource file (at `/res/values/arrays.xml`):
	`<string-array name="flight_sort_options">`
	    `<item>Total Cost</item>`
	    `<item># of Stops</item>`
	    `<item>Airline</item>`
	`</string-array>`
	You must place this entry in `/res/values/arrays.xml`.

android:entryValues	Defines the key, or value, for each item. In our list preference, you set the entryValues to a string array defined in the `arrays.xml` file.
	    `<string-array name="flight_sort_options_values">`
	        `<item>0</item>`
	        `<item>1</item>`
	        `<item>2</item>`
	    `</string-array>`
	Note that each item has some text and a value. The text is defined by entries and the values are defined by entryValues.
	You must place this entry in `/res/values/arrays.xml`.

android:dialogTitle	The title of the dialog—used if the view is shown as a modal dialog.
android:defaultValue	The default value of the list. In our case, you set it to 0 to indicate Total Cost. `<string name="flight_sort_option_default_value">0</string>` You must place this entry in `/res/values/string.xml`.

As we said earlier, the Android framework also takes care of persisting preferences. For example, when the user selects a sort option and clicks OK, Android stores the selection in an XML file within the application's /data directory (see Figure 11-2).

Figure 11-2. *Path to an application's saved preferences*

The actual file path is /data/data/[PACKAGE_NAME]/shared_prefs/[PACKAGE_NAME]_ preferences.xml. Listing 11-2 shows the com.syh_preferences.xml file for our example.

Listing 11-2. *Saved Preferences for Our Example*

```
<?xml version='1.0' encoding='utf-8' standalone='yes' ?>
<map>
    <string name="selected_flight_sort_option">1</string>
</map>
```

You can see that for a list preference, the preferences framework persists the selected item's value using the list's key attribute. Note also that the selected item's *value* is stored—not the text. To read the saved preference, you would use this code:

```
SharedPreferences sp = getPreferenceManager().getDefaultSharedPreferences(this);
String option = sp.getString("selected_flight_sort_option", null);
```

From an activity that extends PreferenceActivity, you obtain a reference to the preference manager. From there, get a hold of the default shared-preference instance and then use the various methods to obtain saved preferences. As shown in the preceding code snippet, you read the saved flight option by calling the getString() method with a key to the list preference defined in Listing 11-1. Note that the second parameter to the getString() method is the default value for the key preference. In this case, you pass null because you want null returned if the preference does not exist in the preference store.

It goes without saying that you might need to access the actual preference controls programmatically. For example, what if you need to provide the entries and entryValues for the ListPreference at runtime? You can define and access preference controls similar to the way you define and access controls in layout files and activities. For example, to access the list preference defined in Listing 11-1, you would call the findPreference() method of PreferenceActivity, passing the preference's key (note the similarity to findViewById()). You would then cast the control to ListPreference and then go about manipulating the control. For example, if you want to set the entries of the ListPreference, call the setEntries() method, and so on.

So now you know how preferences work in Android. You know that Android provides prebuilt UIs to show preferences and also takes care of persisting them. In addition, Android provides the android.preference.PreferenceActivity class that you extend when implementing preferences within your application. This class provides APIs for you to load preferences and allows you to tie into and extend the preferences framework.

We showed you how to use the ListPreference view; now let's examine the other UI elements within the Android preferences framework. Namely, let's talk about the CheckBoxPreference view and the EditTextPreference view.

Understanding CheckBoxPreference

You saw that the ListPreference preference displays a list as its UI element. Similarly, the CheckBoxPreference preference displays a check-box widget as its UI element.

To extend the flight-search example application, suppose you want to let the user set the list of columns he wants to see with the result set. This preference displays the available columns and allows the user to choose the desired columns by marking the corresponding check boxes. The user interface for this example is shown in Figure 11-3 and the preferences XML file is shown in Listing 11-3.

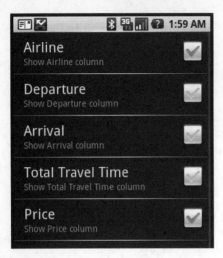

Figure 11-3. *The user interface for the check-box preference*

Listing 11-3. *Using a CheckBoxPreference*

```
// chkbox.xml (store at res/xml/chkbox.xml)
<?xml version="1.0" encoding="utf-8"?>
    <PreferenceScreen
        xmlns:android="http://schemas.android.com/apk/res/android"
                android:key="flight_columns_pref"
                android:title="Flight Search Preferences"
                android:summary="Set Columns for Search Results">
        <CheckBoxPreference
                android:key="show_airline_column_pref"
                android:title="Airline"
                android:summary="Show Airline column" />
        <CheckBoxPreference
                android:key="show_departure_column_pref"
                android:title="Departure"
                android:summary="Show Departure column" />
        <CheckBoxPreference
                android:key="show_arrival_column_pref"
                android:title="Arrival"
                android:summary="Show Arrival column" />
        <CheckBoxPreference
                android:key="show_total_travel_time_column_pref"
                android:title="Total Travel Time"
                android:summary="Show Total Travel Time column" />
```

```
        <CheckBoxPreference
                android:key="show_price_column_pref"
                android:title="Price"
                android:summary="Show Price column" />

</PreferenceScreen>

// CheckBoxPreferenceActivity.java

import android.os.Bundle;
import android.preference.PreferenceActivity;

public class CheckBoxPreferenceActivity extends PreferenceActivity
{
    @Override
    protected void onCreate(Bundle savedInstanceState) {
        super.onCreate(savedInstanceState);
        addPreferencesFromResource(R.xml.chkbox);
    }
}
```

Listing 11-3 shows the preferences XML file, chkbox.xml, and a simple activity class that loads it using addPreferencesFromResource(). As you can see, the UI has five check boxes, each of which is represented by a CheckBoxPreference node in the preferences XML file. Each of the check boxes also has a key, which—as you would expect—is ultimately used to persist the state of the UI element when it comes time to save the selected preference. Note that the UI does not define an OK/Cancel button as you saw in the ListPreference example. With the CheckBoxPreference, the state of the preference is saved when the user sets the state. In other words, when the user checks or unchecks the preference control, its state is saved. Listing 11-4 shows the preference data store for this example.

Listing 11-4. *The Preferences Data Store for the Check-Box Preference*

```
<?xml version='1.0' encoding='utf-8' standalone='yes' ?>
<map>
    <boolean name="show_total_travel_time_column_pref" value="false" />
    <boolean name="show_price_column_pref" value="true" />
    <boolean name="show_arrival_column_pref" value="false" />
    <boolean name="show_airline_column_pref" value="true" />
    <boolean name="show_departure_column_pref" value="false" />
</map>
```

Again, you can see that each preference is saved through its key attribute. The data type of the CheckBoxPreference is a boolean, which contains a value of either true or false: true to indicate the preference is selected, and false to indicate otherwise. To read the value of one of the check-box preferences, you would get access to the shared preference and then call the getBoolean() method, passing the key of the preference.

Now let's have a look at the EditTextPreference.

Understanding EditTextPreference

The preferences framework also provides a free-form text preference called EditTextPreference. This preference allows you to capture raw text rather than ask the user to make a selection. To demonstrate this, let's assume you have an application that generates Java code for the user. One of the preference settings of this application might be the default package name to use for the generated classes. So here, you want to display a text field to the user and allow her to set the package name for the generated classes. Figure 11-4 shows the UI and Listing 11-5 shows the XML.

Figure 11-4. *Using the EditTextPreference*

Listing 11-5. *An Example of an EditTextPreference*

```
// packagepref.xml
<?xml version="1.0" encoding="utf-8"?>
<PreferenceScreen
        xmlns:android="http://schemas.android.com/apk/res/android"
                android:key="package_name_screen"
                android:title="Package Name"
                android:summary="Set package name">

        <EditTextPreference
                android:key="package_name_preference"
                android:title="Set Package Name"
                android:summary="Set the package name for generated code"
                android:dialogTitle="Package Name" />

</PreferenceScreen>

// EditTextPreferenceActivity.java

import android.os.Bundle;
import android.preference.PreferenceActivity;
```

```
public class EditTextPreferenceActivity extends PreferenceActivity{

    @Override
    protected void onCreate(Bundle savedInstanceState) {
        super.onCreate(savedInstanceState);

        addPreferencesFromResource(R.xml.packagepref);
    }

}
```

You can see that Listing 11-5 defines a PreferenceScreen with a single EditTextPreference as a child. The generated UI for the listing features the PreferenceScreen on the left and the EditTextPreference on the right (see Figure 11-4). When the user selects "Set Package Name," she is presented with a dialog to input the package name. When she clicks the OK button, the preference is saved to the preference store.

As with the other preferences, you can obtain the EditTextPreference from your activity class by using the preference's key. Once you have the EditTextPreference, you can manipulate the actual EditText by calling getEditText()—if, for example, you want to apply validation, preprocessing, or postprocessing on the value that the user types in the text field.

Now let's look at the preferences framework's RingtonePreference.

Understanding RingtonePreference

RingtonePreference deals specifically with ringtones. You'd use it in an application that gives the user an option to select a ringtone as a preference. Figure 11-5 shows the UI of the RingtonePreference example and Listing 11-6 shows the XML.

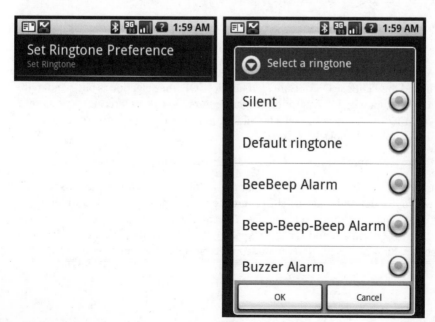

Figure 11-5. *The RingtonePreference example UI*

Listing 11-6. *Defining a RingtonePreference Preference*

```xml
// ringtone.xml (store at res/xml/ringtone.xml)
<?xml version="1.0" encoding="utf-8"?>
<PreferenceScreen
        xmlns:android="http://schemas.android.com/apk/res/android"
                android:key="flight_option_preference"
                android:title="My Preferences"
                android:summary="Set Flight Option Preferences">
    <RingtonePreference
        android:key="ring_tone_pref"
        android:title="Set Ringtone Preference"
        android:showSilent="true"
        android:ringtoneType="alarm"
        android:summary="Set Ringtone" />
</PreferenceScreen>
```

```java
// RingtonePreferenceActivity.java

import android.os.Bundle;
import android.preference.PreferenceActivity;

public class RingtonePreferenceActivity extends PreferenceActivity
{
    @Override
    protected void onCreate(Bundle savedInstanceState) {
        super.onCreate(savedInstanceState);
        addPreferencesFromResource(R.xml.ringtone);
    }
}
```

When the user selects "Set Ringtone Preference," the preferences framework displays a ListPreference containing the ringtones on the device (see Figure 11-5). The user can then select a ringtone and then choose OK or Cancel. If he clicks OK, the selection is persisted to the preference store. Note that with the ringtones, the value stored in the preference store is the URI of the selected ringtone—unless he selects "Silent," in which case the stored value is an empty string. An example URI looks like this:

```xml
<string name="ring_tone_pref">content://media/internal/audio/media/26</string>
```

Finally, the RingtonePreference shown in Listing 11-6 follows the same pattern as the other preferences you've defined thus far. The difference here is that you set a few different attributes, including showSilent and ringtoneType. You can use showSilent to include the silent ringtone in the ringtone list, and ringtoneType to restrict the types of ringtones displayed in the list. Possible values for this property include ringtone, notification, alarm, and all.

Organizing Preferences

The preferences framework provides some support for you to organize your preferences into categories. If you have a lot of preferences, for example, you can build a view that shows high-level categories of preferences. Users could then drill down into each category to view and manage preferences specific to that group.

You can implement something like this in one of two ways. You can introduce nested `PreferenceScreen` elements within the root `PreferenceScreen`, or you can use `PreferenceCategory` elements to get a similar result. Figure 11-6 and Listing 11-7 show how to implement the first technique: grouping preferences by using nested `PreferenceScreen` elements.

Figure 11-6. *Creating groups of preferences by nesting PreferenceScreen elements*

The view on the left of Figure 11-6 displays two preference screens, one with the title "Meats" and the other with the title "Vegetables." Clicking a group takes you to the preferences within that group. Listing 11-7 shows how to create nested screens.

Listing 11-7. *Nesting PreferenceScreen Elements to Organize Preferences*

```xml
<?xml version="1.0" encoding="utf-8"?>
<PreferenceScreen
        xmlns:android="http://schemas.android.com/apk/res/android"
                android:key="using_categories_in_root_screen"
                android:title="Categories"
                android:summary="Using Preference Categories">

    <PreferenceScreen
        xmlns:android="http://schemas.android.com/apk/res/android"
                android:key="meats_screen"
                android:title="Meats"
                android:summary="Preferences related to Meats">
```

```
    <CheckBoxPreference
            android:key="fish_selection_pref"
            android:title="Fish"
            android:summary="Fish is great for the healthy" />
    <CheckBoxPreference
            android:key="chicken_selection_pref"
            android:title="Chicken"
            android:summary="A common type of poultry" />
    <CheckBoxPreference
            android:key="lamb_selection_pref"
            android:title="Lamb"
            android:summary="Lamb is a young sheep" />

</PreferenceScreen>
<PreferenceScreen
    xmlns:android="http://schemas.android.com/apk/res/android"
            android:key="vegi_screen"
            android:title="Vegetables"
            android:summary="Preferences related to vegetable">
    <CheckBoxPreference
            android:key="tomato_selection_pref"
            android:title="Tomato "
            android:summary="It's actually a fruit" />
    <CheckBoxPreference
            android:key="potato_selection_pref"
            android:title="Potato"
            android:summary="My favorite vegetable" />

</PreferenceScreen>

</PreferenceScreen>
```

You create the groups in Figure 11-6 by nesting PreferenceScreen elements within the root PreferenceScreen. Organizing preferences this way is useful if you have a lot of preferences and you're concerned about having the user scroll to find the preference he is looking for. If you don't have a lot of preferences but still want to provide high-level categories for your preferences, you can use PreferenceCategory, which is the second technique we mentioned. Figure 11-7 and Listing 11-8 show the details.

Figure 11-7. *Using PreferenceCategory to organize preferences*

Figure 11-7 shows the same groups we used in our previous example, but now organized with preference categories. The only difference between the XML in Listing 11-8 and the XML in Listing 11-7 is that you create a PreferenceCategory for the nested screens rather than nest PreferenceScreen elements.

Listing 11-8. *Creating Categories of Preferences*

```xml
<?xml version="1.0" encoding="utf-8"?>
<PreferenceScreen
        xmlns:android="http://schemas.android.com/apk/res/android"
                android:key="using_categories_in_root_screen"
                android:title="Categories"
                android:summary="Using Preference Categories">

    <PreferenceCategory
        xmlns:android="http://schemas.android.com/apk/res/android"
                android:key="meats_category"
                android:title="Meats"
                android:summary="Preferences related to Meats">

        <CheckBoxPreference
                android:key="fish_selection_pref"
                android:title="Fish"
                android:summary="Fish is great for the healthy" />
```

```xml
        <CheckBoxPreference
                android:key="chicken_selection_pref"
                android:title="Chicken"
                android:summary="A common type of poultry" />
        <CheckBoxPreference
                android:key="lamb_selection_pref"
                android:title="Lamb"
                android:summary="Lamb is a young sheep" />

    </PreferenceCategory>
    <PreferenceCategory
        xmlns:android="http://schemas.android.com/apk/res/android"
                android:key="vegi_category"
                android:title="Vegetables"
                android:summary="Preferences related to vegetable">
        <CheckBoxPreference
                android:key="tomato_selection_pref"
                android:title="Tomato "
                android:summary="It's actually a fruit" />
        <CheckBoxPreference
                android:key="potato_selection_pref"
                android:title="Potato"
                android:summary="My favorite vegetable" />

    </PreferenceCategory>

</PreferenceScreen>
```

Summary

In this chapter, we talked about managing preferences in Android. We showed you how to use ListPreference, CheckBoxPreference, EditTextPreference, and RingtonePreference. We also talked about programmatically manipulating preferences and then showed you how to organize preferences into groups.

■ ■ ■

CHAPTER 12

Coming to Grips with 1.5

With the release of Android 1.5, developers now have more functionality at their finger-tips. In the next two chapters, we will introduce you to some of the new features in Android 1.5 and provide you with instructions to set up your development environment for the new release. Specifically, we will show you some additions to the media APIs and introduce you to Android's speech-recognition framework. We will also briefly demonstrate Android's input-method framework.

We will start by showing you how to download and install the Android 1.5 SDK and the new ADT plug-in. Note that the instructions you'll find here will not be as detailed as the ones in Chapter 2, so you might want to quickly review the ADT installation instructions there before continuing.

To start building Android applications for the 1.5 runtime, you'll need to download the 1.5 SDK. Point your browser to the Android 1.5 download site (`http://developer.android.com/sdk/1.5_r1/index.html`) and download the SDK zip file for Windows to `c:\Android1.5ZIP\`. After the download completes, unzip the file to `c:\Android1.5_SDK\`.

Now that you have the SDK, let's move on: you'll download the new ADT plug-in and con-figure Eclipse for 1.5 development.

Installing the ADT Plug-in for Android 1.5 Development

The examples throughout the book have used Eclipse 3.4 (Ganymede), and you'll want to ensure that you use this version when developing for Android 1.5. If you have installed an older version of the ADT plug-in (0.8 or lower), you'll need to uninstall that prior to installing the new ADT plug-in. To do that, launch the Eclipse IDE, select the Help menu item, and then choose the Software Updates… option. In the "Software Updates and Add-ons" window, select the "Installed Software" tab. To remove the previous version of ADT, you'll need to uninstall Android Development Tools and Android Editors. Uninstalling is easy: select an item from the list and click the Uninstall button. The IDE will run a process in the background and then ask you to confirm that you want to uninstall the selected item (see Figure 12-1).

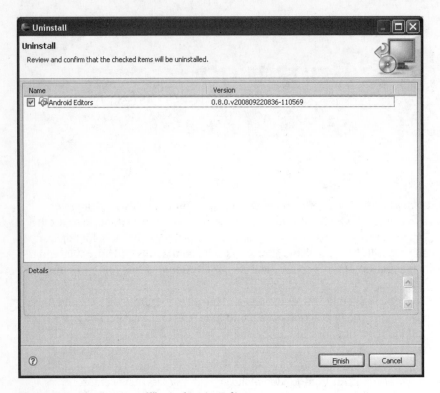

Figure 12-1. *The "Uninstall" window in Eclipse*

Click the Finish button to have the IDE remove the selected feature. After uninstalling an item, Eclipse will display a window recommending that you restart the IDE (see Figure 12-2). But in this case, don't restart Eclipse until you have uninstalled both the Android Development Tools and the Android Editors.

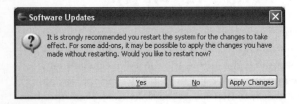

Figure 12-2. *After you uninstall a feature, you are prompted to restart the system.*

Now you are ready to install the new ADT features. You can install ADT by pointing Eclipse to the download site, as you did in Chapter 2, or you can download the ADT archive to your local workstation and then point Eclipse to the archive. Let's do the latter. Download version 0.9.1 of the ADT plug-in from `http://developer.android.com/sdk/adt_download.html`. Store the .zip file at `c:\ADTPluginFor1.5`.

To install it, launch Eclipse, go to Help ➤ Software Updates..., and then select the "Available Software" tab. In the "Available Software" tab, click the Add Site button and then the Archive button. Eclipse will display the "Repository archive" window, from which you'll need to select the ADT archive (which you downloaded to `c:\ADTPluginFor1.5`). After you select the .zip file, you'll be taken back to the "Add Site" window. Click OK. Eclipse will now load a new entry in the "Available Software" tab showing the new ADT version in the list of available software. Select the new ADT .jar file from the list, and make sure the items below the .jar file are also selected (see Figure 12-3). Then click the Install button.

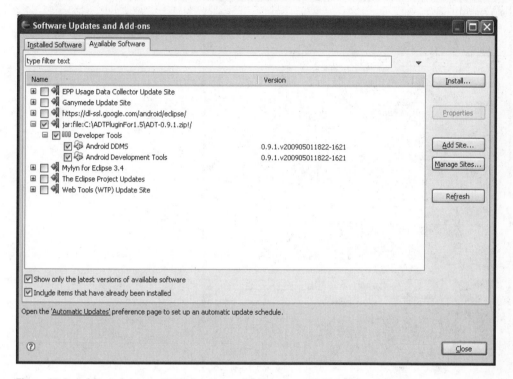

Figure 12-3. *Adding the new ADT plug-in to the list of available add-ons*

Eclipse will then begin downloading the features from the Web, and after a minute or so, you'll be presented with a window to confirm that you want to install the features. Click the Next button to confirm and then accept the terms and license agreements that follow. Click the Finish button to have Eclipse install the new features. The install will take a minute, and then you'll be asked to restart the system. Click the Yes button when prompted to restart.

Before you can begin building applications with the Android 1.5 SDK, you'll need to point Eclipse to the path of the new SDK. Select Window ➤ Preferences ➤ Android. In the Android preferences window, set the SDK location path to `c:\Android1.5_SDK` and then click OK.

Getting Started with Android 1.5

Now you are ready to begin building Android 1.5 applications. Let's quickly create a new Android application to test the new SDK. Select File ➤ New ➤ Project ➤ Android. In the "New Android Project" window (see Figure 12-4), set the project name to **HelloAndroid1.5**, the application name to **Hello Android**, and the package name to **com.syh**. Mark the "Create Activity" check box and set the activity name to **MainActivity**. You'll notice the new "Target" portion of the screen that lets you choose between Android SDK versions. Set the SDK Target to Android 1.5. You can also specify a "Min SDK Version," which is the minimum required Android runtime that your application needs. Leave this setting at its default value of 3. Now click Finish.

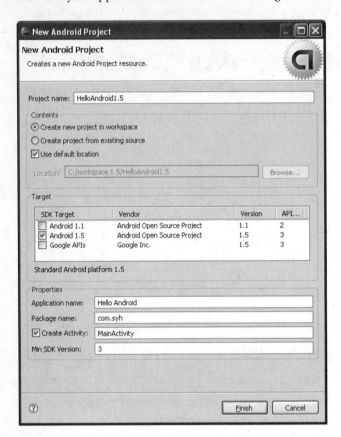

Figure 12-4. *The "New Android Project" window*

When you select Android 1.5 as the target SDK, the Min SDK Version is defaulted to 3, and when you select Android 1.1, the Min SDK Version is defaulted to 2. For now, you'll want to leave the Min SDK Version at 3 when writing Android 1.5 applications unless you have a good reason to specify that your application can run on a device that is running Android 1.1.

Also realize that selecting the Google APIs in the SDK Target list will include mapping functionality in your application, while selecting Android 1.5 will not. In the previous versions of the SDK, the mapping classes were included with android.jar, but they've since been moved to a separate .jar file called maps.jar. When you select Google APIs, your Min SDK Version is defaulted to 3 (for Android 1.5) and the ADT plug-in will include the maps.jar file in your project. In other words, if you are building an application that is using the mapping-related classes, you'll want to set your SDK Target to Google APIs. Note that you still need to add the maps uses-library (<uses-library android:name="com.google.android.maps" />) entry to your AndroidManifest.xml file.

One of the first things you'll notice when you create a new application is a few changes to the project structure, as shown in Figure 12-5.

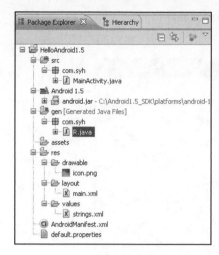

Figure 12-5. *Project structure of the HelloAndroid1.5 application*

As shown in Figure 12-5, the R.java file now resides under the gen folder, and you now have a default.properties file at the root of the project. You are very familiar with R.java, but you should know that the ADT plug-in auto-generates the default.properties file, which you need not modify. Also know that the gen folder is meant to contain code generated by the ADT plug-in. This means, for example, that the AIDL-based Java interfaces would also go into the gen folder.

One of the additions to the ADT plug-in is that you now have a wizard that helps you generate resource files quickly. Let's try this feature by creating a new layout file. In Eclipse, select File ➤ New ➤ Other. In the "New" dialog box, select Android ➤ Android XML File (see Figure 12-6).

Figure 12-6. *The "New" item window*

Alternatively, you can select the green icon with the "+" sign from the toolbar. Either way, you should see the "New Android XML File" window (see Figure 12-7).

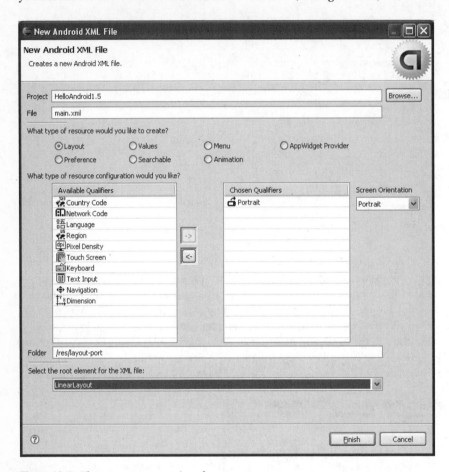

Figure 12-7. *The new resource wizard*

As you can see, the wizard helps you create resource files (such as layouts and strings), menus, preferences, animations, and so on. Moreover, you can customize the generated files by selecting qualifiers specific to the type of resource that you are creating. For example, to create a layout file with a LinearLayout as the root element, you would first set the type of resource to Layout by selecting the corresponding radio button. Then select Orientation from the list of Available Qualifiers and move that to the list of Chosen Qualifiers (by selecting the right-facing arrow). You would then select Portrait from the Screen Orientation drop-down and LinearLayout from the root-element drop-down. To generate the file, you would click the Finish button at the bottom of the "New Android XML File" window.

Creating an Android Virtual Device

To run an application in the emulator requires a bit of setup with the new ADT plug-in. Specifically, before you can run an application in the emulator, you'll have to create at least one Android Virtual Device (AVD). An AVD represents a device configuration. For example, you could have an AVD representing an Android device running version 1.5 of the SDK with a 32MB SD card. The idea is that you create AVDs you are going to support and then point the emulator to one of those AVDs when developing and testing your application. As you'll see shortly, specifying (and changing) which AVD to use is very easy and makes testing with various configurations a snap. Note that the current version (0.9.1) of the ADT plug-in does not provide a UI for you to create an AVD, so you'll have to create it using the command line.

To create an AVD, you'll use a batch file named `android.bat` under the `tools` directory (`c:\Android1.5_SDK\tools\`). `android.bat` allows you to create a new AVD and manage existing AVDs. For example, you can view existing AVDs, move AVDs, and so on. You can see the options available for using `android.bat` by running `android -help`. For now, let's just create an AVD. The first step is to create a folder where the AVD image will be stored, so create a folder at `c:\avd\`. The next step is to run the `android.bat` file to create the AVD:

```
android create avd -n DefaultAVD -t 2 -c 32M -p C:\AVD\DefaultAVD\
```

The parameters passed to the batch file are listed in Table 12-1.

Table 12-1. *Parameters Passed to the android.bat Tool*

Argument/Command	Description
`create avd`	Tells the tool to create an AVD.
`n`	The name of the AVD.
`t`	The target runtime. Use 1 to specify Android 1.1 and 2 to specify Android 1.5.
`c`	Size of the SD card.
`p`	The path to the generated AVD.

Executing the preceding command will generate an AVD; you should see output similar to what's shown in Figure 12-8. Note that when you run the `create avd` command, you are asked if you want to create a custom hardware profile. Answer "no" to this question for now.

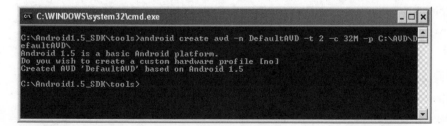

Figure 12-8. *Creating an AVD yields this android.bat output.*

With that, you have what you need to run an Android application in an emulator. Go back to Eclipse now so you can run the example application you created earlier. Select the Run menu, followed by the Run Configurations… option. In the "Run Configurations" window, select Android Application ➤ HelloAndroid1.5 on the left side of the screen. Leave the defaults in the "Android" tab and then choose the "Target" tab. As shown in Figure 12-9, you can now select the AVD you want to use. Because we only have one AVD, set the "Device Target Selection Mode" to Automatic and then choose DefaultAVD from the list of AVDs. To the run the application in the emulator, click the Run button.

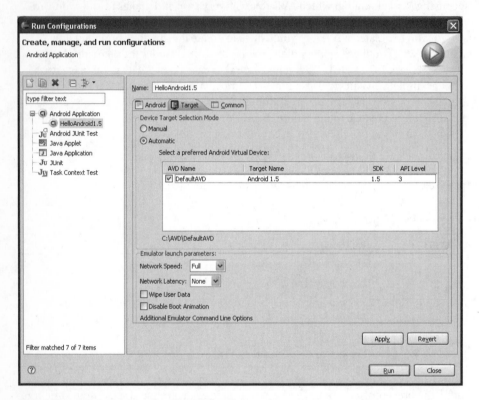

Figure 12-9. *Setting the preferred AVD for the emulator*

Now you are ready to begin developing with the Android 1.5 SDK. In the sections that follow, we are going to introduce some of the new functionality that is packaged with Android 1.5. We will begin by showing you how to use the new video-capture functionality.

Exploring Improvements to the Media Framework

Android 1.5 has some exciting changes to the media APIs. In this section, we are going to show you how to use the MediaRecorder class to implement video capture. We are also going to introduce you to the MediaStore class, and then show you how to scan an Android device for media content. Let's start with video capture.

Using the MediaRecorder Class for Video Capture

If you recall from Chapter 9, video recording was not possible with older versions of the SDK. With 1.5, you can begin to capture video using the media framework. Listing 12-1 demonstrates this. Note that we assume that you have read Chapter 9 and understand how to use the APIs from the media framework. If you have not read Chapter 9, you should do so before continuing with this section. Also realize that Listing 12-1 will not work on an emulator because video recording requires a hardware-encoder module, which is not available with version 1.5 of the SDK. Therefore, you'll have to deploy to a real device to test Listing 12-1.

Listing 12-1. *Using the MediaRecorder Class to Capture Video*

```
import android.app.Activity;
import android.media.MediaRecorder;
import android.os.Bundle;

public class MainActivity extends Activity {
    private MediaRecorder recorder;

    @Override
    public void onCreate(Bundle savedInstanceState) {
        super.onCreate(savedInstanceState);
        setContentView(R.layout.main);

    }

    private void recordVideo() throws Exception {
        if(recorder!=null)
        {
                                        recorder.stop();
            recorder.release();
        }
        recorder = new MediaRecorder();
        recorder.setVideoSource(MediaRecorder.VideoSource.CAMERA);
        recorder.setAudioSource(MediaRecorder.AudioSource.MIC);
        recorder.setOutputFormat(MediaRecorder.OutputFormat.THREE_GPP);
        recorder.setVideoSize(176, 144);
        recorder.setVideoFrameRate(30);
        recorder.setVideoEncoder(MediaRecorder.VideoEncoder. MPEG_4_SP);
        recorder.setAudioEncoder(MediaRecorder.AudioEncoder.AMR_NB);
        recorder.setOutputFile("/sdcard/output.3gpp");
        recorder.prepare();
        recorder.start();
    }
}
```

Listing 12-1 shows an activity class that provides a method to record video content from the device's camera to the SD card. Recall from Chapter 9 that the MediaRecorder requires you to set the recorder properties before calling prepare(). As shown, we set the MediaRecorder's video source to the device's camera, the audio source to the microphone, the output format to 3GPP, and so on. We also set the audio and video encoders and a path to the output file on the SD card before calling the prepare() and start() methods.

Listing 12-1 will capture video content from the camera and output it to the SD card in a file named output.3gpp. As you can see, video recording is fairly easy, as is the audio recording that we showed you in Chapter 9. Note that currently you cannot manipulate the content from the camera before encoding and saving it—you'll have to wait for that, possibly in a later release.

Another notable media-related upgrade is in the android.provider.MediaStore class. Let's explore this class next.

Exploring the MediaStore Class

The MediaStore class provides an interface to the media that is stored on the device (in both internal and external storage). MediaStore also provides APIs for you to act on the media. These include mechanisms for you to search the device for specific types of media, intents for you to record audio and video to the store, ways for you to establish playlists, and more. Note that this class was part of the older SDKs, but it has been greatly improved with the 1.5 release.

Because this class supports intents for you to record audio and video, and the MediaRecorder class does also, an obvious question is, when do you use MediaStore vs. MediaRecorder? As you saw with the preceding video-capture example and with the audio-recording examples in Chapter 9, MediaRecorder allows you to set various options on the source of the recording. These options include the audio/video input source, video frame rate, video frame size, output formats, and so on. MediaStore does not provide this level of granularity, but you are not coupled directly to the MediaRecorder if you go through the MediaStore's intents. More important, content created with the MediaRecorder is not available to other applications that are looking at the media store. If you use MediaRecorder, you'll want to add the recording to the media store using the MediaStore APIs. To that end, let's see how we can leverage the MediaStore APIs.

If you recall from Chapter 9, recording audio was easy, but it gets much easier if you use an intent from the MediaStore. Listing 12-2 demonstrates how to use an intent to record audio.

Listing 12-2. *Using an Intent to Record Audio*

```
import android.app.Activity;
import android.content.Intent;
import android.net.Uri;
import android.os.Bundle;
import android.view.View;
import android.view.View.OnClickListener;
import android.widget.Button;
```

```java
public class UsingMediaStoreActivity extends Activity {
    @Override
    protected void onCreate(Bundle savedInstanceState) {
        super.onCreate(savedInstanceState);

        setContentView(R.layout.record_audio);

        Button btn = (Button)findViewById(R.id.recordBtn);
        btn.setOnClickListener(new OnClickListener(){

            @Override
            public void onClick(View view) {

                startRecording();

            }});
    }

    public void startRecording() {
        Intent intt = new Intent("android.provider.MediaStore.RECORD_SOUND");
        startActivityForResult(intt, 0);
    }

    @Override
    protected void onActivityResult(int requestCode, int resultCode, Intent data) {

        switch (requestCode) {
        case 0:
            if (resultCode == RESULT_OK) {
                Uri recordedAudioPath = data.getData();
                int i=0;
            }
        }
    }
}
// record_audio.xml layout file
<?xml version="1.0" encoding="utf-8"?>
<LinearLayout xmlns:android="http://schemas.android.com/apk/res/android"
    android:orientation="vertical"
    android:layout_width="fill_parent"
    android:layout_height="fill_parent"
    >
 <Button android:id="@+id/btn"
            android:text="Record Audio"
            android:layout_width="wrap_content"
            android:layout_height="wrap_content" />

</LinearLayout>
```

Listing 12-2 creates an intent requesting the system to begin recording audio. The code launches the intent against an activity by calling `startActivityForResult()`, passing the intent and the `requestCode`. When the requested activity completes, `onActivityResult()` is called with the `requestCode`. As shown in `onActivityResult()`, we look for a `requestCode` that matches the code that was passed to `startActivityForResult()` and then retrieve the URI of the saved media by calling `data.getUri()`. You could then feed the URI to an intent to listen to the recording if you wanted to. The UI for Listing 12-2 is shown in Figure 12-10.

Figure 12-10. *Built-in audio recorder before and after a recording*

Figure 12-10 contains two screenshots. The image on the left displays the audio recorder before the recording has started, and the image on the right shows the activity UI after the recording has been stopped.

Similar to the way it provides an intent for audio recording, the `MediaStore` also provides an intent for you to take a picture. Listing 12-3 demonstrates this.

Listing 12-3. *Launching an Intent to Take a Picture*

```
import android.app.Activity;
import android.content.Intent;

import android.os.Bundle;
import android.provider.MediaStore;
import android.view.View;
import android.view.View.OnClickListener;
import android.widget.Button;
```

```java
public class MainActivity extends Activity {

    @Override
    public void onCreate(Bundle savedInstanceState) {
        super.onCreate(savedInstanceState);
        setContentView(R.layout.main);

        Button btn = (Button)findViewById(R.id.btn);

        btn.setOnClickListener(new OnClickListener(){

            @Override
            public void onClick(View view)
            {
                captureImage();
            }});

    }
    private void captureImage()
    {
        Intent intt = new Intent(MediaStore.ACTION_IMAGE_CAPTURE);
        startActivityForResult(intt, 0);

    }
    @Override
    protected void onActivityResult(int requestCode, int resultCode, Intent data) {
        if(requestCode==0 && resultCode==Activity.RESULT_OK)
        {
            Intent inn = new Intent(Intent.ACTION_VIEW);
            inn.setData(data.getData());
            startActivity(inn);
        }
        super.onActivityResult(requestCode, resultCode, data);
    }

}

// main.xml layout file
<?xml version="1.0" encoding="utf-8"?>
<LinearLayout xmlns:android="http://schemas.android.com/apk/res/android"
    android:orientation="vertical"
    android:layout_width="fill_parent"
    android:layout_height="fill_parent"
    >
```

```
<Button android:id="@+id/btn"
        android:text="Take Picture"
        android:layout_width="wrap_content"
        android:layout_height="wrap_content" />
```

```
</LinearLayout>
```

The activity class shown in Listing 12-3 defines the captureImage() method. In this method, an intent is created where the action name of the intent is set to MediaStore.ACTION_ IMAGE_CAPTURE. When this intent is launched, the camera application is brought to the foreground and the user takes a picture. After the picture is taken, onActivityResult() is called with an intent that holds the URI of the picture. In Listing 12-3, we create another intent with the URI of the photo and start an activity to view the picture.

Now that was easy. MediaStore also has a video-capture intent that behaves similarly. You can use MediaStore.ACTION_VIDEO_CAPTURE to capture video.

Scanning the Media Store for Media Content

One of the other features provided by Android's media framework is the ability to search the media store for media content via the MediaScannerConnection class. Let's see how this works (see Listing 12-4).

Listing 12-4. *Scanning the SD Card for Media*

```
import android.app.Activity;
import android.content.Intent;
import android.media.MediaScannerConnection;
import android.media.MediaScannerConnection.MediaScannerConnectionClient;
import android.net.Uri;
import android.os.Bundle;
import android.view.View;
import android.view.View.OnClickListener;
import android.widget.Button;

public class MediaScannerActivity extends Activity implements ➥
MediaScannerConnectionClient
{
    private static final String SCAN_PATH = "/sdcard/";
    private static final String FILE_TYPE = "image/jpeg";

    private MediaScannerConnection conn;

    @Override
    protected void onCreate(Bundle savedInstanceState) {
        super.onCreate(savedInstanceState);
        setContentView(R.layout.scan);

        Button scanBtn = (Button)findViewById(R.id.scanBtn);
```

```
        scanBtn.setOnClickListener(new OnClickListener(){

            @Override
            public void onClick(View view)
            {
                startScan();
            }});
    }

    private void startScan()
    {
        if(conn!=null)
        {
            conn.disconnect();
        }

        conn = new MediaScannerConnection(this,this);
        conn.connect();

    }


    @Override
    public void onMediaScannerConnected() {
        conn.scanFile(SCAN_PATH, FILE_TYPE);
    }

    @Override
    public void onScanCompleted(String path, Uri uri) {
        try {
            if (uri != null) {
                Intent intent = new Intent(Intent.ACTION_VIEW);
                intent.setData(uri);
                startActivity(intent);
            }
        } finally {
            conn.disconnect();
            conn = null;
        }
    }
}

// scan.xml layout file
<?xml version="1.0" encoding="utf-8"?>
<LinearLayout
  xmlns:android="http://schemas.android.com/apk/res/android"
  android:layout_width="wrap_content"
  android:layout_height="wrap_content">
```

```
            <Button android:id="@+id/scanBtn"
                android:text="Scan for Photos"
                android:layout_width="wrap_content"
                android:layout_height="wrap_content" />
</LinearLayout>
```

Listing 12-4 shows an activity class that scans the device's SD card for JPEGs. After the search, the results are displayed to the user via an intent.

Now let's move on to something different. In the next section, we are going to introduce you to Android's voice-recognition framework.

Exploring Voice Recognition

Android 1.5 includes a voice-recognition framework, and one of its popular toys is the RecognizerIntent class. The activity class in Listing 12-5 demonstrates this intent.

Listing 12-5. *Using the RecognizerIntent*

```
import java.util.List;

import android.app.Activity;
import android.content.Intent;
import android.os.Bundle;
import android.speech.RecognizerIntent;
import android.util.Log;
import android.view.View;
import android.view.View.OnClickListener;
import android.widget.Button;

public class RecognizeSpeechActivity extends Activity
{
    /** Called when the activity is first created. */
    @Override
    public void onCreate(Bundle savedInstanceState) {
        super.onCreate(savedInstanceState);
        setContentView(R.layout.main);

        Button btn = (Button)findViewById(R.id.btn);

        btn.setOnClickListener(new OnClickListener(){

            @Override
            public void onClick(View v)
            {
                startVoiceRecognition();
            }});
    }
```

```
    public void startVoiceRecognition()
    {
        Intent intent = new Intent(RecognizerIntent.ACTION_RECOGNIZE_SPEECH);
        startActivityForResult(intent, 0);
    }
    @Override
    protected void onActivityResult(int requestCode, int resultCode, Intent data) {
        super.onActivityResult(requestCode, resultCode, data);

        if(requestCode==0 && resultCode == Activity.RESULT_OK)
        {
            List<String> text = data.getStringArrayListExtra(➥
RecognizerIntent.EXTRA_RESULTS);
            // do something with the result

        }
    }
}


//  main.xml layout file
<?xml version="1.0" encoding="utf-8"?>
<LinearLayout xmlns:android="http://schemas.android.com/apk/res/android"
    android:orientation="vertical"
    android:layout_width="fill_parent"
    android:layout_height="fill_parent"
    >
 <Button android:id="@+id/btn"
            android:text="Speech Recognition"
            android:layout_width="wrap_content"
            android:layout_height="wrap_content" />

</LinearLayout>
```

Listing 12-5 displays a button in the UI that is meant to trigger the launching of the intent. In the click-handler method, the startVoiceRecognition() method is called. This method creates an intent with the action RecognizerIntent.ACTION_RECOGNIZE_SPEECH and then passes that to startActivityForResult(). This launches the speech-recognition activity, which prompts the user for speech. After the user submits speech data, the speech-recognition activity passes the data through a speech-recognizer component. The result of the activity is sent to the onActivityResult method, as shown.

That's obviously a lot of functionality for very little coding. It gets better. The framework also contains an intent action that executes a web search based on the result of the speech recognizer and displays the findings. Very powerful. You can try this by setting the intent action to

```
RecognizerIntent.ACTION_WEB_SEARCH
```

Note that because the preceding action will need to go to the Internet, you will need to add the Internet permission (<uses-permission android:name="android.permission.INTERNET"/>) to your AndroidManifest.xml file.

Now let's move on and discuss the input-method framework.

Introducing the Input-Method Framework

An exciting feature delivered with Android 1.5 is an input-method framework (IMF) implementation. IMF is actually a Java specification that decouples, for example, a text field from the mechanism that delivers text to the component. Example uses of an IMF include interpreters that translate speech into text, translators that convert text written with a pen device into regular text, interpreters that map characters from the Western alphabet table to characters in various east Asian languages (such as Korean and Japanese), and so on. One of the reasons for implementing an input-method framework in Android is to support phones that will ultimately be used in non-English-speaking countries, particularly Korea, China, and Japan. There are other obvious reasons, too. For example, you need an IMF implementation to support voice dialing, soft keyboards, and so on.

The 1.5 SDK actually has several input-method editors and engines. If you are interested in this specialized framework, have a look at the InputMethodService class to get started.

Summary

In this chapter, we introduced you to Android 1.5. We began by showing how to download and install the new SDK along with the associated ADT plug-in. We then showed you some of the new features in the Android 1.5 SDK. Specifically, we talked about video capture and other media-related intents. We also discussed the MediaStore class and showed you how to scan your device for media. We then explored the speech-recognition engine and concluded with a brief introduction to the input-method framework.

In the next chapter, we are going to discuss changes to the OpenGL APIs and show you how to create live folders, which allow developers to expose content providers on a device's home page.

CHAPTER 13

■ ■ ■

Simplifying OpenGL and Exploring Live Folders

In this chapter, we will primarily talk about simplifying OpenGL and introduce a new concept called *live folders* that has attracted a lot of recent attention within the Android developer community. You will need the Android 1.5 SDK to take advantage of the material covered in this chapter. As this is the last chapter of the book, we will also briefly look at the future prospects for the Android OS and how the evolving SDK releases will contribute to that future.

As we pointed out in Chapter 10, the Android SDK needs a simplified framework for beginning OpenGL programmers, and we introduced one such framework loosely based on Android 1.1 samples. In release 1.5, the Android team recognized this need as well, and subsequently introduced a similar framework to hide the OpenGL setup. In the first section of this chapter, we will talk about this framework and introduce you to the set of new OpenGL classes. We will then reimplement the simple triangle-drawing example introduced in Chapter 10 using these new 1.5 SDK classes.

After that, we'll delve into live folders, an important concept introduced in Android 1.5. Live folders allow developers to expose content providers such as contacts, notes, and media on the device's default opening screen (which we will refer to as the device's "home page"). When a content provider such as Android's `contacts` content provider is exposed as a live folder on the home page, this live folder will be able to refresh itself as contacts are added, deleted, or modified in the contacts database. We will explain what these live folders are, how to implement them, and how to make them "live."

In the last section of this chapter, we will explore how the Android OS is set to power the next generation of PCs—not only smartphones, but also netbooks and other Internet-enabled devices that are capable of general-purpose computing.

Let us now take a detailed look at the *improved* OpenGL capabilities in the Android 1.5 SDK.

Simplifying OpenGL

The OpenGL-related changes in the Android 1.5 SDK are primarily aimed at providing a simplified interface to the OpenGL drawing capabilities. This simplification will make OpenGL a lot more approachable to beginning OpenGL programmers. We discussed this need in Chapter 10, and to address it, we designed an OpenGL test harness that exhibits the following characteristics:

- Hide how one needs to initialize and get an EGLContext

- Hide the complexities of drawing on a SurfaceView using a secondary thread

- Expose only the interfaces that are dedicated to the core OpenGL drawing APIs

In that framework, you only needed to worry about inheriting from an AbstractRenderer to start drawing. The changes in the 1.5 SDK follow a similar pattern, introducing these key new classes and interfaces into the android.opengl package:

- GLSurfaceView: This class is responsible for drawing on a surface view using a secondary thread. It's equivalent to the OpenGLTestHarness and GLThread classes covered in Chapter 10.

- GLSurfaceView.Renderer: This is an interface that defines a contract for the inheriting drawing classes. All rendering subclasses need to implement this interface.

With these classes and interfaces, you should use OpenGL like this:

1. Implement the Renderer interface and provide the necessary OpenGL setup such as the OpenGL camera. Then override the onDraw method to draw.

2. Instantiate a GLSurfaceView and associate it with the subclassed Renderer from step 1.

3. Set the GLSurfaceView object in the activity.

You should familiarize yourself with the Renderer interface (see Listing 13-1) because it's the primary contract that developers will use to implement their drawing code.

Listing 13-1. *The 1.5 SDK Renderer Interface*

```
public static interface GLSurfaceView.Renderer
{
    void onDrawFrame(GL10 gl);
    void onSuraceChanged(GL10 gl, int width, int height);
    void onSurfaceCreated(GL10 gl, EGLConfig config);
}
```

As you might have noticed, this renderer resembles the Renderer interface that we introduced in Chapter 10 (see Listing 10-10). The methods in both interfaces have similar responsibilities, so we won't explain what each method does.

By further following the test harness in Chapter 10, we can gain even more simplicity by having all our renderers inherit from an AbstractRenderer. This would let us factor out the code that is common to all renderers and place it in the AbstractRenderer. Let us implement this AbstractRenderer using the new standardized 1.5 SDK Renderer interface (see Listing 13-2).

Listing 13-2. *AbstractRenderer Source Code*

```java
//filename: AbstractRenderer.java
public abstract class AbstractRenderer
implements GLSurfaceView.Renderer
{
    public int[] getConfigSpec() {
        int[] configSpec = {
                EGL10.EGL_DEPTH_SIZE, 0,
                EGL10.EGL_NONE
        };
        return configSpec;
    }

    public void onSurfaceCreated(GL10 gl, EGLConfig eglConfig) {
        gl.glDisable(GL10.GL_DITHER);
        gl.glHint(GL10.GL_PERSPECTIVE_CORRECTION_HINT,
                GL10.GL_FASTEST);
        gl.glClearColor(.5f, .5f, .5f, 1);
        gl.glShadeModel(GL10.GL_SMOOTH);
        gl.glEnable(GL10.GL_DEPTH_TEST);
    }

    public void onSurfaceChanged(GL10 gl, int w, int h) {
        gl.glViewport(0, 0, w, h);
        float ratio = (float) w / h;
        gl.glMatrixMode(GL10.GL_PROJECTION);
        gl.glLoadIdentity();
        gl.glFrustumf(-ratio, ratio, -1, 1, 3, 7);
    }

    public void onDrawFrame(GL10 gl)
    {
        gl.glDisable(GL10.GL_DITHER);
        gl.glClear(GL10.GL_COLOR_BUFFER_BIT | GL10.GL_DEPTH_BUFFER_BIT);
        gl.glMatrixMode(GL10.GL_MODELVIEW);
        gl.glLoadIdentity();
        GLU.gluLookAt(gl, 0, 0, -5, 0f, 0f, 0f, 0f, 1.0f, 0.0f);
        gl.glEnableClientState(GL10.GL_VERTEX_ARRAY);
        draw(gl);
    }
    protected abstract void draw(GL10 gl);
}
```

As you can see, the AbstractRenderer in Listing 13-2 takes care of the settings for an OpenGL scene (see the Chapter 10 discussion about setting up the OpenGL camera).

We are now in a good position to show you how to use these 1.5 OpenGL classes with the AbstractRenderer effectively. We will first implement a simple drawing class by bringing over the SimpleTriangleRenderer class that we introduced in Chapter 10. This will demonstrate the simple inheritance required to start drawing in OpenGL. We will also introduce a simple activity to test this SimpleTriangleRenderer. We will then close this OpenGL topic by showing how you can use these classes for introducing animation. Again, we will demonstrate this animation through a working sample along with source code.

■Note We are not recommending that you circumvent the Android 1.5 OpenGL approach in favor of the Android 1.1 test harness that we built in Chapter 10. By simply adding the AbstractRenderer to the classes in 1.5, you will arrive at the equivalent of the Chapter 10 test harness. You can use this resulting 1.5 test harness for most of your beginning needs. As you become more skilled with OpenGL, you can derive classes similar to AbstractRenderer as necessary. Or you can just ignore the AbstractRenderer and implement that functionality directly in the class you derive from the Renderer.

Now let's proceed to draw the simple OpenGL triangle.

Reimplementing the Simple Triangle OpenGL Drawing

Now that the AbstractRenderer is in place, we'll show you how to create a small activity that draws the same simple OpenGL triangle you drew in Chapter 10. We will use the following files to demonstrate this exercise:

- AbstractRenderer.java
- SimpleTriangleRenderer.java
- OpenGL15TestHarnessActivity.java

We presented the code for AbstractRenderer in the preceding section (see Listing 13-2), so now we'll show you the code for SimpleTriangleRenderer.

SimpleTriangleRenderer.java

The code for the SimpleTriangleRenderer class (see Listing 13-3) is the same as the code for the corresponding class in Chapter 10 (see Listing 10-12), except that the classes inherit from a different AbstractRenderer.

Listing 13-3. *SimpleTriangleRenderer Source Code*

```
//filename: SimpleTriangleRenderer.java
public class SimpleTriangleRenderer extends AbstractRenderer
{
   //Number of points or vertices we want to use
   private final static int VERTS = 3;
```

```java
    //A raw native buffer to hold the point coordinates
    private FloatBuffer mFVertexBuffer;

    //A raw native buffer to hold indices
    //allowing a reuse of points.
    private ShortBuffer mIndexBuffer;

    public SimpleTriangleRenderer(Context context)
    {
        ByteBuffer vbb = ByteBuffer.allocateDirect(VERTS * 3 * 4);
        vbb.order(ByteOrder.nativeOrder());
        mFVertexBuffer = vbb.asFloatBuffer();

        ByteBuffer ibb = ByteBuffer.allocateDirect(VERTS * 2);
        ibb.order(ByteOrder.nativeOrder());
        mIndexBuffer = ibb.asShortBuffer();

        float[] coords = {
                -0.5f, -0.5f, 0, // (x1,y1,z1)
                 0.5f, -0.5f, 0,
                 0.0f,  0.5f, 0
        };
        for (int i = 0; i < VERTS; i++) {
            for(int j = 0; j < 3; j++) {
                mFVertexBuffer.put(coords[i*3+j]);
            }
        }
        short[] myIndecesArray = {0,1,2};
        for (int i=0;i<3;i++)
        {
            mIndexBuffer.put(myIndecesArray[i]);
        }
        mFVertexBuffer.position(0);
        mIndexBuffer.position(0);
    }

    //overridden method
    protected void draw(GL10 gl)
    {
        gl.glColor4f(1.0f, 0, 0, 0.5f);
        gl.glVertexPointer(3, GL10.GL_FLOAT, 0, mFVertexBuffer);
        gl.glDrawElements(GL10.GL_TRIANGLES, VERTS,
                GL10.GL_UNSIGNED_SHORT, mIndexBuffer);
    }
}
```

OpenGL15TestHarnessActivity.java

Now we'll show you the code for a simple activity (see Listing 13-4) that demonstrates how to use the SimpleTriangleRenderer in Listing 13-3 to draw using the 1.5 GLSurfaceView class.

Listing 13-4. *OpenGL15TestHarnessActivity Source Code*

```java
//filename: OpenGL15TestHarnessActivity.java
public class OpenGL15TestHarnessActivity extends Activity {
    private GLSurfaceView mTestHarness;
    @Override
    protected void onCreate(Bundle savedInstanceState) {
        super.onCreate(savedInstanceState);

        mTestHarness = new GLSurfaceView(this);
        mTestHarness.setEGLConfigChooser(false);
        mTestHarness.setRenderer(new SimpleTriangleRenderer(this));
        mTestHarness.setRenderMode(GLSurfaceView.RENDERMODE_WHEN_DIRTY);
        setContentView(mTestHarness);
    }
    @Override
    protected void onResume()    {
        super.onResume();
        mTestHarness.onResume();
    }
    @Override
    protected void onPause() {
        super.onPause();
        mTestHarness.onPause();
    }
}
```

In Listing 13-4, we first instantiate a GLSurfaceView. Through setEGLConfigChooser(false), we advise the SDK to choose a configuration as close to 16-bit RGB as possible, with or without an optional depth buffer as close to 16 bits as possible. Refer to the 1.5 SDK documentation on this method for more advanced options.

We then set the triangle renderer in the GLSurfaceView. GLSurfaceView has two rendering modes: RENDERMODE_CONTINUOUSLY, which allows animation, and RENDERMODE_WHEN_DIRTY, which draws only when necessary. The former is the default setting, whereby the renderer is called again and again. So we indicate otherwise by choosing the latter. Once the GLSurfaceView is set up this way for on-demand rendering, we set the GLSurfaceView in the activity.

You can use the code in Listing 13-5 to run this activity from any menu option.

Listing 13-5. *Invoking an Activity*

```java
private void invoke15SimpleTriangle()
{
    Intent intent = new Intent(this,OpenGL15TestHarnessActivity.class);
    startActivity(intent);
}
```

Of course, you will have to register the activity in the `AndroidManifest.xml` file (see Listing 13-6).

Listing 13-6. *Specifying an Activity in the AndroidManifest.xml file*

```
<activity android:name=".OpenGL15TestHarnessActivity"
              android:label="OpenGL 15 Test Harness"/>
```

When you run this code, you will see the triangle that's shown in Figure 10-3 (see Chapter 10).

As you can see, the Android 1.5 SDK significantly simplifies OpenGL drawing. It simplifies animation as well, as you'll see in the next section.

OpenGL Animation Example

You can easily accommodate OpenGL animation in the new Android release by changing the rendering mode on the `GLSurfaceView` object (see Listing 13-7).

Listing 13-7. *Specifying Continuous-Rendering Mode*

```
//get a GLSurfaceView
GLSurfaceView openGLView;

//Set the mode to continuous draw mode
openGLView.setRenderingMode(GLSurfaceView.RENDERMODE_CONTINUOUSLY);
```

(Note that we're showing you how to change the rendering mode here because we had specified `RENDERMODE_WHEN_DIRTY` in the previous section. As we mentioned, `RENDERMODE_CONTINUOUSLY` is in fact the default setting, so animation is enabled by default.) Once the rendering mode is continuous, it is up to the renderer's `onDraw` method to do what's necessary to effect animation. To demonstrate this, we will show you an example where the triangle drawn in the previous example is rotated in a circular fashion. This example has the following two files:

- `AnimatedTriangleActivity.java`, which is a simple activity to host the `GLSurfaceView`

- `AnimatedSimpleTriangleRenderer.java`, which is responsible for animated drawing

Let us consider each of these files.

AnimatedTriangleActivity.java

The `AnimatedTriangleActivity.java` activity resembles the activity in Listing 13-4 that tests a simple triangle drawing, so you should be able to understand it easily. The goal of this activity is to provide a surface to draw on and then show it on the Android screen (see Listing 13-8).

The key line of code in this activity is highlighted in bold font. We basically took the previous activity that we used for a simple drawing (see Listing 13-4) and commented out the rendering mode. This lets the `GLSurfaceView` default to continuous-rendering mode, which accommodates repeated calls to the `onDraw` method of the renderer, in this case `AnimatedSimpleTriangleRenderer`.

Listing 13-8. *AnimatedTriangleActivity Source Code*

```java
//filename: AnimatedTriangleActivity.java
public class AnimatedTriangleActivity extends Activity {
   private GLSurfaceView mTestHarness;
   @Override
   protected void onCreate(Bundle savedInstanceState) {
       super.onCreate(savedInstanceState);

       mTestHarness = new GLSurfaceView(this);
       mTestHarness.setEGLConfigChooser(false);
       mTestHarness.setRenderer(new AnimatedSimpleTriangleRenderer(this));
       //mTestHarness.setRenderMode(GLSurfaceView.RENDERMODE_WHEN_DIRTY);
       setContentView(mTestHarness);
   }
   @Override
   protected void onResume()    {
       super.onResume();
       mTestHarness.onResume();
   }
   @Override
   protected void onPause() {
       super.onPause();
       mTestHarness.onPause();
   }
}
```

Now let's look into the AnimatedSimpleTriangleRenderer class, which appears in Listing 13-8. It's responsible for drawing the rectangle at frequent intervals to simulate animation.

AnimatedSimpleTriangleRenderer.java

The AnimatedSimpleTriangleRenderer class is very similar to the SimpleTriangleRenderer (see Listing 13-3), except for what happens in the onDraw method. In this method, we set a new rotation angle every four seconds. As the image gets drawn repeatedly, you will see the triangle spinning slowly. Listing 13-9 contains the complete implementation of the AnimatedSimpleTriangleRenderer class.

Listing 13-9. *AnimatedSimpleTriangleRenderer Source Code*

```java
//filename: AnimatedSimpleTriangleRenderer.java
public class AnimatedSimpleTriangleRenderer extends AbstractRenderer
{
   private int scale = 1;
   //Number of points or vertices we want to use
    private final static int VERTS = 3;

    //A raw native buffer to hold the point coordinates
    private FloatBuffer mFVertexBuffer;
```

```java
    //A raw native buffer to hold indices
    //allowing a reuse of points.
    private ShortBuffer mIndexBuffer;

    public AnimatedSimpleTriangleRenderer(Context context)
    {
        ByteBuffer vbb = ByteBuffer.allocateDirect(VERTS * 3 * 4);
        vbb.order(ByteOrder.nativeOrder());
        mFVertexBuffer = vbb.asFloatBuffer();

        ByteBuffer ibb = ByteBuffer.allocateDirect(VERTS * 2);
        ibb.order(ByteOrder.nativeOrder());
        mIndexBuffer = ibb.asShortBuffer();

        float[] coords = {
                -0.5f, -0.5f, 0, // (x1,y1,z1)
                 0.5f, -0.5f, 0,
                 0.0f,  0.5f, 0
        };
        for (int i = 0; i < VERTS; i++) {
            for(int j = 0; j < 3; j++) {
                mFVertexBuffer.put(coords[i*3+j]);
            }
        }
        short[] myIndecesArray = {0,1,2};
        for (int i=0;i<3;i++)
        {
            mIndexBuffer.put(myIndecesArray[i]);
        }
        mFVertexBuffer.position(0);
        mIndexBuffer.position(0);
    }

//overridden method
 protected void draw(GL10 gl)
 {
    long time = SystemClock.uptimeMillis() % 4000L;
    float angle = 0.090f * ((int) time);

    gl.glRotatef(angle, 0, 0, 1.0f);

    gl.glColor4f(1.0f, 0, 0, 0.5f);
    gl.glVertexPointer(3, GL10.GL_FLOAT, 0, mFVertexBuffer);
     gl.glDrawElements(GL10.GL_TRIANGLES, VERTS,
            GL10.GL_UNSIGNED_SHORT, mIndexBuffer);
 }
}
```

Now that you have both the AnimatedTriangleActivity.java and AnimatedSimpleTriangleRenderer.java files, you can invoke this animated activity from any menu item by calling the method identified in Listing 13-10.

Listing 13-10. *Invoking the Animated Activity*

```
private void invoke15SimpleTriangle()
{
  Intent intent = new Intent(this,AnimatedTriangleActivity.class);
  startActivity(intent);
}
```

Don't forget to register the activity in the AndroidManifest.xml file (see Listing 13-11).

Listing 13-11. *Registering the New Activity in the AndroidManifest.xml File*

```
<activity android:name=".AnimatedTriangleActivity"
            android:label="OpenGL Animated Test Harness"/>
```

The changes outlined here make OpenGL a lot more approachable in the Android 1.5 SDK. However, you should still review the background information we provided in Chapter 10, which is essential for working with OpenGL on Android. And the recommendation to refer to external OpenGL resources still holds.

Now let's move on. It's time to explore live folders in the Android 1.5 SDK.

Exploring Live Folders

A live folder in Android is to a content provider what an RSS reader is to a publishing web site. Let us explain. We said in Chapter 3 that content providers are similar to web sites that provide information based on URIs. As web sites proliferated, with each publishing its information in a unique way, there arose a need to aggregate information from multiple sites so that a user could follow the developments through a single reader. To this end came the design of RSS. RSS forced us to see a common pattern among disparate sets of information. Having a common pattern lets you design a reader once and use it to read any type of content, as long as the content is presented in a uniform way.

Live folders are not that different in concept. As an RSS reader provides a common interface to published web-site content, a live folder defines a common interface to a content provider in Android. As long as the content provider can satisfy this protocol, Android can create a live folder on the device's home page to represent that content provider. When a user clicks this live folder, the system will contact the content provider. The content provider is then expected to return a cursor. According to the live-folder contract, this cursor must have a predefined set of columns. This cursor is then visually presented through a ListView or a GridView.

Based on this common-format idea, live folders work like this:

1. First you create an icon on the home page representing a collection of rows coming from a content provider. You make this connection by specifying a URI along with the icon.

2. When a user clicks that icon, the system takes the URI and uses it to call the content provider. The content provider returns a collection of rows through a cursor.

3. As long as this cursor has columns expected by the live folder (such as name, description, and the program to invoke when that row is clicked), the system will present these rows as a ListView or a GridView.

4. Because the ListViews and GridViews are capable of updating their data when the underlying data store changes, these views are called "live"—hence the name "live folders."

So two key principles are at work in live folders. The first is the set of same column names across cursors. The second is that the views know how to look for any updates and change themselves accordingly. This second point is not unique to live folders, but quite natural to all views in the Android UI.

Now that you have some idea of what live folders are, we'll systematically explore the live-folder framework a bit more. We will do that in two subsections. In the first subsection, we will examine the overall end-user experience of a live folder. This should further solidify your understanding of the concept.

In the second subsection, we will show you how to build a live folder correctly so that it is actually "live." It does take some extra work to make a live folder "live," so we will explore this not-so-obvious aspect of live folders.

How a User Experiences Live Folders

Live folders are exposed to end users through the device's home page. Users make use of the live folders using a sequence like this:

1. Access the device's home page.

2. Go to the context menu of the home page.

3. Locate a context-menu option called "Folders" and click it to show any live folders that might be available.

4. Click the live folder you want to expose. This creates an icon on the home page representing the chosen live folder.

5. Click the live-folder icon on the home page to bring up the rows of information in a ListView or a GridView.

6. Click one of the rows to invoke an application that knows how to display that row of data.

7. Use further menu options displayed by that application to view or manipulate a desired item. You can also use the application's menu options to create any new items allowed by that application.

8. Note that the live-folder display automatically reflects any changes to the item or set of items.

We'll walk you through these steps, illustrating them with screenshots. We will start with step 1: a pristine Android 1.5 home page (see Figure 13-1).

Figure 13-1. *Android 1.5 home page*

If you long-click this home page, you will see its context menu (see Figure 13-2).

Figure 13-2. *Context menu on the Android 1.5 home page*

If you click the Folders suboption, Android will open another menu showing any live folders that are available (see Figure 13-3). We will build a live folder in the next section, but for now assume that the live folder we want has already been built. Assume that the live folder we want is called "New live folder" (see Figure 13-3).

Figure 13-3. *Viewing the list of live folders available*

If you click this "New live folder," Android creates an icon on the home page representing the live folder. In our example, the name of this folder will be "Contacts LF," short for "Contacts Live Folder" (see Figure 13-4). This live folder will display contacts from the contacts database. (We'll discuss how to name this folder later, when we describe the AllContactsLiveFolderCreatorActivity class shown in Listing 13-13.)

You will learn in the next section that an activity is responsible for creating the Contacts LF folder. For now, as far as the user experience is concerned, you can click the Contacts LF icon to see a list of contacts displayed in a ListView (see Figure 13-5).

Figure 13-4. *Live-folder icon on the home page*

Figure 13-5. *Showing live-folder contacts*

Depending on the number of contacts you have, this list might look different. You can click one of the contacts to display its details (see Figure 13-6).

Figure 13-6. *Opening a live-folder contact*

You can click the Menu button at the bottom to see how you can manipulate that individual contact (see Figure 13-7).

Figure 13-7. *Menu options for an individual contact*

If you choose to edit the contact, you will see the screen shown in Figure 13-8.

Figure 13-8. *Editing contact details*

To see the "live" aspect of this live folder, you can delete this contact or create a new one. Then when you go back to the live-folder view of Contacts LF, you will see those changes reflected. You can do this by clicking the Back button repeatedly until you see the Contacts LF folder.

Building a Live Folder

Now that you know what live folders are, you can learn to build one. After that, you'll learn how to drag an icon onto the home page to use that live folder. We will also show you how the "live" part works.

To build a live folder, you need two things: an activity and a content provider. The activity is responsible for creating the live folder on the home page. The content provider is responsible for returning a cursor that conforms to a live-folder contract. Typically, you package these two entities in an application and then deploy that application onto the device. You will also need some supporting files to make all this work. We will explain and demonstrate these ideas using a sample, which contains the following files:

- `AndroidManifest.xml`: This file defines which activity needs to be called to create the definition for a live folder.

- `AllContactsLiveFolderCreatorActivity.java`: This activity is responsible for supplying the definition for a live folder that can display all contacts in the contacts database.

- `MyContactsProvider.java`: This content provider will respond to the live-folder URI that will return a cursor of contacts. This provider internally uses the contacts content provider that ships with Android.

- `MyCursor.java`: This is a specialized cursor that knows how to perform a `requery` when underlying data changes.

- `BetterCursorWrapper.java`: This file is needed by `MyCursor` to orchestrate the requery.

- `SimpleActivity.java`: This simple activity is needed for the creation of an Android project.

We'll describe each of these files to give you a detailed understanding of how live folders work.

AndroidManifest.xml

You're already familiar with `AndroidManifest.xml`; it's the same file that is needed for all Android applications. The live-folders section of the file, which is demarcated with a comment, indicates that we have an activity called `AllContactsLiveFolderCreatorActivity` that is responsible for creating the live folder (see Listing 13-12). This fact is expressed through the declaration of an intent whose action is `android.intent.action.CREATE_LIVE_FOLDER`.

The label of this activity, "New live folder," will show up in the context menu of the home page (see Figure 13-3). As we explained in the "How a User Experiences Live Folders" section, you can get to the context menu of the home page by long-clicking the home page.

Listing 13-12. *AndroidManifest.xml File for a Live-Folder Definition*

```xml
<?xml version="1.0" encoding="utf-8"?>
<manifest xmlns:android="http://schemas.android.com/apk/res/android"
      package="com.ai.android.livefolders"
      android:versionCode="1"
      android:versionName="1.0">
  <application android:icon="@drawable/icon" android:label="@string/app_name">
      <activity android:name=".SimpleActivity"
              android:label="@string/app_name">
          <intent-filter>
              <action android:name="android.intent.action.MAIN" />
              <category android:name="android.intent.category.LAUNCHER" />
          </intent-filter>
      </activity>

      <!-- LIVE FOLDERS -->
      <activity
          android:name=".AllContactsLiveFolderCreatorActivity"
          android:label="New live folder "
          android:icon="@drawable/icon">
```

```
        <intent-filter>
            <action android:name="android.intent.action.CREATE_LIVE_FOLDER" />
            <category android:name="android.intent.category.DEFAULT" />
        </intent-filter>
    </activity>

    <provider android:authorities="com.ai.livefolders.contacts"
    android:multiprocess="true"
        android:name=".MyContactsProvider" />

</application>
<uses-sdk android:minSdkVersion="3" />
<uses-permission android:name="android.permission.READ_CONTACTS"></uses-permission>
</manifest>
```

Another notable point of the code in Listing 13-12 is the provider declaration, which is anchored at the URI content://com.ai.livefolders.contacts and serviced by the provider class MyContactsProvider. This provider is responsible for providing a cursor to populate the ListView that opens when the corresponding live-folder icon is clicked (see Figure 13-5).

According to the live-folder protocol, the CREATE_LIVE_FOLDER intent will allow the home page's context menu to show the AllContactsLiveFolderCreatorActivity as an option titled "New live folder" (see Figure 13-3). Clicking this menu option will create an icon on the home page, as shown in Figure 13-4.

It is the responsibility of AllContactsLiveFolderCreatorActivity to define this icon, which will consist of an image and a label. In our case, the code in AllContactsLiveFolderCreatorActivity specifies this label as "Contacts LF." So let us take a look at the source code for this live-folder creator.

AllContactsLiveFolderCreatorActivity.java

The AllContactsLiveFolderCreatorActivity class has one responsibility: to serve as the generator or creator of a live folder (see Listing 13-13). Think of it as a template for the live folder. Every time this activity is clicked (through the Folders option in the home page's context menu), it will generate a live folder on the home page.

This activity accomplishes its task by telling the invoker—the home page or live-folder framework, in this case—the name of the live folder, the image to use for the live-folder icon, the URI where the data is available, and the display mode (list or grid). The framework, in turn, is responsible for creating the live-folder icon on the home page.

■**Note** For all the contracts needed by a live folder, see the Android 1.5 SDK documentation for the android.provider.LiveFolders class.

Listing 13-13. *AllContactsLiveFolderCreatorActivity Source Code*

```java
public class AllContactsLiveFolderCreatorActivity extends Activity
{
    @Override
    protected void onCreate(Bundle savedInstanceState)
    {
        super.onCreate(savedInstanceState);

        final Intent intent = getIntent();
        final String action = intent.getAction();

        if (LiveFolders.ACTION_CREATE_LIVE_FOLDER.equals(action))
        {
            setResult(RESULT_OK,
                    createLiveFolder(MyContactsProvider.CONTACTS_URI,
                            "Contacts LF",
                            R.drawable.icon)
                    );
        } else
        {
            setResult(RESULT_CANCELED);
        }
        finish();
    }

    private Intent createLiveFolder(Uri uri, String name, int icon)
    {
        final Intent intent = new Intent();
        intent.setData(uri);
        intent.putExtra(LiveFolders.EXTRA_LIVE_FOLDER_NAME, name);
        intent.putExtra(LiveFolders.EXTRA_LIVE_FOLDER_ICON,
                Intent.ShortcutIconResource.fromContext(this, icon));
        intent.putExtra(LiveFolders.EXTRA_LIVE_FOLDER_DISPLAY_MODE,
                LiveFolders.DISPLAY_MODE_LIST);
        return intent;
    }
}
```

The createLiveFolder method essentially sets values on the intent that invoked it. When this intent is returned to the caller, the caller will know the following:

- The live-folder name
- The image to use for the live-folder icon
- The display mode: list or grid
- The data or content URI to invoke for data

This information is sufficient to create the live-folder icon as shown in Figure 13-4. When a user clicks this icon, the system will call the URI to retrieve data. It is up to the content provider identified by this URI to provide the standardized cursor. We'll now show you the code for that content provider: the MyContactsProvider class.

MyContactsProvider.java

MyContactsProvider has the following responsibilities:

1. Identify the incoming URI that looks like content://com.ai.livefolders.contacts/contacts.

2. Make an internal call to the Android-supplied contacts content provider identified by content://contacts/people/.

3. Read every row from the cursor and map it back to a cursor like MatrixCursor with proper column names required by the live-folder framework.

4. Wrap the MatrixCursor in another cursor so that the requery on this wrapped cursor will make calls to the contacts content provider when needed.

The code for MyContactsProvider is shown in Listing 13-14. Significant items are highlighted.

Listing 13-14. *MyContactsProvider Source Code*

```
public class MyContactsProvider extends ContentProvider {

    public static final String AUTHORITY = "com.ai.livefolders.contacts";

    //Uri that goes as input to the live-folder creation
    public static final Uri CONTACTS_URI = Uri.parse("content://" +
            AUTHORITY + "/contacts"   );

    //To distinguish this URI
    private static final int TYPE_MY_URI = 0;
    private static final UriMatcher URI_MATCHER;
    static{
      URI_MATCHER = new UriMatcher(UriMatcher.NO_MATCH);
      URI_MATCHER.addURI(AUTHORITY, "contacts", TYPE_MY_URI);
    }

    @Override
    public boolean onCreate() {
        return true;
    }

    @Override
    public int bulkInsert(Uri arg0, ContentValues[] values) {
      return 0; //nothing to insert
    }
```

```java
//Set of columns needed by a live folder
//This is the live-folder contract
private static final String[] CURSOR_COLUMNS = new String[]
{
  BaseColumns._ID,
  LiveFolders.NAME,
  LiveFolders.DESCRIPTION,
  LiveFolders.INTENT,
  LiveFolders.ICON_PACKAGE,
  LiveFolders.ICON_RESOURCE
};

//In case there are no rows
//use this stand-in as an error message
//Notice it has the same set of columns of a live folder
private static final String[] CURSOR_ERROR_COLUMNS = new String[]
{
  BaseColumns._ID,
  LiveFolders.NAME,
  LiveFolders.DESCRIPTION
};


//The error message row
private static final Object[] ERROR_MESSAGE_ROW =
     new Object[]
     {
      -1, //id
      "No contacts found", //name
      "Check your contacts database" //description
     };

//The error cursor to use
private static MatrixCursor sErrorCursor = new ➥
MatrixCursor(CURSOR_ERROR_COLUMNS);
static
{
  sErrorCursor.addRow(ERROR_MESSAGE_ROW);
}

//Columns to be retrieved from the contacts database
private static final String[] CONTACTS_COLUMN_NAMES = new String[]
{
  People._ID,
  People.DISPLAY_NAME,
  People.TIMES_CONTACTED,
  People.STARRED
};
```

```java
public Cursor query(Uri uri, String[] projection, String selection,
                        String[] selectionArgs, String sortOrder)
{
   //Figure out the uri and return error if not matching
   int type = URI_MATCHER.match(uri);
   if(type == UriMatcher.NO_MATCH)
   {
     return sErrorCursor;
   }

   Log.i("ss", "query called");

   try
   {
     MatrixCursor mc = loadNewData(this);
     mc.setNotificationUri(getContext().getContentResolver(),
                        Uri.parse("content://contacts/people/"));
     MyCursor wmc = new MyCursor(mc,this);
     return wmc;
   }
   catch (Throwable e)
   {
     return sErrorCursor;
   }
}

public static MatrixCursor loadNewData(ContentProvider cp)
{
   MatrixCursor mc = new MatrixCursor(CURSOR_COLUMNS);
   Cursor allContacts = null;
   try
   {
     allContacts = cp.getContext().getContentResolver().query(
       People.CONTENT_URI,
       CONTACTS_COLUMN_NAMES,
       null, //row filter
       null,
       People.DISPLAY_NAME); //order by

     while(allContacts.moveToNext())
     {
       String timesContacted = "Times contacted: "+allContacts.getInt(2);
```

```
            Object[] rowObject = new Object[]
            {
                allContacts.getLong(0),     //id
                allContacts.getString(1),    //name
                timesContacted,              //description
                Uri.parse("content://contacts/people/"
                                    +allContacts.getLong(0)), //intent
                cp.getContext().getPackageName(), //package
                R.drawable.icon    //icon
            };
            mc.addRow(rowObject);
        }
      return mc;
    }
    finally
    {
       allContacts.close();
    }
}


@Override
public String getType(Uri uri)
{
  //indicates the MIME type for a given URI
  //targeted for this wrapper provider
  //This usually looks like
  // "vnd.android.cursor.dir/vnd.google.note"
  return People.CONTENT_TYPE;
}

public Uri insert(Uri uri, ContentValues initialValues) {
    throw new UnsupportedOperationException(
          "no insert as this is just a wrapper");
}

@Override
public int delete(Uri uri, String selection, String[] selectionArgs) {
      throw new UnsupportedOperationException(
      "no delete as this is just a wrapper");
}

public int update(Uri uri, ContentValues values,
          String selection, String[] selectionArgs)
{
      throw new UnsupportedOperationException(
      "no update as this is just a wrapper");
}
}
```

The set of columns shown in Listing 13-15 includes the standard columns that a live folder needs.

Listing 13-15. *Columns Needed to Fulfill the Live-Folder Contract*

```
private static final String[] CURSOR_COLUMNS = new String[]
{
  BaseColumns._ID,
  LiveFolders.NAME,
  LiveFolders.DESCRIPTION,
  LiveFolders.INTENT,
  LiveFolders.ICON_PACKAGE,
  LiveFolders.ICON_RESOURCE
};
```

Most of these fields are self-explanatory, except for the INTENT item. This field points to an intent or a URI that needs to be invoked when a user clicks the item in the live folder.

Also note that the content provider executes the code in Listing 13-16 to tell the cursor that it needs to watch the data for any changes.

Listing 13-16. *Registering a URI with a Cursor*

```
MatrixCursor mc = loadNewData(this);
mc.setNotificationUri(getContext().getContentResolver(),
                 Uri.parse("content://contacts/people/"));
```

It should be an interesting fact that the URI to watch is not the URI of our MyContactsProvider content provider, but the URI of the Android-supplied content provider for contacts. This is because MyContactsProvider is just a wrapper for the "real" content provider. So this cursor needs to watch the underlying content provider instead of the wrapper.

It is also important that we wrap the MatrixCursor in our own cursor, as shown in Listing 13-17.

Listing 13-17. *Wrapping a Cursor*

```
MatrixCursor mc = loadNewData(this);
mc.setNotificationUri(getContext().getContentResolver(),
           Uri.parse("content://contacts/people/"));
MyCursor wmc = new MyCursor(mc,this);
```

To understand why you need to wrap the cursor, you must examine how views operate to update changed content. A content provider typically tells a cursor that it needs to watch for changes by registering a URI as part of implementing the query method. This is done through cursor.setNotificationUri. The cursor then will register this URI and all its children URIs with the content provider. Then when an insert or delete happens on the content provider, the code for the insert and delete operations needs to raise an event signifying a change to the data in the rows identified by a particular URI.

This will trigger the cursor to get updated via requery, and the view will update accordingly. Unfortunately, the MatrixCursor is not geared for this requery. SQLiteCursor is geared for it, but we can't use SQLiteCursor here because we're mapping the columns to a new set of columns.

To accommodate this restriction, we have wrapped the MatrixCursor in a cursor wrapper and overridden the requery method to drop the internal MatrixCursor and create a new one with the updated data.

You will see this illustrated in the following two classes.

MyCursor.java

Notice how MyCursor is initialized with a MatrixCursor in the beginning (see Listing 13-18). On requery, MyCursor will call back the provider to return a MatrixCursor. Then the new MatrixCursor will replace the old one by using the set method.

We could have done this by overriding the requery of the MatrixCursor, but that class does not provide a way to clear the data and start all over again. So this is a reasonable workaround. (Note that MyCursor extends BetterCursorWrapper; we'll discuss the latter in the next subsection.)

Listing 13-18. *MyCursor Source Code*

```java
public class MyCursor extends BetterCursorWrapper
{
    private ContentProvider mcp = null;

    public MyCursor(MatrixCursor mc, ContentProvider inCp)
    {
        super(mc);
        mcp = inCp;
    }
    public boolean requery()
    {
        MatrixCursor mc = MyContactsProvider.loadNewData(mcp);
        this.setInternalCursor(mc);
        return super.requery();
    }
}
```

Now you'll look at the BetterCursorWrapper class to get an idea of how to wrap a cursor.

BetterCursorWrapper.java

The BetterCursorWrapper class (see Listing 13-19) is very similar to the CursorWrapper class in the Android database framework. But we need two additional things that CursorWrapper lacks. First, it doesn't have a set method to replace the internal cursor from the requery method. Second, CursorWrapper is not a CrossProcessCursor. Live folders need a CrossProcessCursor as opposed to a plain cursor because live folders work across process boundaries.

Listing 13-19. *BetterCursorWrapper Source Code*

```
public class BetterCursorWrapper implements CrossProcessCursor
{
    //Holds the internal cursor to delegate methods to
    protected CrossProcessCursor internalCursor;

    //Constructor takes a crossprocesscursor as an input
    public BetterCursorWrapper(CrossProcessCursor inCursor)
    {
        this.setInternalCursor(inCursor);
    }

    //You can reset in one of the derived class's methods
    public void setInternalCursor(CrossProcessCursor inCursor)
    {
        internalCursor = inCursor;
    }

    //All delegated methods follow
    public void fillWindow(int arg0, CursorWindow arg1) {
        internalCursor.fillWindow(arg0, arg1);
    }
    // ..... other delegated methods
}
```

We haven't shown you the entire class, but you can easily use Eclipse to generate the rest of it. Once you have this partial class loaded into Eclipse, place your cursor on the variable named internalCursor. Right-click and choose Source ➤ Generate Delegated Methods. Eclipse will then populate the rest of the class for you. Let us now show you the simple activity you need to complete this sample project.

SimpleActivity.java

SimpleActivity.java (see Listing 13-20) is not an essential class for live folders, but its inclusion in the project gives you a common pattern for all your projects. Plus, it allows you to deploy the application and see it onscreen when you are debugging through Eclipse.

Listing 13-20. *SimpleActivity Source Code*

```
public class SimpleActivity extends Activity
{
    @Override
    public void onCreate(Bundle savedInstanceState)
    {
        super.onCreate(savedInstanceState);
        setContentView(R.layout.main);
    }
}
```

You can use any simple XML layout that you would like for the main.xml identified by R.layout.main. Listing 13-21 shows an example.

Listing 13-21. *Simple XML Layout File*

```
<?xml version="1.0" encoding="utf-8"?>
<LinearLayout xmlns:android="http://schemas.android.com/apk/res/android"
    android:orientation="vertical"
    android:layout_width="fill_parent"
    android:layout_height="fill_parent"
    >
<TextView
    android:layout_width="fill_parent"
    android:layout_height="wrap_content"
    android:text="Live Folder Example"
    />
</LinearLayout>
```

Now you have all the classes you need to build, deploy, and run the sample live-folder project through Eclipse. Let us conclude this section on live folders by showing you what happens when you access the live folder.

Exercising Live Folders

Once you have all these files for the live-folder project ready, you can build them and deploy them to the emulator. When you deploy this application through Eclipse, you will see the simple activity show up on the emulator. You are now ready to make use of the live folder that we have constructed.

Navigate to the device's home page; it should look like the screen in Figure 13-1. Follow the steps outlined at the beginning of the section, "How a User Experiences Live Folders." Specifically, locate the live folder you created and create the live-folder icon as shown in Figure 13-4. Click the Contacts LF live-folder icon, and you will see the contact list populated with contacts, as shown in Figure 13-5.

As we come to the conclusion of this book, let us shift our attention to the future of Android and how the 1.5 SDK is enabling some of those expectations.

The Future of Android and the 1.5 SDK

You can already run Android applications on these types of devices:

- T-Mobile G1

- Android Dev Phone 1

- GiiNii Movit

The T-Mobile G1 was one of the first products to be released based on the Android 1.0 SDK. It has most of the bells and whistles of a general-purpose computing device, with a phone attached. At that point, Android did not support a virtual onscreen keyboard (otherwise known as a "soft" keyboard). Android 1.5 does offer this feature, and it's possible that future releases of these devices won't have a physical keyboard at all.

Google has also released the Android Dev Phone 1 so developers can test their applications. This device, which costs around $400, offers the following features:

- Touch screen
- Track ball
- Megapixel camera
- WiFi
- Physical keyboard
- SD card

The GiiNii Movit (`http://www.giinii.com/movit_detail.html`), marketed as an Internet device, comes with the following features:

- WiFi
- Skype
- Microphone/speaker
- Video/audio
- Built-in support for MySpace, Twitter, and Facebook

This device truly marks a shift toward netbooks, whereby smaller computers are powered by the Android OS. The manufacturers that are anticipated to follow this trend include the following:

- Hewlett-Packard (HP)
- Dell
- ASUSTeK Computer Inc. (ASUS)

To support this new push, the Android 1.5 SDK comes with the following key features:

- Virtual ("soft") keyboard
- Home-screen widgets
- Music player
- Calendar
- Picasa
- YouTube
- Google Talk
- Improved Gmail

The following cell-phone manufacturers are expecting to release new devices that support the Android OS:

- HTC Corp.

- LG Electronics

- Motorola

- Samsung

- Sony Ericsson

With all these advances, the future of Android looks quite bright.

Key Online Resources for the 1.5 SDK

We would like to conclude this chapter by listing some key URLs that will come in handy as you discover more about the 1.5 SDK and future releases of Android.

- *Android Developers home page* (http://developer.android.com): This is the main entry page for Android developers. As new SDKs are announced, this page will lead you to the right URLs.

- *The Developer's Guide* (http://developer.android.com/guide/): This is the Android Dev Guide for the most current release. Currently this documentation covers the Android 1.5 SDK.

- *Cupcake Roadmap* (http://source.android.com/roadmap/cupcake): The 1.5 release is sometimes referred to as "cupcake," although the two are in fact distinct. Most of the features from cupcake have been rolled into the 1.5 SDK. You can use this URL to learn more about cupcake's features.

- *Android 1.5 Platform Highlights* (http://developer.android.com/sdk/android-1.5-highlights.html): You can use this URL to find out about the new features in 1.5.

- *SDK downloads* (http://developer.android.com/sdk/1.5_r1/index.html): You can download the Android 1.5 SDK from this site.

- *Android Open Source Project* (http://source.android.com/): If you are looking for Android SDK source code, you will find it here.

- *Google I/O Developer Conference* (http://code.google.com/events/io/): This site contains content from the Google I/O conference, including material from sessions about Android.

- *Android Roadmap* (http://source.android.com/roadmap): This is where Google publishes roadmaps for upcoming releases.

- *Git* (http://git-scm.com/): To work with Android code, you need to use Git, an open source version-control system that accommodates large, distributed projects.

- *"Future-Proofing Your Apps"*: (http://android-developers.blogspot.com/2009/04/future-proofing-your-apps.html): This blog post describes backward-compatibility mechanisms you can use while developing your applications.

Summary

This chapter covered two important aspects of the Android 1.5 SDK: OpenGL, and live folders. We offered background information about both concepts along with working samples. We also described how Android is well-positioned for growth due to its adaptability for netbooks and other computing appliances. Finally, we hope that the URLs we provided prove useful as you continue your exploration of Android.

Index

You Need the Companion eBook